Palgrave Socio-Legal Studies

The Palgrave Socio-Legal Studies series is a developing series of monographs and textbooks featuring cutting edge work which, in the best tradition of socio-legal studies, reach out to a wide international audience.

Wenting Cheng

# China in Global Governance of Intellectual Property

## Implications for Global Distributive Justice

palgrave
macmillan

Wenting Cheng
College of Law
Australian National University
Canberra, ACT, Australia

ISSN 2947-9274 ISSN 2947-9282 (electronic)
Palgrave Socio-Legal Studies
ISBN 978-3-031-24369-1 ISBN 978-3-031-24370-7 (eBook)
https://doi.org/10.1007/978-3-031-24370-7



This Palgrave Macmillan imprint is published by the registered company Springer Nature Switzerland AG
The registered company address is: Gewerbestrasse 11, 6330 Cham, Switzerland

*To my parents,*
*for the bravery and perseverance*
*you taught me through words and deeds.*

# Preface

Writing a book is like a journey, and this book is a long journey for me. I started my Ph.D. at the Australian National University in Early 2014 when there was not much discussion on China in global governance or China's intellectual property (IP) issues. My Ph.D. thesis focused on the question of how China has engaged in global IP governance since its WTO accession in 2001. In March 2018, two weeks after I received feedbacks on the final draft of my thesis, the US Trade Representative issued Section 301 *Report on China's Acts, Policies, and Practices Related to Technology Transfer, Intellectual Property, and Innovation.* The allegations in this report on unfair trade practices and IP theft became the trigger for the US-China trade war. I was fortunate that my Ph.D. degree was conferred without having to incorporate this development. But book revision became an ever-expanding project—with the accelerated US-China decoupling, the 2020 US-China Phase One trade agreement consists of 16-page on IP as its Chapter 1 and the systematic IP law revision in China. In 2020, China promulgated four IP laws and regulations and issued six judicial interpretations, yet it was still condemned engaging IP theft by the US. I kept waking up in the night wondering whether my conclusions in the Ph.D. thesis are still valid and how I can contribute a useful understanding of China in global IP governance.

It took me another four years to update the data and navigate a deeper interpretation of the findings from the cases, but I think it is time worth taking. As will show in this book, the Chinese IP system increasingly resembles those of the US and/or the EU, and IP protection is emphasised in

China's grand strategies such as innovation-driven development. China has recognised the instrumental value of IP in stimulating innovation and facilitating economic transformation. It has started focusing on cultivating an IP culture that respects the intrinsic value of IP, setting the target of building itself as a global IP power by 2035. All these development makes it imperative to understand not only whether China's large-scale deployment of IP in various markets would make itself a global IP regulatory power, but also what China would deliver in its enhanced participation in global IP governance.

While the global COVID-19 pandemic and climate catastrophes are disruptive in many ways, these crises urged the rethinking of IP from its beginning and the fundamentals. The history of the industrialisation of different nations and their IP laws has confirmed Ha-Joon Chang's claim that, by harmonising international IP law, technologically advanced countries have kicked away the ladder for economic development for technologically retarded countries. On the other hand, any view on IP needs to be associated with a broader paradigm of distributive justice (Chapter 1), either as a barrier to knowledge dissemination (egalitarianism), as monopolies for a limited period to stimulate innovation (utilitarianism), or as quasi-property rights (entitlement-based principles). Each paradigm includes not only the principles but also the original caveats that faded in their self-evolvement. In one way or another, none of the paradigms indicates that IP is an inviolable property right even though it has been a dominant discourse since the TRIPS Agreement. These paradigms not only provide frameworks to reflect on the popular allegation of IP theft or to justify law reform when IP conflicts with access to health in a pandemic; they also offer this book a new angle for implications from China's global IP engagement. They provoked questions of what sort of IP rules China would like to promote in its participation in global governance and how China would treat other countries when itself reaches the top of the ladder of technology and industrial development.

Based on five case studies, this book analyses how China has engaged in global IP governance and the implication of its engagement for global distributive justice. It approaches the topic through a regulation-oriented interdisciplinary approach by examining key actors, principles and strategies of China's global IP engagement. Drawing on principles of global distributive justice nationally and internationally, this book contributes to a critical understanding of what China's rising role in global IP governance means for the rest of the world.

This book will not be possible without the love and supports from many people—my supervisors, colleagues, friends and family. I acknowledge my informants to provide valuable information and sometimes clues for such information and other colleagues in China who facilitated my fieldwork during the Ph.D. I was so fortunate to have both Professor Peter Drahos and Professor Susan Sell as my Ph.D. supervisors, who provided continuous supports and guidance on this topic during and after my Ph.D. I thank Professor Sally Wheeler for helping me positioning this book in the broader area of socio-legal studies. I thank Dr Hazel Moir for reading various versions of the manuscript, reminding me of incidences in the history of international IP law that I had otherwise missed. Post-Ph.D. book revision was a solitude, and I appreciate daily message check-ins with my colleague and friend Anne McNaughton to fight against procrastination. I thank my husband and my daughter for their love and support in this marathon like journey. I am grateful to the School of Regulation and Global Governance of the Australian National University to nurture me to be an interdisciplinary regulatory scholar during the Ph.D. period. I also appreciate the fund provided by the Australian Centre on China in the World to support the copyediting of this book—it was a great relief during the COVID-19 lockdown when I also needed to engage home-schooling. I thank Jan Borrie for copyediting my book. I thank Professor David Cowan for including this book in this prestigious Palgrave Series on Socio-Legal Studies. Last but not least, I appreciate Palgrave Macmillan publishing team, particularly Josie Taylor, Saranya Siva and Kanchan Latambale for their seamless support.

Canberra, Australia Wenting Cheng

# Contents

# Abbreviations

| | |
|---|---|
| 1G | The First Generation of Wireless Cellular Technology |
| 2G | The Second-generation Cellular Network |
| 3G | The Third Generation of Wireless Mobile Telecommunications Technology |
| 3GPP | The Third Generation Partnership Project |
| 4G | The Fourth Generation of Broadband Cellular Network Technology |
| 5G | The Fifth-generation Technology Standard for Broadband Cellular Networks |
| ABS | Access and Benefit-Sharing |
| ACTA | The Anti-Counterfeiting Trade Agreement |
| AD | Active Defensive |
| AIIB | The Asian Infrastructure Investment Bank |
| AmCham China | The American Chamber of Commerce in China |
| AP | Active Promotion |
| APEC | The Asia-Pacific Economic Cooperation |
| API | Active Pharmaceutical Ingredient |
| AQSIQ | General Administration of Quality Supervision, Inspection and Quarantine of China (dissolved in 2018) |
| ASEAN | The Association of Southeast Asian Nations |
| AVS | Audio Video coding Standards |
| Beijing Treaty | The Beijing Treaty on Audio-Visual Performance |
| Berne Convention | The Berne Convention for the Protection of Literary and Artistic Works |

| | |
|---|---|
| BRI | The Belt and Road Initiative |
| BRICS | Brazil, Russia, India, China and South Africa |
| CBD | The Convention on Biological Diversity |
| CBWIPSG | China Broadband Wireless IP Standard Group |
| CCP | The Chinese Communist Party |
| CCPIT | China Council for the Promotion of International Trade |
| CDMA2000 | Code-Division Multiple Access 2000 |
| CESI | China Electronic Standardization Institute |
| CETA | Canada-EU Comprehensive Economic and Trade Agreement |
| CFDA | China Food and Drug Administration |
| CHIPS and Science ACT | Creating Helpful Incentives to Produce Semiconductors and Science Act of the US |
| CNIPA | China National Intellectual Property Administration |
| CNY | The Chinese Yuan |
| CoCom | The Coordinating Committee for Multilateral Export Controls |
| COVAX | Covid-19 Vaccines Global Access |
| COVID-19 | Coronavirus Disease 2019 |
| CPTPP | Comprehensive and Progressive Agreement for Trans-Pacific Partnership |
| DG AGRI | Directorate-General for Agriculture and Rural Development |
| DMCA | The US Digital Millennium Copyright Act |
| DSB | Dispute Settlement Body |
| DSM | Dispute Settlement Mechanism |
| DVD | Digital Versatile Disc |
| EC | The European Community |
| EEC | The European Economic Community |
| EFOW | The European Federation of Origin Wines |
| EFTA | The European Free Trade Association |
| EPO | The European Patent Office |
| EU | The European Union |
| FAO | Food and Agriculture Organization |
| FDI | Foreign Direct Investments |
| FRAND | The Principle of Fair, Reasonable and Non-Discrimination |
| FTA | Free Trade Agreement |
| FTAAP | Free Trade Area of the Asia-Pacific |
| G-77 | The Group of 77 |
| GATT | General Agreement on Tariffs and Trade |
| GCC | Gulf Cooperation Council |
| GDP | Gross Domestic Product |

| | |
|---|---|
| GI | Geographical Indication |
| GI Extension | Extending Higher-Level Protection to Products Beyond Wines and Spirits |
| GI Register | A Multilateral System for Notifying and Registering GIs for Wines and Spirits |
| GPA | The WTO Governmental Procurement Agreement |
| GVC | Global Value Chain |
| ICT | Information Communication Technologies |
| ID5 | Industrial Design 5 (a regulatory framework for industrial designs) |
| IEC | The International Electrotechnical Commission |
| IEEE | The Institute of Electrical and Electronics Engineers |
| IP | Intellectual Property |
| IP5 | The Five (Largest) Patent Offices |
| IPC | The International Patent Classification |
| IPO | Initial Public Offering |
| IPR2 | EU China Project on the Protection of Intellectual Property Rights (2007–2011) |
| IRCC | Internationally Recognized Certificate of Compliance |
| IRPL | Implementation Rules of the Patent Law of China |
| ISO | The International Standard Organization |
| ISP | Internet service provider |
| ITPGRFA | International Treaty on Plant Genetic Resources for Food and Agriculture |
| ITU | International Telecommunications Union |
| IUPGR | International Undertaking on Plant Genetic Resources |
| IWNComm | China IWNCOMM Co., Ltd |
| JCCT | The Joint Commission on Commerce and Trade between the US and China |
| JTC | (The ISO and The IEC) Joint Technical Committee |
| KOREU FTA | South Korea-EU FTA |
| KORUS FTA | South Korea-US FTA |
| LAC | Legislative Affairs Committee of the National People's Congress of China |
| LAO | Legislative Affair Office of the State Council of China |
| Lisbon Agreement | Lisbon Agreement for the Protection of Appellations of Origin and their International Registration |
| LMMC | Like-Minded Megadiverse Countries |
| LTE | Long-Term Evolution |
| Madrid Agreement | Madrid Agreement Concerning the International Registration of Marks |
| Madrid Protocol | The Protocol Relating to the Madrid Agreement Concerning the International Registration of Marks |
| MEE | The Ministry of Ecology and Environment of China |

| | |
|---|---|
| MEP | The Ministry of Environmental Protection of China |
| MFA | Ministry of Foreign Affairs of China |
| MFN | The Most Favoured Nation |
| MII | The Ministry of Information Industry of China |
| MIIT | The Ministry of Industry and Information Technology of China |
| MNC | Multinational Corporation |
| MOA | The Ministry of Agriculture of China |
| MOC | The Ministry of Culture of China |
| MOF | The Ministry of Finance of China |
| MOFCOM | The Ministry of Commerce of China |
| MOST | The Ministry of Science and Technology of China |
| MOU | Memorandum of Understanding |
| MPIA | Multiparty Interim Appeal Arbitration Arrangement |
| MSF | Médecins Sans Frontières |
| NAFTA | The North American Free Trade Agreement |
| Nagoya Protocol | Nagoya Protocol on Access to Genetic Resources and the Fair and Equitable Sharing of Benefits Arising from their Utilization to the Convention on Biological Diversity |
| NB | National Body |
| NBS | The National Bureau of Statistics of China |
| NCAAC | National Certification and Accreditation Administration Committee of China |
| NCAC | The National Copyright Administration of China |
| NDB | The New Development Bank |
| NDRC | The National Development and Reform Commission of China |
| NGO | Non-Governmental Organisation |
| NMPA | The National Medical Products Administration of China |
| OEM | Original Equipment Manufacturer |
| oriGIn | Organization for an International Geographical Indications Network |
| PAIC | Provincial Administration for Industry and Commerce |
| Paris Convention | Paris Convention for the Protection of Industrial Property |
| PC | Personal Computer |
| PCCP | The Politburo of Chinese Communist Party |
| PCT | Patent Cooperation Treaty |
| PD | Passive Defensive |
| PDMFSIBS | Provisions on the Definitions of Main Functions, Setup of Internal Bodies and Staffing for Chinese ministries |
| PDO | Protected Designation of Origin |

| | |
|---|---|
| PGI | Protected Geographical Indication |
| PGRFA | Genetic Resources for Food and Agriculture |
| PIC | Prior Informed Consent |
| PIPA | The Protect Intellectual Property Act of the US |
| PLT | Patent Law Treaty |
| PPH | Patent Prosecution Highway |
| PRC | The People's Republic of China |
| QUAD | The Coalition of Canada, the EC, Japan and the US in TRIPS Negotiations |
| R&D | Research and Development |
| RAND | Reasonable and Non-Discrimination |
| RCEP | Regional Comprehensive Economic Partnership |
| Rome Convention | International Convention for the Protection of Performers, Producers of Phonograms and Broadcasting Organizations |
| RTA | Regional Trade Agreement |
| S&ED | The US-China Strategic and Economic Dialogue |
| SAC | The Standard Administration Committee of China |
| SAIC | The State Administration for Industry and Commerce of China |
| SARS | Severe Acute Respiratory Syndrome |
| SBQTS | State Bureau of Quality and Technological Supervision of China |
| SC | Subcommittee |
| SCIO | State Council Information Office of China |
| SCT | The WIPO Standing Committee on the Law of Trademarks, Industrial Designs and Geographical Indications |
| SCTK | WIPO Standing Committee on Intellectual Property and Genetic Resources, Traditional Knowledge and Traditional Cultural Expressions |
| SEP | Standard Essential Patent |
| SFA | The State Forestry Administration of China |
| SIPO | The State Intellectual Property Office of China |
| SOPA | The Stop Online Piracy Act of the US |
| SPC | The Supreme People's Court of China |
| SPLT | Substantive Patent Law Treaty |
| SPO | The State Patent Office of China (the predecessor of SIPO) |
| SSO | Standard-Setting Organization |
| TBT | Technical Barriers to Trade (of the WTO) |
| TCMPD | Traditional Chinese Medicine Patent Database |
| TD-CDMA | Time-Division-Code-Division Multiple Access |
| TKDL | Traditional Knowledge Digital Library |

| | |
|---|---|
| TNC | The WTO Trade Negotiations Committee |
| TP | TRIPS-Plus |
| TPP | Trans-Pacific Partnership |
| TRIPS | The Agreement on Trade-Related Aspects of Intellectual Property Rights |
| TTIP | Transatlantic Trade and Investment Partnership |
| TV | Television |
| UNCTAD | The United Nations Conference on Trade and Development |
| UNESCO | United Nations Educational, Scientific and Cultural Organization |
| UNICTTF | The United Nations Information and Communication Technologies Task Force |
| UPOV | The International Union for the Protection of New Varieties of Plants |
| UPOV Convention | International Convention for the Protection of New Varieties of Plants |
| US | The United States |
| USCETA | The US China Economic and Trade Agreement |
| USITC | The US International Trade Commission |
| USITO | The US Information Technology Office |
| USPTO | The US Patent and Trademark Office |
| USSR | The Union of Soviet Socialist Republics |
| USTR | The US Trade Representative |
| WAPI | WLAN Authentication and Privacy Infrastructure |
| WCDMA | Wideband Code-Division Multiple Access |
| WCT | WIPO Copyright Treaty |
| WEP | The Wired Equivalent Privacy |
| WHO | The World Health Organization |
| Wi-Fi | Wireless Fidelity, a family of standards based on IEEE 802.11 |
| WIPI | The Wireless Internet Platform for Interoperability |
| WIPO | The World Intellectual Property Organization |
| WIPO IGC | WIPO Intergovernmental Committee on Intellectual Property and Genetic Resources, Traditional Knowledge and Folklore |
| WLAN | Wireless Local Area Network |
| WPA | Wi-Fi Protected Access |
| WPPT | WIPO Performances and Phonograms Treaty |
| WTO | The World Trade Organisation |
| ZTE | Zhongxing Telecommunication Equipment Corporation |

# List of Figures

# List of Tables

# Part I

## Setting the Scene

# 1

# Introduction

## 1.1 China: Between IP Theft and Assertive IP Power

Intellectual property (IP) has deeply impacted the ways people use ideas, information, knowledge, symbols, place names, and the list goes on. For example, vaccines and medicines are among the most effective measures to address the global pandemic, yet strong globalised IP protection in the form of patents, trade secrets, and data exclusivity has prevented the rapid and wide dissemination of valuable knowledge and information about these critical resources (Thambisetty *et al.*, 2022). Discussion concerning IP and equitable access to life-saving vaccines and medicines has escalated, revealing broader and more critical perspectives on IP and global distributive justice (Erfani *et al.*, 2021; Sekalala *et al.*, 2021; Wijesinghe *et al.*, 2022).

China is the largest developing-country and the second-largest economy in the world. Chinese IP has been a controversial issue for decades. China has been condemned as constantly conducting IP theft. China established its IP system under US pressure and amended its IP laws in 2000 on the eve of its accession to the World Trade Organisation (WTO). After entering the WTO, China was sued by the European Union (EU) and the United States (US) at the WTO for violations of the *Agreement on Trade-Related Aspects of*


W. Cheng, *China in Global Governance of Intellectual Property*, Palgrave Socio-Legal Studies, https://doi.org/10.1007/978-3-031-24370-7_1

*Intellectual Property Rights* (TRIPS Agreement).[1] In the US-China trade war starting in 2018, the US has accused China of IP theft, and the subsequent US-China Economic and Trade Agreement (USCETA 2020) included the most stringent IP enforcement standards among all US bilateral agreements (Upreti & Vásquez Callo-Müller, 2020).

On the other hand, the number of IP applications from Chinese residents has surged since China's WTO accession in 2001. In 2001, the Chinese Trademark Office registered more trademarks than any other office in the world, and in 2011 the State Intellectual Property Office of China (SIPO)[2] became the world's biggest patent office, receiving the largest number of patent applications. IP has been promoted as a priority in China's national agenda. In 2008, China released its *National IP Strategy*.[3] Since 2012, the Chinese government has incorporated IP as an integral part of a broader strategy of Innovation-driven Development,[4] seeking to transform China into the world's leading IP power. *The Diplomat* commented that 'overall, through a mix of market incentives and political pressure, China appears to be emerging as a global intellectual property leader' (Zukus, 2017). Nonetheless, the rising number of IP registrations does not necessarily lead to the rising regulatory power of China in global IP governance—the globalisation of the market and the globalisation of regulation are contingent but independent processes (Drahos, 2017). China's industrious implementation of IP rules modelled those of developed countries does not qualify it as a global IP leader, either.

In the last decade, China has actively negotiated IP rules in its bilateral and regional trade agreements, such as the Regional Comprehensive Economic Partnership (RCEP) and has participated in IP initiatives in arrangements such as the Belt and Road Initiative (BRI). Observing these activities, Yu (2019) argued that China is becoming increasingly assertive in global IP governance.

---

[1] WTO Dispute Settlements, DS362: China—Measures Affecting the Protection and Enforcement of Intellectual Property Rights; DS542: China—Certain Measures Concerning the Protection of Intellectual Property Rights; DS549: China—Certain Measures on the Transfer of Technology; DS611: China—Enforcement of Intellectual Property Rights.

[2] The English translation for this Chinese IP regulator was revised to China National Intellectual Property Administration (CNIPA) in March 2018. As this book mainly covers the period before 2018, SIPO will be consistently used to avoid confusion.

[3] The State Council of China, *Outline of the National Intellectual Property Strategy* 国家知识产权战略纲要, No. 18, 2008.

[4] Innovation-driven Development 创新驱动发展 was a concept first proposed in Section 4.2 of the Report of the 18th Chinese Communist Party (CCP) National Congress.

China's increasing 'assertiveness' in global IP governance is often discussed as an example of China's rising power, which is further linked to the question informed by the power transition theory—to what extent its potential leadership revises or upholds the international *status quo*—a long-lasting debate among international relations scholars (Feng, 2009; He *et al.*, 2021; Kastner & Saunders, 2012; Pan, 2004; Yuliantoro & Dinarto, 2019). Stories of China imposing revisionist challenges on the US or Western-led *status quo* have proliferated since the US-China trade war started in 2018. International lawyers have also focused on whether China is a norm-taker, norm-shaper, norm-shaker, or norm-maker across different realms of global governance (Burnay & Chaisse, 2020; Shaffer & Gao, 2020; Wang, 2017). These debates deepen the unduly binary division between the West and China (Turner & Nymalm, 2019).

The COVID-19 pandemic and climate change have shown that global governance in its current form cannot adequately respond to these existential threats (Drahos, 2021; Ekström *et al.*, 2021; Zürn, 2021). In this context, there are deeper questions about the role that China plays in global governance. More important than perceiving China as a disrupter of the liberal international order (Weiss & Wallace, 2021) or a threat to US global pre-eminence (Nymalm, 2019) is the question of what China has delivered in its participation in global governance. Similarly, more important than defining China as a rule-taker or rule-maker is the question of how China's efforts in ruletaking or rulemaking processes have contributed to global governance.

This book investigates the role of China in global IP governance and implications of its engagement for global distributive justice. It contributes to research-based insights on China's role in global governance that cross the traditional boundaries of revisionist versus *status quo* and rule-maker versus rule-taker. Similarly, it also complements extant IP research with under-explored yet important cases from a regulation-oriented approach (Braithwaite & Drahos, 2000). Through case studies, this book analyses how China has engaged in global IP governance, in particular after its WTO accession; which actors are involved; what principles have guided its engagement; and how potential contestations of the principles are managed. The findings of this book will shed light on broad questions such as the principles of distributive justice to which China has appealed in its international IP engagement. These implications are particularly relevant to understand China's vision for global IP governance and its positions on crucial IP issues such as the ideal level of IP protection nationally as well as broader issues including IP and equitable access to COVID-19-related vaccines and medicines.

## 1.2 The Development of Global IP Governance

IP law emerged in Western states as part of the positivist legal order. In the form of statutory law, most types of IP law are granted and enforced by the power of sovereign states, which makes them territorial. One exception is that indigenous people construct IP through custom and secrecy, where secrecy allows owners of knowledge to achieve monopolistic control of certain knowledge without support from the state. From a social constructivist perspective, what is defined as intellectual property depends on the outcome of the competition between different interests in a given time at a given place, which further depends on the prevailing social, economic, and legal conditions (George, 2010).

Before the WTO, states had the freedom to define the scope of IP privileges or rights to serve their domestic policy objectives. Many now developed countries that support strong IP protection only accorded incomplete and weak IP protection during their early stages of industrialisation (Chang, 2001). As an extreme case, both the Netherlands and Switzerland abolished their patent systems to enhance the cross-border flow of knowledge to promote domestic industrialisation in the second half of the nineteenth century. Swiss dyeing and chemical industries particularly benefited from this process (Machlup & Penrose, 1950; Schiff, 1971). Germany also chose to protect only methods of manufacture (not chemical compounds) and became a global power in chemicals (Dutfield, 2003). Similar practices were observed in copyright law. While the US is now at the forefront of strong copyright protection, particularly in cyberspace, it refused to protect the copyright of foreign authors in the late nineteenth century. Prominent English writers like Charles Dickens struggled to push the passage of US copyright law because even though he was more popular in the US than in the UK, his work was published in the US without permission or payment of royalties (Hudon, 1964). It was not until 1988 that the US acceded to *the Berne Convention for the Protection of Literary and Artistic Works* (Berne Convention).

Chang (2002) argues that IP is one of the institutions that developed countries use to kick away the ladder after they have climbed to the top—every developed country had actively engaged in 'illegitimate' practices by the current standards when they were developing their own industries. This process of 'kicking away the ladder' has been achieved by the gradual harmonisation of international IP regulation. Once territorial and fragmented IP laws in Western Europe were harmonised by two conventions that fostered reciprocal IP protection, namely, the 1883 *Paris Convention for the Protection of Industrial Property* (Paris Convention) and the 1886 Berne Convention. IP laws were further introduced to colonial territories in the imperial context as part of grand empire building projects involving the expansion of trade and markets in the late nineteenth century (Drahos, 2002; Okediji, 2004). After World War II, newly independent developing countries were encouraged to pursue multilateral IP agreements to assimilate into the global economic order. They expected their enhanced capacity of IP regulation would be accompanied by increased inflows of foreign direct investment, which motivated them to conclude trade and investment treaties including strong IP protection requirements.

More recently, the increase of the global IP protection standards has evolved into a mechanism, the global IP ratchet, rather than a simple process of rule harmonisation. The global IP ratchet comprises a spiral of bilateral, multilateral, and occasionally plurilateral IP agreements, where new agreements never derogate from existing standards and very often set new ones (Drahos, 2002). The TRIPS Agreement, concluded as part of the *Final Act Embodying the Results of the Uruguay Round of Multilateral Trade Negotiations* and coming into force in 1995, was one of the most important multilateral agreements that set 'minimum' international standards for IP protection and enforcement. The TRIPS Agreement was by and large a compromise between powerful initiators, in particular the US, the EC, and their powerful corporations (Gervais, 2003; Sell, 2003). As part of the rules-based international order under the WTO framework, the TRIPS Agreement requires compliance by every WTO member. Suspicious non-compliance can be sued via the WTO's Dispute Settlement Mechanism (DSM). The TRIPS Agreement, however, is not the end of the global IP ratchet. More than a quarter of a century has passed since the TRIPS Agreement, during which there has been a continuous ratcheting up of international IP protection standards through bilateral and plurilateral agreements (Drahos, 2001; Morin & Şurbeck, 2020; Sell, 2010b).

The global IP ratchet has increasingly circumscribed the freedom of developing countries to set suitable IP standards for developing their infant industries. Many recent developments have echoed the observation that 'the global environment is fundamentally arranged in a manner that makes it highly unlikely that developing countries can respond in any meaningful way to the aggressive erosion of their capacity to regulate IP rights for domestic interests' (Okediji, 2004, p. 139). For instance, developing countries have attempted to frame IP as a development-related issue, because high IP protection standards inconsistent with development levels would prevent them from establishing innovative industries. This view was consolidated in the developing countries' proposal for the Development Agenda at the

World Intellectual Property Organisation (WIPO), arguing that development should be WIPO's central concern (May, 2007). The Development Agenda was soon countered by developed countries' forum-shifting strategy to set even higher global IP enforcement standards in plurilateral agreements, such as the *Anti-counterfeiting Trade Agreement* (ACTA) and bilateral trade agreements (Sell, 2010a). This brief history has illustrated the dynamics between the continuous external pressure for higher IP protection and a state's regulatory sovereignty over IP to keep its policies consistent with its stage of economic and technological development.

The development of global IP governance had profound ramifications for countries that have just started industrialisation. The flexibility to design a domestic IP law that fit their stage of economic and technological development, one that industrialised countries enjoyed in the nineteenth century, is no longer available with the TRIPS Agreement. These countries had little influence on the emergence of the TRIPS paradigm; when TRIPS negotiations concluded, they faced the dilemma of either taking it or being excluded from the benefits of trade liberalisation brought by the WTO. They could not afford not belonging to the WTO, so they incorporated TRIPS standards in their national IP law. While they have long been warned that they need to take the lead in policy experimentation and IP innovation to offset overly protectionist tendencies in the developed countries (Maskus & Reichman, 2004), they were nonetheless further disadvantaged by the global IP ratchet after TRIPS. Such imbalance makes the discussion on IP and global distributive justice a salient issue.

## 1.3 IP and Distributive Justice

While the global IP ratchet trend is still prevalent, the global COVID-19 pandemic has intensified conflicts between IP rules and the dissemination of technology for vaccines, medicines, and other life-saving medical equipment. The current WTO proposals for an IP waiver manifested the call from poor countries to address vaccine inequality through restrictions on IP rights (Thambisetty *et al.*, 2022). These debates have brought IP under scrutiny from distributive justice perspectives, at both national and international levels.

Before the global COVID-19 pandemic, the analysis of IP through the lens of distributive justice was 'almost entirely overlooked if not actively suppressed' (Yanisky-Ravid, 2017, pp. 1–2). Discussion on the IP and distributive justice relation has been divided by the externalist view and the internalist view. Externalism contends that distributive justice is external to IP norms, and there is space for principles of distributive justice to intervene in IP norms when they represent competing values (Blankfein-Tabachnick, 2020; Chander & Sunder, 2006; Kapczynski, 2012). The internalist view maintains that distributive justice was built into IP norms (Hughes & Merges, 2016; Van Houweling, 2004), so distributive justice can be achieved through the internal adjustment of IP norms. A recent proposal for a third approach argues that IP and distributive justice interoperate between internalism and externalism (Yanisky-Ravid, 2017). However, these discussions have not sufficiently understood that the starting point of the discussion is the nature of intangible objects including knowledge and information.

The objects discussed under distributive justice are goods, which can be defined broadly or narrowly (Olsaretti, 2018). Most goods are *private* in the sense that their consumption is directly associated with a payment in exchange for them, and once consumed they cannot be consumed again. By contrast, *public* goods have two features: They are non-excludable as once they are provided no one can be excluded from consuming them, and they are non-rivalrous in consumption in a sense that one person's consumption of them does not prevent others' consumption (Grunberg *et al.*, 1999). Public health is a typical example of public goods—no one can be excluded from benefiting from a reduction in risk of COVID-19, and one person's benefit from this reduction does not prevent others from enjoying the benefit either.

Knowledge and information, the objects of both IP and distributive justice, are also public goods. If not restricted, no one is excluded from their benefits from knowledge and information; one person's use of knowledge does not interfere with others' use. IP is an institution that creates scarcity for knowledge and information by constructed monopoly or private right. Such created scarcity further restricted the free availability of knowledge and information, and their enjoyment can only be made conditional on payment. The key to the relationship between IP and distributive justice is to understand the impact of the IP system on the distribution of public goods including information and knowledge and to guide the IP system by distributive justice principles to achieve broader values embodied by such principles.

This relationship, however, is further complicated by the plurality of normative principles for distributive justice and the divergence between distributive justice principles at national and international levels (Hinsch, 2001). A detailed examination of propositions of principles of distributive justice is beyond the scope of this book. The purpose of discussing these principles is not to advocate any particular principle or to consider how ideal societies would operate under them. Rather, it is to understand how real societies have followed different distributive justice principles historically and at present and how IP systems operate under and interact with these principles. Principles of distributive justice provide a useful lens to understand what value(s) China has appealed to in its IP engagement and the implications of China's increasingly active IP engagement for the rest of the world. Four broad principles of distributive justice are discussed below, with a focus on how each principle interacts with the IP system.

### 1.3.1 Egalitarian Principle of Distributive Justice

Egalitarianism includes broad structural theories of distributive justice: strict egalitarianism (Nielsen, 1979), luck egalitarianism (Anderson, 1999; Dworkin, 2003), and Rawls' difference principle (Rawls, 2001). Strict egalitarianism is one of the simplest forms of egalitarianism, arguing that all members of a society should have the same level of benefits and burdens. Luck egalitarianism is based on the idea that equality should not be influenced by arbitrary factors, and people should be compensated for undeserved bad luck that affect their interests, such as suffering from accidents and illness. The difference principle permits inequalities in resource allocation so long as the outcome would make the well-being of the least advantaged in a society materially better off than they would be under the strict egalitarianism. While egalitarian-based distribution can be conveniently achieved for information and knowledge as compared with private goods due to their non-rivalry and non-excludability, IP law has restricted the egalitarian distribution of knowledge. As will be discussed in Sect. 1.4.1, China followed strict egalitarianism, allowing communal ownership of knowledge; it abolished patent and copyright regulation before the Cultural Revolution. Furthermore, while most developed countries nowadays do not appeal to the egalitarian distribution of knowledge, they have argued for an egalitarian distribution of other related resources. For instance, genetic resources and associated traditional knowledge had been considered till the 1970s 'the common heritage of humankind'—global public goods that should be equally distributed (Gepts, 2004). Therefore, the egalitarian principle of distributive justice is particularly important to understand the tension behind the issue of disclosure obligation to be discussed in Chapter 3. More recently, proponents for equitable distribution of COVID-19 vaccines and medicines have also appealed to the egalitarian principle from different angles. For instance, luck egalitarianism underpins the argument that people in wealthy nations have significant duties to people in poorer nations who are subject to unchosen disadvantages (Jecker *et al.*, 2021). COVID-19 vaccines are also argued to be considered 'primary goods' by Rawls, of which the distribution should be to the greatest benefit of the least advantaged (Collste, 2022). These principles provide a critical lens to understand what is at stake in the ongoing WTO IP waiver negotiations (Chapter 6).

### 1.3.2 Utilitarian Principle of Distributive Justice

The utilitarian principle aims to achieve the greatest good for the greatest number. Based on the axiom of Bentham and Stuart, utilitarianism constitutes a basis for creating an IP monopoly. Utilitarianism recognises the function of IP in yielding greater utility for society—creating monopolistic power to stimulate innovation. Specifically, authors and inventors can enjoy an absolute privilege to their works and inventions for a limited period so that they are adequately remunerated. This is greater than the consequences of not recognising IP, that is a lack of provision of knowledge as public goods due to inadequate compensation (Snow, 2021). Within IP law, the utilitarian principle is manifested as incentive theory (Blair & Cotter, 2005; Derclaye & Taylor, 2013) or reward theory (Oddi, 1995). For instance, through constructed monopoly for a limited period, innovators can be rewarded for the knowledge they created, and free riding of information and knowledge can be prevented.

However, utilitarianism has its prominent problems. First, because the system maximises only economic aspects of utility, a utilitarianism-based IP system could lead to the mal-distribution of resources and wealth which may incur substantial social costs, such as setting the price for medicines out of the reach of the poor (Gosseries *et al.*, 2008). Second, the key conditions for balancing different interests in its original design, such as the concept of 'a limited period' for the IP monopoly, are dishonoured. The evergreening strategy is often used for pharmaceutical patents, which extends the life of a patent monopoly by surrounding an original inventive patent with numerous additional patents and further delays generic entry to the market (Moir, 2021). Third, while the utility of the patent institution in stimulating innovation is supported by some empirical evidence, it is not without disagreement—Jaffe and Lerner (2011) found that changing patenting practices in the US have endangered innovation and economic productivity. Despite such criticism, there has been increasing advocacy for maximising IP protection (longer terms, broader protection, and enhanced punishment for violations) (Halbert, 2011) based on a reductionist understanding of utilitarianism that more IP protection would lead to more utility. Again, there is no empirical evidence supporting this hypothesis.

Utilitarianism was introduced to China as essential regulatory knowledge through transnational networks of technocrats and epistemic communities. Based on its original interpretation, China further developed IP instrumentalism as a rationale for its domestic IP regulation (Chapter 8). China's global IP engagement has been a continuous balancing of this principle and its foreign policy principles (Chapter 9).

### 1.3.3 Entitlement-Based Principle of Distributive Justice

The entitlement-based principle considers IP a quasi-property entitlement, despite knowledge and information being public goods by nature. It originated from the Lockean proviso that a person may legitimately acquire property rights by mixing his labour with resources held in common if, after the acquisition, there is enough and as good left in common for others (Locke, 2015 [1690]). The Lockean justification is also related to the sense of desert and respect for individual autonomy and sovereignty (Moore, 2012). Following this theory, if someone uses their intellect to create something, they also deserve to have property rights in that creation. Nozick further combined the Lockean notion of property with his idea of just acquisition and transfer (Nozick, 1974), and this has set the foundation for the contemporary entitlement-based theory that upholds IP as private property rights. The entitlement-based theory has been recently expanded as an embodiment of natural right and fairness through its acquisition of property rights from the fruit of an individual's creation (Merges, 2011).

Nonetheless, applying the Lockean theory to IP has been criticised because legal scholars engaging in such Lockean explorations have ignored the challenges raised against them in the philosophical literature. For one thing, the condition that there should be enough and as good left in common for others in the Lockean theory gradually faded when the entitlement-based theory was developed for IP. For another, the Lockean theory of property was concerned with physical objects. The metaphysical difference between physical objects and non-physical objects of knowledge and information which are non-rivalrous and non-excludable has further led to the question of the boundary of the property right in non-physical objects. Once these differences are carefully considered, a Lockean theory implies that IP should be more limited than in current reality (Chatterjee, 2020). Furthermore, recognising IP as a species of natural right has also faced conceptual difficulties and rights conflict; one illustration of the conflict is that property in expression through copyright conflicts with freedom of expression (Drahos, 1998).

Globally, the TRIPS Agreement is considered a manifestation of the entitlement-based principle, reconceptualising IP as a property right to knowledge and information (which are framed as commodities instead of public goods) rather than an incentive for innovation (Dreyfuss & Frankel, 2014). The recent campaign towards cultivating an IP culture in China has leaned towards the entitlement theory to advocate intrinsic respect for IP (Chapter 8).

### 1.3.4 Global Distributive Justice and the Confucian Golden Principle

While traditionally, it is assumed that the scope of distributive justice should be confined to the national level, there is an emerging literature advocating principles of global distributive justice. There are different approaches to global distributive justice, for instance: 1) cosmopolitanism argues that distributive justice principles should operate globally, and duties of distributive justice thus apply to all human beings (but not states); 2) nationalism is a state-centric approach, emphasising special duties to fellow-nationals; 3) the society-of-states approach considers principles of global distributive justice violate state independence and sovereignty; and 4) realism claims global distributive justice is utopian and advises states to advance their national interests (Caney, 2001). These global distributive justice principles may not be well operationalised when applying to IP. Cosmopolitanism has extended egalitarianism at the global level, but this individual-oriented approach may not capture the central tension in global distributive justice and IP—seeking just distribution of information between states at different levels of industrial development. Nationalism and the society-of-states approach may not provide clear guidance for states to act without associating with any specific distributive justice principles at the national level. By denying global distributive justice, realism only implies state should endure the rule of the jungle instead of calling for change.

In the current international IP system, people in lower-income countries have to accept high IP enforcement standards which may impede their access to primary goods such as textbooks in education (Chon, 2006) and medicines in health care (Fisher & Syed, 2006), in order to provide sufficient incentives or property rights to knowledge creators in wealthy countries. As pointed out by Thomas Pogge:

> The heavily trading opportunities the rich countries afford the poor do not come for free. To obtain them, poor countries must spend large amounts on enforcing the intellectual property rights of the rich, thereby depriving their own populations of access to cheap generic versions of patented seeds and life-saving medicines. (Pogge, 2005a)

Pogge further argued that bilateral and multilateral IP treaties have played a central role through which wealthy countries impose their aggressive IP enforcement standards on poor countries, and participation in the imposition of such social rules may constitute a human right violation (Pogge, 2005b). Combining the social imperatives and the history of global IP governance (Sect. 1.2), a global distributive justice principle in relation to IP should concern just distribution of information and knowledge in the interactions among states, in particular focusing on how to retain the regulatory sovereignty of poor and technologically retarded states in formulating IP laws consistent with their domestic conditions. On the other side of the coin, such a principle requires rich and technologically advanced states to take a more conservative approach to international IP rulemaking by not universalising their domestic utilitarian or entitlement-based distributive justice principles at the global level. Imposing high IP enforcement standards through coercion contravenes this principle, despite it being the practice of some Western countries for decades (Drahos, 2007).

There is nothing new under the sun when we appreciate the plurality of world views in global societies. The above principle of non-imposition in many ways coincides with the Confucian golden principle '己所不欲 勿施于人 never do unto others what you would not like them to do onto you'.[5] According to Confucianism, the cultivation of one's own character sets the foundation for political stability and enduring peace for all under heaven (Zhao, 2006). In this sense, the Confucian golden principle can extend its application globally.

While the principle of non-imposition is similar to the nationalist approach in global distributive justice by focusing on the duties of states, it is distinct from the Western golden rule reasoning that 'we should treat others as we should have them treat us' (Duxbury, 2008). The negative formulation implies the virtue of modesty and forgiveness in Confucianism (Allinson, 1985) with a moral obligation of *not* imposing one's standards on fellow nations. As China has increasingly explored its native resources and culture, it is essential to understand to what extent China has appealed to this principle of non-imposition in its global IP engagement, in particular, whether China's

[5] The Analects of Confucius 论语 XII, 2.

increasingly active global IP engagement has also featured the imposition of Chinese IP enforcement standards on others.

In summary, the principle of non-imposition resonates with various issues of global IP governance discussed in this chapter. It recognises the nature of information and knowledge as public goods and the territoriality of IP law, without contravening a distributive justice principle upheld domestically. In addition, the historical account of global IP governance and industrialisation may also signal the suitability of understanding the principle of non-imposition from an inter-generational perspective of distributive justice—states arriving at industrialisation now should be treated equally in terms of IP protection as the earlier achievers some centuries ago. While this may evoke broader debates about IP and distributive justice, the central focus of this book is the Chinese case—what principles of distributive justice China has appealed to at different stages and to what extent China's global IP engagement has aligned with the Confucian golden principle.

## 1.4 A Brief History of IP in China

There was no indigenous Chinese concept equivalent to that of intellectual property in Western Europe. While in the GI case, the imperial tributary system created significant name-place recognition for some products, there was no regulatory regime institutionalising such a connection as a privilege or property right. Alford (1993) raised the question of why ancient China had not, over a very long period, developed a statutory copyright law. Specifically, Alford argues that even if there was evidence in ancient China concerning restrictions on the unauthorised reproduction of books, symbols, and products, they were instituted for ideological control rather than for the protection of property rights. This argument was reinforced in his book *To Steal a Book Is an Elegant Offense* (Alford, 1995), which has a significant impact beyond academia as it set the foundation for the US negotiators to frame China as a 'born pirate' in the US-China bilateral negotiations from 1989 to 1996 (Wu, 2009). More recently, the allegation of China's theft of US IP (USTR, 2018) triggered the US-China trade war in 2018 and led to the first phase agreement USCETA 2020.

Like other countries that were once colonised, China accepted IP standards at the beginning of the twentieth century. It made the sovereign decision to abandon IP entirely when the People's Republic of China (PRC) was established as a socialist state. It embraced IP again after its reform to become a socialist market economy.

This penultimate section offers a brief account of Chinese IP history. It provides specific social, economic, and cultural contexts for China's global IP engagement. It also clarifies the starting point for the discussion of case studies. Prominently, China has been a regulatory importer of IP rules for a century, which sets the foundation for this book to investigate China's more active and constructive engagement in recent times.

### 1.4.1 IP in China's Modern History and the Maoist Era

China's experience with IP in its modern history (1840–1949) was linked to memories of a century of humiliation and acceptance of Western IP models in bilateral agreements. IP was not a prominent issue for foreign businesses in China until the *Shimonoseki Treaty* (1895) between the Qing government (1644–1912) and Japan, which allowed foreign businesses to engage in manufacturing in China. As all colonists shared privileges, other Western powers also started manufacturing in China. Western business people soon found that trademarks were an effective instrument for them to secure their interests in the Chinese market. Meanwhile, trademark disputes between Chinese and foreign businesses, as well as among foreign businesses, increased dramatically.

In response to business demands, Western powers began to seek opportunities to push the Qing government to legalise trademark rights (Cai & Wang, 2005). The chance came in 1902 when the Qing government was involved in the negotiation of bilateral friendship and commerce treaties after the *Xinchou Treaty* (also known as the Boxer Protocol). After the settlement of the Boxer Rebellion in 1900, the Xinchou Treaty was signed between the Qing government and the Eight-Nation Alliance. Article 11 of the Xinchou Treaty provided that 'the Chinese Government has agreed to negotiate the amendments deemed necessary by the foreign Governments to the Treaties of Commerce and Navigation and the other subjects concerning commercial relations with the object of facilitating them'. The UK, the US, Japan, Portugal, and Germany separately negotiated commercial and navigation treaties with the Qing government, and IP was put on the agenda in these bilateral negotiations. The Qing government agreed to introduce IP laws in its last few years of ruling after it negotiated with the UK, the US, and Japan on the following treaties[6]:

[6] Negotiations with Germany and Portugal were not finalised before the collapse of the Qing Government.

- *New Commercial Treaty of 1902 between the UK and China* (the Mackay Treaty), which included provisions on trademarks;
- *Treaty between the US and China for the Extension of the Commercial Relations between Them* (1903), which included provisions on trademarks, patents, and copyright;
- *Japan–China Additional Treaty of Commerce and Navigation* (1903), which included provisions on trademarks and copyright (Wang, 2008).

These three treaties directly pushed China into IP lawmaking. By implementing these treaties, the Qing government started a legal reform process and formulated laws including the *Copyright Code of the Great Qing Dynasty* (1910). The Qing Dynasty collapsed in 1912 before its trademark law and patent law were finalised. Since China was not colonised by a single Western power, it did not completely transplant the legal system from a specific Western state. Signing unequal treaties with different Western powers allowed the Qing government to have a certain level of flexibility in selecting to transplant an IP law from a certain jurisdiction. Despite constant wars and changes in regimes, three copyright laws, four patent laws, and three trademark laws were promulgated in the first half of the twentieth century. China's international IP engagement in its modern history has been, by and large, a process of regulatory importation from different sources. The early IP laws have contributed to accelerating the waning of China's ancient traditions and values, including those related to the production and diffusion of knowledge.

After the establishment of the PRC in 1949, China was able to make sovereign decisions on domestic issues for the first time in a century. China shifted to a system of knowledge regulation following the model of the Union of Soviet Socialist Republics (USSR) till 1978. After four years of economic recovery from 1950 to 1953, China initiated its socialist transformation. Through public-private partnerships, private ownership in sectors including agriculture, handicrafts, and commerce was transformed into socialist public ownership. During this period of economic recovery and socialist transformation, IP was first adopted as a proprietary right to encourage domestic capitalists to invest in innovation, as well as to attract foreign investment and stimulate technology importation.[7] Once the socialist transformation was accomplished in 1956, however, the IP system quickly lost legitimacy. On the eve of the Cultural Revolution which began in 1966, patent regulations

[7] Finance and Economic Committee of the Administrative Council of the Central Government of China, *The Provisional Regulations on the Protection of Inventors' Right and Patent Right* 保障发明权与专利权暂行条例, 17 August 1950.

were completely abolished.[8] In terms of copyright, while the right of attribution was retained, the economic right to get remuneration was abolished in 1960 (Lu, 2008, p. 26).

Although communal ownership might have been suitable domestically, China had a weak industrial base and still needed to introduce technologies from other countries to achieve technological catch-up. When the Capitalist Bloc embargoed exports to China through the Coordinating Committee for Multilateral Export Controls (CoCom) (Hunt, 1982), China followed the foreign policy of 'leaning to one side' to the USSR to ally with the Communist Bloc in the 1950s (Guan, 2009; Niu, 1999). This enabled China to receive technical assistance from the USSR and Eastern Europe. In this decade, China introduced 156 major projects from the USSR and Eastern Europe in areas of energy, national defence, and mechanical industries. Guided by the ideology of communal ownership, no patent fees were paid by China in these contracts (Xiao & Wu, 2015). The USSR also helped train the first generation of Chinese technicians and engineers by dispatching over 8000 experts to China who trained over 7000 Chinese technicians. However, when the China-USSR alliance broke up in the early 1960s, the USSR stopped technical assistance and recalled its experts immediately.

Consequently, China began to diversify its technology importation, endeavouring to import technology and equipment from Japan and Western Europe (Zhang *et al.*, 2005, pp. 374–375). After US President Richard Nixon visited Beijing in 1972, China started seeking technology transfers from the US. The second wave of technology importation occurred in 1973, with 26 projects on fibre, fertiliser, petrochemicals, integrated coal mining, and power stations (Chen, 2005). This wave of technology importation became a stimulus for China to integrate into the international IP system because it could no longer ignore patents. In keeping with the communal ownership of knowledge, technologies imported to China were further disseminated to domestic companies at no extra cost. Due to the lack of patent protection, some foreign companies were only willing to export sets of equipment to China without the associated technologies. Chinese companies were trapped in a cycle of 'equipment importation, equipment ageing, and equipment re-importation'.

[8] State Council, *Regulations on Remuneration for Inventions* 发明奖励条例, 3 November 1963. Article 23 stipulates that 'The ownership of inventions belongs to the State. Any individual or institution may not monopolise the invention. Any institution (including the collectively owned institution) in the State can use an invention when it needs to'.

### 1.4.2 China's Re-integration into the International IP System

China started to re-integrate into the international IP system following the normalisation of US-China bilateral foreign relations and China's domestic reform towards a market economy. The four decades since 1979 can be further divided into three stages with the following two milestones: China's WTO accession in 2001 and China's promulgation of its National IP Strategy in 2008.

Cooperation in science and technology was the starting point for the normalisation of US-China relations, and IP was a priority in the negotiation of the US-China Agreement on High Energy Physics and the US–China Agreement on Trade Relations, both concluded in 1979 following DENG Xiaoping's visit to the US. The US and China then concluded four bilateral Memorandum of Understanding (MOUs) on IP from 1988 to 1996.[9] Establishing an IP system and consistently improving it became a treaty obligation for China. In parallel, IP was also central to China's 15-year negotiations to resume its position in General Agreement on Tariffs and Trade (GATT) from 1986 to 2001. Under external pressure, the PRC promulgated its first *Trademark Law* in 1982, *Patent Law* in 1984, and *Copyright Law* in 1990.

There was continuous pressure to enhance protection standards in Chinese IP laws. China was on the priority watch list in its *Special 301 Report* based on Section 301 of the US Trade Act of 1974, a unilateral measure that the US has used since 1989 to pressure foreign countries to change their IP laws to protect US business interests (Palmedo, 2020). Bilateral negotiations followed when China was put on the Special 301 watch list. China was also pressured to enhance its IP standards as it was a precondition for China's accession to the WTO. Although China's ultimate aim for the GATT negotiation was to be accepted by the multilateral trade system, the negotiations concerning market entry were taken bilaterally. After signing *US-China Bilateral Agreement on China's Entry into the WTO* in which the US agreed to support China's WTO accession, China's GATT negotiation with other countries has considerably accelerated. In addition, the US-China Joint Commission on

[9] China–United States Memorandum of Understanding on Enactment and Scope of PRC Copyright Law on 19 May 1989, China–United States Memorandum of Understanding on the Protection of Intellectual Property on 17 January 1992, China–United States Agreement Regarding Intellectual Property Rights Memorandum of Understanding on 26 February 1995; and China's Implementation of the 1995 Intellectual Property Rights Agreement on 17 June 1996. The Chinese literature often mentions three MOUs instead of four, as the one in 1996 was considered a unilateral clarification to implement the 1995 agreement, not a bilateral MOU per se.

Commerce and Trade (JCCT) was co-organised by the US Trade Representative (USTR) and the Chinese Ministry of Commerce in 1983, which became a major bilateral forum for US-China IP communication after 1996.

China was in a weak bargaining position in these bilateral IP negotiations. China needed access to science and technology, while the US had the most advanced science and technology; China wanted to attract foreign investment, and US multinational corporations were the major investors worldwide; China was eager to enter the WTO, but it had to go through market access negotiations with the US first to achieve this. The deterioration of foreign relations after the Tiananmen Square event in 1989 compounded the pressure on IP negotiations. While fundamental issues such as human rights bedevilling the overall US-China relations appeared beyond solution, IP was still a legitimate topic for bilateral bargaining (Maruyama, 1999, p. 172). China responded to the US pressure with two strategies: one was to take the TRIPS Agreement as a baseline in its bilateral negotiations with the US, and the other was to use its domestic market as leverage for retaliation. China's participation in TRIPS negotiations[10] allowed it to have direct access to the Draft Final Act (1991)[11] (Otten, 2015). Since 1991, Chinese negotiators have adjusted their position in US-China bilateral IP negotiations by defending the Draft Final Act (1991) as a new baseline to resist the higher standards pushed by the US (Wang & Wu, 2001). For instance, under the Chinese Patent Law (1984), chemicals and pharmaceuticals were not subject to patent protection, but they became patentable subject matter in the amended Patent Law (1992) (Wen, 1992). Although this was apparently amended to comply with the US-China MOU (1992), China accepted such a standard also because it expected itself to become a GATT member when it would make the amendment anyway (Zheng, 1998).

The decade from 1996 to 2007 was often referred to as a honeymoon period (Harris, 2008) for US-China bilateral IP relations. In this decade, China mainly focused on domestic IP law amendment and other issues for TRIPS compliance. This was often referred to as China's second IP law amendment, including Patent Law (2000), Trademark Law (2000), and Copyright Law (2000). The amended laws adopted the same language as the TRIPS Agreement to guarantee compliance (Wen, 2002). Chinese market

---

[10] China was one of the co-sponsors for the GATT proposal MTN.GNG/NG11/W/71,14 May 1990. This proposal represented the developing countries' position in the TRIPS negotiation.

[11] Uruguay Round, Trade Negotiations Committee, *Draft Final Act Embodying the Results of the Uruguay Round of Multilateral Trade Negotiations*, 20 December 1991, MTN.TNC/W/FA. The text of the TRIPS Agreement made two minor changes on the basis of this Draft Final Act (1991): '(1) the addition to Article 64 of paragraphs 2 and 3 on non-violation disputes and (2) the addition of the language in Article 31(c) in regard to semiconductor technology'.

entities also began to use IP to protect their innovation. Patent applications submitted to SIPO increased by 26% annually from 2000 (WIPO, 2011), and SIPO became the world's biggest patent office in 2011. In this decade, China developed a positive relationship with WIPO, signed 17 WIPO-administered IP treaties (Appendix 1), and joined other developing countries in submitting proposals to the TRIPS Council in the Doha Round.

Bilaterally, IP emerged on the agenda of EU-China relations in 1999, which further developed into special EU-China cooperation projects for IP protection (Crookes, 2013). Wyzycka and Hasmath (2017) argue that technical assistance programmes have been among the most effective soft power instruments in shaping the EU's influence on China, for example in exporting *sui generis* protection for GIs.

The honeymoon ended when the US sued China at the WTO in 2007. China had to amend domestic IP laws to comply with the panel's decision.[12] In addition to Special 301, the US International Trade Commission (USITC) initiated another unilateral measure, 337 investigations under Section 337 of the US Tariff Act of 1930. Since 2005, 337 investigations targeting Chinese companies for IP infringement have accounted for 30% of total annual investigations. Among these investigations, patent infringement has been the major cause of action (Ran, 2017).

### 1.4.3 China's Global IP Engagement in the New Era

After 2008 China promulgated its National IP Strategy (2008), and IP transitioned into an instrument to serve the Chinese domestic policy objective of innovation promotion from an institution responsive to external coercion. The National IP Strategy set IP targets to be achieved in 2013 and 2020 and specified tasks for their implementation. The National IP Strategy has significantly improved the priority of IP through institution-building and implementation. Institutionally, the Inter-Ministerial Joint Meeting for Implementing the National IP Strategy (Inter-Ministerial Joint Meeting) was established. With its general office affiliated with and located in the State Council, the Inter-Ministerial Joint Meeting has all 31 IP regulators as members (Appendix 2). After achieving its mid-term targets in 2013, China released the *Action Plan on Further Implementing the* National IP Strategy (2014–2020)[13] (National IP Strategy 2.0) as the second stage of its National

---

12 WTO, China—Measures Affecting the Protection and Enforcement of Intellectual Property Rights, 2009 (WT/DS362/R).

13 State Council General Office, *Circular of the General Office of the State Council on Forwarding the Action Plan by SIPO and Other Departments on the Further Implementation of the National Intellectual*

IP strategy. The National IP Strategy 2.0 sets specific, measurable, and time-based targets for invention patent applications, patent applications via the *Patent Cooperation Treaty* (PCT), trademark and copyright registrations, as well as IP services and financing (Appendix 3). In 2015, China further clarified its IP target of building itself as an IP power of the world and the role of IP in its innovation-driven development strategy.[14] IP is recognised as an important instrument to enhance the technological competitiveness of China, stimulate innovation, and facilitate industrial development.

A prominent outcome of implementing these strategies is surging patent filings by Chinese applicants. In 1999, WIPO's Patent Cooperation Treaty (PCT) system received 276 applications from China. By 2019, that number had risen to 58,990 (WIPO, 2020). Underpinning this 200-fold increase in 20 years are not only patent subsidies provided by the government but also genuinely enhanced innovation capacities. In 2019, China surpassed the US as the biggest user of the PCT.

Even with such progress, China has still been condemned by the US for ineffective IP enforcement and for engaging in IP theft, which led to a new bilateral agreement USCETA 2020. In this agreement, China agreed to enact the highest level of IP protection among all US bilateral and plurilateral agreements, including provisions on patent linkage, patent term extension, data exclusivity, trade secrets, and enhanced criminal sanctions for IP infringements. It seems that, despite the exponential increase in IP numbers, the US-China bilateral IP relations still resemble that in the late 1980s. In the meanwhile, China further progressed its own agenda in building itself as a global IP power. In the *Outline of Building a Powerful Intellectual Property Country (2021–2035)*,[15] China sets the target of building itself into a global IP power in 2035:

> By 2035, China's comprehensive IP competitiveness will be among the top countries in the world; its IP system will be complete; IP will promote the vigorous development of innovation and entrepreneurship; the cultural awareness of IP of the whole society will be basically formed; China will fully participate in international IP cooperation and global IP governance

*Property Strategy (2014–2020)* 国务院办公厅关于转发知识产权局等单位深入实施国家知识产权战略行动计划 (2014–2020年) 的通知. No. 64 (2014).

[14] State Council, *Several Opinions on Accelerating Building China as a Powerful IP Country under New Conditions* 关于新形势下加快知识产权强国建设的若干意见 No. 71 (2015). In 2016, the State Council issued another notice to disaggregate tasks mandated by the above opinions.

[15] The Central Committee of the CCP and the State Council, *Outline for Building a Powerful Intellectual Property Country (2021–2035)* 知识产权强国建设纲要 (2021–2035年).

at multiple levels; China will become a global IP power with Chinese characteristics.

In summary, China's century-long engagement with IP, has involved conflicts, colonialism, rejection, communist models, market opening, re-integration into global capitalism, regulatory importation, and emerging initiatives. The focus of the book is the last two decades after China's WTO accession.

## 1.5 Case Selection, Analytical Framework, and Key Findings

This book has three parts. This chapter is the first part, setting the scene by introducing the historical background of both global and Chinese IP governance and theoretical foundations for key issues to be discussed in this book. Part II includes five case studies: geographical indications (GIs) (Chapter 2), the requirement to disclose sources of genetic resources in patent applications (the disclosure obligation) (Chapter 3), IP and standardisation (Chapter 4), and China's international IP engagement at the bilateral level (Chapter 5) and multilateral level (Chapter 6). Part III further analyses factors that influenced China's international IP engagement based on the case studies, including actors (Chapter 7), contesting principles (Chapter 8), and managing strategies (Chapter 9). Chapter 10 concludes. This section explains the rationale for case selection, the analytical framework of the discussion chapters, and the key findings of the book.

### 1.5.1 Selection of Cases

The central question of how China has engaged in global IP governance drives the empirical exploration of this book and sets selection criteria for case studies. This book analyses China's global IP engagement in five cases: GIs, the disclosure obligation, IP and standardisation, China's bilateral IP engagement, and its multilateral IP engagement. The first three cases are thematic. The TRIPS Agreement is the starting point to analyse China's global IP engagement where China has assimilated TRIPS rules as domestic law on major IP types including patents, trademarks, and copyright. From this default position of modelling TRIPS rules, this book selects cases where international IP rules are not yet settled—either fragmented, contested, or under negotiation at various forums. Only in these cases does China have the opportunity to participate and make a meaningful contribution to agenda-setting.

*The Doha WTO Ministerial Declaration* has set the agenda for IP negotiations in the post-TRIPS era:

> We agree to negotiate the establishment of a multilateral system of notification and registration of geographical indications for wines and spirits by the Fifth Session of the Ministerial Conference. We note that issues related to the extension of the protection of geographical indications provided for in Article 23 to products other than wines and spirits will be addressed in the Council for TRIPS pursuant to paragraph 12 of this declaration... We instruct the Council for TRIPS, ... to examine, inter alia, the relationship between the TRIPS Agreement and the Convention on Biological Diversity, the protection of traditional knowledge and folklore, and other relevant new developments...[16]

This supports the selection of GIs and the disclosure obligation as cases for this book, the latter being a central issue for the relationship between the Convention on Biological Diversity (CBD) and the TRIPS Agreement. China, as the world's factory, also initiated its technological standards in the wireless local-area network (WLAN) after lessons from its earlier experience. The case of IP and standardisation is, therefore, selected as a third thematic case to see how the Chinese initiatives are received by the rest of the world.

These cases illustrate China's active engagement in global IP governance beyond accepting TRIPS standards. Specific engagement activities varied with issues and changes over time. In the case of GIs, China initially transplanted rules both from the US and from the EU. After its three domestic GI regulatory regimes were established, China actively participated in negotiations at the WTO and bilateral FTAs. However, the agreements that China concluded with the EU and the US, respectively, in 2020 included competing mandates concerning foreign GIs registered in China, putting China in a compliance dilemma. In the case of the disclosure obligation, the discussions at the WTO in the early 2000s facilitated China's understanding of the issue. The Chinese Patent Law (2008) incorporated holistic provisions on the disclosure obligations for plant, animal, and human genetic resources with its institutional innovation. After this milestone in domestic law, China actively promoted disclosure obligations in international negotiations. The failed attempts of China's promotion of its WLAN standards both as national and international

---

[16] WTO, Ministerial Declaration, WT/MIN(01)/Dec/1, 20 November 2001, Paras. 18 and 19.

standards demonstrated that to be an agenda setter in global governance China needed more than market power and an impressive patent portfolio.

China's bilateral engagement through free trade agreements (FTAs) and its multilateral engagement with the WTO and WIPO provide an opportunity to investigate agendas China attempted to promote at different forums, and the implications of China's engagement for global distributive justice. By and large, China seldom initiated alternative IP rulemaking. When it did so, its initiatives were often challenged or ignored. Nonetheless, China generally supported agendas that either safeguarded TRIPS standards or were proposed by developing countries. It also joined other developing countries to respond to the global IP ratchet (Cheng, 2019).

### 1.5.2 Analytical Framework and Main Findings

The analytical framework in Part III models that of *Global Business Regulation* (Braithwaite & Drahos, 2000). Braithwaite and Drahos analysed global business regulation through actors, principles, and mechanisms. This book adapts its analysis to actors, principles, and strategies instead. The change of focus from mechanisms to strategies is mainly because of the need to understand how China participated in global IP governance rather than the mechanisms of global IP governance.

An important context for the analysis is the international regime complexity. International IP regulation has increasingly interacted with regulatory regimes on related issues, such as genetic resources, public health, and human rights (Helfer, 2009, 2015; Muzaka, 2011; Raustiala & Victor, 2004; Yu, 2007). The dense overlaps of non-hierarchical international institutions at different levels, often referred to as international regime complexity, have profound implications for global IP governance. As international regime complexity provides opportunities for forum-shopping, forum-shifting, and new forum creation, weak actors can circumvent oppositions or promote their preferred policies internationally (Helfer, 2004). International IP regime complexity also means there is no general rule-maker or rule-taker across all forums of global IP governance. Problem-solving is not straightforward for any actor, powerful or powerless (Alter & Raustiala, 2018). Both cases of GIs and disclosure obligation put China in the context of the international regime complexity, focusing not only on the issues that China has put on the agenda (what) but also on the strategies China has employed to achieve its preferred objectives (how), and the choice of forum to advance its proposition (where).

Following the analytical framework, the main findings in terms of actors, principles, and management strategies concerning China's international IP engagement are as follows:

**Lack of coordination among actors**

Over 30 ministries are involved in China's domestic IP regulation (Appendix 2). These substate actors and non-state actors, including the IP epistemic communities and private actors, are all involved in China's international IP engagement. Instead of consolidated efforts, the substate actors show a spectrum of positions behind China's international IP engagement. Chinese IP regulators and epistemic communities have close connections with their counterparts from developed countries and with international organisations. Over time, they have been inclined to absorb various legal approaches and ideas about IP, especially those underpinned by utilitarianism and entitlement-based theory. The lack of coordination among actors has partly contributed to the inconsistency of China's positions on the same issue at different forums and its reluctance to actively advance an egalitarian agenda for unconstrained public access to information, such as IP waiver negotiation at the WTO.

**Contesting principles**

China's IP engagement has been guided and bounded by various principles. There are two groups of principles: IP instrumentalism and China's foreign policy principles. IP instrumentalism is a manifestation of the utilitarian approach with Chinese characteristics. It recognises the value of IP in stimulating innovation, fostering economic transformation, and enhancing technological competitiveness. On the other hand, China's foreign policy principles require it to take sides with developing countries, support multilateralism, and not make alliances with other countries. There are internal tensions and potential contestations between these two groups of principles. Consequently, China's global IP engagement, in a sense, is a manifestation of its managing strategies to reconcile the contestation between different principles.

**Managing strategies**

China has taken strategies of modelling and balancing to implement the above principles or minimise their potential conflicts. Following foreign policy objectives, modelling is a strategy that China has used in all three cases. In the case of GIs, China followed both the US and the EU models for GI protection. In the case of the disclosure obligation, China actively learned from diverse proposals submitted to the WTO and WIPO and promulgated domestic legislation that modelled these proposals when international negotiation was still in progress. Modelling led to compliance and institutional isomorphism, and China has increasingly taken similar positions to developed countries on many IP issues. China has used the strategy of balancing to address the potential contestation in principles. It includes three specific strategies: reticence, serving the foreign policy priority, and rule coexistence and complexity.

In addition to managing the contesting principles domestically, China faces external challenges in the context of international regime complexity. China's forum and agenda-related strategies include multi-forum engagement, dissembling, and more cohesive responsive engagement. Specifically, multi-forum engagment is a strategy via which China participated in IP negotiations and discussions in all relevant forums rather than prioritising one forum over another. China has used the dissembling strategy in many cases—China takes one position in one international forum at one time, but positions on the same issue at different forums are inconsistent. This strategy takes advantage of international regime complexity and addresses potential contestation in principles. In addition, China has a clearer and more cohesive agenda in its responsive engagement than actively promoting its agenda.

Implications of China's IP engagement for distributive justice and global distributive justice vary from case to case. These are discussed at the end of each case study. However, two general observations can be made as follows.

### China's diminishing resistance to global IP ratchet

While traditionally China has resisted TRIPS-plus standards with other developing countries concertedly, recent bilateral agreements with developed countries clearly indicate that China's resistance to high IP protection standards is diminishing. Rather than resisting the global IP ratchet, China becomes part of it—by cultivating an IP culture domestically and by collaborating with WIPO to enhance IP capacity in developing countries. This can be explained by China's enhanced innovative capacities. The proposition that the IP system needs to be aligned with the development stage of a country (Chang, 2001) implies that once the country has graduated from the early stage of economic development and becomes an innovator itself, it may increasingly benefit from extensive IP protection. The paradox is that the more advanced a country is in its innovative capacity, the more reluctant it can be in promoting unconstrained dissemination of knowledge following the egalitarian principle. With enhanced innovative capacity, China has increasingly appealed to the entitlement-based theory. Its diminishing resistance to high IP protection standards, in particular the USCETA 2020, means developing countries have lost China as part of the coalition in resisting the global IP ratchet. Once divided, they are easier to be conquered—the US has indeed started using this agreement as a template IP chapter for subsequent trade agreements.

**The principle of non-imposition**

The Confucian golden principle of non-imposition is an ethical restriction that has not been followed by Western powers when it comes to intellectual property. This principle of non-imposition is manifested in China's global IP engagement, in particular in its bilateral FTAs. While China can accept high IP standards itself, it did not further request high IP standards in its trade agreements. The fact that most Chinese FTAs safeguard the TRIPS standards, either implicitly or explicitly without incorporating TRIPS-plus standards, indicates an approach of non-imposition. This approach makes it possible for Chinese FTA partners to maintain policy space for their domestic IP law. However, following the principle of non-imposition does not necessarily mean that China would support the more equitable distribution of knowledge at the global level. It has exerted its influence indirectly. For instance, as China becomes a technological exporter itself, it collaborated with WIPO to enhance IP capacities in the BRI countries and waved its own transnational networks with technocrats of these countries to enhance IP awareness and protection.

### 1.5.3 A Focus on Engagement

Engagement is the focus of analysis in this book, which brings new insights to address the research questions. Engagement refers to an actor's conscious and purposive interaction with a system. Engagement enables an inductive approach to examine scattered activities in China's global IP engagement in the framework of actors, principles and strategies, and distributive justice principles. This process of discovery may reveal a broader range of behaviour among emerging participants in global governance than that of the global governors who create issues, set agendas, establish and implement rules, and evaluate outcomes (Avant *et al.*, 2010).

Engagement emphasises processes more than outcomes, which helps to disentangle the 'how' question which facilitates a more nuanced understanding of the role that China plays in global IP governance than the dichotomy of rule-taker or rule-maker. With increasing legal fragmentation and rule complexity in international regime complexity, no state in the world can remain an IP rule-maker on every issue at every forum. Meanwhile, discussions of outcomes immediately put the issue under the radar of political and economic diplomacy, leading to a confrontation between winners and losers instead of a concerted effort to address the common challenges for global governance. The focus on engagement, instead, provides an opportunity to escape from the binary division and observe continuous dynamics between China and other actors in global IP governance. It is not a once-and-for-all deal, but many repeated interactions starting from small steps.

China's engagement in global IP governance is a complex and cross-cutting issue, and there is no linear storyline. The accusation of China's conduct of IP theft can be established only in the paradigm of rigid entitlement-based theory; the rise of China as an IP rule-maker can be an alert only when viewing China as a revisionist in the current international order. This chapter presented pluralistic views of IP based on different principles of distributive justice and historical observations. Against this backdrop, the rest of the book will show there is much more to the Chinese IP story than the well-known caricatures.

## References


Alford, W. P. (1993). Don't Stop Thinking About Yesterday—Why There Was No Indigenous Counterpart to Intellectual Property Law in Imperial China. *Journal of Chinese Law, 7*(1), 3–34.

Alford, W. P. (1995). *To Steal a Book Is an Elegant Offense: Intellectual Property Law in Chinese Civilization.* Stanford University Press.

Allinson, R. E. (1985). The Confucian Golden Rule: A Negative Formulation. *Journal of Chinese Philosophy, 12*(3), 305–315.

Alter, K. J., & Raustiala, K. (2018). The Rise of International Regime Complexity. *Annual Review of Law and Social Science, 14*(1), 329–349.

Anderson, E. S. (1999). What Is the Point of Equality? *Ethics, 109*(2), 287–337.

Avant, D. D., Finnemore, M., & Sell, S. K. (2010). *Who Governs the Globe?* Cambridge University Press.

Blair, R. D., & Cotter, T. F. (2005). *Intellectual Property: Economic and Legal Dimensions of Rights and Remedies.* Cambridge University Press.

Blankfein-Tabachnick, D. (2020). Maximizing Intellectual Property: Optimality, Synchronicity, and Distributive Justice. *St. John's Law Review, 94*(1), 1–66.

Braithwaite, J., & Drahos, P. (2000). *Global Business Regulation.* Cambridge University Press.

Burnay, M., & Chaisse, J. (2020). Global Commons as an Emerging Arena of Contestation of Global Governance Structures and Norms. *International Community Law Review, 22*(5), 533–558.

Cai, X., & Wang, G. (2005). Foreign-Related Trademark Dispute in Late Qing Dynasty 晚清时期的涉外商标侵权纠纷. *Academic Research 学术研究, 9*, 101–105.

Caney, S. (2001). International Distributive Justice. *Political Studies, 49*(5), 974–997.

Chander, A., & Sunder, M. (2006). Is Nozick Kicking Rawls's Ass-Intellectual Property and Social Justice. *U.C. Davis Law Review, 40*, 563–579.

Chang, H.-J. (2001). Intellectual Property Rights and Economic Development: Historical Lessons and Emerging Issues. *Journal of Human Development, 2*(2), 287–309.

Chang, H.-J. (2002). *Kicking Away the Ladder: Development Strategy in Historical Perspective.* Anthem Press.

Chatterjee, M. (2020). Lockean Copyright Versus Lockean Property. *Journal of Legal Analysis, 12*, 136–182.

Cheng, W. (2019). China Engages with the Global Intellectual Property Governance: The Recent Trend. *The Journal of World Intellectual Property, 22*(3–4), 1–16.

Chen, J. (2005). *Narratives and Memoir on the Big Events of China 国事忆述*. CCP History Publishing House 中国党史出版社.

Chon, M. (2006). Intellectual Property from Below: Copyright and Capability for Education. *U.C. Davis Law Review, 40*(3), 803–854.

Collste, G. (2022). 'Where You Live Should Not Determine Whether You Live'. Global Justice and the Distribution of COVID-19 Vaccines. *Ethics & Global Politics, 15*(2), 43–54.

Crookes, P. I. (2013). Resetting EU–China Relations from a Values-Based to an Interests-Based Engagement. *International Politics, 50*(5), 639–663.

Derclaye, E., & Taylor, T. (2013). Happy IP: Replacing the Law and Economics Justification for Intellectual Property Rights with a Well-Being Approach. *European Intellectual Property Review, 37*(4), 197–209.

Drahos, P. (1998, November 9). The Universality of Intellectual Property Rights: Origins and Development. *Intellectual Property and Human Rights*. Panel Discussion Organized by the World Intellectual Property Organization (WIPO), in Collaboration with the Office of the United Nations High Commissioner for Human Rights (OHCHR) (pp. 13–41).

Drahos, P. (2001). BITs and BIPs. *The Journal of World Intellectual Property, 4*(6), 791–808.

Drahos, P. (2002). Developing Countries and International Intellectual Property Standard-Setting. *The Journal of World Intellectual Property, 5*(5), 765–789.

Drahos, P. (2007). Weaving Webs of Influence: The United States, Free Trade Agreements and Dispute Resolution. *Journal of World Trade, 41*(1), 191–210.

Drahos, P. (2017). Regulatory Globalisation. In P. Drahos (Ed.), *Regulatory Theory: Foundations and Applications* (p. 249).

Drahos, P. (2021). *Survival Governance: Energy and Climate in the Chinese Century.* Oxford University Press.

Dreyfuss, R., & Frankel, S. (2014). From Incentive to Commodity to Asset: How International Law Is Reconceptualizing Intellectual Property. *Michigan Journal of International Law, 36*(4), 557–562.

Dutfield, G. (2003). *Intellectual Property Rights and the Life Science Industries: A Twentieth Century History.* Routledge.

Duxbury, N. (2008). Golden Rule Reasoning, Moral Judgment, and Law. *Notre Dame Law Review, 84*(4), 1529–1606.

Dworkin, R. M. (2003). Equality, Luck and Hierarchy. *Philosophy & Public Affairs, 31*(2), 190–198.

Ekström, A. M., Berggren, C., Tomson, G., Gostin, L. O., Friberg, P., & Ottersen, O. P. (2021). The Battle for COVID-19 Vaccines Highlights the Need for a New Global Governance Mechanism. *Nature Medicine, 27*(5), 739–740.

Erfani, P., Binagwaho, A., Jalloh, M. J., Yunus, M., Farmer, P., & Kerry, V. (2021). Intellectual Property Waiver for COVID-19 Vaccines Will Advance Global Health Equity. *BMJ, 374*, n1837.

Feng, H. (2009). Is China a Revisionist Power? *Chinese Journal of International Politics, 2*(3), 313–334.

Fisher, W., & Syed, T. (2006). Global Justice in Healthcare: Developing Drugs for the Developing World. *U.C. Davis Law Review, 40*(3), 581–678.

George, A. E. (2010). The Construction of Intellectual Property: A Study in Applied Legal Philosophy.

Gepts, P. (2004). Who Owns Biodiversity, and How Should the Owners Be Compensated? *Plant Physiology, 134*(4), 1295–1307.

Gervais, D. J. (2003). *The TRIPS Agreement: Drafting History and Analysis.* Sweet & Maxwell.

Gosseries, A., Marciano, A., & Strowel, A. (2008). *Intellectual Property and Theories of Justice*. Springer.

Grunberg, I., Kaul, I., & Stern, M. A. (1999). *Global Public Goods: International Cooperation in the 21st Century*. Oxford University Press.

Guan, J. (2009). Review of Research Concerning "Leaning to One Side" Policy at the Initial Stage of the PRC 新中国成立初期"一边倒"政策研究综述. *Beijing CCP History 北京党史, 5*, 30–34.

Halbert, D. (2011). The Politics of IP Maximalism. *The WIPO Journal, 3*(1), 81–93.

Harris, D. P. (2008). The Honeymoon Is over: Evaluating the United States' WTO Intellectual Property Complaint Against China. *Fordham International Law Journal, 32*(1), 96–187.

He, K., Feng, H., Chan, S., & Hu, W. (2021). Rethinking Revisionism in World Politics. *The Chinese Journal of International Politics, 14*(2), 159–186.

Helfer, L. R. (2004). Regime Shifting: The TRIPs Agreement and New Dynamics of International Intellectual Property Lawmaking. *Yale Journal of International Law, 29*(1), 1–84.
Helfer, L. R. (2009). Regime Shifting in the International Intellectual Property System. *Perspectives on Politics, 7*(1), 39–44.
Helfer, L. R. (2015). Mapping the Interface Between Human Rights and Intellectual Property. In C. Geiger (Ed.), *Research Handbook on Human Rights and Intellectual Property* (pp. 6–16). Edward Elgar Publishing.
Hinsch, W. (2001). Global Distributive Justice. *Metaphilosophy, 32*(1–2), 58–78.
Hudon, E. G. (1964). Literary Piracy, Charles Dickens and the American Copyright Law. *American Bar Association Journal*, 1157–1160.
Hughes, J., & Merges, R. P. (2016). Copyright and Distributive Justice. *Notre Dame Law Review, 92*(2), 513–578.
Hunt, C. (1982). Multilateral Cooperation in Export Controls—The Role of CoCom. *University of Toledo Law Review, 14*(4), 1285–1298.
Jaffe, A. B., & Lerner, J. (2011). *Innovation and Its Discontents: How Our Broken Patent System Is Endangering Innovation and Progress, and What to Do About It*. Princeton University Press.
Jecker, N. S., Wightman, A. G., & Diekema, D. S. (2021). Vaccine Ethics: An Ethical Framework for Global Distribution of COVID-19 Vaccines. *Journal of Medical Ethics, 47*(5), 308–317.
Kapczynski, A. (2012). The Cost of Price: Why and How to Get Beyond Intellectual Property Internalism. *UCLA Law Review, 59*(4), 970–1026.
Kastner, S. L., & Saunders, P. C. (2012). Is China a Status Quo or Revisionist State? Leadership Travel as an Empirical Indicator of Foreign Policy Priorities. *International Studies Quarterly, 56*, 163–177.
Locke, J. (2015 [1690]). *The Second Treatise of Civil Government*. Broadview Press.
Lu, B. (2008). The Change of the Remuneration System for Copyright: A Review of the Publishing Industry Three Decades After Reform and Opening-Up 稿酬制度嬗变中的时代映像—出版业改革开放三十年的片段追忆. *China Publishing Journal 中国出版, 5*, 26–28.
Machlup, F., & Penrose, E. (1950). The Patent Controversy in the Nineteenth Century. *The Journal of Economic History, 10*(1), 1–29.
Maruyama, W. H. (1999). US-China IPR Negotiations: Trade, Intellectual Property, and the Rule of Law in a Global Economy. In M. A. Cohen, A. E. Bang, & S. J. Mitchell (Eds.), *Chinese Intellectual Property Law and Practice* (pp. 165–212). Kluwer Law International.
Maskus, K. E., & Reichman, J. H. (2004). The Globalization of Private Knowledge Goods and the Privatization of Global Public Goods. *Journal of International Economic Law, 7*(2), 279–320.
May, C. (2007). World Intellectual Property Organization and the Development Agenda. *Global Governance, 13*(2), 161–170.
Merges, R. P. (2011). *Justifying Intellectual Property*. Harvard University Press.

Moir, H. V. (2021). Pharmaceutical Patents and Evergreening. *SSRN*. https://papers.ssrn.com/sol3/papers.cfm?abstract_id=3975947
Moore, A. D. (2012). A Lockean Theory of Intellectual Property Revisited. *San Diego Law Review, 49*(4), 1069–1104.
Morin, J.-F., & Surbeck, J. (2020). Mapping the New Frontier of International IP Law: Introducing a TRIPS-plus Dataset. *World Trade Review, 19*(1), 109–122.
Muzaka, V. (2011). Linkages, Contests and Overlaps in the Global Intellectual Property Rights Regime. *European Journal of International Relations, 17*(4), 755–776.
Nielsen, K. (1979). Radical Egalitarian Justice: Justice as Equality. *Social Theory and Practice, 5*(2), 209–226.
Niu, J. (1999). The Formation and the Major Characteristics of the Foreign Policy of the PRC 新中国外交的形成及其主要特征. *Historical Research 历史研究, 5*, 23042.
Nozick, R. (1974). *Anarchy, State, and Utopia*. Basic Books.
Nymalm, N. (2019). The Economics of Identity: Is China the New 'Japan Problem' for the United States? *Journal of International Relations and Development, 22*(4), 909–933.
Oddi, A. S. (1995). Un-Unified Economic Theories of Patents—The Not-Quite-Holy Grail. *Notre Dame Law Review, 71*(2), 267–327.
Okediji, R. L. (2004). Back to Bilateralism? Pendulum Swings in International Intellectual Property Protection. *University of Ottawa Law & Technology Journal, 1*, 125–148.
Olsaretti, S. (2018). *The Oxford Handbook of Distributive Justice*. Oxford University Press.
Otten, A. (2015). The TRIPS Negotiations: An Overview. In J. Watal & A. Taubman (Eds.), *The Making of the TRIPS Agreement: Personal Insights from the Uruguay Round Negotiations* (pp. 55–78). WTO Online Bookshop.
Palmedo, M. (2020). *Analysis of Special 301 Listings, 2009–2020*. Shamnad Basheer IP/Trade Fellow White Paper, Texas A&M University School of Law. https://papers.ssrn.com/sol3/papers.cfm?abstract_id=3680332
Pan, C. (2004). The "China Threat" in American Self-Imagination: The Discursive Construction of Other as Power Politics. *Alternatives: Global Local, Political, 29*(3), 305–331.
Pogge, T. (2005a). *Poverty and Human Rights*. Office of the High Commissioner for Human Rights or the United Nations Human Rights Office. https://www2.ohchr.org/english/issues/poverty/expert/docs/Thomas_Pogge_Summary.pdf
Pogge, T. W. (2005b). Human Rights and Global Health: A Research Program. *Metaphilosophy, 36*(1–2), 182–209.
Ran, R. (2017). Summary of Chinese Enterprises' Response to the 337 Investigation in 2016 (Part I) 2016年度中国企业应诉美国337调查综述(上). *Chinese Lawyer 中国律师, 4*, 72–76.
Raustiala, K., & Victor, D. G. (2004). The Regime Complex for Plant Genetic Resources. *International Organization, 58*(2), 277–309.

Rawls, J. (2001). *Justice as Fairness: A Restatement.* Harvard University Press.

Schiff, E. (1971). *Industrialization Without National Patents: The Netherlands, 1869–1912; Switzerland, 1850–1907*. Princeton University Press.

Sekalala, S., Forman, L., Hodgson, T., Mulumba, M., Namyalo-Ganafa, H., & Meier, B. M. (2021). Decolonising Human Rights: How Intellectual Property Laws Result in Unequal Access to the COVID-19 Vaccine. *BMJ Global Health, 6*(7), e006169.

Sell, S. K. (2003). *Private Power, Public Law: The Globalization of Intellectual Property Rights.* Cambridge University Press.

Sell, S. K. (2010a). *The Global IP Upward Ratchet, Anti-Counterfeiting and Piracy Enforcement Efforts: The State of Play*. American University Washington College of Law.

Sell, S. K. (2010b). TRIPS Was Never Enough: Vertical Forum Shifting, FTAS, ACTA, and TTP. *Journal of Intellectual Property Law, 18*(2), 447–478.

Shaffer, G., & Gao, H. (2020). A New Chinese Economic Order? *Journal of International Economic Law, 23*(3), 607–635.

Snow, N. (2021). Moral Bars to Intellectual Property: Theory & Apologetics. *UCLA Entertainment Law Review, 28*(1), 75–126.

Thambisetty, S., McMahon, A., Mcdonagh, L., Yoon Kang, H., & Dutfield, G. (2022). Addressing Vaccine Inequity During the COVID-19 Pandemic: The TRIPS Intellectual Property Waiver Proposal & Beyond. *Cambridge Law Journal, 81*(2), 384–416.

Turner, O., & Nymalm, N. (2019). Morality and Progress: IR Narratives on International Revisionism and the Status Quo. *Cambridge Review of International Affairs, 32*(4), 407–428.

Upreti, P. N., & Vásquez Callo-Müller, M. (2020). Phase One US-China Trade Deal: What Does It Mean for Intellectual Property? *GRUR International, 69*(4), 389–393.

USTR. (2018). *Findings of the Investigation into China's Acts, Policies, and Practices Related to Technology Transfer, Intellectual Property, and Innovation Under Section 301 of the Trade Act of 1974.* https://ustr.gov/sites/default/files/Section%20301%20FINAL.PDF

Van Houweling, M. S. (2004). Distributive Values in Copyright. *Texas Law Review, 83*(6), 1535–1580.

Wang, L. (2008). *Research of the First Intellectual Property Negotiation Between China and Foreign Countries in the Late Qing Dynasty 晚清中外首次知识产权谈判研究* (Ph.D.). Suzhou University.

Wang, L., & Wu, H. (2001). *China-US Intellectual Property Negotiation Review 披尽黄沙始见金 — 中美知识产权谈判再回顾*. http://www.cpo.cn.net/zscqb/zhuanban/t20011116_2735.htm. Accessed 4 May 2017.

Wang, Z. (2017). The Economic Rise of China: Rule-Taker, Rule-Maker, or Rule-Breaker? *Asian Survey, 57*(4), 595–617.

Weiss, J. C., & Wallace, J. L. (2021). Domestic Politics, China's Rise, and the Future of the Liberal International Order. *International Organization, 75*(2), 635–664.

Wen, X. (1992). China's Patent System Improved During Reform and Opening-Up 中国的专利制度在改革开放中完善. *International Trade 国际贸易, 6*, 9–11.

Wen, X. (2002). Introduction to the Second Revision of the Chinese Patent Law 中国专利法的第二次修改介绍. *Intellectual Property 知识产权, 5*, 6–10.

Wijesinghe, S., Adikari, C., & Ariyaratna, R. (2022). The Proposal for Waiver of WTO's TRIPS Agreement to Prevent, Contain and Treat COVID-19: Investigating the Benefits and Challenges for Low- and Middle-Income Countries. *Journal of Intellectual Property Law & Practice, 17*(2), 179–192.

WIPO. (2011). *World Intellectual Property Indicators*. http://www.wipo.int/edocs/pubdocs/en/intproperty/941/wipo_pub_941_2011.pdf

WIPO. (2020). *China Becomes Top Filer of International Patents in 2019 Amid Robust Growth for WIPO's IP Services, Treaties and Finances*. https://www.wipo.int/pressroom/en/articles/2020/article_0005.html (Accessed).

Wu, H. (2009). *The Contestation of the Great Powers 大国的较量*. Changjiang Literature and Art Publishing House 长江文艺出版社.

Wyzycka, N., & Hasmath, R. (2017). The Impact of the European Union's Policy Towards China's Intellectual Property Regime. *International Political Science Review, 38*(5), 549–562.

Xiao, X., & Wu, L. (2015). The Introduction of Technology During the Initial Stage of Industrialization of the PRC 略论新中国工业化起步时期的技术引进. *Research on Development 开发研究, 1*, 150–156.

Yanisky-Ravid, S. (2017). The Hidden Though Flourishing Justification of Intellectual Property Laws: Distributive Justice, National Versus International Approaches. *Lewis & Clark Law Review, 21*(1), 1–44.

Yuliantoro, N. R., & Dinarto, D. (2019). Between Revisionist and Status Quo: The Case of China's Leadership in the AIIB. *Jurnal Hubungan Internasional, 7*(2), 169–177.

Yu, P. K. (2007). International Enclosure, the Regime Complex, and Intellectual Property Schizophrenia the International Intellectual Property Regime Complex. *Michigan State Law Review, 1*, 1–34.

Yu, P. K. (2019). The Rise of China in the International Intellectual Property Regime. In Z. Ka (Ed.), *Handbook of the International Political Economy of China*. Edward Elgar.

Zhang, B., Yao, F., Zhang, J., & Jiang, L. (2005). *The Technology Transfer from USSR to China 苏联技术向中国的转移 (1949–1966)*. Shandong Education Press 山东教育出版社.

Zhao, T. (2006). Rethinking Empire from a Chinese Concept 'All-under-Heaven' (Tian-xia). *Social Identities, 12*(1), 29–41.

Zheng, C. (1998). The TRIPS Agreement and Intellectual Property Protection in China. *Duke Journal of Comparative & International Law, 9*(1), 219–228.

Zukus, J. (2017). *How China Is Emerging as a Leader in Global Innovation and IP Rights*. https://thediplomat.com/2017/07/how-china-is-emerging-as-a-leader-in-global-innovation-and-ip-rights/. Accessed 17 May 2018.

Zürn, M. (2021). COVID-19 and the Legitimacy Crisis of Global Governance. In *The Crises of Legitimacy in Global Governance* (pp. 37–52). Routledge.

# Part II

## Case Studies

# 2

# China Engages in International Regulation of Geographical Indications

## 2.1 Introduction

Geographical indications (GI)s are essentially place names that are used for products. Typical examples are Champagne, Feta, Parma ham, Longjing tea, and Colombian coffee. The EU successfully promoted GIs as a type of intellectual property so that producers from the designated place can exclude producers outside of that place from using the name for their similar products. However, for generations, European immigrants brought these names, as part of their culture, to new places where they live, for example, the US, Australia, New Zealand and Canada. In these countries, these names became generic product names that everyone was free to use. The conflict has escalated when products bearing the same name but from different places meet in a globalised market.

There are two primary legal mechanisms for the protection of GIs: *sui generis* protection promoted by the EU and trademark protection promoted primarily by the US. The first difference between the two is that a registered GI is a description associated with products from a particular geographical location, while a trademark must be distinctive—that is, it cannot use ordinary words that should be left free for other producers to use. Descriptive terms, such as place names, cannot fulfil the distinctiveness requirement in trademark registration. Second, all producers from the demarcated geographical location have the right to use the GI label and exclude wrongful appropriation of a GI, while an individual trademark holder has sole exclusive rights over that trademark. Third, a GI is usually seen as a guarantee



W. Cheng, *China in Global Governance of Intellectual Property*, Palgrave Socio-Legal Studies, https://doi.org/10.1007/978-3-031-24370-7_2

of quality, with producer associations responsible for quality monitoring. Trademarks may also be relevant to quality, but this relationship is built on the accumulated reputation rather than on the special characteristics of the geographical location. Finally, a GI is not freely transferable due to the required association with the geographical location (Blakeney, 2012).

The conflict between common versus proprietary ownership and the issue of distinctiveness have been reconciled by the introduction of certification or collective marks within the trademark mechanism. However, this does not reconcile the competition between the *sui generis* and the trademark mechanisms. The EU proposed a stringent *sui generis* mechanism that could be justified by: 1) the concept of *terroir* as the core of a GI (Josling, 2006); 2) the necessity of using GIs to preserve cultural diversity (Broude, 2005); and 3) the benefits of GIs for regional and local development (van Caenegem & Cleary, 2017). Since 2006, GIs have become a 'must-have' in EU trade agreements (Engelhardt, 2015). However, empirical evidence on the economic benefits of GI protection is insufficient (Török *et al.*, 2020), and the EU's rulemaking has been consistently resisted by New World countries such as the US, Australia, and Chile, who argue that collective or certification trademarks are sufficient to protect place names (Watson, 2016). Based on the trademark rationale, the US rejects the EU's GI regulation because certain names either have already been registered as trademarks or have become generic and thus lost distinctiveness (Goebel & Groeschl, 2014).

The EU has convinced many developing countries of the positive effect of GIs on local and regional development, and they have joined the EU in promoting GI-related negotiations at the WTO and WIPO in the post-TRIPS era. As a response, the US expanded its competing standards on GIs through its trade agreements based on a trademark system to indicate the origin of goods. The EU–US GI contestation in international rulemaking has led to an increasing divergence in global regulation and inevitable fragmentation in domestic legal systems in countries that accepted GI-related standards from both the EU and the US.

GIs present a unique case in IP law in which the US and the EU disagree in its global governance. Their fundamental disagreement not only contributed to international GI regime complexity but also has profound ramifications for third countries. This chapter focuses on how China has navigated international GI regulation in the context of regime complexity. Specifically, it will discuss how the international GI regulation influences China and whether robust domestic institution building has stimulated any 'Chinese agenda' in international GI regulation. If so, how has this agenda manifested itself?

## 2.2 International GI System: Regime Complexity and Power Contestation

Internationally, GIs have been governed by multiple regimes at both bilateral and multilateral levels (Blakeney, 2012; Cortés Martín, 2004; Gangjee, 2016; Gervais, 2010; Okediji, 2007). The international GI governance presents as regime complexity (Alter & Raustiala, 2018; Orsini *et al.*, 2013) with these dense yet non-hierarchical regimes.[1] There are considerable implications of international regime complexity for actors within it, such as introducing legal fragmentation and rule ambiguity, facilitating opportunistic forum shopping, forum shifting, and other feedback effects (Gomez-Mera, 2015). Since the conflicting GI agendas of the EU and the US have been institutionalised over the years in various international GI regimes, it is essential to examine how international GI regime complexity has impacted China, in particular, the challenge of legal fragmentation when China was considering legal transplantation and opportunities for cross-forum strategies of which it could take advantage.

### 2.2.1 Mapping International GI Regime Complexity

The existence of different terms and definitions that refer to concepts in different regimes is an illustration of international GI regime complexity. The Paris Convention protects 'indications of source or appellations of origin'; the Madrid Agreement Concerning the International Registration of Marks (Madrid Agreement) protects 'indications of source'. 'Indications of source' are briefly mentioned in Articles 1(2) and 10 of the Paris Convention and throughout the Madrid Agreement. However, these two treaties do not provide any definition of the term. The Paris Convention only specifies protection for 'indications of source', in Article 10(1), which provides the obligation to seize imported 'goods bearing false indications as to their source' (Correa, 2007, p. 214). Article 10*bis* further provides against unfair competition by prohibiting the use of confusing, false, or misleading names. Because WTO members are also committed to complying with the Paris Convention and the TRIPS Agreement does not specify how WTO members should protect GIs, theoretically, the Paris Convention can be one of the mechanisms for WTO members to adopt to protect GIs.

[1] There is emerging literature on this topic, and some earlier research used the term 'regime complexity' alternatively.

The Madrid Agreement and the Madrid Protocol create an international registration system for trademarks that enables the filing of one application with the International Bureau that can be considered as effective as national filings in the individual contracting member states. As of 9 June 2022, the Madrid Union has had 112 members covering 128 countries and represented more than 80% of world trade. The Madrid Agreement and the Madrid Protocol aim to protect sources of origin (quality-neutral indications), the scope of which is broader than GIs.

The Lisbon Agreement for the Protection of Appellations of Origin and their International Registration (Lisbon Agreement) is a special and optional agreement based on Article 19 of the Paris Convention and is administered by WIPO. The Lisbon Agreement protects 'appellations of origin'—a form of labelling with a narrower scope than GIs and the link between an appellation and the place of origin is stronger than in the case of GIs. According to Article 2(1) of the Lisbon Agreement, 'Appellation of origin means the geographical name of a country, region, or locality, which serves to designate a product originating therein, the quality and characteristics of which are due exclusively or essentially to the geographical environment, including natural and human factors.' The Lisbon Agreement has not been a notable success for the international protection of GIs (Josling, 2006) until recently as it was marginalised after the TRIPS Agreement given its small membership. A proposal emerged to reinvent the Lisbon Agreement through a TRIPS GI Register (Gervais, 2010). The revival of interest in the Lisbon Agreement was mainly due to the deadlock in the WTO GI negotiations. Furthermore, developing countries rich in GIs on a broad scope of products other than wines and spirits prefer the Lisbon Agreement, because it provides equal protection to all agricultural products and foodstuffs (Vivas-Eugui, 2001). Its level of protection equals that of Article 23 of the TRIPS Agreement, but its scope extends beyond wines and spirits—Article 3 of the Lisbon Agreement provides that member states of WIPO shall ensure protection against 'any usurpation or imitation, even if the true origin of the product is indicated or if the appellation is used in a translated form or accompanied by terms such as "kind", "type", "make", "imitation", or the like'. The WIPO Working Group on the Development of the Lisbon System facilitated the adoption of the highly controversial Geneva Act of the Lisbon Agreement at a diplomatic conference on 20 May 2015 (Gervais & Slider, 2017). However, the influence of the Lisbon Agreement remains limited due to its small number of contracting parties.

### 2.2.2 TRIPS Provisions on GIs and Post-TRIPS GI Negotiations

In the Uruguay Round, the EU successfully incorporated the concept of GIs, as well as relevant regulatory rules, into the TRIPS Agreement. The TRIPS Agreement is the first multilateral agreement that protects GIs as a separate category of intellectual property and establishes 'minimum' standards for GI protection. The TRIPS Agreement has a broader membership than previous WIPO treaties and is more effective because it can be enforced through the WTO. Articles 22 to 24 of the TRIPS Agreement deal with GIs. Article 22.1 of the TRIPS Agreement defines GIs as 'indications which identify a good as originating in the territory of a Member, or a region or locality in that territory, where a given quality, reputation, or other characteristic of the good is essentially attributable to its geographical origin.' Furthermore, according to Articles 2–4 of the TRIPS Agreement, provisions of the Paris Convention and the National Treatment and Most Favoured Nation clauses also apply to GIs.

Article 22.1 of the TRIPS Agreement defines GIs without clarifying specific mechanisms for WTO members to implement their protection. Basic protection is granted to agri-food products other than wines and spirits to prevent the use of certain indications that would mislead consumers. Article 23 of the TRIPS Agreement provides higher/additional protection for wines and spirits 'even if misuse would not cause the public to be misled'. The difference between the basic and higher protections for GIs granted by the TRIPS Agreement can be illustrated by the following example: a label 'Parma ham, produced in Canberra' is allowed under TRIPS Article 22 because ham is not a wine or spirit, and the real origin of the product is indicated. However, 'Champagne, produced in Canberra' is not permitted under TRIPS Article 23 'even where the true origin of the goods is indicated or the geographical indication is used in translation or accompanied by expressions such as "kind", "type", "style", "imitation" or the like'. Consequently, although the TRIPS Agreement allows flexibility to implement GI protection for agri-food products in Article 22, Article 23 requires a higher minimum protection standard for GIs for wines and spirits. Nonetheless, Articles 24.4, 24.5, and 24.6 of the TRIPS Agreement are grandfathering provisions that allow the continuous practice of a WTO member concerning certain aspects of GIs before the TRIPS Agreement (Heald, 1996). The differentiated protection for wine and spirit GIs was also an EC–US compromise in the TRIPS negotiations to cover both basic trademark model proposed by the US and the *sui generis* model proposed by the EC that offers higher protection.

GI provisions in the TRIPS Agreement present a constructive inconsistency. The TRIPS Agreement includes provisions to reconcile legal issues between *sui generis* protection and trademark protection, such as using GIs as generic terms and the coexistence between earlier trademarks and GIs. As the EU was not satisfied with the TRIPS outcomes, GI negotiations continued at the WTO in the post-TRIPS era to establish a multilateral system for notifying and registering GIs for wines and spirits (the GI Register) and extending higher-level protection to products beyond wines and spirits (the GI Extension).

### 2.2.3 Post-TRIPS GI Negotiations at the WTO

Negotiations on the GI Register and GI Extension started in 1997, and no consensus has yet been reached on either issue. Considering most of these discussions or negotiations occurred after China's WTO accession in 2001, they provided an international context to understand China's position on GIs at the multilateral level (Sect. 2.4).

GI Register negotiations aimed to create a compulsory multilateral system for notifying and registering GIs for wines and spirits. It is a built-in agenda because TRIPS Article 23.4 clearly requires WTO members to enter further negotiations on a multilateral registration system for wines and spirits. Major disagreements in the negotiations included different interpretations of the required participation and the legal basis for protecting a name as a GI. The US-led proposals for a voluntary multilateral GI Register that could provide appropriate protection based on domestic law but not introduce additional burdens beyond the TRIPS Agreement.[2] In contrast, the EU-led proposals for a compulsory multilateral register with *prima facie* legal effect internationally.[3]

GI Extension discussions aimed to extend higher-level protection to products beyond wines and spirits. This was a more controversial issue than the GI Register among WTO members (WTO, 2008). Since the GI Extension is not explicitly mandated as a built-in agenda in Article 24.1 of the TRIPS Agreement, the primary disagreement was not substantive but centred on whether

[2] WTO, 'Proposed Draft TRIPS Council Decision on the Establishment of a Multilateral System of Notification and Registration of Geographical Indications for Wines and Spirits—Submission by Argentina, Australia, Canada, Chile, Costa Rica, Dominican Republic, Ecuador, El Salvador, Guatemala, Honduras, Israel, Japan, South Korea, Mexico, New Zealand, Nicaragua, Paraguay, the Separate Customs Territory of Taiwan, Penghu, Kinmen and Matsu, and South Africa and the United States', 31 March 2011, TN/IP/W/10/Rev.4.

[3] WTO, 'Geographical Indications—Communication from the European Communities', 14 June 2005, WT/GC/W/547; TN/C/W/26 and TN/IP/W/11.

this issue should be put on the agenda for negotiation at all. Supporters of the GI Extension argued that there was no justification for the hierarchical differences in protection between wines and spirits and agri-food products. Opponents maintained the Doha Ministerial Declaration did not provide a mandate for negotiations because it may introduce new rights and obligations for WTO members beyond the TRIPS Agreement. The initial proponents of the GI Extension were primarily developing countries. When the European Commission (EC) joined as a co-sponsor, both sides began to harden their positions (Rangnekar, 2002). The US even sued the EC at the WTO over its GI regulations.[4] Since 2011, there has been no substantive progress in WTO negotiations on either issue (Kongolo, 2011; Mwape, 2010).

### 2.2.4 GI-Related Initiatives at WIPO

WIPO has been a major forum for promoting international GI rule harmonisation after the Madrid and Lisbon agreements. WIPO established a Committee of Experts on the International Protection of Appellations of Origin and Other Indications of Source, which prepared a draft Treaty on the Protection of GIs for the WIPO International Bureau in 1975 (TAO/II/2),[5] which was never adopted. It was followed by two WIPO proposals for revising the Paris Convention to address specific issues related to GIs in the late 1970s, and both proposals also failed. In 1990, a new Committee of Experts on the International Protection of GIs was established to initiate a treaty[6]—an attempt that failed as well.[7] The EC later adopted a strategy of forum shifting. Instead of furthering WIPO negotiations, it incorporated GI as an item for TRIPS negotiations in the Uruguay Round. TRIPS provisions on GIs demonstrated the success of this strategy.

In the post-TRIPS era, WIPO remains an important forum for multilateral GI negotiations. The Standing Committee on the Law of Trademarks, Industrial Designs, and Geographical Indications (SCT) was established in 1998 to address issues related to trademarks, industrial designs, GIs, and appellations of origin. Specific to GIs, the SCT aimed to be 'the forum to discuss

[4] WTO, 'European Communities—Protection of Trademarks and Geographical Indications for Agricultural Products and Foodstuffs', WT/DS174, WT/DS290.

[5] WIPO Committee of Experts on the International Protection of Appellations of Origin and Other Indications of Source, Second Session, *Draft Treaty on the Protection of Geographical Indications*, TAO/II/2, 25 August 1975.

[6] WIPO Committee of Experts on the International Protection of Geographical Indications, First Session, *The Need for a New Treaty and Its Possible Contents*, GEO/CE/I/2, 9 April 1990.

[7] WIPO SCT, Sixth Session, *Geographical Indications: Historical Background, Nature of Rights, Existing System for Protection and Obtaining Effective Protection on Other Countries*, SCT/6/3, 25 January 2001.

issues, facilitate coordination and provide guidance concerning the progressive international development of the law of trademarks, industrial designs and geographical indications, including the harmonization of national laws and procedures'.[8] The SCT had 44 sessions before 2022. GIs were intensively discussed in the first ten sessions, but the US and its alliance proposed keeping GIs as a second-level priority thereafter. From the 30th session of the SCT in 2013, GIs returned to the agenda, but no substantive achievement has been made. Recent discussions in the SCT have focused on collecting information about how national and regional systems can protect GIs and legal issues on the use and misuse of GIs, country names, and geographical terms on the Internet and as domain names.[9]

With the stagnation of GI negotiations at the WTO,[10] both the EU and the US have engaged in a strategy of vertical forum shifting. GI negotiations, like other IP negotiations, gradually shifted from multilateral to plurilateral and bilateral forums (Sell, 2010).

### 2.2.5 Failed GI Proposal in the Anti-Counterfeiting Trade Agreement

The Anti-Counterfeiting Trade Agreement (ACTA) (Blakeney, 2012; Kaminski, 2011) became another forum for IP negotiations from 2008 at the plurilateral level. Some European non-governmental organisations (NGOs) and industrial associations—such as origin and the European Federation of Origin Wines (EFOW)—lobbied the European Commission to include GIs as part of the agenda for ACTA negotiations. Among the eight ACTA negotiating parties, Switzerland and Mexico also supported the EU proposal on GIs. However, their proposal was rejected by the US and Australia. The final text of ACTA focuses only on IP enforcement and contains no provisions on GIs (Blakeney, 2012, pp. 92–95). Given ACTA was rejected by the European

---

[8] WIPO SCT, First Session, *Organizational Markets and Overview of the Issues to be Considered by the Standing Committee on the Law of Trademarks, Industrial Designs, and Geographical Indications*, SCT/1/2, 12 March 1998.

[9] WIPO SCT, Fortieth Session, *Compilation of the Replies to Questionnaire I on the National and Regional Systems that can Provide a Certain Protection to Geographical indications*, (SCT/40/5) and *Compilation of the Replies to Questionnaire II on the Use/Misuse of Geographical Indications, Country Names and Geographical Terms on the Internet and in the DNS* (SCT/40/6), 12–16 November 2018.

[10] See TRIPS Council Special Session, *Multilateral System of Notification and Registration of Geographical Indications for Wines and Spirits*, Report by the Chairman, Ambassador Alfredo Suescum (Panama), TN/IP/22 (2014).

Parliament in 2012 and will not come into force, the forums for GI negotiations were further moved to the bilateral level (Omachi, 2019), in particular in various Free Trade Agreements (FTAs).

### 2.2.6 GIs in Bilateral FTAs

The EU and the US both incorporated GI provisions in their FTAs or other bilateral arrangements such as on the mutual recognition of GIs. When WTO trade negotiations encountered a deadlock, both parties intensified GI negotiations at the bilateral level.

The EU has negotiated specialised wine and spirit agreements with some New World countries (such as Australia, Mexico, and South Africa) in parallel with the TRIPS negotiations (Blakeney, 2014). In these early agreements, the EU succeeded in preventing the use of EU place names as generic names in the New World countries. This was realised through the provision of a 'phasing-out period'. For instance, the *European Community–Australia Wine Agreement* of 1994 provided a 'phasing-out' period for various types of Australian wines, after which the use of the EU name of origin was prohibited (Dechent & Sadler, 2010). After the TRIPS Agreement, the EC incorporated GI provisions in its FTAs and regional trade agreements (RTAs) with South Korea, the Andean Community, Central American countries, Ukraine, Georgia, Moldova, South Africa, Canada, Singapore, Vietnam, Japan, and China (Engelhardt, 2015; Huysmans, 2020; Moir, 2017). The EU has generally achieved its negotiating objectives for GIs in these agreements, including: 1) establishing a list of EU names to be protected directly and indefinitely by the trading partner; 2) extending higher-level protection granted by Article 23 of the TRIPS Agreement to products beyond wines and spirits; 3) providing for the coexistence of GIs with prior trademarks; 4) phasing out prior uses of names originating in the EU (Engelhardt, 2015). GIs became a deal breaker for the Comprehensive Economic and Trade Agreement between the EU and Canada (CETA), as both Greece and Italy had threatened not to ratify CETA due to insufficient GI protection (Huysmans, 2020).

As a response, the US strategically incorporated GI provisions in its own FTAs and RTAs (Omachi, 2019), so the EU model of *sui generis* protection would not become a default global standard. In practice, US trade agreements with Australia, Central American countries, Chile, Jordan, Morocco, and Singapore incorporate provisions to protect place names following the trademark model (Pugatch, 2007). For instance, in the United States-Korea Free Trade Agreement (KORUS FTA), GIs were stipulated under the heading 'Trademarks including GIs'.

GI provisions in EU-led FTAs and those in US-led FTAs are incompatible (O'Connor, 2014). For example, after the signing of the Korea–European Union Free Trade Agreement (KOREU FTA), 162 GI-designated EU products became protected as GIs in South Korea, while 64 South Korean GI-designated products became protected as GIs in the EU. The US dairy industry was concerned because the *sui generis* protection of various EU cheeses may impair its producers' use of identical names as generic terms, thus affecting US sales in the Korean market (Cooper *et al.*, 2011). South Korea agreed with the US to allow the generic use of GIs (KORUS FTA: Article 18.2.3). A side letter of the KORUS FTA also confirms the legitimacy of the generic use of components of multicomponent terms—for example, 'grana', 'parmigiana', 'provolone', or 'Romano'—even if Grana Padano, Parmigiano Reggiano, Provolone Valpadana, and Pecorino Romano are listed as GIs in the KOREU FTA.[11] It will be difficult for South Korea to simultaneously meet the obligation for certain names to both: 1) provide higher-level protection equivalent to Article 23 of the TRIPS Agreement to specified EU agricultural products as required in the KOREU FTA and 2) guarantee generic use of geographical names as required in the KORUS FTA. Unless the EU and the US reach a compromise in forums such as the Transatlantic Trade and Investment Partnership (TTIP), countries having trade negotiations with both the EU and the US will, like South Korea, have to commit to both mechanisms (Frankel, 2017; O'Connor & de Bosio, 2017).

In summary, international GI regime complexity has led to rule ambiguity. Various international treaties introduced different concepts—appellations of origin, sources of origin, and GIs—but their compatibility is rarely addressed except that the TRIPS Agreement incorporates relevant provisions in the Paris Convention. Post-TRIPS negotiations on GIs continue for both the GI Register and the GI extension. However, both the EU and the US initiated vertical forum shifting in their bilateral FTAs with third countries due to fruitless negotiations at the WTO. These FTAs inevitably led to further legal fragmentation—most prominently, the proliferation of competing GI provisions has made it difficult for some third countries to reconcile their treaty obligations. Nonetheless, the EU–US GI contestation manifests the competing interests of the Old World and the New World countries and potentially provides opportunities for a third country to have some influence on global GI governance.

[11] 'Letter from Jong-Hoon Kim, South Korean Minister for Trade, to USTR Ron Kirk', 20 June 2011. In this letter, South Korea clarified its GI provisions in the KOREU FTA to the satisfaction of the USTR.

The following sections will discuss how international GI regime complexity and continuous EU–US GI contestation have shaped China's international GI engagement and to what extent China has taken the opportunity of EU–US disagreements to advance its domestic policy objectives.

## 2.3 GIs in China: Legal Fragmentation and Regulatory Competition

Although GIs are generally considered a European form of intellectual property (van Caenegem *et al.*, 2014), they are not uncommon in the traditional Chinese tributary system (Zhang & Buzan, 2012). *Shangshu* 尚书, one of the Five Classics of ancient China, recorded that Xilü 西旅 (a tributary state) submitted their regional specialties as a tribute to the new emperor of Zhou in the year 1,046 BC.[12] This record demonstrated that the concept of regional specialties, which emphasised the place-product link by using place names as part of product names, has existed in China for over 3,000 years. The tributary system lasted until the end of the Qing Dynasty in 1911, and more than 3,000 types of objects were submitted as tributes to ancient Chinese empires, including food, fabrics, exotic beasts and birds, traditional Chinese medicines, and musical instruments (Hu, 1996). While the traditional use of geographical names in Chinese tributary systems differed from GIs in the modern intellectual property system, they later became valuable resources when China decided to import the regulatory system of GIs. Indeed, Chinese GI applicants still refer to the history of a product submitted as a tribute in their application documents as evidence of the product's premium quality or other characteristics. A reputation built on regional specialties in the past is well recognised by Chinese consumers.

In the early twentieth century, Portugal sought to add GIs to its Agreement of Friendship and Navigation with the Qing Dynasty (Wang, 2008), but the negotiation was never finalised. The PRC has not concerned with GIs till the 1980s, following China's Reform and Opening-up which enhanced foreign trade and introduced foreign investment to China. Because of complaints from EU GI rightholders, China encountered the concept of European-style GIs for the first time in its history.

---

12 It read: 'The intelligent kings paid careful attention to their virtue, and the wild tribes on every side acknowledged their subjection to them. The nearer and the more remote all presented the regional specialties, such as robes, food, and vessels for use 明王慎德, 四夷咸宾. 无有远迩, 毕献方物, 惟服食器用.' See Shangshu Zhoushu Lv'ao 尚书·周书·旅獒.

This section will discuss how China managed the competing EU and US GI demands over time, the problems of legal fragmentation and regulatory competition caused by such practices, and the holistic approach of the China National Intellectual Property Administration (CNIPA) to address the problem.

### 2.3.1 From No Protection to Case-by-Case Protection

Before the 1980s, geographical names and related labels were not recognised as a type of IP rights in China. Under the Chinese *Trademark Law* (1982), geographical names were naturally excluded from trademark registration. In 1986, the State Administration for Industry and Commerce (SAIC) issued a reply to local trademark regulators[13] to prohibit the use of geographical names of administrative divisions at or above the county level as trademarks on four grounds according to Paragraph 1 of the reply:

> First, it is the international custom not to use place names of administrative divisions as trademarks. Secondly, geographical names of an administrative division should not be used by a specific enterprise or individual which excludes usage by other enterprises or individuals from the same region of the same name in the same or similar products. Thirdly, using geographical names of administrative divisions at or above the county level as trademarks in a manner that is contradictory to the protection of origins. Fourthly, place names of administrative divisions at or above the county level can only indicate the source of origin of a product, which is a lack of distinctiveness when using as a trademark.'

There are four levels of administrative division in China: provincial, prefectural, county, and township. There were 2,862 counties in China as of 2004, which means the reply has enacted a considerable prohibition on using these place names as GIs. These grounds essentially clarified the principle of distinctiveness in trademark registration, and the balance of public and private interests—as place names could not meet the criteria of distinctiveness, they should not be appropriated as private property. This rationale was later challenged when the SAIC was confronted by foreign complaints. While protection for geographical names was not justified because of the anticompetition effect of a GI (Ground 2) and the lack of distinctiveness in trademark

[13] SAIC, *Reply Concerning Issues of Using Names of Administrative Divisions above the County Level* 国家工商行政管理局商标局就县级以上行政区划名称做商标等问题的复函 (1986).

registration (Ground 4), foreign companies conducting business in China still required exclusivity of their names based on the Paris Convention.

China became a contracting party of the Paris Convention in 1984. While the Chinese Trademark Law (1982) was clear that geographical names of administrative divisions at or above the county level were not protected, some foreign entities argued that based on Article 10*bis* of the convention, contracting members were mandated to protect geographical names for anti-competition purposes. Therefore, even if domestic place names were not protected, foreign place names should be to fulfil China's international obligations under the Paris Convention. This happened both individually (in the case of Danisa 丹麦牛油曲奇) and collectively (in the case of the consortium of Champagne 香槟). As a response to the complaint, SAIC issued an opinion to the Beijing Provincial Administration of Industry and Commerce (PAIC) to investigate the false use of the translated Chinese characters of Danisa by a food company in Beijing in 1987. The Beijing PAIC ordered the company to stop using Danisa immediately because it was an appellation of origin and China should comply with the Paris Convention.[14] In a 2018 anti-competition dispute in China, it was revealed that while Danisa used the term 'endorsed by the Denmark Royal family' and implied the place of production was Denmark, its products were actually produced in Indonesia.[15] In the context of Chinese GI regulation in the 1980s, the outcry over 'Danisa' as an appellation of origin worked, as the Chinese Trademark Office at that time presumed good faith in the complaint and could not verify information outside China. In another case of Champagne, SAIC ordered PAICs to protect the French name in 1989, after repeated complaints from French Champagne producers.[16] According to this order, Chinese enterprises cannot use 'Champagne' or its Chinese translation, '香槟', on any wines or spirits. Although these two cases illustrated China's efforts to comply with the Paris Convention, this case-based protection approach was an interim response before an institution was built to cover all products.

[14] SAIC, *Letter Concerning the Protection of Appellation of Origin* 国家工商行政管理局商标局关于保护原产地名称的函 (1987).

[15] Beijing Intellectual Property Court (2018) *Jing 73 Min Zhong* No. 538 Civil Judgement 北京知识产权法院 (2018) 京73民终538号民事判决书.

[16] SAIC, *Notice on Prohibiting Using '香槟' or Champagne for Wines* 国家工商行政管理局关于停止在酒类商品上使用香槟或 champagne 字样的通知 (1989).

### 2.3.2 EU and US Influences on the Building of Chinese GI Institutions

The case-by-case protection of foreign GIs led to 'supernational treatment' because, in effect, only foreign place names were protected, while domestic place names were not. For instance, the SAIC instructed the Shandong PAIC, in 1988, that 'Longkou 龙口' could not be registered as a trademark for vermicelli, because it has long been used as a name for the vermicelli produced within the area of Longkou and should not be exclusively owned by one company.[17] The differentiated treatment of domestic and foreign place names stimulated extensive research on legal mechanisms for protecting GIs.

China began to follow the international debates on GIs and explore different mechanisms for GI regulation, including *sui generis* and trademark protection.

Some European countries also took the initiative to disseminate their regulatory practices to their Chinese counterparts. In 1995, the then State Bureau of Quality and Technological Supervision (SBQTS) started to cooperate on GIs with the French Ministry of Agriculture, the Cognac Association, and the Chinese Ministry of Finance through personnel exchange and training. In 1997 and 1998, China and France signed the *Sino-French Statement on the Establishment of the Cooperative Committee on Agriculture and Foodstuffs* (Liu, 2015) which expedited China's establishment of *sui generis* protection for GIs (AQSIQ, 2007). This was led by the General Administration of Quality Supervision, Inspection and Quarantine (AQSIQ), the successor of the SBQTS. After the EU began bilateral cooperation with China, bilateral GI communication was moved to the regional level in EU–China bilateral IP cooperation projects (Wyzycka & Hasmath, 2017). This happened contemporaneously with China's large-scale rule-amending and rulemaking to comply with WTO requirements.

During the early EU push for GI recognition, the US influence on China's GI rulemaking was less visible, as the US was in a position of responding defensively, advocating for lower-level protection for GIs. In the US-China bilateral negotiations before the TRIPS Agreement, GIs were not mentioned. Still, China was aware of the US way of regulating geographical names through the trademark system.

The Madrid Agreement provides parties with an opportunity to use collective or certification marks to protect geographical names. China signed this

[17] SAIC, *Opinions Concerning the Name of 'Longkou'* 国家工商行政管理局商标局关于'龙口'名称的意见 (1988). Longkou Vermicelli later became a registered GI and was listed in China–EU GI mutual recognition program.

agreement in 1989 and established a system to protect geographical names as collective and certification marks in 1994.[18] One important feature of this 1994 regulation was that it did not provide higher-level protection to wines and spirits. It has another function of ending supernational treatment by introducing equal protection for domestic and foreign GIs. It also filled the gap in domestic law as domestic disputes about geographical names increased in this period. The famous Jinhua ham case highlights such domestic conflicts (Lü & Wu, 2006). Internationally, the issue of TRIPS Article 23 compliance only emerged after China's WTO accession in 2001.

### 2.3.3 TRIPS Compliance and Post-TRIPS GI Divergence

China amended its IP laws comprehensively after its WTO accession. Article 16 was added to the Chinese *Trademark Law 2001*, in which Paragraph 2 adopted the exact definition of GIs from Article 22 of the TRIPS Agreement—a move to guarantee that Chinese law fully complies with the TRIPS requirement. It provides that if a trademark contains a place name but the product does not originate in that area (thus misleads the public), the geographical name should not be registered or used. However, a grandfathering exception is provided that if a trademark has already been registered in good faith in such circumstances, it remains valid. This exception is particularly relevant for foreign GIs because GI protection in a third country is underpinned by a reputation accumulated in that market, not *terroir* in the origin country. This was later clarified by the *Administrative Regulations Concerning the Registration of Collective Marks and Certification Marks* (Collective and Certification Marks Regulation 2003), which repealed the collective and certification mark regulation of 1994. The Collective and Certification Marks Regulation 2003 protects all products (including handcrafts) equivalent to TRIPS Article 22. In particular, Article 12 of the regulation provides a TRIPS Article 23-level protection for wines and spirits.

The influence of the EU led to two further *sui generis* systems in China in the post-TRIPS era. First, AQSIQ established a *sui generis* system to protect 'GI Products' under the *Provisions on the Protection of GI Products* (2005),[19] which protects both products grown and bred in a place and products of which all the raw materials come from the place after which the product is named or some of the raw material comes from other places but

---

[18] SAIC, *Administrative Regulations Concerning the Registration of Collective Marks and Certification Marks* 集体商标、证明商标注册和管理办法, by Order No. 22 (1994).

[19] AQSIQ, *Provisions on the Protection of GI Products* 地理标志产品保护规定, Order No. 78 (2005).

is produced and processed within the named place using special techniques. The second category extends protection beyond agriculture and foodstuffs to handcrafts. This is an institutional creation to accommodate the *sui generis* system to China's competitive advantage in handicrafts such as embroidery and ceramics. With the regulatory strength of the AQSIQ on quality control of GI products (Article 22), such products must conform to stringent quality standards and production techniques. The use of GI will be relinquished if a producer fails to conform to these requirements (Article 23).

Second, the Chinese Ministry of Agriculture (MOA) issued a regulation in 2007 to protect 'Agricultural GI Products'—defined as primary agricultural products, including plants, animals, microorganisms, and products obtained from agricultural activities.[20] A *sui generis* protection under the MOA was mainly justified by the fact that, in the European Union, GIs are regulated under the Directorate-General for Agriculture and Rural Development (DG AGRI). In addition, given the scope of Chinese GI Products is broader than agricultural products, it seems necessary to have a specialised system dedicated to agricultural products. However, a dedicated GI system for forestry products could also make sense if there can be one for agricultural products. In 2013, the State Forestry Administration (SFA) proposed establishing a system resembling that of the MOA to protect 'GIs for forestry products'.[21] This proposal, however, was not approved by the State Council.

Previous studies, in both Chinese and English, have already discussed the details of these three parallel systems (Wang & Huang, 2006; Wang & Kireeva, 2007; Zhang, 2007). For present purposes, it is only necessary to understand the architecture of the three systems (Fig. 2.1) and their relationship with one another.

First, the three systems under three ministries in China are completely independent of each other, leading to duplicate or even triplicate applications by certain users. It is not only a waste of public resources but also contributes to consumer confusion. Second, the US and the EU exported GI regulations through technocratic networks similar to the pattern of their influence in patent regulation (Drahos, 2008). The three domestic systems indicate how the EU–US power contestation at the international level eventually

20 MOA, *Measures for the Administration of Geographical Indications for Agricultural Products* 农产品地理标志管理办法, Order No. 11 (2007). 'GIs for agricultural products', which are the subject of these protection measures, refers to special agricultural product indications named after geographical place names and whose purpose is to note that the indicated agricultural products are from a specific area and the quality and major characteristics of the products lie mainly in the natural environment as well as the cultural and historical factors of the area (Article 2).

21 SFA, *Measures for the Administration of GIs for Forestry Products (Draft for Comments)* 林产品地理标志管理办法 (征求意见稿) (2013).

GI Trademarks (SAIC) | GI Protected Products (AQSIQ) | Agricultural GI Products (MOA)

**Fig. 2.1** Special signs for GIs regulated by SAIC, AQSIQ, and the MOA

contributed to Chinese GI regulatory competition. Third, there are deviations in the law transplanted to China and the original model of trademark or *sui generis* protections. In terms of trademark law, the amended Article 12 of the Collective and Certification Marks Regulation (2003) provides a TRIPS Article 23 level of protection for wines and spirits. While this means Chinese trademark law complies with TRIPS standards, such protection could not be justified by trademark law theories. In terms of *sui generis* protection, the problem lies in prohibited activities. Article 21 of the *Provisions on the Protection of GI Products* (2005) prohibits the following behaviour: 1) using without authorisation or forging the place name and the special sign of a GI-protected product, 2) using a place name for a product without conforming to the GI-protected product standards or management specifications, or 3) using signs similar to the special signs of GI-protected products and similar misleading names to the place name or using letters or signs that can mislead consumers to believe that similar products with the signs are GI-protected products. The third category does not further stipulate the criteria to determine similarity, so it can be difficult to implement. Furthermore, consumer confusion or the use of similar signs follows the trademark rationale. It seems a bit confusing that this rationale is applied in the Chinese *sui generis* mechanism. This brings a further problem of expanding the scope of protection in this Chinese *sui generis* mechanism because originally the European *sui generis* mechanism protects only place names, not associated signs. It is also not clear how the behaviour described in item 3) relates to TRIPS Article 23 prohibiting the use of place names for

> products not originating in the place indicated by the geographical indication in question … even where the true origin of the goods is indicated or the geographical indication is used in translation or accompanied by expressions such as 'kind', 'type', 'style', 'imitation' or the like.

The EU has two systems for GIs—the Protected Designation of Origin (PDO) and the Protected Geographical Indication (PGI). It is not clear which the Chinese 2005 regulation resembles. The two systems differ in: 1) the extent to which raw materials come from the designated place and the extent to which processing stages take place in the designated place; 2) PDOs are underpinned by the concept of *terroir* while PGIs are based on a product's reputation over time. Concerning the first issue, the Chinese GI regulation requires all or most of the raw material to come from the designated place and all production processes to occur in the designated place. These are stringent requirements that resemble the PDO system, as PGI only requires at least one phase of the production process to occur in the designated place. However, concerning *terroir*, it is hard to tell how the place–product link in the Chinese context is related to *terroir*, even though the supporting documents[22] must include an explanation of the relationship between the perceived characteristics of the products and the natural and human factors of the place of production.

### 2.3.4 Implementing GI Regulation to China's Advantage

Despite the above theoretical problems, the Chinese GI systems have been tailored to protect Chinese regional specialties, some of which have built their reputation by tracing back to the tributary system in imperial China. GIs could allow local communities to exploit such reputation of regional specialties accumulated over 3,000 years. GIs have also been internalised and incorporated into Chinese agricultural policies to promote higher quality agricultural products. For instance, SAIC has developed the *Strategy for the Prosperity of Farmers*, an integral part of which is the use of certification trademarks or collective trademarks to protect GIs.

There have been reports of success stories. For instance, Guanxi Pomelo 琯溪蜜柚 is a pomelo named after the little creek of 'Guanxi' in the town of Xiaoxi in Pinghe County, Zhangzhou Prefecture, Fujian Province. According to a survey, 635,000 tonnes of Guanxi Pomelos were sold in China in 2009,

[22] According to Article 10 of the *Provisions on the Protection of GI Products* (2005), the application should be supported by: 1) an application form for GI-protected products; 2) a description of the product name, category, production area, and geographical features; 3) a description of the physical, chemical, sensory, and other characteristics of the product and its relationship with the natural and human factors of the place in which it is produced; 4) technical specifications (including product processing technology, safety and health requirements, technical requirements for processing); 5) the reputation of the product, including product production and sales data, and the historical reputation of the place of production; and 6) technical standards of the GI-protected products.

destined for major cities such as Beijing, Tianjin, Shanghai, Nanjing, and Ningbo. Meanwhile, 120,000 tonnes of Guanxi Pomelos were exported to Hong Kong, Macau, the EU, Central Asia, and South-East Asia. As one of the 10 Chinese GIs in the EU–China mutual recognition project (Sect. 2.4.3), 60% of the exported Guanxi Pomelos were sold on the EU market. In Guanxi, more than 99% of pomelo producers used the collective trademark 'Pinghe Guanxi Pomelo'. With annual farmer per capita income exceeding CNY4,700 (almost US$800), Guanxi Pomelo becomes a typical example of GIs contributing to regional prosperity (Sun, 2016).

China has witnessed a surge in GI applications across the three systems. In 2013, 3,210 GIs have been registered across the three parallel systems, with an economic value of CNY1.3 trillion (US$213 billion) (Liu, 2013). GI registrations in 2020 more than doubled compared with 2013 (Fig. 2.2). The large scale of registration reflects that the traditional Chinese regional specialties from its ancient tributary system have revived through the new, transplanted GI mechanism.

Data on the internal distribution of the applications demonstrate regulatory competition in the three Chinese GI systems. By the end of 2020, there has been 3,352 GI trademarks, 2,174 agricultural GI products, and 1,299 GI-protected products. Figure 2.3 shows a considerable overlap of registrations where nearly 1,400 products were protected by two systems, and 198 (2.35%) products are protected by all three systems. Most users seeking dual protections submitted applications for trademarks and one of the two *sui generis* systems. Double or triple registration is a waste of resources, which perhaps

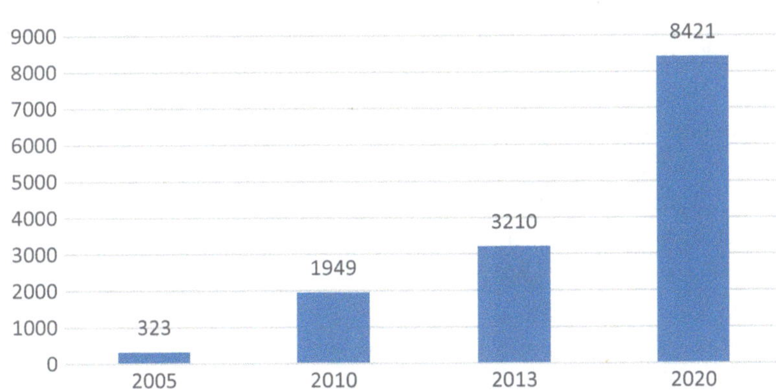


**Fig. 2.2** Registered GIs in China, (2005–2020) (*Source* Central County Research Institute 中郡研究所 [2020] *The Fourth National Survey on the Number of Geographical Indications* 第四次全国地理标志数量调研报告)

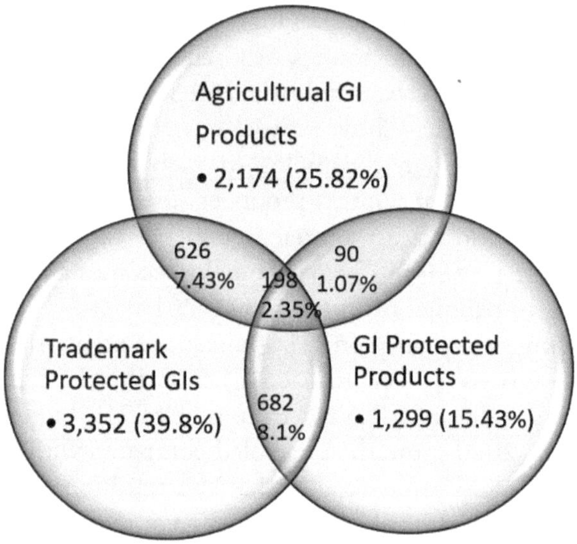


**Fig. 2.3** GI Registrations in the three Chinese systems (*Source* Central County Research Institute 中郡研究所 [2020] *The Fourth National Survey on the Number of Geographical Indications* 第四次全国地理标志数量调研报告)

explains why a fourth system, for the protection of GIs for forestry products, has not been approved.

### 2.3.5 Regulatory Competition and CNIPA's Holistic Approach to GI Regulation

While each GI mechanism has been promoted as a way to enhance regional prosperity, there are three competent regulators in charge of GIs simultaneously. In China, regulatory power on a specific issue is allocated among ministries of the State Council based on mandates stipulated in their *Provisions on the Definitions of Main Functions, Setup of Internal Bodies and Staffing* (PDMFSIBS). Regulatory competition arises when there is an overlap or ambiguity in the PDMFSIBS mandate statement or an emerging regulatory subject that can be tangentially regulated by more than one regulator. The emergence of GIs as a new regulatory subject with no prescription in any PDMFSIBS is the cause of domestic GI regulatory competition.

The major problem with this regulatory competition is the wasting of public resources to maintain triplicate systems, the extra costs for applicants who pursue more than one label (Fig. 2.2), and consumer confusion. The institutional integration of central regulators created an opportunity to address this problem. After an institutional reshuffle in 2018, both SAIC and AQSIQ were dissolved, and their mandates on GI-related issues were integrated into the CNIPA. There was no change of mandate concerning the regulation of GIs for the MOA.

This semi-partial integration seems to be counterintuitive. Logically, one would expect the two *sui generis* systems (under AQSIQ and the MOA) to merge, and with this merged institution coexisting with the trademark system; an alternative option would be to relinquish either the trademark system or the *sui generis* system in its entirety. The first scenario did not happen because, while the establishment of the *sui generis* and trademark systems were under the influence of the EU and the US, respectively, each regulator also followed the hierarchy of the State Council where SIPO was sub-ministerial and MOA was ministerial; it would be very difficult for SIPO to integrate the GI mandate from the MOA. Second, the influence of the EU and the US is already deeply rooted and institutionalised, making the ending of either system impossible.

Although the 2018 institutional integration did not resolve regulatory competition, it led to a more holistic approach to GI regulation. However, CNIPA faces a theoretical problem as a single regulator in charge of two GI systems, one trademark and one *sui generis*. To address these challenges, CNIPA has implemented a series of measures to streamline the two systems. In 2019, CNIPA issued the *Revised Measures for the Protection of Foreign GI-Protected Products*,[23] which modified 2016 measures issued by AQSIQ[24] which designated AQSIQ as the regulator of foreign GIs. The revision confirms CNIPA as the regulator of foreign GI products in China.

Secondly, CAINA introduced a uniform application platform (CNIPA, 2019) and a uniform sign for both trademark and *sui generis* GIs that replaces previous GI Trademark and GI Protected Products signs (Fig. 2.1). According to the *Administrative Measures on Using Special Signs of GIs*,[25] GI-protected products under the *sui generis* system should bear this new sign together with the name of 'GI product', as well as associated GI standard or GI product registration number; GIs registered as certification or collective marks should use this sign together with the trademark and indicate the trademark registration number. The social credit number of the enterprise should also be included as part of the sign. In addition to these major changes in rules, signs,

[23] CNIPA, *Measures on the Protection of Foreign GI-Protected Products* 外国地理标志产品保护办法 (2019).

[24] AQSIQ, *Measures on the Protection of Foreign GI-Protected Products* 外国地理标志产品保护办法 (2016).

[25] CNIPA, *Administrative Measures on Using Special Signs for GIs (Trial Implementation)* 地理标志专用标志使用管理办法(试行) (2020).

and application procedures, CNIPA has collected statistics on GI registrations in each system and integrated these into its quarterly statistical reports.[26] It also promotes social awareness of GIs by initiating special enforcement campaigns for GI protection during the Chinese New Year (Xiong, 2019) and for seasonal products[27] such as tea or crabs.

A uniform application platform and a uniform sign for both *sui generis* and trademark-protected GIs demonstrate CNIPA's efforts to coordinate the once fragmented and overlapping systems. These measures, however, may not mitigate the theoretical concerns of integration. It remains to be seen whether this integration will eventually create tiered protection for GIs—like the relationship between inventions and utility models in the Chinese patent system. The requirements for inventive steps and examination processes are different as utility models do not require substantive examination. The number of trademark-protected GIs was more than that of registered GI products after the integration, partly due to less control of the production process in voluntary self-regulation (for collective marks) or third-party regulation by the consortium (for certification marks) than in the *sui generis* system.

## 2.4 China's Engagement with International GI Regulation

The TRIPS Agreement was part of the most complex set of agreements in t*he Final Act Embodying the Results of the Uruguay Round of Multilateral Trade Negotiations*. The complexity and range of these agreements meant probably only a few players had any real understanding of them as a package (Drahos, 2001). China was a latecomer to the international IP system, and it took a long process for China to understand the trade-offs in TRIPS GI negotiations. The same is true of Chinese engagement with WIPO. China has been a member of WIPO since June 1980 and joined the Paris Convention in December 1984, the Madrid Agreement in October 1989, and the Madrid Protocol in December 1995. When China became a party to these international agreements, their texts had already been negotiated. So, it was a game of take it or leave it. Nonetheless, once China established its three domestic GI regulatory mechanisms, it engaged more actively with international GI regulations at various levels.

---

[26] CNIPA, *Circular of the CNIPA General Office on Carrying Out a Survey of Geographical Indications Resources* 国家知识产权局办公室关于开展地理标志保护资源普查的通知 (2019).

[27] CNIPA, *Notice of the General Office on Strengthening the Protection of Geographical Indications in Autumn 2019* 国家知识产权局办公室关于加强2019年秋季地理标志保护工作的通知.

### 2.4.1 China's Position at the WTO

China was not fully involved in the post-TRIPS negotiations in the first few years after its WTO accession in 2001. This was partly because it did not yet have a nuanced understanding of previous negotiations. Another reason was that compliance with the TRIPS Agreement was China's priority at that time, so its entire focus was on establishing domestic legislation. China amended or formulated its domestic IP laws to comply with TRIPS standards (Hu, 2002; Li, 2002), including GI regulations discussed in Sect. 2.3.2. Recognising that GI protection aligned with its national interests particularly in enhancing regional prosperity, China began to engage in international GI negotiations, not to promote its own agenda but to monitor that prospect international law does not contravene its domestic GI objectives.

As mentioned, the GI Register and GI Extension have been major issues on the WTO's agenda since the TRIPS Agreement. The GI Register aims to establish a multilateral notification and registration system for wines and spirits; the GI Extension aims to extend the higher-level protection standard to products beyond wines and spirits. Table 2.1 provides a summary of the contesting positions on these two issues in post-TRIPS negotiations.

Although Table 2.1 shows the EU and developing countries have taken similar positions on both issues, this consensus was reached only in 2008 when 108 WTO members jointly submitted proposal TN/C/W/52[28] to the WTO. Before that, the GI Register proposals were mainly sponsored by the EU while developing countries supported the GI Extension proposals. China was a co-sponsor for the TN/C/W/52 proposal—the only proposal China has submitted to the WTO on GI-related issues. Therefore, this proposal provides a unique opportunity to investigate China's GI engagement at the WTO.

The TN/C/W/52 proposal intended to provide modalities to kick off text-based negotiations to amend the TRIPS Agreement. On GI Register, the proposal clarified that the 'register shall be considered as *prima facie* evidence' based on the definition of GIs in TRIPS Article 22.1, and participation in the multilateral notification and registration system is mandatory. On GI Extension, the proposal recommended initiating text-based negotiations in special sessions to begin TRIPS amendments. This proposal incorporates both the EU's position on the GI Register and the developing countries' proposal

[28] WTO Trade Negotiations Committee, *Draft Modalities for TRIPS Related Issues*, Communication from Albania, Brazil, China, Colombia, Ecuador, the European Community, Iceland, India, Indonesia, the Kyrgyz Republic, Liechtenstein, the Former Yugoslav Republic of Macedonia, Pakistan, Peru, Sri Lanka, Switzerland, Thailand, Turkey, the African, Caribbean, Pacific Group, and the African Group, TN/C/W/52, 19 July 2008.

**Table 2.1** Major disagreements in the post-TRIPS negotiation of GIs

| Topics | Issues | US<br>Representing the New World | EU<br>Representing the Old World | Developing countries (including China) |
|---|---|---|---|---|
| GI Register | Participation | Voluntary and non-burdensome | Compulsory | Compulsory |
| | Legal criteria to protect a foreign GI | Domestic law | International Law/<br>Prima facie based on TRIPS Article 22.1 | Prima facie based on TRIPS Article 22.1 |
| GI Extension | Procedural | GI Extension was not a built-in issue in post-TRIPS negotiations | Not clear | – GI Extension to be addressed in regular TRIPS Council meetings as a priority<br>– Text-based negotiations shall be undertaken |
| | Substance | GI Extension will create difficulties because:<br>– the distribution of GIs is not balanced among WTO members<br>– Article 22 provides sufficient protection<br>– GI extension will impair the use of genetic terms<br>– GI Extension would incur substantial costs | – all GIs should be protected equally<br>– protection equivalent to Article 23 TRIPS should be extended to all products | – all GIs should be protected equally<br>– protection equivalent to Article 23 TRIPS should be extended to all products |

on the GI Extension. It was a strategic coalition between the EU and the developing-country members of the WTO to advance GI negotiations.

As China co-sponsored this proposal, it can be difficult to distinguish a Chinese position based only on the proposal's text. However, co-sponsoring TN/C/W/52 per se indicated that China considered GIs aligning with its national interests—in particular, the tradition of using place names as product names in its tributary system. In addition, China welcomed WTO negotiations on both GI Register and GI Extension.

More specifically, China's position on both issues was expressed by Chinese negotiators via contributions to Chinese academic publications. WAN Yiting, the Vice-Division Director in the WTO Department of the Ministry of Commerce (MOFCOM), co-authored a journal article Wang and Wan (2010) that analyses China's position and strategy in the GI negotiations at the WTO in that context. As indicated in its first footnote, the article was an output of 'the research project assigned by MOFCOM, and the results of the project have been adopted by the MOFCOM in the WTO Doha Negotiations'. Given the difficulty in accessing interviewees, the following analysis is mainly based on this article.

According to Wang and Wan (2010), China held the following positions on GI-related issues in proposing TN/C/W/52. First, China intended to strike a balance between the EU and the US positions on the controversial issue of GIs. On the one hand, China joined with the EU in supporting the TN/C/W/52 proposal on GI Register and GI Extension. On the other hand, China did not join the EU in blaming US firms for using EU GIs as generic names. Instead, China referred to the principle of mutual respect for each state's sovereignty and non-interference in one another's internal affairs. According to this principle, the legitimacy of US firms using EU GIs is an internal US affair, and China respects the sovereignty of the US in regulating this issue based on its domestic laws and regulations.

Second, China strategically made a procedural proposal to show its substantive preference: China was more interested in GI Extension than GI Register. This was because China is a country rich in regional specialties, many of which are internationally renowned products; however, most of these products are agricultural products, not wines and spirits. To promote its preference for GI Extension, China proposed binding together the negotiations on both issues, even though the TRIPS Agreement did not initially give them equal priority. GI Register had a higher priority than the GI Extension according to Paragraph 18 of the Doha Ministerial Declaration:

> With a view to completing the work started in the TRIPS Council on the implementation of Article 23.4, we agree to negotiate the establishment of a multilateral system of notification and registration of geographical indications for wines and spirits by the Fifth Session of the Ministerial Conference. We note that issues related to the extension of the protection of geographical indications provided for in Article 23 to products other than wines and spirits will be addressed in the Council for TRIPS pursuant to paragraph 12 of this declaration.[29]

As revealed in this quotation, GI Register was a built-in issue that committed WTO members to continuous negotiation after the TRIPS Agreement, while the GI Extension was not so the possibility of negotiation was uncertain. China proposed binding the negotiations on these issues together to increase the priority of the GI Extension; however, this could slow the progress of negotiations on the GI Register, due to the strong resistance of the US to the Extension (in particular, by its dairy industry). Prioritising GI Extension was likely a condition of China and other developing members for co-sponsoring the proposal with the EU; if the EU wanted the coalition on GIs to work, it had to support the developing-country positions on GI Extension.

Third, concerning GI Register, while China generally agreed that the multilateral register on wines and spirits should be compulsory, it preferred greater flexibility. Comparing the Chinese position as manifested by Wang and Wan (2010) with the text of the TN/C/W/52 proposal, there were three differences regarding GI Register. To start with, they proposed different governing laws concerning whether a geographic name can be protected as a GI. While the TN/C/W/52 proposal maintained that such a decision should be made based on international law, China's position was that the decision should be based on domestic law. Second, the TN/C/W/52 proposal put forward a restrictive enforcement mechanism for the multilateral register to protect the interests of rightsholders, but China proposed a principle of sufficient notification, following which there would be more flexibility in enforcement; if an infringer used the GIs because they were unaware of the registration, they would be exempt from punishment. Third, while the TN/C/W/52 proposal did not mention third parties, China proposed that the rights of a third party should be protected by allowing them to sue in

---

29 Doha Ministerial Declaration, 20 November 2001, WT/MIN(01)/DEC/1.

a domestic court of a WTO member (Wang & Wan, 2010). Interestingly, some of these Chinese positions bore more similarity to those of the US than the EU (Table 2.1).

In summary, although China made the TN/C/W/52 proposal with the EU and other developing countries, it did not take the same position as the EU. China's preference for GI Extension was expressed in a subtle way—through the suggestion to bind together the negotiations on GI Register and GI Extension to raise the priority of the latter. This subtlety was caused by the limited benefits to China from negotiations on GI Register (Wang & Wan, 2010) and China's preference for GI Extension because it would increase the value and reputation of Chinese products, especially its regional specialties, by granting them a higher standard of protection.

### 2.4.2 China and the WIPO SCT

China has not yet signed the Lisbon Agreement, the major international agreement on GIs administered by WIPO. In May 2015, the Diplomatic Conference for the Adoption of a New Act of the Lisbon Agreement for the Protection of Appellations of Origin and their International Registration was held in Geneva. Since China is not yet a contracting party to this agreement, it dispatched only an observer delegation to the conference. In June 2016, the WIPO Working Group for the Preparation of Common Regulations under the Lisbon Agreement and the Geneva Act held its first meeting, and China again dispatched an observer delegation.[30] The Geneva Text took effect in early 2020. Domestically, there has been no indication that China is interested in joining the Lisbon Agreement.

Notwithstanding its prudence in the latest progress, Chinese representatives regularly participated in the WIPO SCT meetings, a longstanding forum for GI negotiations and discussions (Sect. 2.2.2). Looking through SCT conference minutes, China rarely expresses an opinion and has never been involved in the debate. On the few occasions a Chinese delegation has expressed an opinion, the representative made sure not to introduce any controversy. For instance, at the SCT's sixth session, the Chinese delegation said:

[30] WIPO Working Group for the Preparation of Common Regulations under the Lisbon Agreement and the Geneva Act of the Lisbon Agreement, First Session, *Summary by the Chair*, LI/WG/PCR/1/5, 9 June 2016.

> China was in support of examining the protection of geographical indications because its country was currently revising its legislation in marks and the relationship between geographical indications and trademarks appeared to be a problem that needed to be overcome. The Delegation said that it would appreciate a continuing discussion and that awaiting the outcome of the work that was currently undertaking [sic] on geographical indications within the Council for TRIPS was not necessarily satisfactory.[31]

China also took the STC forum as an opportunity to demonstrate achievements in its domestic GI registration and protection, as well as how GIs had boosted its agricultural sector. For instance, SAIC and WIPO organised the seventh biennial *International Symposium on Geographical Indications* in Beijing in 2007 (WIPO, 2007), during which the Chinese representatives made clear: 'China is systematically engaged in the exploitation of GIs as a means of adding value to her agricultural products and boosting her rural economy' (March, 2007).

SAIC represented China in its international engagement on GI-related issues at the WIPO SCT till the institutional integration in 2018.[32] Domestically, it was in charge of China's GI protection under the trademark mechanism. Therefore, it was difficult for SAIC, a trademark regulator, to provide substantive inputs to the GI Extension negotiations which aimed to expand the scope of *sui generis* protection. However, SAIC was active in disseminating its achievements by using trademarks to protect GIs. In China's 2018 institutional reshuffle, SAIC was dissolved and the function of trademark regulation in its entirety was merged into CNIPA. It is not clear so far to what extent this has impacted China's engagement on GI-related issues at WIPO, where it used to maintain a general interest in the progress of negotiations and conferences through observers while remaining quiet in all these sessions.

[31] WIPO SCT, Sixth Session, *Report*, SCT/6/6, 5 December 2001.

[32] This is demonstrated in the 2010 Memorandum between SAIC and WIPO to Further Strengthen Cooperation 工商总局和世界知识产权组织关于进一步加强合作的谅解备忘录. The text of the memorandum in Chinese is available at: http://www.gov.cn/gzdt/2010-04/27/content_1593670.htm.

## 2.4.3 China's Bilateral GI Engagement with the EU and US

### 2.4.3.1 EU–China GI Mutual Recognition

So far, the major achievement on GIs between the EU and China is the '10+10 Project', which was finalised in 2012. The project was a reciprocal scheme in which 10 Chinese geographical names were registered and protected in the EU and labelled either PDO or PGI. Meanwhile, 10 EU geographical names were registered in China as GI products in its *sui generis* mechanism.[33] Following this pilot project, a similar '100+100 Project', in which 100 geographical names would receive recognition and protection in each territory, was proposed in March 2011. In July 2017, the 100 GI names from each side were published,[34] with the expectation that an agreement would be straightforward with another one or two rounds of negotiations (Hu, 2018). The EU–China GI Agreement[35] was eventually signed in September 2020, with the list of GIs for mutual recognition extending to 275 from each side. This agreement is politically significant for both the EU and China.

The EU–China GI Agreement demonstrates some key features of their bilateral GI cooperation. First, it provides a channel for deeper integration. The relevant Chinese and EU GI regulators and users—rather than ministries in charge of trade and foreign affairs—met and discussed GI issues and mutual recognition directly. A dedicated bilateral agreement only on GIs, with the intensive involvement of Chinese IP regulators, means this cooperation can be less influenced by the broader considerations and trade-offs that typically occur in formal international cooperation through the MOFCOM. Initially, AQSIQ and the EC DG AGRI and DG Trade signed conference

[33] The 10 EU GIs protected in China are Grana Padano, Prosciutto di Parma, Roquefort, Pruneaux d'Agen/Pruneaux d'Agen mi-cuits, Priego de Cordóba, Sierra Mágina, Comté, White Stilton Cheese/Blue Stilton Cheese, Scottish Farmed Salmon, and West Country Farmhouse Cheddar. The Chinese list of GIs protected in the EU comprises: Dongshan bai lu sun 东山白芦笋 (asparagus), Guanxi mi you 琯溪蜜柚 (honey pomelo), Jinxiang da suan 金乡大蒜 (garlic), Lixian ma shan yao 蠡县麻山药 (yam), Longjing cha 龙井茶 (tea), Pinggu da tao 平谷大桃 (peach), Shaanxi ping guo 陕西苹果 (apple), Yancheng long xia 盐城龙虾 (crayfish), Zhenjiang xiang cu 镇江香醋 (vinegar), and Longkou fen si 龙口粉丝 (vermicelli).

[34] EU DG AGRI and MOFCOM China, *Joint Communiqué on the Negotiation of the Agreement on Cooperation on, and Protection of, Geographical Indications, 2 June 2017* 欧盟委员会农业和农村发展总局与中华人民共和国商务部关于《地理标志合作与保护协定》谈判的联合声明 (2017年6月2日), https://ec.europa.eu/agriculture/sites/agriculture/files/newsroom/2017-06-02-joint-comm.pdf (last retrieved 28 May 2021).

[35] EU and China, Agreement on Cooperation on, and Protection of, Geographical Indications, OJ L 408I, 4 December 2020, pp. 3–43.

minutes on bilateral GI cooperation in October 2006 (AQSIQ, 2007). When MOFCOM became the coordinator for intellectual property, it replaced AQSIQ as the key negotiator of EU–China GI mutual recognition. Second, the EU–China GI cooperation manifested the pragmatism of the two parties. Since AQSIQ was only a ministry under the State Council, it did not have the authority to sign international agreements. The 10+10 Project was an experiment in what mutual GI recognition would look like and what difficulties the two parties would encounter before a formal agreement was negotiated. Based on the successful experience of the 10+10 Project, further progress was made towards a bilateral agreement, with larger numbers of geographical names mutually recognised in each territory.

#### 2.4.3.2 GIs in the US-China Economic and Trade Agreement

In the first-phase agreement of the current US-China trade war, USCETA 2020, China promised to import no less than US$12.5 billion worth of agricultural products from the United States in 2020 and no less than US$19.5 billion in 2021 (Article 6.2.1(b)). This made GI a salient issue for the US to compete in the Chinese agricultural market. In the USCETA, various provisions were in place to counteract the EU-style mutual recognition agreement (Ribeiro de Almeida, 2020), including objection and cancellation procedures (Article 1.15.2), and provisions on determining generic terms. The USCETA defines a generic name as 'a term customary in the common language as the common name for the associated good' and provides four criteria for China to consider whether a geographic name is a generic term. In addition, China must ensure its domestic regulations are in place so that 1) any geographical indication may become generic over time and may be subject to cancellation on that basis (Article 1.16.1 (b)), and 2) an individual component of a compound term shall not be protected as a GI if the component is generic (Article 1.17.1). These two mechanisms allow relevant stakeholders, not only from the US but also from other third countries, to challenge the EU GIs (mutually recognised as Chinese GIs) as generic names in Chinese courts. The opposition and cancellation procedures guarantee the right to sue on the above and other grounds.

The USCETA further requires China to ensure that US access to its markets relying on trademarks and generic names in the future will not be undermined by 'any measures taken in connection with pending or future requests from any other trading partner for recognition or protection of a geographical indication according to an international agreement'

(Article 1.15.1). It is not clear how this outcome-oriented provision can be implemented in a Chinese court.

Further domestic conflicts in implementing both 2020 agreements with the US and the EU remain to be seen, but various provisions discussed above indicate that there is limited policy space for China to manoeuvre in this new context of vertical forum-shifting.

### 2.4.4 GI Provisions in Other Chinese FTAs/RTAs

Since 2003, China has signed over 20 FTAs (Chapter 5), including nine Chinese FTAs with GI provisions: China-Chile FTA (2008), China-Peru FTA (2009), China-Costa Rica FTA (2010), China-New Zealand FTA (2008), China-Iceland FTA (2013), China-Switzerland FTA (2013), China-South Korea FTA (2015), China-ASEAN FTA (2002, upgraded in 2015), and China-Australia FTA (2015) and China-Georgia FTA (2017). The nine Chinese FTAs mentioning GIs can be divided into three categories.

#### 2.4.4.1 Category I: FTAs Mentioning GIs in the Definition of Intellectual Property Rights

In China's FTAs with New Zealand, Iceland, South Korea, and ASEAN, GIs are mentioned in the definition of intellectual property. For instance, Article 63.2 of China–Iceland FTA provides:

> For the purpose of this Chapter, the term 'intellectual property rights' refers to copyright and related rights, rights in trademarks, geographical indications, industrial designs, patents, undisclosed information, layout designs of integrated circuits, and rights in plant varieties as defined in TRIPS.

This provision defines the concept of IP rights by referring to the TRIPS Agreement. Since South Korea, Iceland, New Zealand, and ASEAN countries are all members of the WTO, GI protection should be consistent with the standards in Articles 22–24 of the TRIPS Agreement. In particular, without special mutual GI recognition mechanisms in these four FTAs, geographical names from one party must go through the formal process of registration and examination by the other party to be recognised as GIs in the other party.

#### 2.4.4.2 Category II: Listing GIs for Mutual Recognition

China's FTAs with Chile, Peru, and Costa Rica list specific GIs of one party to be recognised and protected in the territory of the other party. Article 116 of China–Costa Rica FTA designates 10 Costa-Rican GIs to be protected in China, but the Chinese GIs to be protected in Costa Rica are not yet confirmed in the FTA text. Article 146 of China–Peru FTA lists 22 Chinese GIs to be protected in Peru and four Peruvian GIs to be protected in China. Article 10 in China–Chile FTA lists two Chinese GIs to be protected in Chile and one Chilean GI to be protected in China. The standards of protection granted to these listed products are equivalent to those under the TRIPS Agreement. Some of the listed products are wines, including Shaoxing Wine, Pisco Perú, and Chilean Pisco, so they are granted higher-level protection as stipulated in Article 23 of the TRIPS Agreement.

These FTAs expand the scope of Chinese bilateral cooperation on GIs, and their text shares similarities. For instance, both China–Peru FTA and China–Costa Rica FTA contain a provision for the possible extension of the geographical names on the list through future consultation by mutual consent of the parties. Furthermore, China–Costa Rica FTA includes a provision on GI regulatory collaboration through information exchange, cooperation on technical mechanisms, and registration procedures.

The practice of including a list of GIs to be mutually recognised by the other party follows the EU model of GI provisions in FTAs (Engelhardt, 2015; Moir, 2017). Interestingly, although Chile has vigorously opposed the proposed GI Register (TN/IP/W/10) and GI Extension (IP/C/W/386) at the WTO, it managed to reach a bilateral mutual recognition arrangement for GIs with China.

#### 2.4.4.3 Category III: Miscellaneous

China's FTAs with Switzerland, Georgia, and Australia further demonstrate the diversity and flexibility of its bilateral GI arrangement. The Chinese FTAs with Switzerland and Georgia foresee future opportunities for mutual recognition, while China–Australia FTA confirms the legitimacy of trademark protection for GIs.

In the FTA with Switzerland, the definition of GIs is the same as in the TRIPS Agreement. In addition, it introduces the concepts of appellations of origin and indications of sources. Footnote 18 of China–Switzerland FTA clarifies that appellations of origin in Switzerland can be protected as GIs in China. Footnote 19 thereof confirms indications of source are part of IP protection in Switzerland; however, it does not further clarify the relationship between indications of source and GIs. Considering the scope of indications of source is broader than that of GIs, this leaves space for further interpretation of whether indications of source can be recognised as intellectual property in China. Georgia FTA largely follows the pattern of China–Switzerland FTA.

If China's FTA with Switzerland represents extensive protection of GIs, China–Australia FTA represents the most flexible protections for GIs of any Chinese agreement. Article 11.15 of China–Australia FTA provides: 'Each Party recognises that geographical indications may be protected through a trademark or *sui generis* system or other legal means.' In practice, GIs (except for wine GIs) are protected by the trademark system in Australia. Since FTAs may not exempt a party from its TRIPS obligations, the term 'may be protected' cannot be interpreted as providing a choice of whether to provide such protection. Instead, it should be interpreted as a choice of trademark or *sui generis* mechanism to use to implement such protection.

The flexibility of trademark or *sui generis* protection in China–Australia FTA, while compatible with the Chinese domestic systems, may cause problems with China's commitment to China–Switzerland FTA. Imagine the following examples: 1) a type of cheese that is protected as a GI in Switzerland (Product A) is exported to the Chinese market and has been registered and approved as a GI to be protected in China and 2) an Australian cheese (Product B) using the same geographical name as Product A is also exported to China. To comply with China–Switzerland FTA (Article 11.13.3), China should prevent Product B from using the registered Swiss name. Meanwhile, China is also committed to allowing imports into China under the MFN principle. Product B has legally used a generic name in Australia, and a restriction on imports to China may constitute discrimination based on the origin of the product. The same difficulty in reconciliation is seen in South Korea's FTAs with the EU and the US (O'Connor, 2014).

GI provisions in Chinese FTAs provide a valuable opportunity to explore China's true interests in GIs and its willingness to engage with bilateral rule-making. Instead of a uniform template, the GI provisions in Chinese FTAs demonstrate different patterns with different parties. This diversity indicates China's pragmatism in FTA negotiations—something that is also evident in FTAs in which GIs are intentionally not dealt with in detail. With considerable similarities in cultural traditions and language, Chinese and South Korean producers have already been in conflict over certain names. For instance, South Korean kimchi has been listed as a cultural heritage item by the United Nations Educational, Scientific and Cultural Organization

(UNESCO) and registered as a GI in South Korea, but an identical and/or similar process of seasoning vegetables has been used extensively in north-eastern China for centuries, and Hanguo paocai 韩国泡菜 is used as a generic name in China (Cheng, 2014) to differentiate the north-eastern style from seasoned vegetables in other parts of China—for instance, Sichuan paocai. While this is a different issue from GIs as it concerns the use and misuse of a country name, it highlights the language and cultural nexus behind GIs between China and its neighbouring countries. In another example, Chinese Ginseng, Changbaishan renshen 长白山人参, is a registered GI in China, and South Korean Ginseng is a registered GI in South Korea (Na & Wei, 2013). Nonetheless, their characteristics attribute very similar climate and ecological environment of the Changbaishan on China–North Korea border. In other words, the geographical conditions determining the qualities or other characteristics of the products are the same, but they are registered as different GIs in different countries only because the same origin is demarcated by state borders. In this case, recognition of the ginseng GI by either party will impair the competitive advantage of their domestic counterpart. In the final text of China–South Korea FTA, the two parties shelved these controversies and only ambiguously mentioned the term 'geographical indications' in the definition of intellectual property.

#### 2.4.4.4 GI in Chinese Regional Trade Agreements: RCEP

Concluded on 15 November 2020, RCEP is the latest RTA in which China has participated. Its members include 10 ASEAN member states, Australia, China, Japan, New Zealand, and South Korea. India participated in the initial negotiations but later withdrew to protect its domestic market from being flooded with imports with no gains in services (Gaur, 2020). With the creation of a popular trading area and enhancement of interregional investment at its centre, RCEP also has an IP chapter that includes some TRIPS-plus provisions (Callo-Müller & Upreti, 2021).

Given RCEP's aims for deeper integration based on existing bilateral FTAs among its participants, it is worth focusing on what RCEP has added in GI provisions compared with existing provisions in the bilateral FTAs signed by China and its RCEP signatory parties, including ASEAN, Australia, New Zealand, and South Korea. The little that has been added is located in Article 11.29 to Article 11.35 of the IP Chapter. Interestingly, without the EU's participation in this RTA, one can observe some provisions resembling the US position on GIs—in particular, the protection of multicomponent terms (Article 11.32). This provision confirms that

> an individual component of a multi-component term that is protected as a geographical indication shall not be protected in a Party if that individual component is a term customary in the common language as the common name for the associated good in the territory of that Party.

This provision follows the side letter in the KORUS FTA as well as the USCETA (2020). It is likely that both South Korea and China promoted this provision to be consistent with their domestic regulation. However, it is difficult to distinguish China's position on GIs in the RCEP given the secrecy of the negotiation process (Chander & Sunder, 2018).

## 2.5 Conclusion

The international GI system is characterised by regime complexity and legal fragmentation. This has everything to do with the contestation between the EU and the US over protection standards and which legal mechanism (*sui generis* or trademark) should have priority. The hegemonic stability that characterised the origins of the TRIPS Agreement has been replaced with fractured hegemony. It is difficult to impose fine-grained positive rules on states under such conditions. As pointed out by Braithwaite and Braithwaite and Drahos (2000, p. 27), 'when the US and EC can agree on which direction global regulatory change should take, that is usually the direction it does take'. Arguably, when the US and the EU cannot agree, there are more flexibility for a third country to navigate the system. However, this case study shows China had to adopt both models from the EU and the US, which led to domestic legal fragmentation.

Despite the domestic legal fragmentation, China has navigated its way in international GI engagement. At multilateral forums such as the WTO and WIPO, China takes a pro-development position in supporting the agenda proposed by developing countries. The developing countries' interests deviate from the EU's narrow focus on using GIs to protect agri-food stuffs and continuously enhancing global protection standards. China's support for the GI Extension agenda could help China and other developing countries have their competitive advantages in handicrafts recognised. China's proposal to link the negotiations on GI Extension and GI Register at the WTO also helped enhance the priority of the GI Extension agenda that aligned with developing countries' interests. At the national level, GIs have also been increasingly used to increase farmers' income, reducing poverty in rural areas. Products with traditionally accumulated reputation through the tributary system have had their reputation legally recognised through the GI systems.

From a perspective of distributive justice, efforts at both multilateral and domestic levels are gestures appealing to the egalitarian principle, so that the global GI system reflects the interests of developing countries and the domestic GI system benefits the disadvantaged (farmers in rural areas).

At the bilateral level, China has been flexible about GI rules in its trade agreements following the principle of reciprocity. There are no uniform templates for GIs in Chinese FTAs. China has experimented GI mutual recognition with the EU, and three FTA partners including Peru, Chile, and Costa Rica. On the other hand, it has been flexible in China–Australia FTA, in which trademark protection for GIs is sufficient. Arguably, with thousands of domestic GIs, China could benefit more from a more extensive mutual recognition of GIs in its bilateral agreements than they currently are. However, the versatile FTAs analysed in this chapter indicate that, unlike the EU, China does not impose GI standards on its trading partners. It is particularly important for trading partners such as Australia, which does not have a *sui generis* system for GI protection. By contrast, GIs have been a controversial issue in the ongoing negotiations of the Australia–EU FTA.

Responsively, China has established dual protection systems for GIs under the influence of both the EU and the US. Three independent systems for GI protection were established, under the regulation of SAIC, AQSIQ, and the MOA. After the 2018 institutional reshuffle, there are still two GI regulatory mechanisms. This is a typical case of how regime complexity at the international level has introduced legal fragmentation into national laws. Fragmented domestic GI regulatory systems may have potential problems. First, dual systems tend to provide overprotection for rightholders. Some producers are registered with all three of the GI systems, which is a waste of public resources. In addition, parallel domestic protection mechanisms have led to regulatory competition. China delegated representatives from different ministries to negotiate on GIs at different international forums. WTO-related issues are generally negotiated by, while WIPO SCT negotiations have been undertaken by SAIC and (and after 2018, CNIPA). Bilaterally, SAIC developed its transnational cooperation with countries that support the use of the trademark system for GIs, while AQSIQ (and, after 2018, CNIPA) cooperated with countries that have interests in the *sui generis* system. This has hindered China from making concerted efforts to promote law reform with other developing countries.

China accepted competing GI mandates in its 2020 bilateral agreements with the EU and the US. Broadly speaking, these agreements illustrate that Chinese and international legal fragmentation in GIs have gone further, creating a dilemma in that complying with one agreement means breaking the other. This is caused by deeper EU–US disagreement in global GI governance, which they refuse to confront each other or resolve the problem directly. Nonetheless, if there is one 'third country' in the world that could leverage the EU and the US to face the compliance dilemma in GIs, it could be China. China is a large export market for agri-food products from both the EU and the US, and it is familiar with both the EU and the US regulatory regimes for GI protection. Chinese GIs are not in direct competition with either EU or US names. China could have highlighted the impossibility of complying with both bilateral agreements at multilateral forums, such as the TRIPS Council and the WIPO SCT. It could have advanced global distributive justice further by resisting the imposed standards and questioning the legitimacy of the competing GI demands from the EU and the US for third countries. China is better resourced in many respects than other developing countries to raise this issue. This is not about rulemaking or rule-shaking. Rather, it is about defending regulatory sovereignty and making disconnected domestic rules consistent in the context of regime complexity. Without such initiatives, China's 2020 agreements with the EU and the US mean that the GI-related provisions in these agreements may become templates for other bilateral agreements, and more countries will be trapped by the compliance dilemma.

## References

Alter, K. J., & Raustiala, K. (2018). The Rise of International Regime Complexity. *Annual Review of Law and Social Science, 14*(1), 329–349.

AQSIQ. (2007). *A Substantial Progress Has Been Made in the Cooperation Between the AQSIQ and the EU on the Protection of Geographical Indication Products. The First Batch of 10 Chinese and 10 European Geographical Names Are Expected to Be Protected in Each Other's Territory 国家质检总局与欧盟地理标志产品保护合作取得实质性进展 首批中欧各10个产品可望受到专门保护*. http://www.aqsiq.gov.cn/zjxw/zjxw/zjftpxw/200707/t20070712_33478.htm. Accessed 10 May 2018.

Blakeney, M. (2012). *Intellectual Property Enforcement: A Commentary on the Anti-Counterfeiting Trade Agreement (ACTA)*. Edward Elgar Publishing.

Blakeney, M. (2014). *The Protection of Geographical Indications: Law and Practice*. Edward Elgar Publishing.

Braithwaite, J., & Drahos, P. (2000). *Global Business Regulation*. Cambridge University Press.

Broude, T. (2005). Taking Trade and Culture Seriously: Geographical Indications and Cultural Protection in WTO Law. *University of Pennsylvania Journal of International Economic Law, 26*(4), 623–692.

Callo-Müller, M. V., & Upreti, P. N. (2021). RCEP IP Chapter: Another TRIPS-Plus Agreement? *GRUR International, 70*(7), 667–671.

Chander, A., & Sunder, M. (2018). The Battle to Define Asia's Intellectual Property Law: TPP to RCEP. *UC Irvine Law Review, 8*(3), 331–362.

Cheng, S. (2014). China's Strategies Based on FTA Geographical Indications 基于FTA中地理标志的中国策略. *Journal of Xinjiang University of Finance & Economics 新疆财经大学学报, 2*, 16–20.

CNIPA. (2019). *The Uniform Electronic Application Platform for the Protection of Geographical Indication Products Is Launched Where Two Types of Applications are Integrated in One Webpage with Six Functions 一个网页、六大功能、两种申请!地理标志产品保护统一申请电子平台启动.* https://www.cnipa.gov.cn/art/2019/12/5/art_1390_91758.html. Accessed 9 October 2022.

Cooper, W. H., Jurenas, R., Platzer, M. D., & Manyin, M. E. (2011). EU-South Korea Free Trade Agreement and Its Implications for the United States. *Russia, China and Eurasia, 27*(3), 561–594.

Correa, C. M. a. (2007). *Trade Related Aspects of Intellectual Property Rights: A Commentary on the TRIPS Agreement.* Oxford University Press.

Cortés Martín, J. M. (2004). The WTO TRIPS Agreement: The Battle Between the Old and the New World over the Protection of Geographical Indications. *The Journal of World Intellectual Property, 7*(3), 287–326.

Dechent, S., & Sadler, P. (2010). Geographical Indications in the Wine Industry. *Legal Issues in Business, 12*, 3–9.

Drahos, P. (2001). The TRIPS Reviews and the CBD: A Dress Rehearsal. In P. Drahos & M. Blakeney (Eds.), *IP in Biodiversity and Agriculture: Regulating the Biosphere* (pp. 53–67). Sweet & Maxwell Ltd.

Drahos, P. (2008). "Trust Me": Patent Offices in Developing Countries. *American Journal of Law & Medicine, 34*(2–3), 151–174.

Engelhardt, T. (2015). Geographical Indications Under Recent EU Trade Agreements. *IIC-International Review of Intellectual Property and Competition Law, 46*(7), 781–818.

Frankel, S. (2017). Geographical Indications and Mega-Regional Trade Agreements and Negotiations. In I. Calboli & W. L. Ng-Loy (Eds.), *Geographical Indications at the Crossroads of Trade, Development, and Culture: Focus on Asia-Pacific* (pp. 147–167). Cambridge University Press.

Gangjee, D. S. (2016). *Research Handbook on Intellectual Property and Geographical Indications.* Edward Elgar Publishing.

Gaur, P. (2020). India's Withdrawal from RCEP: Neutralising National Trade Concerns. *Journal of the Asia Pacific Economy, 27*(2), 270–288.

Gervais, D. J. (2010). Reinventing Lisbon: The Case for a Protocol to the Lisbon Agreement (Geographical Indications). *Chicago Journal of International Law, 11*(1), 67–126.

Gervais, D. J., & Slider, M. (2017). The Geneva Act of the Lisbon Agreement: Controversial Negotiations and Controversial Results. In W. van Caenegem & J.

Cleary (Eds.), *The Importance of Place: Geographical Indications as a Tool for Local and Regional Development* (pp. 15–46). Springer International Publishing.

Goebel, B., & Groeschl, M. (2014). The Long Road to Resolving Conflicts Between Trademarks and Geographical Indications. *The Trademark Reporter, 104*(4), 829–866.

Gomez-Mera, L. (2015). International Regime Complexity and Regional Governance: Evidence from the Americas. *Global Governance, 21*(1), 19–42.

Heald, P. J. (1996). Trademarks and Geographical Indications: Exploring the Contours of the TRIPS Agreement. *Vanderbilt Journal of Transnational Law, 29*(3), 635–660.

Hu, S. (1996). Authentic Herbs and Local Records and Tributes 道地药材与方志和贡品. *Chinese Pharmaceutical Journal 中国药学杂志, 31*(8), 496–499.

Hu, W. (2018). *Reciprocity and Mutual Benefits: EU-China Cooperation on and Protection of Geographical Indications* (CEPS No. 2018/04). http://aei.pitt.edu/94154/1/RR2018_04_WHu_GIs.pdf

Huysmans, M. (2020). Exporting Protection: EU Trade Agreements, Geographical Indications, and Gastronationalism. *Review of International Political Economy, 29*(3), 979–1005.

Hu, Z. (2002). The Influence of the Accession to the WTO on China's Legal System of Intellectual Property 加入WTO对我国知识产权法律制度的影响. *Juridical Science Journal, 23*(2), 22–23.

Josling, T. (2006). The War on "Terroir": Geographical Indications as a Transatlantic Trade Conflict. *Journal of Agricultural Economics, 57*(3), 337–363.

Kaminski, M. E. (2011). An Overview and the Evolution of the Anti-Counterfeiting Trade Agreement. *Albany Law Journal of Science and Technology, 21*(3), 385–444.

Kongolo, T. (2011). Any New Developments with Regard to GIs Issues Debated Under WTO. *European Intellectual Property Review (EIPR), 33*(2), 83–90.

Li, S. (2002). TRIPs and China's Legal System of Intellectual Property TRIPs 与我国的知识产权法律制度. *Technological Achievements 科技成果纵横, 1*, 15–17.

Liu, F. (2013). *Geographical Indication Development Research Report 中国地理标志发展报告*. China Land Press 中国大地出版社.

Liu, Z. (2015, January 25). The Insight of the GIs Protection System in France: Memorizing the China-France GIs Cooperation in 20 Years 法国地理标志产品保护制度的启示—纪念中法地理标志制度交流20周年. *Guangming Daily 光明日报*, p. 5.

Lü, G., & Wu, D. (2006). Improvement of Legal System of Geographical Indications in China 我国地理标志法律制度的完善. *Legal Science 法学, 1*, 154–160.

March, E. (2007). Geographical Indications from Darjeeling to Doha. *WIPO magazine* (4).

Moir, H. V. (2017). Understanding EU Trade Policy on Geographical Indications. *Journal of World Trade, 51*(6), 1021–1042.

Mwape, D. (2010). *Multilateral System of Notification and Registration of Geographical Indications for Wines and Spirits*. https://www.wto.org/English/tratop_e/trips_e/chairreport_trip20_e.pdf

Na, L., & Wei, D. (2013). GIs in FTAs and China's Option 论FTA 中的地理标志与中国的选择. *Jiang-Huai Tribune 江淮论坛, 4*, 120–125.

O'Connor, B. (2014). The European Union and the United States: Conflicting Agendas on Geographical Indications—What's Happening in Asia? *Global Trade and Customs Journal, 9*(2), 66–69.

O'Connor, B., & de Bosio, G. (2017). The Global Struggle Between Europe and United States over Geographical Indications in South Korea and in the TPP Economies. In W. van Caenegem & J. Cleary (Eds.), *The Importance of Place: Geographical Indications as a Tool for Local and Regional Development* (pp. 47–79). Springer International Publishing.

Okediji, R. L. (2007). The International Intellectual Property Roots of Geographical Indications. *Chicago-Kent Law Review, 82*(3), 1329–1368.

Omachi, M. (2019). A Tale of Two Approaches: Analysis of Responses to EU's FTA Initiatives on Geographical Indications (GIs). *Chicago-Kent Journal of Intellectual Property, 18*(1), 153–206.

Orsini, A., Morin, J.-F., & Young, O. (2013). Regime Complexes: A Buzz, a Boom, or a Boost for Global Governance? *Global Governance: A Review of Multilateralism and International Organizations, 19*(1), 27–39.

Pugatch, M. P. (2007). *A Transatlantic Divide? The US and EU's Approach to the International Regulation of Intellectual Property Trade-related Agreements*. European Centre for International Political Economy (ECIPE) Working Paper.

Rangnekar, D. (2002). *Geographical Indications: A Review of Proposals at the TRIPS Council: Extending Article 23 to Products Other Than Wines and Spirits*. UNCTAD/ICTSD Capacity Building Project on Intellectual Property Rights and Sustainable Development. https://unctad.org/system/files/official-document/ictsd2003ipd4_en.pdf

Ribeiro de Almeida, A. (2020). Geographical Indications Versus Trade Marks and Generic Terms: The US–China Agreement. *IIC—International Review of Intellectual Property and Competition Law, 51*(3), 277–281.

Sell, S. K. (2010). TRIPS Was Never Enough: Vertical Forum Shifting, FTAS, ACTA, and TTP. *Journal of Intellectual Property Law, 18*(2), 447–478.

Sun, Q. (2016). Geographical Indication Products and Economic Development at the County Level 地理标志产品与县域经济发展. *Journal of Nanjing Agricultural University (Social Sciences Edition) 南京农业大学学报(社会科学版), 12*(1), 37–42.

Török, Á., Jantyik, L., Maró, Z. M., & Moir, H. V. (2020). Understanding the Real-World Impact of Geographical Indications: A Critical Review of the Empirical Economic Literature. *Sustainability, 12*(22), 9434.

van Caenegem, W., & Cleary, J. (2017). *The Importance of Place: Geographical Indications as a Tool for Local and Regional Development*. Springer.

van Caenegem, W., Cleary, J. A., & Drahos, P. (2014). Pride and Profit: Geographical Indications as Regional Development Tools in Australia. *Journal of Economic & Social Policy, 16*(1), 90–114.

Vivas-Eugui, D. (2001). Negotiations on Geographical Indications in the TRIPS Council and Their Effect on the WTO Agricultural Negotiations. *The Journal of World Intellectual Property, 4*(5), 703–728.

Wang, L. (2008). *Research of the First Intellectual Property Negotiation between China and Foreign Countries in the Late Qing Dynasty 晚清中外首次知识产权谈判研究*. Suzhou University.

Wang, L., & Huang, Z. (2006). Debate on the Protection Model of Geographical Indications and the Choice for China in Law-making 地理标志保护模式之争与我国的立法选择. *Journal of the East China University of Political Science and Law 华东政法学院学报, 6*, 44–53.

Wang, X., & Kireeva, I. (2007). Protection of Geographical Indications in China: Conflicts, Causes and Solutions. *The Journal of World Intellectual Property, 10*(2), 79–96.

Wang, X., & Wan, Y. (2010). The Position and Strategies for China to Participate in the WTO Negotiations on Geographical Indications 我国参加WTO地理标志谈判的立场和对策. *Intellectual Property 知识产权, 20*(115), 47–51.

Watson, K. W. (2016). *Reign of Terroir: How to Resist Europe's Efforts to Control Common Food Names as Geographical Indications*. https://www.cato.org/sites/cato.org/files/pubs/pdf/pa787.pdf

WIPO. (2007). *International Symposium on Geographical Indications*. International Symposium on Geographical Indications. http://www.wipo.int/meetings/en/details.jsp?meeting_id=13243. Accessed 9 October 2022.

WTO. (2008). *Intellectual Property (TRIPS) Geographical Indications Background and the Current Situation*. https://www.wto.org/english/tratop_e/trips_e/gi_background_e.htm. Accessed 9 October 2022.

Wyzycka, N., & Hasmath, R. (2017). The Impact of the European Union's Policy Towards China's Intellectual Property Regime. *International Political Science Review, 38*(5), 549–562.

Xiong, H. (2019). *The State Intellectual Property Office Has Launched a Special Campaign to Regulate the Use of Geographical Indications During the Spring Festival 国家知识产权局部署春节期间开展地理标志使用专项整治工作*. http://www.gov.cn/xinwen/2019-02/08/content_5363295.htm (Accessed).

Zhang, Y. (2007). The Nature of Geographical Indications and the Choice of Protection Model 地理标志的性质和保护模式选择. *Law Science Magazine 法学杂志, 6*, 6–11.

Zhang, Y., & Buzan, B. (2012). The Tributary System as International Society in Theory and Practice. *The Chinese Journal of International Politics, 5*(1), 3–36.

# 3

# China Engages in International Regulation of Disclosure Obligation

## 3.1 Introduction

This chapter will explore how China has engaged in international regulation concerning the disclosure of the origin or source of genetic resources in patent applications. Genetic resources are any material from a plant, animal, microbe, or other organism containing functional units of heredity that have actual or potential value (Schei & Tvedt, 2010).[1] 'Disclosure obligation' refers to the mandatory requirement to disclose the origin or source of genetic resources in a patent application if the invention is accomplished by relying on genetic resources. The disclosure obligation issue is situated at the intersection of the international regulation of genetic resources and the international IP regulation. Discussions and negotiations concerning the disclosure obligation have taken place at various levels. At the multilateral level, disclosure of the origin of genetic resources was negotiated at the WTO TRIPS Council and the WIPO Intergovernmental Committee on Intellectual Property and Genetic Resources, Traditional Knowledge and Folklore (IGC). At the bilateral level, the protection of genetic resources was mentioned in

[1] WIPO Intergovernmental Committee on Intellectual Property and Genetic Resources, Traditional Knowledge and Folklore [hereinafter IGC], *Consolidated Document Relating to Intellectual Property and Genetic Resources*, WIPO/GRTKF/IC/29/4, 30 November 2015. The CBD tends to interpret the concept of genetic resources more broadly: the genetic structure per se can be utilised or the information encapsulated in the nucleotide sequence of the genetic material can be read and digitalised and easily acquired.


W. Cheng, *China in Global Governance of Intellectual Property*, Palgrave Socio-Legal Studies, https://doi.org/10.1007/978-3-031-24370-7_3

the IP chapters of several Chinese FTAs. At the national level, the disclosure obligation was adopted in the Chinese *Patent Law* (2008).

Disclosing the origin of genetic resources is part of a broader issue in international law. Along with the expansion of colonialism, nineteenth century international law tended to consider genetic resources as the 'common heritage of humankind', so the exploitation of genetic resources was free for everyone. For instance, during the nineteenth century, kiwifruit originating in China was first taken by missionaries to New Zealand (Zhang, 2008), and international law at that time did not prohibit such a practice. The free exploitation of genetic resources from the territory by indigenous communities continued after World War II. Countries rich in genetic resources began to realise their importance and condemn the taking of such resources without authorisation from local communities as misappropriation or biopiracy (Robinson, 2010, p. 21). Typical cases of misappropriation also include Basmati rice, Bolivian habanero pepper, and *Artemisia judaica* (Judean wormwood) (Robinson, 2012). When big pharmaceutical companies seek patent monopolies on inventions using genetic resources and the traditional knowledge often associated with them (Schei & Tvedt, 2010), contestations over 'who owns the genetic resources' intensifies. The so-called megadiverse countries formed a coalition to promote the overarching principle of state sovereignty over genetic resources.

State sovereignty over genetic resources was established as a principle in the 1992 Convention on Biological Diversity (CBD),[2] the revised International Undertaking on Plant Genetic Resources (IUPGR), and the International Treaty on Plant Genetic Resources for Food and Agriculture (ITPGRFA) (Gerstetter *et al.*, 2007). State sovereignty does not equate to state ownership of genetic resources (Roa-Rodríguez & Van Dooren, 2008); rather, it confirms that states have regulatory power over the genetic resources within their jurisdiction. The CBD also sets access and benefit-sharing (ABS)[3] as one of its objectives, requiring authorisation for any exploitation of genetic resources. Specifically, prior informed consent (PIC) must be obtained from relevant government authorities and local communities (Perrault *et al.*, 2006). PIC is also the basis on which local communities can claim benefit sharing

[2] CBD: Para. 5, Preamble, and Article 3.

[3] Access and benefit-sharing refer to the way genetic resources may be accessed and how benefits resulting from their use are shared between the people or countries using the resources (users) and the people or countries providing them (providers). ABS is based on prior informed consent (PIC) being granted by a provider to a user and negotiations between both parties. ABS is one of the three objectives of the CBD and is stipulated in detail in the Nagoya Protocol on Access to Genetic Resources and the Fair and Equitable Sharing of Benefits Arising from their Utilization to the Convention on Biological Diversity (Nagoya Protocol).

of genetic resources once they generate value. Considering that the value of genetic resources is often crystallised in a patent, the principle of state sovereignty over plant genetic resources in the CBD and ITPGRFA further intersects with IP rules, in particular, the TRIPS Agreement and the International Convention for the Protection of New Varieties of Plants (UPOV Convention). Raustiala and Victor (2004) described this interaction as the international regime complexity for plant genetic resources.

CBD is a framework treaty, which means it cannot achieve the ABS objective by itself. It needs to be implemented by a more detailed system of rules that help clarify ownership issues, rights to use genetic resources, and remedies for violations. Based on the CBD's principle of state sovereignty over genetic resources, the next step is to set rules on obtaining authorisation from local communities. The disclosure obligation is one set of rules to guarantee such authorisation with the threat of invalidating patents relying on genetic resources in cases of non-disclosure or misrepresentation. There have long been debates and negotiations over how the disclosure obligation can operate in reality (Sect. 3.2.1).

The disclosure obligation is an appropriate case study for this book to observe China's international IP engagement. First, China is one of the 17 megadiverse countries in the world. According to the *National Biodiversity Conservation Strategy and Action Plan* (2011–2030), China is home to territorial ecosystems covering forests, shrubland, meadows, steppe, desert, wetland, as well as marine ecosystems, including the Yellow Sea, East China Sea, South China Sea, and Kuroshio Basin. China has up to 34,984 species of higher plants, ranking it third in the world; 6,445 vertebrate species, accounting for 13.7% of the global total; and more than 10,000 species of fungi, making up 14% of the global total.[4]

These statistics indicate that China has clear interests in protecting its genetic resources from misappropriation and in joining multilateral negotiations on the disclosure obligation. For instance, China is one of the Like-Minded Megadiverse Countries (LMMC),[5] willing to actively promote international negotiations on disclosure obligation. China is aligned with

4 Ministry of Environment Protection, Notice Concerning Issuing the National Biodiversity Conservation Strategy and Action Plan of China (2011–2030) 关于印发《中国生物多样性保护战略与行动计划》(2011–2030年) 的通知, No. 106 (2010).

5 The LMMC was set up in 2002 by 17 countries: Bolivia, Brazil, China, Colombia, Costa Rica, Democratic Republic of Congo, Ecuador, India, Indonesia, Kenya, Madagascar, Malaysia, Mexico, Peru, Philippines, South Africa, and Venezuela. These countries are home to about 70% of the Earth's species. The LMMC was established to promote consultation and cooperation on the preservation and sustainable use of biological diversity.

other LMMC to promote rival standards with a strong disclosure obligation to which the US disagrees. This standard has also been opposed by other developed countries or countries less endowed with genetic resources such as Australia, Canada, Japan, and South Korea. The EU has taken a hedging position by proposing a weak disclosure agenda (Sect. 3.2.2). The debates and negotiations on the disclosure obligation provide a unique opportunity to explore how China, as one of the megadiverse countries and a major economic power, joins other LMMC to promote the rival standard and actively engages as a latecomer in international IP rulemaking. As the disclosure obligation is one of the few issues that remain unsettled in relation to patent regulation, this is also a valuable case to observe how the Chinese Patent Law (2008) was informed by relevant international debates and negotiations and how China has developed its agenda to engage in alternative rulemaking.

## 3.2 Multilateral Negotiations on the Disclosure Obligation

The disclosure of the origin of genetic resources has been an issue on which the US, the EU, and megadiverse countries disagreed. Multilateral negotiations on the disclosure obligation have been characterised by fierce debates about whether such a requirement is necessary and how to implement it. Different understandings of these issues present a spectrum of positions in multilateral negotiations and guide various domestic practices.

### 3.2.1 Debates Over the Disclosure of the Origin of Genetic Resources

So far, the debates concerning the disclosure requirement have focused on three issues: 1) whether embedding disclosure requirements into patent law is the solution to guarantee ABS; 2) whether disclosure should be voluntary or mandatory; and 3) whether international consent on this issue is necessary.

#### 3.2.1.1 Is Patent Law a Solution to Guarantee ABS?

Disclosure has been one of the fundamental principles in the history of patent law. According to social contract theory, patentholders can only obtain a certain period of monopoly for an invention under the condition of adequate disclosure of the technical information encapsulated within the invention. TRIPS provisions on disclosure largely followed US law. Although the working obligation proposed by developing countries was reflected in the Brussels Text of December 1990, it was not incorporated in the final text of the TRIPS Agreement (Yamane, 2011). An early draft of the Substantive Patent Law Treaty (SPLT) negotiated at the WIPO included a rule requiring 'sufficiently clear and complete disclosure for the invention to be carried out by a person skilled in the art'.[6] Given that negotiations on the SPLT have been on hold since 2006, this proposal has never been implemented. The disclosure requirement negotiated at these multilateral forums, however, is a general patent law requirement to balance the interests of the rightholders and the public, which is different from disclosing the origin of genetic resources used in an invention, as discussed in this chapter.

Megadiverse countries proposed using disclosure of the origin of genetic resources to prevent misappropriation through the patent system.[7] They proposed that once a patent relying on genetic resources has been published, the relevant indigenous community can check whether this access to genetic resources was based on PIC and so open the way to claim for benefit-sharing. In other words, information disclosed in the patent application is the key evidence as to whether there are benefit-sharing obligations under the condition that the national law has already established the ABS mechanism. Within the patent system, megadiverse countries proposed the disclosure of the origin of genetic resources should be part of the substantive requirement in patent examination. This means that in the case of non-disclosure, the patent will not be granted for an application under examination or a patent already granted will be invalidated. However, the US opposed this proposal that links the protection of genetic resources with patent status. It proposed a contract-based approach that considers PIC a contract between the external exploiter of a genetic resource and the local community, the idea being that the local community can claim ABS later based on this contract.

#### 3.2.1.2 Voluntary Disclosure Versus Mandatory Disclosure

Dutfield (2005) distinguished two types of disclosure requirements: mandatory disclosure (disclosure obligation) and voluntary disclosure according to

[6] SPLT, Articles 11, Alternative A. See WIPO Standing Committee on the Law of Patents [hereinafter SCP], Fifth Session, *Draft Substantive Patent Law Treaty*, SCP/5/2, 4 April 2001.

[7] WTO TRIPS Council, *The Relationship between the TRIPS Agreement and the Convention on Biological Diversity: Summary of Issues Raised and Points Made*, Note by the Secretariat, IP/CIW/368/Rev.1, 8 February 2006.

**Table 3.1** Possible arrangement in patent law for the disclosure of origin

| | Voluntary disclosure | Mandatory disclosure (disclosure obligation) |
|---|---|---|
| National law | Disclosure of the origin of genetic resources is voluntary: | Disclosure of the origin of genetic resources is mandatory |
| | - no statutory requirement for disclosure;<br>- non-disclosure is a breach of contract if disclosure is provided as a contractual obligation. | In the case of non-disclosure:<br>- patent application rejected; granted patent invalidated or unenforceable; or<br>- other civil and criminal consequences result from non-compliance. |
| International law | Not necessary | Proof of legal acquisition |

burdens on patent applicants. The disclosure obligation requires disclosure of the origin of genetic resources in a patent application, and non-compliance has legal consequences. A voluntary mechanism mainly involves the contract-based approach in which disclosure is optional and depends on the terms and conditions that the parties agreed to in a contract. There are no other legal consequences other than a breach of contract (Table 3.1).

The proponents of voluntary disclosure argue a binding mechanism is not the only way to achieve the goal of ABS. The US proposed 'national-based approaches' to the WTO,[8] which included permits, contractual obligations, visa systems, and civil and criminal penalties for non-compliance. This approach essentially relies on the contract. The problem with this—as pointed out by some of the megadiverse countries—is that equitable and fair benefit sharing is unlikely to be achieved because of asymmetric negotiating power and a lack of transparency.

### 3.2.1.3 International Law Versus National Law

The lawmaking on the disclosure obligation starts at the national level. For instance, the Indian *Patent Act of 2002 (Second Amendment)* provides that non-disclosure or wrongful disclosure of the origin of biological resources in a patent application will lead to rejection of the application or revocation of the patent if it has already been granted. Regionally, the Andean Group established the 'Common Regime on Access to Genetic Resources'

[8] WTO TRIPS Council, IP/CIW/368/Rev.1.

to promote access.[9] These initiatives associate the disclosure of the origin of genetic resources with the general patent law doctrine of disclosure.[10]

However, in most cases, misappropriation is a transnational infringement: patentholders do not come from the country where the genetic resources are sourced, so a mandatory requirement at the national level is not enough. This is why an international consensus on the proof of legal acquisition with complementary international coordination is the best option to tackle the problem (Dutfield, 2005). A binding international law will also help coordinate the various legislation and practices of disclosure—in particular, on issues of whether disclosure should be considered as a substantive or a formal requirement in a patent application, the legal consequences of non-disclosure, and the scope of information to be disclosed. However, such a consensus will be difficult because the US, which is home to many large biopharmaceutical companies, opposes any type of international law to govern this issue.

### 3.2.2 A Spectrum of Positions on the Disclosure Obligation

Given that the disclosure obligation sits at the intersection of genetic resource and IP regulation, clarifying the relationship between relevant treaties in terms of scope and hierarchy is the starting point for negotiations. Article 16.5 of the CBD provides a guide to the relationship between it and IP rights:

> The Contracting Parties, recognizing that patents and other intellectual property rights may have an influence on the implementation of this Convention, shall cooperate in this regard subject to national legislation and international law in order to ensure that such rights are supportive of and do not run counter to its objectives.[11]

At the WTO, megadiverse countries argued that the TRIPS Agreement and the CBD are in conflict. They proposed the disclosure obligation to reconcile that conflict by subordinating IP rights to ABS, one of the objectives of the CBD. Other WTO members, essentially developed countries—did not recognise the conflict because the text of the CBD does not contain a clause

---

[9] Andean Community, *Decision No. 391 Establishing the Common Regime on Access to Genetic Resources*, Decision No. 391, was issued in Caracas, Venezuela, by the Commission of the Cartagena Agreement (the Commission of the Andean Community) on 2 July 1996. It was published in the *Official Gazette of the Cartagena Agreement*, No. 213 of 17 July 1996, in Lima, Peru.

[10] In addition to genetic resources, megadiverse countries also promoted the disclosure of origin of traditional knowledge and traditional knowledge associated with genetic resources.

[11] CBD, Article 16.5.

expressly overriding IP rights in the case of inconsistency. Given there is no conflict, it is therefore not necessary to incorporate the disclosure obligation into international and national laws. Consequently, clarifying the TRIPS–CBD relationship is a prerequisite before addressing specific issues of the disclosure obligation, which itself was a prolonged negotiating process.

The TRIPS–CBD relationship was incorporated as one of the outstanding implementation issues into the Doha Round work programme. The TRIPS Council became the forum for this discussion from 2002, following the Doha Ministerial Declaration.[12] However, these discussions were informal, and the disclosure obligation has not been addressed as an independent issue. India, Brazil, and other megadiverse countries including China endeavoured to promote text-based negotiations on the disclosure obligation,[13] but their efforts failed in 2006. Since then, the discussions have been part of the WTO Director-General's consultation process, and no substantive negotiations have been launched on this issue.

There have been three representative positions on the disclosure obligation among WTO members (Appendix 1). First, it is necessary to have a strong disclosure obligation on the basis that there is an inherent conflict between the TRIPS Agreement and the CBD. India first proposed a disclosure obligation as a solution to the relationship between the TRIPS Agreement and the CBD.[14] Brazil added support to India's initiative by further specifying that Article 27.3 of the TRIPS should be amended to include evidence of PIC as a condition of patentability.[15] After the Doha Ministerial Declaration, additional megadiverse countries supported India and Brazil in calling for a clearer agenda of disclosure of origin by adding a new Article 29*bis* to the TRIPS Agreement, which specifically addresses the disclosure requirement.[16]

The second position is a weak disclosure obligation supported by the European Community (EC), Switzerland and Norway, which argued that although there was no inherent conflict between the two agreements, the

---

[12] *WTO Doha Ministerial Declaration*, Paras 12 and 19.

[13] WTO General Council, Trade Negotiations Committee, TRIPS Council, *Doha Work Programme—The Outstanding Implementation Issue on the Relationship between the TRIPS Agreement and the Convention on Biological Diversity*, Communication from Brazil, China, Colombia, Cuba, Pakistan, Peru, Thailand, and Tanzania, IP/C/W/474 [also circulated as WT/GC/W/564/Rev.2 and TN/C/W/41/Rev.2], 5 July 2006.

[14] WTO TRIPS Council, *Proposals on Intellectual Property Rights Issues*, Communication from India, IP/C/W/195, 12 July 2000, Para 16.

[15] WTO TRIPS Council, *Review of Article 27.3 (b)*, Communication from Brazil, IP/C/W/228, 24 November 2000. See Para. 25 of this communication.

[16] WTO TRIPS Council, *The Relationship between the TRIPS Agreement and the Convention on Biological Diversity and the Protection of Traditional Knowledge*, Communication from Brazil, China, Cuba, Dominican Republic, Ecuador, India, Pakistan, Thailand, Venezuela, Zambia, and Zimbabwe, IP/C/W/356, 24 June 2002. See Para. 10 of this communication.

disclosure requirement could still be included as a formal requirement in patent application. Accompanying this non-conflict position, the EC and Switzerland also proposed that WIPO IGC should be the proper forum for related discussions or negotiations. Nonetheless, both the EC and Switzerland deployed a cross-forum strategy by getting involved in discussions at both WIPO and the WTO.[17] Norway also supported the view that disclosure should be a formal requirement. However, in contrast to the EC and Switzerland, Norway proposed amending the TRIPS Agreement to incorporate the disclosure obligation. In 2008, the EU and Switzerland joined developing countries to support negotiations on the disclosure obligation in the 'Draft Modalities for TRIPS Related Issues' (TN/C/W/52).[18] More than two-thirds of WTO members co-sponsored this proposal. As discussed in Chapter 2, the GI Register and GI Extension were the other two issues included in this proposal, which balanced different positions but kept a certain level of vagueness in the text. It did not mention the discrepancy between megadiverse countries and the EU on this issue but focused on making a joint effort to promote text-based negotiations.

The third position was led by US, which maintained that a contract-based approach could solve the problem of misappropriation.[19] The US also argued the introduction of a disclosure obligation would neither guarantee PIC nor prevent misappropriation; instead, it would add uncertainty to the patent system and introduce administrative burdens.[20] Megadiverse countries opposed the US position, arguing the fact that the disclosure obligation was only one of the elements to prevent misappropriation should not be the reason to abandon this approach at all. They also emphasised that a broader approach is necessary to coordinate the disclosure obligation with issues such as how to distinguish a certain origin when more than one is

17 The EC submitted proposals to the TRIPS Council and the WIPO IGC contemporaneously. See TRIPS Council, IP/C/W/383, 17 October 2002, and WIPO IGC, WIPO/GRTKF/IC/8/11, 17 May 2005. Switzerland first proposed to WIPO to reform the PCT regulations to incorporate disclosure requirement (PCT/R/WG/5/11), then proposed to the TRIPS Council to gain support for this WIPO proposal (IP/C/W/446).

18 WTO Trade Negotiations Committee, *Draft Modalities for TRIPS Related Issues*, Communication from Albania, Brazil, China, Colombia, Ecuador, the European Communities, Iceland, India, Indonesia, Kyrgyz Republic, Liechtenstein, Former Yugoslav Republic of Macedonia, Pakistan, Peru, Sri Lanka, Switzerland, Thailand, Turkey, the ACP [African, Caribbean and Pacific] Group, and African Group, TN/C/W/52, 19 July 2008.

19 WTO TRIPS Council, *Views of the United States on the Relationship between the Convention on Biological Diversity and the TRIPS Agreement*, Communications from the United States, IP/C/W/257, 13 June 2001, pp. 5–6.

20 WTO TRIPS Council, *Article 27.3 (B), Relationship between the TRIPS Agreement and the CBD, and the Protection of Traditional Knowledge and Folklore*, Communication from the United States, IP/C/W/434, 25 November 2004, pp. 2–5.

identified and how to monitor patent publications from other countries and initiate legal procedures. To date, no consensus on the disclosure obligation has been reached in the WTO negotiations, meaning WTO members are free to decide: 1) whether to introduce the disclosure obligation into their domestic law and 2) if so, a specific mechanism for implementing the disclosure obligation, in either its weak or its strong form.

### 3.2.3 Disclosure Obligation Negotiations: From WTO to WIPO

In parallel with the negotiations on disclosure obligation at the TRIPS Council, the WIPO IGC was established in 2001 and gradually became another forum for the disclosure obligation. Disclosure obligation was one of the key issues at the IGC. So far, the IGC has held 46 meetings on issues related to genetic resources, traditional knowledge, and folklore.

The EC and Switzerland first proposed the disclosure obligation to the IGC because this forum could better accommodate their position of recognising disclosure as a formal requirement in patent applications and avoiding discussion of the controversial issue of the TRIPS–CBD[21] Japan, and New Zealand[22] countries that refuse to recognise the TRIPS–CBD conflict.

Developing countries initially opposed negotiations at the WIPO IGC. They emphasised that the IGC and the TRIPS Council have different mandates—in particular, the mandate to examine the relationship between the TRIPS Agreement and the CBD is specific to WTO members,[23] so the TRIPS Council should be the main forum for related negotiations. However, some developing countries also actively followed up with discussions or negotiations at the IGC. There was no obvious progress in the negotiations on the disclosure obligation at the TRIPS Council from 2002 to 2010 because of the consistent opposition from the US. However, the IGC reached an initial agreement to undertake text-based negotiations in March 2010. Since then, countries have started to observe and participate in text-based negotiations.

Notwithstanding the forum shift, negotiations at the IGC have not been any easier than at the TRIPS Council. The participation of the same core

---

[21] WTO TRIPS Council, *Minutes of the Meeting Held in the Centre William Rappard on June 5, 2007*, IP/C/M/54, 26 July 2007, Para. 58.

[22] WTO TRIPS Council, *Minutes of the Meeting Held in the Centre William Rappard on June 8–9*, IP/C/M/60, 28 September 2009, Para. 37.

[23] Ibid., Para. 55.

countries has led to the same pattern of divergence in opinions.[24] In early 2012, delegations of WIPO member states started to negotiate the draft of a consolidated document at IGC meetings.[25] The disclosure obligation has been a controversial issue in this consolidated document despite rounds of revisions and negotiations. For example, in one earlier version, the disclosure obligation was listed as one option in parallel with the defensive protection of genetic resources proposed by Japan through the establishment of related databases.[26] This position basically denied the mandatory nature of disclosure obligation as proposed by megadiverse countries and the EU. This version was later replaced by stipulating the disclosure obligation in an independent article. However, in a footnote, defensive protection remains an alternative for some contracting members.[27]

The IGC negotiations broke down in 2014. The mandates of the IGC, as a non-permanent committee of WIPO, are subject to biennial renewal. However, the renewal of mandates in 2014 was not successful because the US did not agree with its normative work programme (Saez, 2015). In 2015, the African Group proposed promoting the IGC to a standing committee of WIPO (to be called the Standing Committee on Intellectual Property and Genetic Resources, Traditional Knowledge and Traditional Cultural Expressions, or SCTK)[28] to avoid the biennial review of its mandates. The US submitted a counterproposal to discontinue the mandate of the IGC and replace the IGC with seminars, studies, and an expert working group.[29] This showed that IGC is a forum vulnerable to games of delay of negotiations on the disclosure obligation.

---

[24] See, for instance, proposals from the African Group, Like-Minded Countries, European Communities and its Member States, Switzerland, and Japan, WIPO/GRTKF/IC/20/INF/11.

[25] WIPO IGC, Twenty-Third Session, *Consolidated Document Relating to Intellectual Property and Genetic Resources*, document prepared by the Secretariat, WIPO/GRTKF/IC/23/4, 2 November 2012.

[26] See ibid., WIPO/GRTKF/IC/25/5, Article 3.

[27] See WIPO/GRTKF/IC/30/4, Footnote 1.

[28] WIPO General Assembly, Forty-Seventh (22nd Ordinary) Session, *Conversion of WIPO Intergovernmental Committee on Intellectual Property and Genetic Resources, Traditional Knowledge and Folklore (IGC) into a Standing Committee: Proposal by the African Group to the 2015 General Assembly*, document prepared by the Secretariat, WO/GA/47/16, 28 July 2015.

[29] WIPO General Assembly, Forty-Seventh (22nd Ordinary) Session, *Matters Concerning the Intergovernmental Committee on Intellectual Property and Genetic Resources, Traditional Knowledge and Folklore (IGC): Proposal of the United States of America to the WIPO General Assembly*, document prepared by the Secretariat, WO/GA/47/17, 4 September 2015.

## 3.3 China Navigating Multilateral Negotiations on the Disclosure Obligation

China is one of the world's megadiverse countries, and its international engagement on the disclosure obligation has been constrained by the following conditions: as a contracting party of the CBD and Nagoya Protocol on Access to Genetic Resources and the Fair and Equitable Sharing of Benefits Arising from their Utilisation to the Convention on Biological Diversity (Nagoya Protocol), China must establish a legal system to guarantee the achievement of ABS. As a latecomer to the WTO, China must position itself in the context of existing WTO negotiations. As an emerging economy with ambitions to grow its own bioindustries, China also needs to balance the interests of global biopharmaceutical companies, its domestic biopharmaceutical companies, and the development of local and indigenous communities. In particular, the ambition to cultivate a domestic biopharmaceutical industry may lead China to diverge from the position of other megadiverse countries.

### 3.3.1 Context for China's Engagement in the Disclosure Obligation

China is a contracting party to more than 20 multilateral IP treaties (Appendix 1), including the TRIPS Agreement, the UPOV Convention (1978), the Patent Cooperation Treaty (PCT), and other WIPO-administered treaties. China must fulfil its treaty obligations on IP protection by setting domestic implementation mechanisms. On the other hand, China joined the CBD in 1992 and participated in ITPGRFA negotiations, although it has not yet signed the ITPGRFA. These agreements provided opportunities for China to model alternative standards concerning IP and the protection of genetic resources. Some international uncertainties also need a domestic solution—for instance, being a party of both the CBD and the TRIPS Agreement means China must address their relationship in domestic implementation and develop its own position in relevant international negotiations.

So far, there is no compliance pressure for China in the case of the disclosure obligation because no international consensus has yet been reached. China has the flexibility to decide which position it will take without risking a violation of international law. As a megadiverse country, China is interested in strengthening the protection of genetic resources at the multilateral level. As a latecomer to the WTO, while China did not actively contribute to the relevant negotiations that led to the TRIPS Agreement, post-TRIPS disclosure obligation negotiations have provided China with the opportunity to select the most suitable model for its domestic conditions. China learned about the subtle differences between various models in the ongoing debates and negotiations. For instance, China was not aware of the issue upon its WTO accession in 2001. Only six months later, it decided to support other megadiverse countries by co-sponsoring the proposal IP/C/W/356[30] at the TRIPS Council, in June 2002.

Unlike some megadiverse countries that proposed amending the TRIPS Agreement to exclude life forms and parts thereof from patentability,[31] China has the ambition to develop its biotechnology industry. In 2010, China identified seven strategic emerging industries (SEIs) to be the foundation of its industrial modernisation and technological development in the future, one of which is biological breeding.[32] In 2015, the *Made in China 2025*[33] strategy explicitly emphasised the bioindustry as one of the ten high-end industries China needed to gain or maintain its competitive advantage.

According to the WIPO IP Statistics Data Centre, patent grants to Chinese applicants in biotechnology have surged since 2010. The number of patent grants to Chinese applicants first overtook those to US applicants in 2013. With the fluctuation of patent grants to Chinese applicants over the following five years, the number eventually again exceeded that of the US in 2018 (Fig. 3.1).[34]

Given that not all biotechnology patents are related to the use of genetic resources, it is necessary to look into the internal structure of biological patents in China. According to SIPO (2016), a report on China's patenting activities in the biological industry, applications submitted to SIPO followed a similar pattern to those submitted to the US Patent and Trademark Office (USPTO) in the area of biotechnology—with intensive applications in the fields of bio-drugs, biomedical equipment, and biochemical products. China had more applications than the US in the manufacturing of bio-agricultural products and applied environmental management technology (Fig. 3.2).

---

30 WTO TRIPS Council, *The Relationship between the TRIPS Agreement and the Convention on Biological Diversity*, Brazil on behalf of the delegations of Brazil, China, Cuba, Dominican Republic, Ecuador, India, Pakistan, Thailand, Venezuela, Zambia, and Zimbabwe, IP/C/W/356, 24 June 2002.

31 For instance, Bolivia proposed amending Article 27.3(B), which gained support from many megadiverse countries. See WTO TRIPS Council, *Article 27.3(B) and the Legalization of Biopiracy: Trends, Impacts and Why it Needs to be Amended*, Communication from the Plurinational State of Bolivia, IP/C/W/554, 28 March 2011.

32 State Council, *Decision on Accelerating the Development of Strategic Emerging Industries* 国务院关于加快培育和发展战略性新兴产业的决定 No. 32 (2010).

33 State Council, *Notice of the State* Council on Issuing Made in China 2025 国务院关于印发《中国制造2025》的通知, *No 28* (2015), 8 May 2015.

34 WIPO, *Intellectual Property Statistics*, available at: http://www.wipo.int/ipstats/en/. This figure is reproduced under the Attribution 4.0 International CC license (CC BY 4.0).

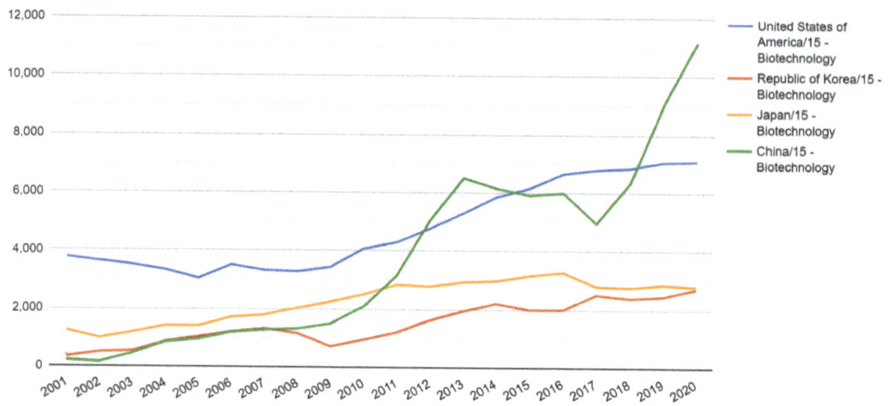


**Fig. 3.1** Patent grants in biotechnology (Counted by filing office and applicant's origin), 2001–2020

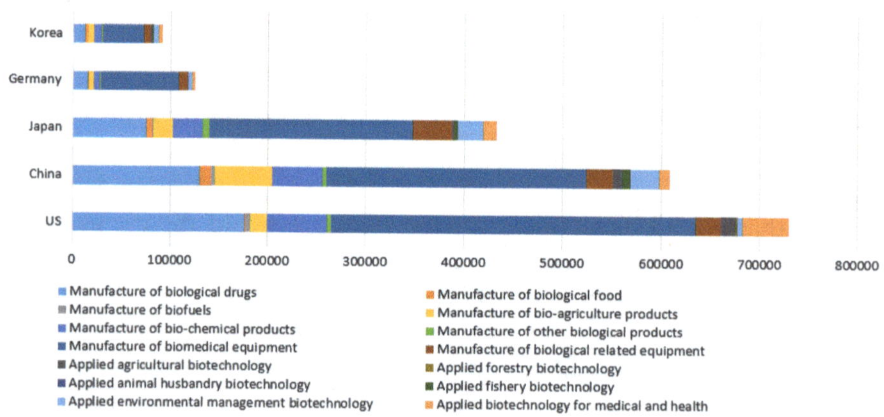


**Fig. 3.2** Technological distribution of patent applications in bioindustry (*Source* SIPO [2016, pp. 62–63])

These figures show China has a clear intention to deploy its own patents in biotechnologies. Therefore, it may not fully agree with the megadiverse countries' position on a strong disclosure requirement. China must balance the legal consequences of non-disclosure with legal certainty for granted patents.

### 3.3.2 China's Position at the TRIPS Council

China first encountered a debate on disclosure requirements at the TRIPS Council after its WTO accession in 2001. This created opportunities for China to learn about various proposals and choose a position that can work in its domestic context. The TRIPS Council started discussions on the TRIPS–CBD relationship in March 2002,[35] three months after China's WTO accession. China was overwhelmed at that time, by the mandate to amend its domestic IP laws to comply with the TRIPS standards. The Chinese representatives at the TRIPS Council were not aware of what was at stake in the discussion on the TRIPS–CBD relationship. At this 2002 March meeting, the Chinese representative said: '[T]he question of potential conflicts between the TRIPS Agreement and the CBD might not be of great importance.' She acknowledged that biological diversity was a 'relatively new concept'[36] and showed interest in the US proposal for the contract-based solution. China later realised the problem of unequal bargaining power in the contract-based approach.

Through a process of learning and adaptation, China soon developed its own position to support the disclosure obligation and active protection of traditional knowledge. However, in the early stages, China vacillated between the strong and the weak forms of the disclosure obligation. On the one hand, China was very cautious in co-sponsoring proposals initiated by other megadiverse countries. Among 16 proposals submitted by megadiverse and developing countries (Appendix 4), China co-sponsored only two (IP/C/W/356 and IP/C/W/474) before 2008 when its domestic Patent Law introduced a standard on the disclosure obligation. China also expressed its support for proposals by other megadiverse countries at the TRIPS Council meetings without being a co-sponsor.

China showed interest in the EU and Norwegian proposals for a weak disclosure obligation as well. Both proposals considered disclosure as a formal requirement in patent applications, with non-compliance not causing the invalidity of a patent already granted. Chinese representatives took advantage of the TRIPS Council meetings to learn the details of these proposals.[37] Such knowledge to a certain extent influenced Chinese domestic rulemaking (Sect. 3.4.2).

China announced its intention to amend its Patent Law in 2005, and the domestic legislative process on the disclosure obligation led to uncertainty in China's position at the TRIPS Council. Before the law amendment

35 WTO TRIPS Council, *Minutes of the Meeting Held in the Center William Rappard on March 5–7, 2002*, IP/C/M/35, 22 March 2002.

36 Ibid., Para. 248.

37 For instance, the Chinese representative to the TRIPS Council posed questions to the European Commission on details of the disclosure obligation regarding the legal consequence of violation, and whether a civil or criminal remedy would be appropriate. See WTO TRIPS Council, *Minutes of the Meeting Held in the Center William Rappard on February 18–19, 2003*, IP/C/M/39, 21 March 2003, Para. 135.

was announced in April 2005, China had clearly expressed its support for the megadiverse countries' proposals.[38] After the announcement, Chinese representatives remained silent in the forty-eighth and forty-ninth TRIPS Council meetings—the only two meetings at which they did not speak on the disclosure obligation. China's silence during these TRIPS meetings showed how careful it was to maintain consistency between its international position and its domestic legislation. After it became clear that the amended Patent Law would introduce rules on the disclosure obligation, China reassumed its engagement at the TRIPS Council. After the promulgation of Patent Law (2008), the Chinese position at the TRIPS Council supporting disclosure obligation became firmer and clearer (Sect. 3.5.1).

## 3.4 Active Learning from Negotiations: Patent Law (2008)

China generally engaged in a learning process, introducing international practices on the disclosure obligation to its Patent Law (2008), but it also provided a broader protection for genetic resources in its patent law. This section will explore relevant provisions *in* Chinese Patent Law (2008)[39] on the disclosure obligation and its regulatory innovation through a comparative analysis. This is an example of actively using the strategy of modelling (Chapter 9) when international rules are not yet in place.

### 3.4.1 The Disclosure Obligation in Patent Law (2008)

Before the Chinese Patent Law (2008), China had already established legislation to protect some genetic resources—for instance, the Law of Seeds

[38] See WTO TRIPS Council, *Minutes of the Meeting Held in the Center William Rappard on 8–9 and 31 March 2005*, IP/C/M/47, 3 June 2005, Para. 57. In this speech, the Chinese representative showed China's support for proposals IP/C/W/442 and IP/C/W/443—specifically: WTO TRIPS Council, *The Relationship between the TRIPS Agreement and the Convention of Biological Diversity (CBD) and the Protection of Traditional Knowledge—Elements of the Obligation to Disclose Evidence of Benefit-Sharing under the Relevant National Regime*, Submission from Bolivia, Brazil, Colombia, Cuba, Dominican Republic, Ecuador, India, Peru, and Thailand, IP/C/W/442, 18 March 2005; and WTO TRIPS Council, *The Relationship between the TRIPS Agreement and the Convention on Biological Diversity (CBD) and the Protection of Traditional Knowledge—Technical Observation on Issues Raised in a Communication by the United States (IP/C/W/434)*, Submission from Brazil and India, IP/C/W/443, 18 March 2005.

[39] The Chinese Patent law was promulgated in 1984, and amended in 1992, 2000, 2008, and 2020, respectively. Patent Law (2008) introduced provisions on genetic resources for the first time. Relevant provisions remain unchanged in the 2020 amendment.

(2000) introduced the principle of state sovereignty over germplasm resources for plant seeds. Although these laws[40] did not clarify the meaning of state sovereignty, they confirmed the regulatory power of Chinese ministries beyond SIPO over genetic resources. This pre–Patent Law landscape influenced China, to some extent, to take its own approach to the disclosure obligation. Nonetheless, these laws only focus on specific types of genetic resources without defining them. The *Implementation Rules of the Patent Law* (*IRPL*) (2010)[41] define genetic resources as 'any material taken from [a] human, animal, plant, or microorganism, containing genetically functioning units with actual or potential value' (*IPRL*: Art. 26.1). This definition is very comprehensive, including genetic resources beyond plants.

The Chinese Patent Law (2008) introduced two provisions on the protection of genetic resources: Article 26.5 on the disclosure obligation, and Article 5.2 which I refer to as the linkage arrangement. In addition, the *IRPL* further stipulated the legal consequences of non-compliance with the disclosure obligation. Articles 26.5 and 5.2 are compared in Table 3.2.

#### 3.4.1.1 Weak Disclosure Obligation

Article 26.5 of Patent Law (2008) specifies that the Registration Form for Indicating the Origin of Genetic Resources should be submitted along with other documents in patent applications:

> [W]ith regard to an invention accomplished by relying on genetic resources, the applicant shall, in the patent application documents, indicate the origin and direct source of the genetic resources. If the applicant cannot indicate the origin, he/she shall state the reason.

This provision confirms the Chinese Patent Law has adopted the model of weak disclosure that treats disclosure a formal requirement in patent applications. According to Article 26.5, examiners will only check whether the Registration Form for Indicating the Origin of Genetic Resources is included, not the truthfulness of the information that has been disclosed. Following this logic, legal consequences are only relevant in the pre-grant stage: for those applications where the form identifying the source of genetic resources is submitted, a patent will be granted; otherwise, if an invention is created

[40] See the Chinese Constitution 宪法, Article 9; Forest Law 森林法, Article 3; Grassland Law 草原法, Article 9; Law on Protection of Wild Animals 野生动物保护法, Article 3; Law on Animal Husbandry 畜牧法, Chapter 2; Seeds Law 种子法, Article 11.

[41] State Council, *Implementation Rules of the Patent Law* 专利法实施细则, 2010.

**Table 3.2** The protection of genetic resources in Patent Law (2008)

| | Disclosure obligation<br>Patent Law 2008: **Article 26.5** | Linkage arrangement<br>Patent Law 2008: **Article 5.2** |
|---|---|---|
| Violation | Not submitting a document disclosing the origin and direct source of the genetic resources in patent applications. | Applying for a patent for an invention relying on genetic resources where those resources have been accessed or used in a way that violates other laws and regulations. |
| Formal examination stage | The applicant should state his/her observations or correct the application within the specified time limit.<br>If the applicant fails to make any response within the specified time limit, the application shall be deemed to have been withdrawn (*IRPL* 2010: Art. 44.2). | The applicant should state his/her observations or correct the application within the specified time limit.<br>If the applicant fails to make any response within the specified time limit, the application shall be deemed to have been withdrawn (*IRPL* 2010: Art. 44.2). |
| Substantive examination stage | Application rejected (*IRPL* 2010: Art. 53.2). | Application rejected (*IRPL* 2010: Art. 53.1). |
| Post-grant | Not mentioned. | Invalidity announcement upon the petition by a third party (*IRPL* 2010: Art. 65.2). |

relying on genetic resources and no form has been submitted in its patent application, the application will be rejected. Since disclosure is a formal requirement and an application without disclosure (where it should have been made) will be rejected before the substantive examination, there are no post-grant legal consequences. However, this provision does not cover the situation of a false statement about the genetic resource origin, for which a post-grant remedy is necessary. Currently, there is no incentive for a patent applicant to submit a false statement about the source of genetic resources because PIC has not yet been established in the Chinese legal system. Nonetheless, misrepresentation could occur after the legal mechanism of ABS is introduced to China.

#### 3.4.1.2 Additional Protection for Genetic Resources: The Linkage Arrangement

Article 5.2 of Patent Law (2008) stipulates that '[p]atent rights shall not be granted for inventions that are accomplished by relying on genetic resources which are obtained or used in violation of the provisions of laws and administrative regulations.' This provision intends to link the Patent Law to other laws and administrative regulations. If other laws have provisions that have been violated, this will invoke the application of Article 5.2.

Article 5.2 has introduced some controversy in its interpretation. Structurally, it is under Article 5, a general provision on *ordre public* and morality. Article 5.1 provides that 'patent rights shall not be granted for any inventions that are against the law, social ethics or impair public interest'. Article 5.2 is part of the Patent Law to maintain Order Public by protecting genetic resources. In this sense, its scope extends beyond the disclosure obligation.

This provision was included in Patent Law (2008) to compensate for the drawbacks of the weak disclosure mechanism in Article 26.5. SIPO may not have the capacity to examine the truthfulness and credibility of the information in the Registration Form for Indicating the Origin of Genetic Resources. As a country planning to boost its bioindustry, China wants certainty in its patent system; however, it also acknowledges that weak disclosure alone is not enough for the effective protection of genetic resources. Therefore, SIPO proposed additional protection for genetic resources in Article 5.2 with the expectation that other laws and regulations will fill the gap by referring to this provision. In short, Article 5.2 provides the legal consequences within the patent system when a certain behaviour in accessing genetic resources (on which a patent relies) has violated other laws and regulations. For such a violation, the legal consequence would be the rejection of a patent application or invalidation when a patent has already been granted.

The ideal scenario for a functioning linkage between various laws and Article 5.2 of Patent Law would be: 1) both the law governing specific types of genetic resources in China and the law of ABS include clear provisions specifying either the *legitimate* ways to access genetic resources or what constitutes a *violation* in accessing genetic resources; 2) the above laws refer to Article 5.2 of Patent Law (2008) for legal consequences in when a patent application is filed relying on genetic resources that were accessed in the illegal ways stipulated in abovementioned 1). However, such an ideal has not yet in operation. The major problem is that while Article 5.2 provides a link between the Patent Law and other laws and regulations, the latter has not yet been formulated. The laws before 2008 only generally stated the principle of state sovereignty over genetic resources (Xue & Cai, 2009), without introducing PIC or specifying what constitutes legitimate access to genetic resources. However, a mere declaration of state sovereignty could not constitute the basis to determine legitimate access in specific cases.

China ratified the Nagoya Protocol in September 2016, which indicates that domestic rulemaking about ABS on plant genetic resources will be enacted in accordance with this Protocol. As China also participated in ITPGRFA negotiations and there were expert recommendations that China should join the treaty (Zhang, 2012), ABS for genetic resources for food and agriculture was also put on the legislative agenda. Given the identified problems of lack of coordination, communication, and mutual support among various regulators on genetic resources (Xue, 2015), there is a long way to go to establish such a linkage. Nonetheless, although the linkage arrangement has so far been an empty promise because the relevant laws and regulations are not in place, China's signature on the Nagoya Protocol means an ABS mechanism (including PIC) will be in place quickly. There is a basis for this conjecture: China started drafting its Biodiversity Conservation Law in 2016 (Xinhuanet, 2016). If this law requires ABS for all types of genetic resources, the linkage will be established. By then, the linkage approach could complement the 'softness' of the weak disclosure obligation in Article 26.5 of Patent Law (2008).

### 3.4.2 Comparison of Chinese Law with Existing Proposals

After analysing the Chinese Patent Law (2008)'s provisions on the protection of genetic resources, this section further explores the origin of these rules through textual analysis. I take a comparative approach in this section, using three proposals on the disclosure obligation submitted to the WTO TRIPS Council or the WIPO IGC[42] as references. I then compare relevant provisions in the Chinese Patent Law (2008) with elements of these proposals. I also refer to publications on SIPO's website to show how active learning has happened.

China undertook active learning to introduce the disclosure obligation into Patent Law (2008). It encountered the discussion on misappropriation at the TRIPS Council and the WIPO IGC and learned from other WTO members how the disclosure obligation could be part of the solution. In contrast to pressure to comply with other aspects of the TRIPS Agreement, China has not received external pressure to establish a domestic law for disclosure obligation.

SIPO started its preparation for the third amendment of the Patent Law in April 2005, and its first draft was submitted to the State Council on 27 December 2006. Megadiverse countries proposed a strong disclosure model (IP/C/W/474) and Norway proposed a weak disclosure model (IP/C/W/473)[43] to the WTO in July 2006 to promote text-based negotiations on the disclosure obligation. These two proposals were submitted during the drafting of China's Patent Law (2008) and China had access to the text of both proposals. In particular, the Chinese representative at the TRIPS Council meeting showed interest in the Norwegian proposal,[44] which was soon translated into Chinese and published in the specialised column on the

[42] See WTO General Council, Trade Negotiation Council, and TRIPS Council, *The Relationship between the TRIPS Agreement, the Convention on Biological Diversity and the Protection of Traditional Knowledge—Amending the TRIPS Agreement to Introduce an Obligation to Disclose the Origin of Genetic Resources and Traditional Knowledge in Patent Applications*, Communication from Norway, IP/C/W/473 [also circulated as WT/GC/W/566 and TN/C/W/42], 14 June 2006; see details for the megadiverse-country proposal (IP/C/W/474) and the EU proposal to the IGC (WIPO/GRTKF/IC/8/11).

[43] Ibid., IP/C/W/473.

[44] WTO TRIPS Council, *Minutes of the Meeting Held in the Center William Rappard on 14–15 June 2006*, IP/C/M/51, 20 September 2006, Para. 85: 'He welcomed Norway's support of the amendment of the TRIPS Agreement to introduce a mandatory disclosure obligation in patent applications, although he had reservations on the effectiveness of sanctions outside the patent system.' WTO TRIPS Council, *Minutes of the Meeting Held in the Center William Rappard on 5 June 2007*, IP/C/M/54, 26 July 2007, Para. 51: 'While welcoming the constructive attitude of Norway, he took note of the substantial difference between Norway's proposal and the joint proposal, particularly with regard to the nature of the disclosure requirements.'

protection of genetic resources on SIPO's website.[45] The translation enabled this proposal to reach decision-makers not proficient in English.

The EU's proposal (WIPO/GRTKF/IC/8/11) demonstrated the nuances of the weak disclosure obligation. Directly, The EU–China IPR2 project provided advice to the amendment of the Chinese Patent Law (2008) (Wyzycka & Hasmath, 2017). It was circulated at a WIPO IGC meeting in 2005 and took a cross-forum strategy by reiterating its position at the TRIPS Council. Although both the Norwegian and the EU proposals promoted a weak disclosure model, they differed in several respects. Table 3.3 provides a detailed comparison of the disclosure obligation in these four documents.

One basic conclusion from the comparison in Table 3.3 is the Chinese Patent Law (2008) bore more similarity with the Norwegian and the EU proposals than with the megadiverse-country proposal because it considered disclosure a formal requirement of patent applications. The scope of information to be disclosed was limited to genetic resources and did not include traditional knowledge. The legal consequences for non-compliance were limited to the pre-grant stage. However, as a co-sponsor of the megadiverse countries' proposal, China realised the problem of weak disclosure and incorporated Article 5.2 into its Patent Law to protect genetic resources.

This comparison demonstrates that the introduction of the disclosure obligation into the Chinese Patent Law was largely a modelling process through learning. Nonetheless, one can still see the creativity of Chinese regulators—in particular, the linkage established in Article 5.2 of Patent Law (2008) to other relevant laws and regulations (Sect. 3.4.1.2). Under this arrangement, Article 5.2 picked up violations relating to the use of genetic resources outside the Patent Law and imposed a penalty (invalidity) within the Patent Law. This broad protection for genetic resources does not exist in the EU and Norwegian proposals for weak disclosure. In this way, the disclosure obligation in Article 26.5 of Patent Law (2008) was consistent with the logic of weak disclosure, where disclosure is still not among the substantive requirements for patentability; patentability is still only decided based on novelty, inventive steps, and applicability. However, the additional protection provided by Article 5.2 of Patent Law (2008) did include the invalidation of a patent as a penalty if certain provisions for the protection of genetic resources are violated.

---

[45] The page for the protection of genetic resources and traditional knowledge on the SIPO website was at: http://www.sipo.gov.cn/ztzl/ywzt/yczyhctzsbh/zlk/ggty/ [this address was not valid when last searched on 6 May 2018]. That section was updated during March 2005 and April 2007—the period of preparation of the Patent Law (2008) amendment. The Norwegian proposal was the only one submitted to the TRIPS Council that has been translated.

**Table 3.3** Disclosure obligation in multilateral proposals and the Chinese Patent Law (2008)

| | Megadiverse country proposal (IP/C/W/474) | Norwegian proposal (IP/C/W/473) | EU proposal WIPO/GRTKF/IC/8/11 | Chinese Patent Law (2008) Article 26.5 |
|---|---|---|---|---|
| Nature of disclosure obligation | Substantive requirement | Formal requirement | Formal requirement | Formal requirement |
| Non-compliance effect (pre-grant) | No granting because of failure to meet patentability | Regarded as withdrawn because of not satisfying formal requirements (para. 7) | Reject or consider as withdrawn | An application shall be rejected if it fails to meet the formal requirement in Article 26.5 (*IRPL* 2010: Art. 53) |
| Non-compliance (post-grant) | Invalidity or unenforceable | Administrative or criminal punishment outside the patent system (para. 8) | Outside the field of patent law | - |
| Information to be disclosed | Source and origin of genetic resources<br>Evidence of PIC<br>Evidence of ABS | Origin of genetic resources | Source of genetic resources and information concerning PIC | Origin and direct source of genetic resources |
| Disclosure of traditional knowledge | Mandatory | Mandatory | Optional to disclose | Not required |
| The relationship between the genetic (biological) resources and the invention patent | Invention derived from or developed with biological resources and/or associated traditional knowledge | - | The invention must be directly based on the specific genetic resources | Invention accomplished by relying on genetic resources |

*Note* Arrangements at the international level are not included in this comparison

In addition to the linkage arrangement, there were minor adjustments to the disclosure obligation. For instance, the disclosure of traditional knowledge was not mentioned in Patent Law (2008). In this respect, it was more cautious than both the Norwegian and the EU proposals on the disclosure of traditional knowledge. The Chinese Patent Law (2008) covered only genetic resources, excluding both traditional knowledge per se (proposed by megadiverse countries and Norway) and associated traditional knowledge (or traditional knowledge associated with genetic resources) (proposed by the EU).

In summary, the inclusion in the Patent Law (2008) of a provision on the disclosure obligation was an outcome of China's multilateral engagement since its WTO accession. China started implementing what it had proposed multilaterally into its domestic law before any consensus had been reached at the multilateral level. This learning process was different from China's efforts to comply with the TRIPS Agreement. Without external coercion or pressure, China incorporated the disclosure obligation through active learning from various proposals at the multilateral level.

## 3.5 China's Engagement After Patent Law (2008)

The disclosure obligation is an issue that demonstrates interactions between China's domestic law-making and its international engagement. Before 2008, China learned from international negotiations to build a disclosure mechanism into its Patent Law. After the disclosure obligation was incorporated into Patent Law (2008), the domestic provision fed back into Chinese multilateral engagement on the issue. The incorporation of the disclosure obligation into Chinese domestic law provided a clear position for China in multilateral negotiations. At the bilateral level, the disclosure obligation is also included in the China–Peru and China–Switzerland FTAs.

### 3.5.1 China Engages in Multilateral Negotiations

Since the introduction of its Patent Law (2008), China has been committed to promoting substantive negotiations on the disclosure obligation at the TRIPS Council. China also supported initiatives at the council to guarantee the implementation of the Nagoya Protocol. China even started forming coalitions with other megadiverse countries at the TRIPS Council from 2013 to 2015. Notably, China's position at the TRIPS Council consolidated as soon as the disclosure obligation was included in the draft of the Patent Law (2008).

#### 3.5.1.1 China Promoting Substantive Negotiations at the TRIPS Council

Just before the promulgation of Patent Law (2008), China co-sponsored the TN/C/W/52 proposal at the WTO, which differed from proposals (IP/C/W/356 and IP/C/W/474) China had previously co-sponsored. The previous two proposals clearly demonstrated the interests of megadiverse countries by promoting a strong disclosure model. TN/C/W/52, however, was a balanced proposal, accommodating the interests of 108 WTO members.[46] Co-sponsored by the EU, Iceland, Switzerland, megadiverse countries, the African Group, and other developing countries, this proposal was a compromise between the weak and the strong disclosure models and consolidated the issue of the TRIPS–CBD relationship, the GI Register, and the GI Extension (see Chapter 2). The main purpose of the proposal was to seek common ground and promote text-based negotiations in the WTO forum. Therefore, controversial issues, such as the nature of the disclosure obligation (a formal or substantive requirement in patent application) and the legal consequences for non-compliance, were intentionally left untouched. Two-thirds of WTO members, including China, supported the proposal because of its generality and ambiguity.

After co-sponsoring the TN/C/W/52 proposal and promulgating its Patent Law (2008), China's position at TRIPS Council meetings became more positive. Before the proposal, the Chinese representative at the TRIPS Council 'encouraged all Members to engage in text-based discussions in informal consultations and to hold focused technical discussions on the amendment proposal at the Council's regular meetings'.[47] After the proposal, the Chinese representative started to 'urge that text-based negotiations on the relationship between the TRIPS Agreement and the CBD be undertaken in Special Sessions of the TRIPS Council immediately'.[48] The underlined text indicates China took a stronger position on supporting negotiations on the disclosure obligation at the TRIPS Council.

46 WTO TRIPS Council, *Minutes of the Meeting Held in the Center William Rappard on 27–28 October and 6 November 2009*, IP/C/M/61, 12 February 2010, Para. 80.

47 WTO TRIPS Council, *Minutes of the Meeting Held in the Center William Rappard on 23–24 October 2007*, IP/C/M/55, 21 December 2007, Para. 112. Underlines added by the author.

48 WTO TRIPS Council, *Minutes of the Meeting Held in the Center William Rappard on 13 March 2008*, IP/C/M/56, 21 May 2008, Para. 37. Underlines added by the author.

After years of negotiations, the Chinese representative at the TRIPS Council started to present a clear position on specific issues to support megadiverse countries. For instance, China insisted that the WTO TRIPS Council should be the major forum for negotiations concerning the disclosure obligation when the US and other developed-country members suggested shifting the negotiations to WIPO IGC.[49] China also rejected the proposal for the defensive protection of genetic resources—a proposal based on the idea of establishing databases as an alternative to the disclosure obligation—because the information contained in databases is limited and may not be accessible by patent examiners. Chinese representatives have clearly developed a more nuanced position compared to the comments they made immediately after China joined the WTO.

#### 3.5.1.2 China Supporting the Implementation of the Nagoya Protocol at the WTO

The Nagoya Protocol was the first multilateral agreement on ABS. After incorporating the disclosure obligation in its Patent Law (2008), China, as a member of the LMMC, supported incorporating the disclosure obligation into the Nagoya Protocol. Although the disclosure obligation was not incorporated into the final text (UNCTAD, 2014), the protocol's achievement on ABS stimulated megadiverse countries to promote further negotiations at the WTO to comply with this aspect of the Nagoya Protocol.

In 2011, Brazil, China, Colombia, Ecuador, India, Indonesia, Peru, Thailand, the African, Caribbean and Pacific Group, and the African Group co-sponsored a new proposal[50] in the Trade Negotiations Committee of the WTO. TN/C/W/59 proposed an updated Article 29*bis* in the TRIPS Agreement on the disclosure obligation. It requires Internationally Recognised Certificates of Compliance (IRCC), part of ABS in the Nagoya Protocol, as a component in the disclosure obligation. This way, the TN/C/W/59 proposal aimed to incorporate the IRCC as a TRIPS requirement to achieve the CBD objective.

Comparison of the TN/C/W/59 proposal with the previous megadiverse-country proposal, IP/C/W/474, on Article 29*bis* of the TRIPS Agreement

---

[49] WTO TRIPS Council, *Minutes of the Meeting Held in the Center William Rappard on 2 March 2010*, IP/C/M/62, 1 June 2010, Para. E.27; WTO TRIPS Council, *Minutes of the Meeting Held in the Center William Rappard on 8–9 June 2010*, IP/C/M/63, 4 October 2010, Para. 64.

[50] WTO Trade Negotiations Committee, *Draft Decision to Enhance Mutual Supportiveness between the TRIPS Agreement and the Convention on Biological Diversity*, Communication from Brazil, China, Colombia, Ecuador, India, Indonesia, Peru, Thailand, ACP [African, Caribbean and Pacific] Group, and African Group, TN/C/W/59, 19 April 2011.

shows TN/C/W/59 proposed weaker legal consequences for non-compliance with the disclosure obligation at the post-grant stage. In TN/C/W/59, the post-grant sanctions for non-compliance included: 1) administrative sanctions, criminal sanctions, fines, and adequate compensation for damages or 2) other measures and sanctions, including revocation. In IP/C/W/474, the revocation or rendering unenforceable of a patent is essential to penalties for post-grant non-compliance. The text of the TN/C/W/59 proposal for Article 29*bis* of the TRIPS Agreement is similar to the Chinese Patent Law. Nonetheless, there is still insufficient data to verify China's influence on the proposal.

#### 3.5.1.3 China as Part of the Coalition to Push Negotiations Forward

After ten years of negotiations, the TRIPS–CBD relationship was still not listed for an early harvest in preparation for the ninth ministerial conference of the WTO in 2013. Since 2013, China has formed coalitions with Indonesia, Brazil, India, Peru, South Africa, Cuba, Ecuador, and other megadiverse countries, proposing text-based negotiations on the disclosure obligation at TRIPS Council meetings. The opening remark by a Chinese representative at a 2013 TRIPS Council meeting that 'China would like to associate itself with the delegations of Indonesia and Brazil'[51] was unprecedented. It was the first time China had announced a coalition (in expressive language) at a TRIPS Council meeting on this issue.

This coalition lasted for two years. From 2013 to 2015,[52] China was one of the main supporters of the disclosure obligation and the exchange of information between the CBD and the TRIPS Agreement. The coalition was opposed by the US, South Korea, Japan, and Canada. Given no prominent progress has been achieved by this coalition, megadiverse countries have focused more on the negotiations at the IGC.

[51] WTO TRIPS Council, *Minutes of the Meeting Held in the Center William Rappard on 5–6 March 2013*, IP/C/M/72, Para. 5.5.

[52] WTO TRIPS Council, *Minutes of the Meeting Held in the Center William Rappard on 11–12 June 2013, Addendum*, IP/C/M/73/add.1, Para. 8; WTO TRIPS Council, *Minutes of the Meeting Held in the Center William Rappard on 10–11 October 2013, Addendum*, IP/C/M/74/Add.1, Para. 15.

### 3.5.2 China Incorporates the Disclosure Obligation into FTAs

In addition to multilateral engagement, the disclosure obligation is also mentioned in Chinese bilateral FTAs. Generally, China actively promoted the protection of genetic resources in its FTA negotiations. The China–Peru and China–Switzerland FTAs include stipulations on the disclosure obligation. As both agreements were signed after the implementation of the Chinese Patent Law (2008), they will allow us to assess the impact of China's domestic law on its FTAs.

#### 3.5.2.1 China–Peru FTA

At the WTO Hong Kong Ministerial Conference in 2005, India, Brazil, and Peru proposed including the disclosure obligation in the final ministerial text, addressing the need for further consultation on implementation issues of the TRIPS–CBD relationship. They proposed to negotiate the disclosure obligation at the WTO. Notwithstanding its position multilaterally, Peru accepted a side letter in its FTA with the US in 2005 in which, although both parties agreed to the protection of genetic resources, Peru agreed to the US position of only using contracts to access genetic resources and traditional knowledge and not requiring the disclosure obligation in patent applications (Gerhardsen & New, 2005). The contract-based approach means the FTA supported non-binding voluntary disclosure, which is different from Peru's original position at the WTO. Moreover, this position also diverged from the position of megadiverse countries—a coalition of which Peru was a leader.

The China–Peru FTA was signed against this background. As the first Chinese FTA that mentions the disclosure obligation, China–Peru FTA stipulates that both parties agree to further discussion of the 'disclosure obligation of the origin or source of genetic resource[s] and/or the prior informed consent'. Although no substantive negotiations are required by this article, mention of the disclosure *obligation* is consistent with Peru's position at the WTO.[53] This provision indicates that Peru attempted to subtly manipulate its positions at different forums—supporting the disclosure obligation at the

[53] WTO TRIPS Council, *Article 27.3(B), Relationship between the TRIPS Agreement and the CBD and Protection of Traditional Knowledge and Folklore*, Communication from Peru, IP/C/W/441, 8 March 2005; WTO TRIPS Council, *Article 27.3(B), Relationship between the TRIPS Agreement and the CBD and Protection of Traditional Knowledge and Folklore*, Communication from Peru, IP/C/W/447, 8 June 2005; WTO TRIPS Council, *Analysis of Potential Cases of Biopiracy*, Communication from Peru, IP/C/W/458, 7 November 2005.

TRIPS Council and in its FTA with China while accepting the contract-based approach in its FTA with the US. Considering this provision appeared only in China–Peru FTA and not any other Chinese FTA, it was probably proposed by Peru. In this case, China supported the position of its FTA partner to promote the disclosure obligation—something that conforms to their common interest.

#### 3.5.2.2 China–Switzerland FTA

The China–Switzerland FTA is the other Chinese FTA mentioning the disclosure obligation. In contrast to the China–Peru FTA, in which both parties actively promoted the disclosure obligation, the focus of the China–Switzerland FTA on the disclosure obligation is the legal consequence of non-compliance. Switzerland has supported the weak disclosure obligation model at both the TRIPS Council and the WIPO IGC.

Switzerland agreed with megadiverse countries that international IP rules should support CBD goals, but it denied there was a conflict between the TRIPS Agreement and the CBD. Switzerland proposed amending the PCT or the SPLT to incorporate the disclosure obligation rather than amending the TRIPS Agreement.[54] Switzerland also co-sponsored the TN/C/W/52

[54] WTO TRIPS Council, *Review of Article 27.3 (b): The View of Switzerland*, Communication from Switzerland, IP/C/W/284, 15 June 2004; WTO TRIPS Council, *Article 27.3(B), the Relationship between the TRIPS Agreement and the Convention on Biological Diversity, and the Protection of Traditional Knowledge*, Communication from Switzerland, IP/C/W/400/Rev.1, 18 June 2003; WTO TRIPS Council, *Additional Comments by Switzerland on its Proposal Submitted to WIPO Regarding the Declaration of Source of Genetic Resources and Traditional Knowledge in Patent Applications*, Communication from Switzerland, IP/C/W/423, 26 June 2003; WTO TRIPS Council, *Further Observations by Switzerland on its Proposals Regarding the Declaration of the Source of Genetic Resources and Traditional Knowledge in Patent Applications*, Communication from Switzerland, IP/C/W/433, 25 November 2004; WTO TRIPS Council, *The Relationship between the TRIPS Agreement and the Convention on Biological Diversity (CBD) and the Protection of Traditional Knowledge and Folklore and the Review of Implementation of the TRIPS Agreement under Article 71.1*, Communication from Switzerland, IP/C/W/446, 30 May 2005; WIPO International Patent Cooperation Union (PCT Union) Working Group on Reform of the Patent Cooperation Treaty (PCT), Fourth Session, *Proposals by Switzerland Regarding the Declaration of the Source of Genetic Resources and Traditional Knowledge in Patent Applications*, PCT/R/WG/4/13, 5 May 2003; WIPO International Patent Cooperation Union (PCT Union) Working Group on Reform of the Patent Cooperation Treaty (PCT), Fifth Session, *Proposals by Switzerland Regarding the Declaration of the Source of Genetic Resources and Traditional Knowledge in Patent Applications*, PCT/R/WG/5/11, 19 November 2003; WIPO International Patent Cooperation Union Working Group on Reform of the Patent Cooperation Treaty (PCT), Sixth Session, *Additional Comments by Switzerland on its Proposals Regarding the Declaration of the Source of Genetic Resources and Traditional Knowledge in Patent Applications*, PCT/R/WG/6/11, 21 April 2004; WIPO International Patent Cooperation Union Working Group on Reform of the Patent Cooperation Treaty (PCT), *Further Observations by Switzerland on its Proposals Regarding the Declaration of the Source of Genetic Resources and Traditional Knowledge in Patent Applications Seventh Session*, PCT/R/WG/7/9, 5 April 2005.

proposal to the WTO Trade Negotiation Committee to promote text-based negotiations on this issue. Although China's Patent Law (2008) generally adopted the formal disclosure approach, provisions on the legal consequences of non-compliance were fragmented in the *IRPL* 2010. The China–Switzerland FTA, therefore, was intended to confirm the legal consequences already existing in the Chinese Patent Law (2008).

Article 11.9.5 of the China–Switzerland FTA provides that:

> Parties may set a time limit by which the applicant must correct the defect. The Parties may refuse the application or consider it withdrawn if the defect according to this paragraph has not been corrected within the set time limit.

This provision is consistent with Article 44.2 of the *IRPL* 2010 (Table 3.2) and the Chinese Patent Examination Guidelines.[55] Since this article merely reiterates the position in Patent Law (2008), it seems this provision does not pose an extra obligation on either party of the FTA. However, this provision can have a lock-in effect so that it is more difficult for China to revise its current domestic law than if there were no such provision in the FTA. Nevertheless, the China–Switzerland FTA uses 'may' in this provision, so the lock-in effect is debatable.

Both China–Peru FTA and the China–Switzerland FTA mention the disclosure obligation, but their impacts on implementation are different. The text of the China–Peru FTA is more ambiguous and tends to reinforce bilateral cooperation on the negotiation and implementation of the disclosure obligation. The China–Switzerland FTA, although seemingly consistent with the current Chinese patent legislation, has the potential to eliminate the freedom for China to amend its domestic regulations on the legal effect of non-compliance.

## 3.6 Conclusion

This chapter investigated how China has engaged in the global governance of genetic resources and patents, with a focus on the disclosure obligation. China established protection for genetic resources in its domestic patent law and engaged in international negotiations at the TRIPS Council, the WIPO IGC, and in its FTAs. Generally, China took a pro-development position

[55] Article 5.3 of the Chinese *Patent Examination Guidelines* 专利审查指南 stipulates that patent applicants can still submit the disclosure form during the substantive examination. If the disclosure obligation is still not fulfilled at this stage, the patent application will be rejected.

to support the disclosure obligation in multilateral negotiations. Along with other megadiverse countries, China promoted text-based negotiations on this issue and supported the proposal to amend Article 29 *bis* of the TRIPS Agreement to implement the Nagoya Protocol and realise the ABS objectives of the CBD. The legislative process of Patent Law (2008) revealed an internal balance between developing its own biotechnology and the protection of genetic resources through adaptation of what it had learned from multilateral negotiations.

This case also shows the dynamics between China's multilateral negotiations and its domestic rulemaking over time. The inclusion of the provisions on the disclosure obligation in Patent Law (2008) was inspired by China's participation in TRIPS Council discussions. After the implementation of Patent Law (2008), China's position at the TRIPS Council was consolidated, and it even formed a coalition with other megadiverse countries to promote text-based negotiations to amend the TRIPS Agreement.

The disclosure obligation is a case of China supporting rival standards to safeguard the interests of local and/or indigenous communities and state sovereignty. It is also a case where implications for global distributive justice can be articulated. Egalitarianism guides to equal or equitable distribution of goods in general. A practice of resorting to different principles of distributive justice for closely related goods per se contravenes this principle. The US market-based approach for disclosure can be considered such a practice—it appeals to the entitlement-based principle for the distribution of patentable knowledge, but it opposes creating similar entitlement via statutory law for genetic resources and/or associated traditional knowledge on which these patent relies. Should the entitlement-based principle be consistently pursued in both patentable knowledge and genetic resources, a disclosure obligation is the necessary first step to provide evidence and set boundaries for different entitlements. As misappropriation of genetic resources often occurs transnationally, efforts of creating disclosure obligation as binding international law align with the cosmopolitan principle for more equitable distribution of gains from genetic resources at the global level. In this sense, China's support for the amendment of Article 29 *bis* in the TRIPS Agreement is part of concerted efforts with other developing countries to enhance global distributive justice.

## References

Dutfield, G. (2005). Thinking Aloud on Disclosure of Origin. *QUNO Occasional Paper, 18*, 131–147.

Gerhardsen, T. I. S., & New, W. (2005) *Peru Attempts Strong WTO Position on Disclosure Despite Weaker US Deal*. Intellectual Property Watch. https://www.ip-watch.org/2005/12/17/peru-attempts-strong-wto-position-on-disclosure-despite-weaker-us-deal/. Accessed 16 May 2018.

Gerstetter, C., Görlach, B., Neumann, K., & Schaffrin, D. (2007). The International Treaty on Plant Genetic Resources for Food and Agriculture Within the Current Legal Regime Complex on Plant Genetic Resources. *The Journal of World Intellectual Property, 10*(3/4), 259–283.

Perrault, A., Herbertson, K., & Lynch, O. J. (2006). Partnerships for Success in Protected Areas: The Public Interest and Local Community Rights to Prior Informed Consent (PIC). *Georgetown International Environmental Law Review, 19*(3), 475–542.

Raustiala, K., & Victor, D. G. (2004). The Regime Complex for Plant Genetic Resources. *International Organization, 58*(2), 277–309.

Roa-Rodríguez, C., & Van Dooren, T. (2008). Shifting Common Spaces of Plant Genetic Resources in the International Regulation of Property. *The Journal of World Intellectual Property, 11*(3), 176–202.

Robinson, D. F. (2010). *Confronting Biopiracy: Challenges, Cases and International Debates*. Routledge.

Robinson, D. F. (2012). Biopiracy and the Innovations of Indigenous Peoples and Local Communities. In P. Drahos & S. Frankel (Eds.), *Indigenous Peoples' Innovation: Intellectual Property Pathways to Development* (pp. 77–94). ANU Press.

Saez, C. (2015). *WIPO General Assemblies to Tackle Budget, Fate of Traditional Knowledge Committee*. Intellectual Property Watch. http://www.ip-watch.org/2015/10/04/wipo-general-assemblies-to-tackle-budget-fate-of-tk-committee/. Accessed 16 May 2018.

Schei, P. J., & Tvedt, M. W. (2010). Genetic Resources in the CBD: The Wording, the Past, the Present and the Future. *Genetics, 6*, 533–543.

SIPO. (2016). *Analysis Report on Patenting in the Biological Industry (Part I) 生物产业专利技术动向分析报告 (上)*. http://www.sipo.gov.cn/docs/pub/old/tjxx/zltjjb/201603/P020160308545887650029.pdf

UNCTAD. (2014). *The Convention on Biological Diversity and the Nagoya Protocol: Intellectual Property Implications, A Handbook on the Interface between Global Access and Benefit Sharing Rules and Intellectual Property*. United Nations Publications.

Wyzycka, N., & Hasmath, R. (2017). The Impact of the European Union's Policy Towards China's Intellectual Property Regime. *International Political Science Review, 38*(5), 549–562.

Xinhuanet. (2016). *The First Meeting for the Drafting of China's "Biodiversity Conservation Law (Proposal)" Was Held in Beijing 我国《生物多样性保护法 (建议稿)》起草研讨会第一次会议在京召开*. http://www.xinhuanet.com/2016-08/22/c_135624413.htm. Accessed 10 May 2018.

Xue, D. (2015). On Establishing the National Synergy Strategy for the Implementation of International Agreements Related to Biodiversity Conservation 建立生物多样性保护相关国际公约的国家履约协同战略. *Biodiversity Science 生物多样性, 23*(5), 673–680.

Xue, D., & Cai, L. (2009). China's Legal and Policy Frameworks for Access to Genetic Resources and Benefit-Sharing from Their Use. *Review of European Community & International Environmental Law, 18*(1), 91–99.

Yamane, H. (2011). *Interpreting TRIPS: Globalisation of Intellectual Property Rights and Access to Medicines.* Bloomsbury Publishing.

Zhang, X. (2008). Study on Access and Benefit-Sharing of Chinese Genetic Resources 我国遗传资源的获取和惠益分享立法研究. *Science of Law (Journal of Northwest University of Political Science and Law 法律科学(西北政法学院学报), 1*, 142–157.

Zhang, X. (2012). Access to Plant Genetic Resources for Food and Agriculture and Benefit-Sharing in China: Legal Framework, Current Practices and Future Developments. *Review of European Community & International Environmental Law, 21*(2), 137–148.

# 4

# China Emerges in International Standardisation

## 4.1 Introduction

This chapter will focus on China's international engagement in standardisation—in particular, how China began to engage in the process of international (and domestic) standardisation and how these attempts were blocked by the US. Standardisation and standard are twin concepts. A standard is a set of technical specifications that adhere to a particular technology and standardisation is the process of developing, ratifying, and implementing a standard. Standardisation is a critical strategy for leading firms in an industry to maintain their competitive advantage. States interested in seeing their firms maintain a dominant position in standards and standardisation have less incentive to restrict the standard-setting capacity of their firms. They prefer this issue to be regulated by their own national laws and unregulated at the international level or loosely regulated by international standard-setting organisations in the form of soft law. In addition, the anticompetition effects are different before and after a standard is set. As pointed out by Farrell *et al.* (2007, p. 607):

> *Ex ante*, before an industry standard is chosen, there are various attractive technologies, but *ex post*, after industry participants choose a standard and take steps to implement it, alternative technologies become less attractive. Thus, a patent covering a standard may confer market power *ex post* that was much weaker *ex ante*. In the extreme, a standard could be built around initially arbitrary choices that become essential once the standard is established.


W. Cheng, *China in Global Governance of Intellectual Property*, Palgrave Socio-Legal Studies, https://doi.org/10.1007/978-3-031-24370-7_4

Typical *ex post* anticompetitive behaviour includes patent hold-up and royalty stacking (Farrell *et al.*, 2007; Lemley & Shapiro, 2006). There is little chance for a latecomer initiative to be successful once a standard for a certain technology is set. Chinese companies in most cases have been latecomers to technology breakthroughs and had to accept and follow the *ex post* standards. That means skyrocketing royalties and little chance to surpass the existing standards due to the high cost of switching to an incompatible standard (Farrell & Klemperer, 2007; Shin & Kim, 2008). As a result, the only chance for an actor to win the standardisation game is to participate in the *ex ante* competition, influencing standardisation from an early stage.

Technically, standardisation and IP (mainly patents) intersect in the form of standard-essential patents (SEPs). But SEPs is not a focus of this chapter. Instead, this chapter examines how standardisation influenced China and Chinese entities, and how China participated in international standardisation in selected cases. This chapter focuses on the latter through the case of China's participation in the standardisation of Wireless Local Area Network (WLAN). Given the strategic significance of standards to various industries, including information and communication technology (ICT), the Chinese government has a clear interest in promoting its domestically developed standards to become compulsory national standards and potential international standards. However, it is a highly contentious area. The Chinese DVD industry tried to survive but was ultimately defeated. Later, China planned to establish a national standard and participate in international standardisation for WLAN. It was also defeated because there is more to the game than just having an impressive patent portfolio. The failed attempts indicate that a country needs a complementary set of institutional, organisational, and negotiating skills if it is to make a standard come alive globally. While both cases predate the contentious Huawei and 5G standard-setting examples, these less well-known cases already revealed the emergence of a US national security state that treats IP more than a trade-related issue (Drahos, 2021).

### 4.1.1 Standardisation as a Survival Kit in Competition

Economically, compatibility is the main justification for standards. On the supply side of a product, the diverse parts or components manufactured by multiple firms must be compatible with one another to produce a product. The process of standardisation makes things similar enough for them to be compatible or interoperable (Farrell, 1989); however, standardisation means more for a firm than just compatibility. For users, standards produce a network externality (Katz & Shapiro, 1985; Liebowitz & Margolis, 1994):

The more users there are in the same network, the cheaper it is for a single user to consume related goods. The network externality can bring increasing returns for firms in the network, a mechanism whereby the more products that are sold, the more profitable it is for the firms involved (Lee & Oh, 2006). The increasing returns further stimulate firms to strategically use standards; once a standard is established in a network, it is likely to continue because the cost of switching to a new and incompatible standard will be remarkably high. Firms, therefore, use standards to exclude the entry of competitors as well as to lock users in.

Looking beyond firms, the roles of standards in both facilitating compatibility and excluding competition have also long been used by governments to secure their competitive advantage in a market where a network externality effect is at work. With the development of international supply chains, the importance of international standardisation has increased. More and more actors are involved in the game of standardisation with the key principle 'winner takes all' (Shin *et al.*, 2015). This explains the fierce competition in elevating potential candidates to a standard. Firms use standards to secure the first-mover advantage; states use standards as non-tariff barriers to trade. As pointed out by Büthe (2010, p. 294), 'standardization is often as intensely political as it is technical'. This principle also explains why, as will be discussed later in this chapter, it is so difficult for China to initiate international standardisation as a latecomer in ICT.

### 4.1.2 The North-South Contestation in International Standardisation

Historically, states acted unilaterally as standard setters for their telegraph systems (Braithwaite & Drahos, 2000, p. 332). With the development of international trade, regional and international standard-setting organisations (SSOs) were created to solve the incompatibility problems among different jurisdictions. Since standardisation has become part of international competition, states have reassumed their roles in the process of international standardisation (Lee & Oh, 2006). The North-South tension in standardisation is increasingly prominent given that: 1) the existing consortia of the ICT sector emerged from alliances of companies from developed countries and 2) companies from emerging countries are increasingly involved in the process of standardisation thanks to their recent technological development. The case of WAPI illustrates the battle over standardisation from the North-South perspective.

As international SSOs gradually gained the normative power of standardisation during their evolution (Büthe, 2010), states cannot directly interfere with the process of international standardisation in the ICT sector as they once did. Nonetheless, a state can still have regulatory power over standardisation within its jurisdiction. States can directly set committee-based de jure standards through the proper procedural channels of national SSOs, and multinational corporations (MNCs) can set market-based de facto standards as the first movers by taking advantage of the network externality of standards (Farrell & Saloner, 1988).

In the post-WTO era, states' power over standardisation has been further limited by the Technical Barriers to Trade (TBT) Agreement, a WTO agreement aiming at ensuring technical regulations and standards do not create unnecessary obstacles to international trade. Under this agreement, WTO members must notify their adoption of certain national standards and guarantee these standards do not constitute a barrier to trade. With major international SSOs as its observers, the TBT Committee also draws up basic principles to guide the procedure of international standardisation. These principles include transparency, openness, impartiality and consensus, effectiveness and relevance, coherence, and consideration of the development dimension.[1]

### 4.1.3 Standardisation as a Lifeline for Chinese ICT Firms

Standards are crucial to the development of Chinese ICT. On the supply side, Chinese manufacturers have long operated on the Original Equipment Manufacturer (OEM) model—a labour-intensive development model that makes them the least profitable in global value chains (GVCs) (Sect. 4.2.3). In recent years, some Chinese companies have begun to focus on innovation, increasing their research and development (R&D) expenditure, and patenting. The number of patents applied for by Chinese ICT companies has reached phenomenal levels; ZTE and Huawei were the top two PCT applicants in 2016 (WIPO, 2017 Figure 14). Their accumulated patents have helped them catch up with the existing giants in the industry. Nonetheless, MNCs often use standards and IP litigation to block the firms from catching up. Standards have become the glass ceiling for Chinese ICT companies.

[1] WTO TBT Committee, *Second Triennial Review of the Operation and Implementation of the Agreement on Technical Barriers to Trade—Decision of the Committee on Principles for the Development of International Standards, Guides and Recommendations with Relation to Articles 2, 5 and Annex 3 of the TBT Agreement*. G/TBT/9, 13 November 2000, para. 20 and Annex 4.

On the demand side, China has become the world's largest mobile phone market, benefiting from the country's population size. This provides China with certain leverage regarding standards regulation: Domestic regulations within its jurisdiction may have a significant impact on MNCs doing business in or selling products to China.

## 4.2 The DVD Case and Its Lessons

### 4.2.1 The Rise and Fall of the DVD Industry in China

The DVD industry in China experienced a rise and fall within a decade (1997–2007). The industry rose because the global supply chain extended to China. It perished because Chinese companies could not afford the patent fees MNCs charged based on their SEPs. Because of this, the Chinese government, Chinese companies, and Chinese academics started to pay attention to standards. China further developed strategic thinking about its position in global value chains (GVCs) and the importance of technology dependence.

Baldwin (2013, p. 16) identified two reasons for the rise of GVCs in the mid-1980s: '[T]he ICT revolution made it possible to coordinate complexity at distance; [and] the vast wage differences between developed and developing nations made separation profitable'. China became the world's factory in many industries because of its comparatively low wages, which directly led to the prosperity of the global DVD industry. The world DVD market was worth only US$1 billion in 1998 when Japanese and European firms dominated the market. After the entry of Chinese firms, the market grew dramatically to US$19 billion in 2004 (Shintaku *et al.*, 2006, p. 18).

Although China quickly developed into a global production base for DVDs, it followed a labour-intensive production mode and most of the DVD patents and standards were owned by Japanese and EU companies. In 2000, patentholders, which had established de facto standards in the DVD industry, started requesting patent royalties from Chinese firms. From 2002 to 2008, the number of licensors increased from one to 37, with the royalty rate increasing from US$4 per unit to US$21.30 per unit (Lu & Gao, 2010, p. 79). Table 4.1 shows the internal structure of the royalties. In addition to paying royalties, Chinese companies imported core components of DVD players such as optical heads, encoder chips, and servo controllers at US$27 per unit (in 2003 prices).

The price of DVD players dropped dramatically from the year 2000: 'Prices for the first (DVD) players in 1997 were $1000 and up'. By the end

**Table 4.1** Licensing fees paid by Chinese DVD manufacturers to multinational corporations (Lu & Gao, 2010)

| Patentholders/alliances | Member companies | Royalty rate (US$/unit) |
|---|---|---|
| DVD6C | Hitachi Consumer Electronics, JVC KENWOOD, Mitsubishi Electric Corporation, Panasonic Corporation, Samsung Electronics, Sanyo Electric Co., Sharp Corporation, Toshiba Corporation, and Warner Brothers | 4 |
| DVD 4C Union | Sony Corporation, Philips Electronics, Pioneer Corporation, and LG Electronics | 5 (3.5 since July 2002) |
| MPEG-2 | The Moving Picture Experts Group (MPEG) is a joint committee of the International Organization for Standardization (ISO) and the International Electrotechnical Commission (IEC). The MPEG-LA consists of 24 different companies | 4 (2.5 since July 2006) |
| Thomson | – | 2 |
| Dolby | – | 4.95 |
| TDS | – | 2–3 |

of 2000, players were available for under $100 at discount retailers. In 2003, players became available for under $50' (Taylor, 2013). Most licensing agreements mentioned above provided fixed licensing rates that did not change with the retail price. While in 2002 there were more than 100 DVD manufacturers in China, the number dropped to 14 in 2007. The Chinese DVD industry quickly perished due to unreasonably high licensing fees that did not reflect the tremendous drop in retail prices of DVD players.

### 4.2.2 Two Lessons from the DVD Case

Chinese DVD manufacturers paid for a lesson in the importance of standards and their control through patents. Implications have gone beyond the DVD industry. The Chinese government and other stakeholders began to find solutions. For instance, the China Electronics Standardization Institute (CESI, 2003) claimed China had fallen victim to a new form of non-tariff barrier—an 'IP-centric technology barrier'. During the discussions that

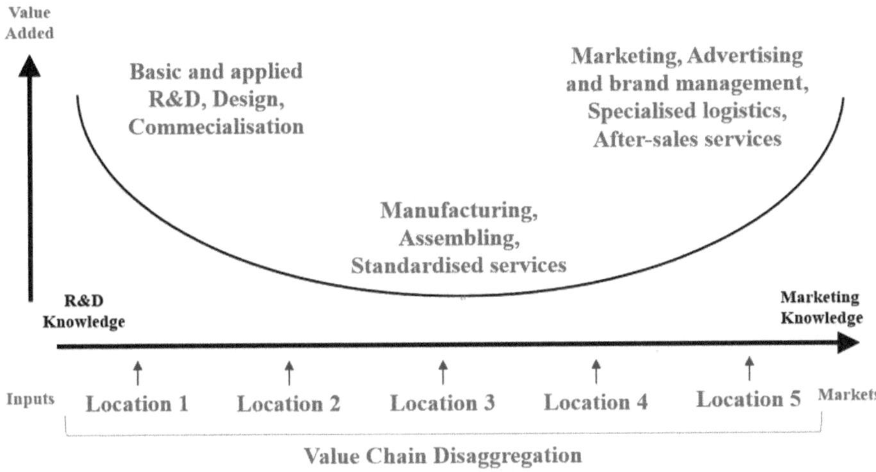


**Fig. 4.1** The smiling curve of value creation. Author's adaption based on Mudambi (2008)

followed, China began to recognise where its companies are positioned in GVCs (Gereffi *et al.*, 2005) and to think strategically about the importance of technological independence.

Studying 560 GVCs from 1995 to 2008, Timmer *et al.* (2014) found that the GVCs had a similar pattern in the distribution of value-added parts when sliced up. Other scholars called the U-shaped value distribution curve 'the smiling curve' (Chen, 2004; Shin *et al.*, 2012; Sunny Li *et al.*, 2010; Wang & Jia, 2010) (Fig. 4.1).

The smiling curve reveals that the greatest value is captured by upstream (R&D) and downstream (marketing) firms, and the lowest value is captured by the assembly firms located in the middle of GVCs (Shin *et al.*, 2012).[2] The value distribution in GVCs generally presents a smiling curve because MNCs have control over the two ends of the curve. They possess product planning capabilities and market access advantages, so they can decide on the distribution of value derived from the GVCs (Chen, 2004). The curve became deeper as Timmer *et al.* (2014) found when the value-added shares of low-skilled workers in emerging economies declined between 1995 and 2008. A typical example of the smiling curve is the GVCs of Apple. According to

[2] It is worth noting that the smiling curve describes the phenomenon of values captured by firms at different locations in a GVC. Chinese manufacturing firms are the often least profitable actors in a GVC; however, for the MNCs, it means their costs in this segment of the curve are low. Mudambi (2008) suggests MNCs can control GVCs by concentrating on R&D and marketing while outsourcing low value-added assembling and processing to firms in emerging economies.

Kraemer *et al.* (2011), Chinese labour accounts for 1.8% of the total value of an iPhone and 2% of the total value of an iPad.

As pointed out by Chen (2004), the smiling curve indicates an underpinning power relation between actors located in a GVC where MNCs are the regulators while the Chinese OEM firms are the regulatees. Since suppliers for MNCs are located at the end of a smiling curve, Chinese OEM firms are dependent on these MNCs. As revealed in the DVD case, the dependence mainly lies in technologies, in particular, those protected by patents and adopted as standards.

### 4.2.3 Strategies to Avoid a Similar Trap

After the DVD case, the Chinese government and Chinese firms became familiar with the doctrine that 'first-class enterprises set standards; second-class enterprises develop technology; [and] third-class enterprises manufacture products'.[3] China responded to the DVD case directly by developing its standards, as exemplified by the Audio Video Coding Standards (AVS). With the development of 3G and 4G wireless networks, DVDs are gradually being replaced with online TVs on which people can watch live programs, sometimes for free. When the market for high-definition digital TVs began to develop potential, China started early to create its own national standards for the industry. In early 2002, China set up the AVS Working Group.[4] AVS has saved Chinese digital TV producers patent royalties amounting to tens of billions of dollars (Huang & Zhang, 2017).

However, the above two lessons revealed more substantial problems with standardisation. The fact that most Chinese firms were in the middle of the smiling curve indicated that they captured the lowest value in GVCs. China began to find ways to support its domestic firms to climb up the smiling curve, either through investing in innovation (towards the input end) or through enhancing the reputation of 'Made in China' (towards the market end) (Fig. 4.1). However, such efforts were not well received by some domestic firms. MNCs come to China for its lower labour costs. To climb up the smiling curve, Chinese firms must abandon the labour-intensive development model, which has so far been the source of their profits. Nonetheless, this meant in the transition they may lose their competitive advantage (low

[3] This slogan, translated from Chinese, has been widely used by the Chinese government and firms regarding what they have learned about the importance of standards. It has been popular in IP training materials with government officials and corporate managers as the audience.

[4] See the official website of the Audio and Video Coding Standard Workgroup of China (AVS Workgroup) for its mission, organisation and history: http://www.avs.org.cn/english/.

labour costs), and some may not survive the transition. This paradox was compounded by the unbalanced development between regions within China (Gao *et al.*, 2017).

China began to develop and deploy standards in all strategic industries because standardisation is also critical to the competitiveness of the state. Chinese President Xi Jinping sent a written message to the Thirty-Ninth ISO General Assembly held in Beijing in 2016:

> China will actively implement the strategy of standardisation. We will promote innovative, coordinated, green, open, and sharing development with the support of standards. Together with all countries in the world, we are ready to deepen cooperation in standards, enhance exchange and mutual learning, and improve the system of international standards. (Gasiorowski-Denis, 2016)

The hosting of the ISO General Assembly and the content of President Xi's message demonstrate the political will of China to participate in international standardisation.

Since 2006, China has also promoted indigenous innovation through the accreditation of indigenous innovative products.[5] Relevant policies measured indigenous innovation by whether a product was accredited as 'indigenous' IP. Specifically, indigenous IP required product patents must be wholly owned by Chinese firms, and trademarks for a branded product must be first registered in China. Products accredited as containing indigenous IP were given preferential treatment in public procurement. These policies were first implemented in 2009 for six selected technology fields (including computer and application equipment, communications products, modern office equipment, software, new energy and equipment, and energy-efficient products), but they were opposed by the US as measures discriminating against MNCs (McGregor, 2010; USITC, 2011). As China was not a member of the WTO Governmental Procurement Agreement (GPA), it could make a sovereign decision about such preferential treatment in public procurement. However, under pressure, the implementation policy for the second round of accreditation was significantly changed in 2010. The requirement for indigenous IP has been abandoned, and a company can be accredited if it has the right to use IP. This way, MNCs could also apply for benefits available for indigenous innovation products. After this change, the indigenous innovation policy was less likely to fulfil its purpose of promoting the technological independence of Chinese companies.

---

[5] MOST, MOF and NDRC (2006), *the Administrative Measures for Accreditation of Indigenous Innovative Products for Trial Implementation* 国家自主创新产品认定管理办法 (试行) No. 539.

Following this failure, China relied on a subtler use of mechanisms of IP law and competition law. In a regulation jointly issued by SAC and SIPO on patents and standards,[6] issues arising from the development of national standards were addressed, such as the disclosure of patent information and using the principle of fair, reasonable, and non-discrimination (FRAND) to determine royalty rates for SEP licensing. The Chinese Anti-Monopoly Law provides a legal basis for investigating unreasonable licensing fees, and regulators have enacted supplemental rules on IP-related issues. For instance, in February 2015, the National Development and Reform Commission (NDRC) completed its investigation into Qualcomm, finding it violating the Anti-Monopoly Law (2007) by abusing its market power—specifically, by attaching an unreasonable requirement for patent licensing. The NDRC-ordered Qualcomm to stop its abuse of market power and imposed a fine equal to 8% of Qualcomm's revenue in 2013—CNY6.088 billion (US$975 million) (King, 2015).

The DVD case was a trigger for China to think about its position in the GVCs that form the basis of modern production, as well as its degree of technological independence after two decades of market reform and opening-up. The DVD case stimulated China to develop strategies to push its own companies to climb the smiling curve and achieve a greater degree of technological independence. To summarise, these strategies include: 1) promoting standardisation as a national strategy, 2) developing indigenous innovation policies, and 3) applying IP and competition laws and regulations to standards. Thus far, the indigenous innovation policies have proved a failure.

## 4.3 WAPI: Failed Attempts at Domestic and International Standardisation

Informed by the DVD case, China deployed standardisation as a key strategy to develop its ICT sector. Of the seven strategic emerging industries in China, next-generation information technology is the only one in which China could have an 'international competitive advantage'. Relevant technologies can be applied to areas including next-generation communication networks, the Internet of Things, integration of telecommunications networks, computer networks and cable television networks, new flat-panel

[6] SAC and SIPO (2013), *Regulations on National Standards that Involve Patents (Temporary)* 国家标准涉及专利的管理规定 (暂行), No. 1.

displays, high-performance integrated circuits and cloud computing. Prominently, China has attempted to adopt its homegrown WLAN standard, the WLAN Authentication and Privacy Infrastructure (WAPI), as a compulsory national standard. When this was unsuccessful, China further promoted WAPI as a candidate for international standardisation. These attempts illustrate how China has engaged with international standardisation and the difficulties it has faced.

### 4.3.1 Failure to Adopt WAPI as a Compulsory National Standard

WLAN standards were developed mainly by the US-based Institute of Electrical and Electronics Engineers (IEEE), a standardization organization in the US. China's WAPI standards were developed by the China Broadband Wireless IP Standard Group (CBWIPSG) to fill the security hole in WLAN standards at that time. Developing WAPI was part of China's indigenous innovation efforts to gain greater technological independence. As pointed out by Gao (2008), China expected its WAPI standards to replace those of the WLAN technologies owned by foreign companies. Table 4.2 illustrates how various Chinese stockholders attempted to promote WAPI standards[7] as compulsory national standards and how their efforts were opposed by the US. The US government and Intel Corporation politicised this issue by putting it on the agenda of bilateral negotiations with China. As a result, the implementation of WAPI as a compulsory national standard was suspended indefinitely in 2004.

Intel was one of the key MNCs opposing WAPI and the biggest winner from its indefinite suspension in April 2004. Intel first introduced its flagship Centrino processor in early 2003, in which its wireless network conforming to Wi-Fi standards was tied to its processor and chipset. Intel was concerned about China's plan to adopt WAPI as compulsory national standards. This

[7] WAPI primarily included two standards: (1) GB15629.11-2003, which refers to 'Information Technology—Telecommunications and Information Exchange between Systems—Local and Metropolitan Area Networks—Specific Requirements—Part 11: Wireless LAN Medium Access Control (MAC) and Physical Layer (PHY) Specification' 信息技术系统间远程通信和信息交换局域网和城域网特定要求第11部分: 无线局域网媒体访问 (MAC) 和物理 (PHY) 层规范; and (2) GB15629.1102-2003, which refers to 'Information Technology—Telecommunications and Information Exchange between Systems—Local and Metropolitan Area Networks—Specific Requirements—Part 11: Wireless LAN Medium Access Control (MAC) and Physical Layer (PHY) Specification: Relatively High Speed Physical Layer of 2.4 GHz Frequency Expanding Specification' 信息技术系统间远程通信和信息交换局域网和城域网特定要求第11部分: 无线局域网媒体访问 (MAC) 和物理 (PHY) 层规范: 2.4 GHz频段较高速物理层扩展规范.

**Table 4.2** Timeline for WAPI to be adopted as a national standard

| Time | Actor | Event |
|---|---|---|
| June 2001 | Ministry of Information Industry (MII)<br>China Broadband Wireless IP Standard Group (CBWIPSG) | The MII announced a research and development plan to draft China's own WLAN standards. In total, 26 research institutes and firms were recruited to implement the plan. They later established the CBWIPSG to undertake a research project to develop a Chinese WLAN standard |
| 12 May 2003 | Standardization Administration of China (SAC) | The SAC announced two standards (GB15629.11-2003 and GB15629.1102-2003) drafted by the CBWIPSG, which are the key WAPI standards |
| 9 July 2003 | Ministries in charge of standardisation | Eight ministries in China, including MII and SAC, organised a promotion and implementation conference in Beijing, which determined the WAPI standards as compulsory national standards. The WAPI standards were to be implemented in China by 1 December 2003 |
| 23 November 2003 | IEEE | Paul Nikolich, IEEE 802 Chair, sent a letter[8] to Li Zhonghai, Chairman of the SAC, and Wang Xudong, Minister for Information Industry, saying the WAPI would unnecessarily fracture the world market for WLAN products |

(continued)

[8] 'Subject: IEEE 802 LMSC and SAC Standards GB15629.11 and GB 1529.1102', Letter from Paul Nikolich, Chair, IEEE 802 Local and Metropolitan Area Network Standards Committee, to Li Zhonghai, Chairman, Standardization Administration of China (SAC), 23 November 2003, available from: http://www.ieee802.org/16/liaison/docs/L80216-03_19.pdf.

**Table 4.2** (continued)

| Time | Actor | Event |
|---|---|---|
| 26 November 2013 | General Administration of Quality Supervision, Inspection and Quarantine (AQSIQ)<br>SAC | The AQSIQ and SAC jointly published a notice stating that China would implement compulsory certification of WLAN products.[9] The WAPI standards would be implemented from 1 December 2003, after which, any importation, production or sale of WLAN products not conforming to the WAPI standards would be prohibited from the Chinese market |
| December 2003 | AQSIQ<br>National Certification and Accreditation Administration Committee (NCAAC) | AQSIQ and NCAAC jointly announced a notice extending the implementation of WAPI as a compulsory national standard until 1 June 2004 |
| March 2004 | US politicians | US Secretary of Commerce Donald Evans, US Secretary of State Colin Powell and US Trade Representative Robert Zoellick jointly sent a letter to Chinese Vice-Premiers Wu Yi and Zeng Peiyan, asking China to reconsider the implementation of WAPI as a compulsory national standard |
| March 2004 | Intel and other US chipmakers | Intel and Broadcom, the major Wi-Fi chipmakers, opposed the WAPI standards by announcing they would stop selling products with Wi-Fi chips in China from 1 June 2004 (Kanellos, 2004) |

(continued)

[9] AQSIQ and SAC (2003), *Notice Concerning the Implementation of the Compulsory National Standards in WLAN* 关于无线局域网强制性国家标准实施的公告, No. 110.

**Table 4.2** (continued)

| Time | Actor | Event |
|---|---|---|
| 22 April 2004 | US and Chinese high-level officials at the Joint Commission on Commerce and Trade (JCCT) in 2004 | At the 2004 JCCT, WAPI was one of the top priorities for the US. China agreed to 'suspend indefinitely its proposed implementation of WAPI as a mandatory wireless encryption standard'. China also expressed its intention to 'participate in international standards bodies on WAPI and wireless encryption for computer networks' (USTR, 2004) |

was because it meant the Centrino featuring Wi-Fi could not enter the Chinese market without installing WAPI.

Intel lobbied the US government to prevent China from adopting WAPI as compulsory national standards and threatened China with an embargo on Wi-Fi chips. In 2004, the US put WAPI at the top of the agenda of the Joint Commission on Commerce and Trade (JCCT)—one of the highest-level US-China bilateral forums. Finally, Chinese Vice-Premier Wu Yi announced that China would indefinitely suspend implementing WAPI as a compulsory national standard.

China's development of WAPI also attracted academic attention in the US, with some arguing that WAPI would constitute a violation of the WTO TBT Agreement and the national treatment principle in GATT (Cromer, 2005; Gibson, 2007). They concluded that WAPI should not be implemented, which in turn justified the US intervention with China's implementation of WAPI as compulsory national standards.

### 4.3.2 The Journey for WAPI to Go Global

The fifteenth JCCT report in 2004 announced that while China had agreed to indefinitely suspend WAPI as compulsory national standards, the US promised to support WAPI to become international standards. China initiated the international standardisation of WAPI two weeks after the announcement of suspending WAPI as a compulsory national standard. The SAC, as a National Body representing China, proposed a WLAN standard (JTC 1

N7506) based on WAPI at the ISO and the IEC Joint Technical Committee (ISO/IEC JTC 1) for information technology. One month after the ISO/IEC JTC 1 received the Chinese proposal, the United Kingdom opposed it and submitted a competing proposal (JTC 1 N7537) based on IEEE 802.11i. China's efforts to promote WAPI as an international standard are illustrated in Table 4.3. The timeline shows the ISO did not treat China's national body equally as it treated the IEEE in the assessment procedure. The Chinese proposal was cancelled in September 2004 and the opportunity to discuss it at the JTC 1 meeting in Orlando, Florida, was missed. The reason for this cancellation—'an administrative error'—was announced three months later, but the proposal was again ignored at the JTC 1 Frankfurt meeting in 2005. After persistent appeals by the Chinese national body, the Chinese and UK proposals were put on a parallel fast-track starting from the same date, despite the Chinese proposal having been submitted one month earlier. The IEEE 802.11 Working Group engaged in intensive lobbying during the five-month balloting process and disseminated detailed arguments against WAPI (EE Times, 2006)—something China appealed but was unsuccessful in the end.

The above timeline also shows that when facing controversies in ISO procedures, the Chinese national body tried to communicate with the ISO and appealed to the Technical Management Board on issues of unfair treatment. For instance, at the Orlando meeting, the Chinese representative addressed a series of events that formed 'a pattern of irregularity, deception, mishandling, discrimination, and obstruction against the China NB [national body] within this group'.[10] These obstacles included: 1) China's request to fast-track the WAPI was ignored; 2) the Resolution Group discarded the SAC's comments and cancelled the Chinese proposal before the end of the review period; and 3) visas for the Chinese delegation to enter the US were denied. After the result of the ballot was announced, the Chinese national body submitted its second appeal, complaining that the ISO balloting was unfairly influenced by the IEEE's unethical behaviour and prejudices. The Chinese national body also expressed its discontent by withdrawing from the Frankfurt meeting and publishing an open comment afterwards. Nonetheless, the Chinese efforts did not change the result: 802.11i was adopted as an international standard. Though China tried to resubmit the WAPI in 2009, it eventually withdrew it in November 2011.

An unbiased procedure would not necessarily have changed the result, but the prejudice demonstrated how China's efforts to make the WAPI a global

[10] *Supra* note 16.

**Table 4.3** Timeline of WAPI's failure as an ISO standard

| Time | Event |
|---|---|
| 27 July 2004 | China's national body, SAC, submitted a proposal for a WAPI security mechanism at ISO/IEC JTC 1 Subcommittee 6 (SC6) and requested a fast-track procedure |
| 2 August 2004 | ISO/IEC JTC 1 SC6 published the Chinese WAPI proposal in document JTC 1 N7506. It took three months for publication and review of the proposal |
| 25 August 2004 | The UK national body submitted to the SC6 a rival standard (JTC 1 N7537) based on IEEE 802.11i |
| Mid-September 2004 | The Chinese proposal was cancelled before the end of the publication and review period without explanation. The UK proposal was published and fast-tracked |
| 8–12 November 2004 | **ISO/IEC JTC 1/SC6 Orlando meeting**<br>The Chinese proposal N7506 was not discussed because it was 'non-existent'<br>Four of the six Chinese delegation members (including three drafters of the WAPI standards) were denied visas to enter the US territory to participate at the Orlando meeting<br>SAC representatives addressed the meeting, revealing the obstacles experienced[11]<br>Because of the resistance from the SAC, the Orlando meeting resolved that 'China's submission and China's comments on 802.11i' would be discussed at the Frankfurt meeting in February 2005[12] |

[11] CBWIPSG (2004), Preliminary Response to "Proposed Resolution of Problems Identified by the Chinese NB in Opening Comments of Chinese NB" at the SC 6/WG 1 Orlando meeting, ISO/IEC JTC 1/SC 06 N12769. Available from http://www.chinabwips.org.cn/doc/N12769.pdf (Accessed: May 10, 2022).

[12] IEEE 802.11 ISO JTC1-SC6 SG1 Ad-Hoc Committee Conference Call, IEEE 802.11/JTC1 Engagement, submission from Jesse Walker, IEEE 802 Liaison to JTC1/SC6, doc.: IEEE 802.11-04/1547/ro, December 2004, Slide 4, available from: https://mentor.ieee.org/802.11/dcn/04/11-04-1547-00-0000-ieee-802-jc1-sc6-engagement.ppt.

| Time | Event |
|---|---|
| December 2004 | The IEEE clarified why the Chinese proposal had been cancelled: 'due to administrative error, the JTC1/SC6 Secretariat removed China's submission' and 'JTC1/SC6/WG1 Project Editor has invited China to resubmit its proposal'[13] |
| | The SAC sent a letter to the SC6 Secretariat, complaining that the resubmission would allow the UK proposal to enter the ballot stage earlier[14] |
| January 2005 | SC6 recommended China first submit the WAPI standard to the IEEE for approval; however, China rejected this recommendation as unnecessary[15] |

(continued)

[13] Slide 5, IEEE 802.11-04/1547/ro.

[14] 'Chinese NB's Urgent Request for Action on 1N7506 and 1N7537', Letter from Chinese National Body to Ms Jooran Lee, 20 December 2004, available from: http://www.chinabwips.org/doc/Chinese%20NB%20Urgent%20Request%20for%20Action%20on%201N7506%20and%201N7537.pdf.

[15] 'Chinese NB Reply about WLAN Proposal', Letter from Zhang Lin, Director General of SAC International Standards Department, to Mrs Lisa Rajchel, 6 February 2005, available from: http://www.sc6.org/doc/Chinese%20NB%20reply%20about%20WLAN%20proposal.pdf.

Table 4.3 (continued)

| Time | Event |
|---|---|
| February 2005 | **ISO/IEC JTC 1/SC6 Frankfurt meeting**<br>The Chinese proposal JTC 1 N7506 was not discussed as planned in the Orlando meeting resolution<br>The SAC withdrew from the meeting halfway and published an announcement protesting the unfair treatment it had received[16] |
| 21 April 2005 | China appealed to the ISO's Technical Management Board,[17] condemning its unfair treatment at the Frankfurt meeting and requesting suspension of the voting for N7537. The voting for N7537 was suspended |
| 15–17 May 2005 | **Geneva meeting (exceptional meeting to address the Chinese appeal)**<br>The ISO formed a special group to resolve the technical issue |

[16] 'Disputes Surrounding N7506 and N7537 Emerged on the First Day Meeting', Letter submitted by the Chinese National Body at the ISO/IEC JTC1 SC6 WK1 Interim Meeting, 22 February 2005, available from: http://www.chinabwips.org/doc/1F03_20050222-ChinaFirstdayrecordsFrankfurtmeeting.pdf; 'Final Statement of the Chinese National Body', Letter submitted by the Chinese National Body at the ISO/IEC JTC1 SC6 WG1 Interim Meeting, 23 February 2005, available from: http://www.chinabwips.org/doc/ATT2-Final%20Statement%20of%20the%20Chinese%20National%20Body,Germany,%202005-02.pdf.

[17] 'A Letter of Appeal to ISO/IEC SMB/TMB from Chinese National Body', Appeal submitted by the Chinese National Body after Frankfurt meeting in 2005, available from: http://www.chinabwips.org/doc/A%20Letter%20of%20Appeal%20to%20ISOIEC%20SMBTMB%20from%20Chinese%20National%20Body.pdf.

| Time | Event |
|---|---|
| 29 August–2 September 2005 | **ISO/IEC JTC 1/SC6 Saint-Paul-De-Vence meeting**<br>The SAC proposed establishing a joint working team to harmonise the two proposals[18]<br>The meeting resolved to undertake a parallel fast-tracking ballot for IEEE802.11i and WAPI with voting for both closing on the same date (Resolution 6.1.6)[19] |
| 7 September 2005 | Despite China's objection to the above resolution of the Saint-Paul-De-Vence meeting, the voting began on 7 September 2005 and lasted five months |
| 22 February 2006 | China sent a letter to all members of the ISO/IEC JTC 1/SC6 about the 'IEEE's unethical activities'[20] during the voting |
| March 2006 | The ISO rejected the Chinese proposal and adopted IEEE 802.11i as an international standard for WLAN |
| 21 April 2006 | The SAC submitted an appeal to the Technical Management Board, the IEC Standardization Management Board and the Central Secretariat of the ISO/IEC[21] |
| 2009 onwards | The SAC resubmitted the WAPI in 2009 but withdrew it in October 2011without disclosing reasons[22] |

[18] 'Action Plan Proposed by Chinese National Body on 30 August 2005', available from: http://jtc1sc6.org/doc/SC6WG1-SPV025-CHN-007-Solutions%20from%20CNB.pdf.

[19] 'SC6 WG1 Resolutions for Closing Plenary of WG1', 31 August 2005, available from: http://www.chinabwips.org/doc/SC6%20WG1%20Resolutions%20for%20Closing%20Plenary%20of%20WG1-v5.pdf.

[20] Chinese National Body, 'Urgent Alert on IEEE's Recent Unethical Activities', available from: http://www.chinabwips.org/doc/Urgent%20Alert%20on%20IEEE%20Recent%20Unethical%20Activities.pdf.

[21] Chinese National Body, 'Unjust Activity, Undue Process, Unfair Results: Ethical and Procedural Violations in WAPI-11i Fast-Track Process', 21 April 2006, available from: http://www.chinabwips.org/doc/Unjust%20Activity,%20Undue%20Process,%20Unfair%20Results.pdf.

[22] IEEE 802 JTC1 Standing Committee (2012), Minutes of JTC1 Standing Committee in Jacksonville in January 2012, Para. 8.c., available from: https://mentor.ieee.org/802.11/dcn/12/11-12-0199-00-0jtc-jacksonville-minutes-jan-2012.doc.

standard has been counteracted by the synergy of various actors. The failure of the WAPI was also due to the fact that China did not form a coalition to support the ballot (Kennedy, 2006). This argument, however, neglects the fact that it was the wide coalition formed by the IEEE that denied basic procedural justice to China.

These events indicated what it means for China to be an IP power in the world. Even if it manages to invent the technologies and develop its own standards, there are other dimensions to winning the standard game. Liaison with the ISO, familiarity with application procedures (including intentional mistakes to delay procedures), subtle influences of the balloting, coalition-building and even small tricks such as visa control to prevent certain Chinese representatives to attend meetings contributed to the win of the 802.11i. For China, having patents is not enough; it is only the first step.

### 4.3.3 The Mobile Phone Market: A New Opportunity for WAPI?

After the indefinite suspension of the WAPI as a compulsory national standard, the marketing expansion of it was slower than that of Wi-Fi in China. Nonetheless, products with WAPI standards were prioritised in government procurement. In addition, the Beijing 2008 Olympic Games exclusively adopted WAPI standards. The WAPI Alliance, the successor of the CBWIPSG, was established in 2006 (Cao, 2006).

WAPI did not completely lose the Chinese market; the suspension worked differently for PCs and mobile phones. This is mainly because the vendors of mobile phone networks in China are the three state-owned telecommunication operators—China Mobile, China Unicom and China Telecom—and the Ministry of Industry and Information Technology (MIIT, the successor to the MIT) tightly controlled market access of mobile phones by issuing a unique identification number for each phone. In April 2009, the MIIT convened a meeting with all mobile phone producers, informing them that to enter the Chinese market, a Wi-Fi–enabled mobile phone should have WAPI installed (Cheng, 2009).

This tie-in strategy proved successful. In 2009, using mobile phones to access the Internet became popular. Motorola, Apple and Samsung competed to enter the huge smartphone market in China. Motorola was the first to comply with the MIIT requirement to install WAPI and became the first to launch wireless Internet-enabled mobile phones in the Chinese market. Apple initially refused to install WAPI on its iPhones, but then agreed and entered the Chinese market in May 2010 (Qin, 2010).

There are several reasons for the effectiveness of the adoption of the WAPI standards in mobile phones. First, the market structure for mobile phones is different from that for PCs. Since the MIIT controls access to the mobile phone market and the interests of vendors are divergent, it is difficult for mobile phone vendors to act collectively. The second factor was the timing. In 2003, Intel was eager to be the first mover in the Chinese market. In 2009, with the widespread use of hotspots, Wi-Fi had become a de facto WLAN standard in China. After losing its first opportunity to expand the market, IWNComm, the major developer of WAPI could not afford to deploy adequate hotspots. This determined Wi-Fi's dominance of the market because a consumer would not choose to use WAPI due to insufficient hotspots. Third, Intel, as a supplier of Wi-Fi-enabled chipsets, did not resist the process in 2009 when the MIIT announced its decision.

### 4.3.4 A Standard Without a Market: The Implementation Game for WAPI

After Internet-enabled mobile phones equipped with WAPI spread in the Chinese market, IWNComm, the leading company in the WAPI Alliance, started collecting royalties for WAPI-related SEP (the patent named 'a method of safe access of mobile device and data security communication in WLAN', patent No. 02139508.X), for which it was the patentholder. However, some mobile phone manufacturers that had WAPI installed on their phones refused to pay royalties. For instance, IWNComm claimed that Sony had refused to engage in or intentionally prolonged substantive negotiations over royalties for WAPI-related SEPs and thus sued Sony in the Beijing IP Court in 2015 for patent infringement.

The court found: 1) the patent at issue was a basic invention in the area of WLAN; 2) the patent had been granted science and technology prizes by the Chinese government and had been adopted as a SEP in the national compulsory standard; and 3) the defendant was at fault in the licensing negotiations. The court argued that the fact the patents at issue were SEPs did not change the criteria to determine infringement. The court further decided that infringement was established, issued an injunction ordering Sony to stop infringement and decided the reasonable royalty rate for WAPI-related SEPs (CNY1 per phone) based on the market price. In addition, the court supported IWNComm's claim for treble damages as well as reasonable costs, which amounted to CNY9.1 million (US$1.32 million) in March 2017.[23] Sony appealed to the Beijing Higher People's Court, but the decision was sustained.[24]

The *IWNComm vs Sony* case was just the start for IWNComm in its pursuit of royalties. From 2010 to 2014, IWNComm licensed the WAPI standard-essential patent to Apple. After the contract expired, the two parties failed to reach a new agreement following up to 16 months of negotiations. IWNComm filed a lawsuit against Apple for patent infringement, claiming damage of 150 million in March 2016. Two months later, Apple submitted to the Board of Patent Re-examination of CNIPA, claiming that the relevant patent in that lawsuit was invalid. Apple further sued the Board of Patent Re-examination at Beijing IP Court when the Board confirmed that the patent at issue was valid. Beijing IP Court sustained the decision of the CNIPA Board of Patent Re-examination in June 2020. In addition to invalidating the relevant patent, Apple also sued IWNComm in an anti-monopoly case, claiming that IWNComm has a dominant position in the market for the patent at issue. IWNComm countersued Apple for abuse of its dominant position in the market as the implementer and patent hold-out. Both anti-monopoly cases were still under investigation at the time of writing. In addition, Apple initiated arbitration against IWNComm in Hong Kong, and IWNComm used Apple for breach of confidentiality.

These lawsuits have escalated disputes on WAPI-related SEPs to a new level of complexity both substantively and procedurally. On the one hand, MNCs cannot afford to defy the court judgement and exit the Chinese market. On the other hand, Apple's cross-forum strategies, paralleling lawsuits of invalidating and anti-monopoly have dragged the disputes for six years without an outcome.

## 4.4 Discussion: Technological Hegemony or Technological Nationalism?

Two decades elapsed between the initiation of the WAPI standard. Various non-state actors—including MNCs, domestic Chinese enterprises and international SSOs—were involved in the process. So far, domestic implementation of WAPI has been partly successful for mobile phones but has failed for

[23] IWNComm versus Sony for infringement upon invention patent (first instance at Beijing Intellectual Property Court) 西电捷通诉索尼发明专利侵权纠纷案 (2015) 京知民初字第1194号.

[24] IWNComm versus Sony for infringement upon invention patent 西电捷通诉索尼发明专利侵权纠纷案 (final decision by Beijing People's High Court) (2017) 京民终454号.

the PC market. The globalisation journey of the WAPI standard has failed. The war for royalty collection for WAPI-related SEPs in domestic Chinese courts has continued, with the WAPI owner winning the first case.

WAPI has been one of the most debated Chinese standards in the ICT sector. In addition to criticism that it could violate the WTO GPA, which China has not yet signed, there have been claims that the WAPI is an exemplar of China's increasing 'neo-technological nationalism' (Suttmeier & Yao, 2004; Suttmeier *et al.*, 2006). Techno-nationalism is not a unique characteristic of China, it has been common for states such as the US, Japan, and various EU states to strengthen their national identity or national security through science and technology policies in their national innovation systems (Kohno, 1995). Yet China has been criticised for neo-technological nationalism, which keeps national interests at the centre and emphasises expanded state commitments (Kim *et al.*, 2020).

However, there can be another explanation that the neo-technological nationalism was due to China's lack of experience in international standardisation. China's attempt to establish a rival standard revealed the limitation of the influence of Chinese economic and regulatory institutions and the paradoxical dynamics of interstate cooperation and rivalry in the political economy (Zhao, 2010). Winning standardisation contests demands a subtle combination of global regulatory influence (e.g. in the ISO), firm dominance (such as that held by Intel), incremental innovation capability, patent capability (the use of the PCT to build a global patent portfolio), negotiating prowess and competent regulators who know the tacit rules of the game. Over time, in the 5G case, scholars have found that China's approach to international standardisation has evolved from techno-nationalism to techno-globalism strengthened global connection and growth orientation, with increasing proximity to techno-nationalism of the Western style (Kim *et al.*, 2020; Kwak *et al.*, 2012).

### 4.4.1 The US Strategy Against WAPI

One of the mysteries of the WAPI case was why China agreed to the US call to indefinitely suspend implementing WAPI as compulsory national standards. There was a speculation that China used WAPI as a bargaining chip so the US would agree to release restrictions on defence technology exports to China. But given the high priority of standardisation on China's national agenda, it seems unlikely it would so easily compromise its national interests over standardisation. A more plausible hypothesis is that a reciprocal arrangement was reached whereby China agreed to the indefinite domestic suspension while the US agreed to support proposals to make WAPI an international standard.

Evidence for such a promise can be found. In 2007, at the ground-breaking ceremony for Intel's manufacturing base in the north-eastern coastal city of Dalian, Vice-Minister for Industry and Information Technology Luo Qinjian said the 'MIIT would promote Intel's cooperation with Chinese enterprises in areas of computer and next-generation communication. Meanwhile, Intel should support WAPI to become an international standard to fulfil the US' promise at the fifteenth JCCT' (Lin, 2009). The address indicated such a promise existed and that the US would support WAPI becoming an international standard. After persuading China to suspend the domestic implementation of WAPI, the US began to exclude the WAPI standards. Domestically, Intel launched its flagship Centrino platform, which tied Wi-Fi access to its processor and chipset, in China. With the popularity of Centrino PCs, Intel's Wi-Fi standard soon became the de facto WLAN standard in the Chinese market. Internationally, IEEE, the national representative for the US at the ISO, blocked WAPI both substantively and procedurally. Substantively, the IEEE argued that WAPI could only become 'an optional standard complementing 802.11i', because

- WAPI implementation [is] still optional under china's policy
- IEEE 802 feels the market can decide when to use which security standard
- Compatibility with the rest of 802.11 [is the] most important issue.[25]

The US Government first urged China to suspend domestic implementation of the WAPI as a compulsory national standard at the fifteenth JCCT. Then, the fact that WAPI was optional in China was used as 'evidence' by the IEEE to suggest that WAPI was not suitable as an international standard. This strategy—complemented by various procedural irregularities, administrative errors and visa denials for Chinese experts to participate in the ISO meetings—made the IEEE achieve its goal of having WAPI rejected and 802.11i adopted as a WLAN standard by the ISO.

The US also delicately shaped public perception of the WAPI standards. The only source found referring to the procedural irregularities (see Table 4.3) around WAPI is the official website of the CBWIPSG. In English, there was little coverage of these procedural issues in the media or academic publications. What was highlighted in the English-language publications was not the technical issues relating to the standard, but rather the origin of the WAPI

[25] Slide 4, IEEE 802.11-04/1547/ro.

in state planning (DeLacey *et al.*, 2006). The underlying concern was that because WAPI was sponsored by the national standardisation body—affiliated with the Chinese government—it was unreliable. This in a way indicates the increasing neo-technological nationalism of the Western governments as well. Should they believe in techno-globalism to reduce global barriers to the transfer and diffusion of technology and enhance global welfare (Kim *et al.*, 2020), they would ask whether WAPI could provide a better solution to the technical problem that it proposed to address and investigate the malpractices to guarantee fair competition.

### 4.4.2 *Ex Ante* Standards and the Compatibility Argument

One of the strongest criticisms of WAPI is that it is not compatible with the existing WLAN standard (Lee & Oh, 2006). The initial standard, the Wired Equivalent Privacy (WEP), had security flaws that led the Wi-Fi Alliance to implement another encryption system, Wi-Fi Protected Access (WPA). When the WPA was still not able to guarantee a satisfactory level of security, Wi-Fi Protected Access II (WPA2, IEEE 802.11i) was developed. Technologically, although WPA and WPA2 are not secure enough to survive hacker attacks, they are compatible with the other WLAN standards. WAPI developed an encryption algorithm that needs double authentication, so its security level is higher than WPA2, which requires only unilateral authentication. However, the compatibility problem was highlighted by the IEEE during the ISO balloting process.

However, this argument exaggerated the need for compatibility *ex ante*. Compatibility can only be an *ex post* problem because, *ex ante*, the market should be open so that candidates for a standard can compete. In the case of WAPI, when it was announced as a compulsory Chinese national standard, the market size of WLAN was very small. Statistics show that even in 2004, the same year WAPI was suspended indefinitely, only 1.29% of US inhabitants and 0.72% of UK inhabitants used Wi-Fi (UNICTTF, 2005). Even though the IEEE's 802.11 standards had been gradually developed since 1999, they were not yet the standards widely used in the market, even in the US. If the market share of the 802.11 standard was only 1%, there was no real basis on which to block the development of other standards. The WLAN market was still in the early stages of standards development. Since the network was not yet established, compatibility was not really the issue. The issue here was *ex ante* competition (Farrell *et al.*, 2007)—competition for market share.

Intel launched its Centrino platform for PC that integrated the Wi-Fi standard at the Chinese market in 2003. If WAPI had been implemented as compulsory national standards, Intel's market would have been lost. Intel lobbied the US government and successfully entered the Chinese market through its intervention in the fifteenth JCCT. After securing the Chinese market, Intel also led public opinion on the compatibility issue and the immaturity of WAPI. In 2006, Intel's Centrino had captured more than two-thirds of the Chinese PC market, meaning Wi-Fi had developed exponentially into a de facto standard. Thereafter, the competition was over, and compatibility did become an issue. Intel then took the position that it was 'up to the market to decide which standard is more feasible' (Xin & Wang, 2006).

The same logic also applies to the process of international WLAN standardisation. When WAPI was first proposed, the WLAN market was not yet established. But the process for WAPI to become an international standard was deeply flawed and ultimately delayed, so China eventually withdrew its application. At the same time, the international market for Wi-Fi was expanding and 802.11i was fast-tracked for balloting. In other words, compatibility was an issue after Wi-Fi was established as a de facto standard, but not initially. The debate over compatibility shows how US technological domination flows from a mix of regulatory, negotiating and organisational capabilities without which an innovative technology cannot of its own accord flower into a global standard.

### 4.4.3 Lessons Learned: China Embracing Inclusive Development in the ICT Sector

Lee and Oh (2008, p. 662) compared WAPI and Wireless Internet Platform for Interoperability (WIPI), a similar WLAN standard ratified in South Korea, and concluded that:

> Despite some similarities of 'aiming for a de jure national standard', [being] 'government-initiated' and 'anticipatory', the outcomes of the two efforts are different. WIPI was ratified in (South) Korea, while WAPI was indefinitely postponed as the national standard and failed to be ratified as an international standard ... Different outcomes (of these two standards) are attributed to differences in the openness of the standards and of institutional processes of standardisation, combined with the government role and the timing of market entry.

Indeed, the lack of transparency and exclusivity to Chinese entities in the drafting of the WAPI standards were the major reasons the US framed WAPI as a thrust of China's neo-technological nationalism. Until 2014, by which time the outcome of the competition between Wi-Fi and WAPI was clear, the US Information Technology Office (USITO) was still recommending the US government raise the issue of WAPI at the JCCT because 'WAPI are developed outside of international norms in an opaque manner that limits foreign participation' (USITO, 2014).

China also realised that WAPI failed because its formulation excluded the incumbent players in the industry—MNCs in particular. China changed course after the WAPI failure. It began to compromise and adopted a more inclusive strategy. For instance, China was inclusive in the development of standards for mobile telecommunications network technologies.

The role of China in the development of the cellular telecommunications networks can be summarised as being absent for 1G, a follower in 2G, making a breakthrough in 3G, catching up in 4G and leaping forward in 5G. In the late 1990s, China did not have any leading technologies in the 2G cellular network and had to pay significant amounts of patent royalties to patentholders like Qualcomm. In the development of 3G, China gained access to the Time Division-Code Division Multiple Access (TD-CDMA) technology standards from Siemens, which helped Chinese companies equip themselves with SEPs in this area. The Chinese TD-SCDMA (Li *et al.*, 2005), based on Siemens' TD-CDMA, was approved by the International Telecommunications Union (ITU) as one of the three standards for 3G, in parallel with the US standard, CDMA2000, and the EU standard, WCDMA (Chen, 2016). In this way, China was able to break through into 3G technology. In the 4G era, Huawei submitted 546 proposals for the core 4G Long-Term Evolution (LTE) standard by the end of 2014, accounting for 25% of the world's total (Huawei, 2015).

China also started early in the 5G standardisation process. In 2014, the MIIT, the NDRC and the Ministry of Science and Technology (MOST) jointly established 'IMT-2020' to promote cooperation with MNCs to develop 5G technologies. This inclusive approach differs from that of WAPI. The standard for 5G is not only technology-intensive but also capital-intensive, which means it can only be implemented in markets large enough to absorb the investment and ensure returns to investors. China Telecom had deployed 5G base stations in six Chinese cities by the end of 2017 (Zhang, 2017).

Despite China's move towards a more transparent and inclusive approach towards technology globalism, the US has embarked on the path of neo-technological nationalism. More broadly, the US has taken technological non-proliferation as a geopolitical strategy (Czerwiec, 2021). The US government perceived Huawei's competitive advantage in 5G and related technologies as a threat to its national interest and a challenge against its long-standing dominance of global communications networks.[26] While there have been concerns about the legitimacy of relevant measures from academics (Greenbaum, 2018), the 2019 Executive Order 13873 banned Huawei from selling 5G equipment to US companies.[27] The US has also enhanced export control since 2019 for dual-use technologies. In 2022, the US CHIPS and Science Act imposes a ten-year ban prohibiting US companies receiving subsidies under the Act from producing chips more advanced than 28 nanometres in China. Intel's Dalian plant founded in 2007 was sold to South Korea's SK Hynix.

## 4.5 Conclusion

Although the Chinese patent office has been the largest in the world for years, it is not enough for China to win the standardisation game only with impressive patent numbers. This case shows inconvenient processes of China's engagement in domestic and international standardisation. If we compare this case with China's international engagement in the regulation of GIs and the disclosure obligation, China's intention to participate in international standardisation was clearer and stronger. This is mainly because standards are crucial to China's objectives to achieve technological catch-up and independence. The DVD case shows standards are the lifeline of industry and allow firms to be positioned at the high ends of the smiling curve. However, for the same reason, standards are crucial for every state to maintain its competitive advantage. Such strategic importance of standards underpins each attempt China has made to promote WAPI as both a national and an international standard. This strategic importance also underpins each counteraction the US took to promote its own Wi-Fi standard. Chinese companies have climbed up the PCT ladder, but they were defeated in the battle over WAPI by a

---

[26] Letter from Aimen N. Mir, Deputy Assistant Secretary, Investment Security, Department of the Treasury, to Mark Plotkin, Covington & Burling LLP and Theodore Kassinger, O'Melveny & Myers LLP (5 March, 2018) available from https://www.sec.gov/Archives/edgar/data/804328/000110465918015036/a18-7296_7ex99d1.htm.

[27] Executive Order 13873 of 15 May 2019, Securing the Information and Communications Technology and Services Supply Chain.

combination of US non-compliance with its JCCT commitment, various procedural irregularities, administrative errors, and visa denials. Nonetheless, China gained a certain amount of leverage from its huge market size in particular for WAPI to become SEP for the mobile phone market. As shown by court decisions on *IWNComm vs Sony* and *IWNComm vs Apple*, Chinese patent regulators and courts have been active in the law implementation game. The thorny questions of FRAND interpretation, damage calculation for SEPs, and applying anti-monopoly law to patent holding-up and patent holding-out will all deepen Chinese regulators' understanding of distributive justice principles in relation to standardisation.

To make a standard come alive globally, a newcomer needs a set of complementary institutional, organisational and negotiating skills. While China has learned from the WAPI case and taken a more inclusive and open approach to its standardisation for 5G, it is still been perceived as taking an approach of neo-technological nationalism. China's 5G technologies have encountered paramount counteractions from the US, including blocking China's international standardisation, containing certain Chinese technology companies from operating in the US market, and restricting technology proliferation. With these counteractions being institutionalised, China's engagement in international standardisation for key technologies can be more difficult than it has experienced in WAPI.

There is considerable uncertainty in terms of the implications of China's engagement in international standardisation for global distributive justice. As the nature of the game is changing in the context of the US and Chinese national security-based imperatives, this is also a case where one needs to acknowledge other moral demands beyond distributive justice. Two observations can be briefly made though. First, while there are indeed hard security concerns that can justify certain measures that each country has taken, it is also important to distil economic protectionism from hard security concerns when measures are applied (Czerwiec, 2021). Second, if Chinese standardisation in 5G networks has indeed taken an open and collaborative approach and provided cost-effective solutions to access modern communications technologies, they can help populations in poor countries and poor regions within wealthy countries to overcome the digital divide. These efforts, therefore, contribute to enhancing global distributive justice following the cosmopolitan principle. This is a helpful way of thinking about global distributive justice as non-US users of 5G networks need to consider their own welfare in the digital economy rather than become collateral damage due to US national security concerns.

## References

Baldwin, R. (2013). Global Supply Chains: Why They Emerged, Why They Matter, and Where They are Going. In D. K. Elms & P. Low (Eds.), *Global Value Chains in a Changing World* (pp. 13–60). WTO Publications.

Braithwaite, J., & Drahos, P. (2000). *Global Business Regulation*. Cambridge University Press.

Büthe, T. (2010). The Power of Norms and the Norms of Power: Who Governs International Electrical and Electronic Technology? In D. D. Avant, M. Finnemore & S. K. Sell (Eds.), *Who Governs the Globe* (pp. 292–332). Cambridge University Press.

Cao, M. (2006). *The WAPI Alliance Was Formed Yesterday and 22 Companies Joined WAPI联盟昨成立22家企业加入* Available at: http://tech.sina.com.cn/t/2006-03-08/0907860767.shtml. Accessed 10 May 2018.

CESI. (2003). *Review on Technology Barriers Related with Intellectual Property*. Chinese Electronic Standards Institute. Available at: http://www.simmtester.com/page/news/showpubnews.asp?num=103. Accessed 11 May 2018.

Chen, J. (2016). *MIAO Yu: Twenty Billion Yuan of TD-SCDMA Investment Was Not Down the Drain 苗圩: 2000亿元的TD-SCDMA投入没有打水漂*. Available at: http://it.people.com.cn/n1/2016/0321/c1009-28215124.html. Accessed 10 May 2018.

Chen, S.-H. (2004). Taiwanese IT Firms' Offshore R&D in China and the Connection with the Global Innovation Network. *Research Policy, 33*(2), 337–349.

Cheng, P. (2009). *Ministry of Industry and Information Technology Releases Domestic Standard and Mobile Phones Can Have Access to Wireless LAN through WAPI 工信部放行国产标准WAPI接入手机无线局域网*. Available at: http://ip.people.com.cn/GB/136672/136680/9480778.html. Accessed 10 May 2018.

Cromer, Z. K. (2005). China's WAPI Policy: Security Measure or Trade Protectionism? *Duke Law & Technology Review, 4*(1), 1–13.

Czerwiec, J. (2021). Reprograming Geopolitical Firewalls: Technological Non-Proliferation and the Future of Investor-State Dispute Settlement. *ITA in Review: The Journal of the Institute for Transnational Arbitration, 3*(3), 57–140.

DeLacey, B. J., Herman, K., Kiron, D., Lerner, J., & Lo, W. S. (2006). *Government Intervention in Standardization: The Case of WAPI*. Available at: https://ssrn.com/abstract=930930

Drahos, P. (2021). *TRIPS Through a Military Looking Glass* (EUI Law Working Paper No. 2). Available at: https://cadmus.eui.eu/bitstream/handle/1814/70598/LAW_2021_02.pdf?sequence=1&isAllowed=y

EE Times. (2006). *ISO Rejects China's WLAN Standard*. Available at: https://www.eetimes.com/document.asp?doc_id=1159974. Accessed 11 May 2018.

Farrell, J. (1989). Standardization and Intellectual Property. *Jurimetrics, 30*(1), 35–50.

Farrell, J., Hayes, J., Shapiro, C., & Sullivan, T. (2007). Standard Setting, Patents, and Hold-up. *Antitrust Law Journal, 74*(3), 603–670.

Farrell, J., & Klemperer, P. (2007). Coordination and Lock-in: Competition with Switching Costs and Network Effects. In M. Armstrong & R. H. Porter (Eds.), *Handbook of Industrial Organization* (pp. 1967–2072).

Farrell, J., & Saloner, G. (1988). Coordination Through Committees and Markets. *The RAND Journal of Economics, 19*(2), 235–252.

Gao, B., Dunford, M., Norcliffe, G., & Liu, Z. (2017). Capturing Gains by Relocating Global Production Networks: The Rise of Chongqing's Notebook Computer Industry, 2008–2014. *Eurasian Geography and Economics, 58*(2), 231–257.

Gao, P. (2008). WAPI: A Chinese Attempt to Establish Wireless Standards and the International Coalition that Resisted. *Communications of the Association for Information Systems, 23*(1), 8.

Gasiorowski-Denis, E. (2016). *Chinese President Calls Standards "Common Language of the World"*. Available at: https://www.iso.org/news/2016/09/Ref2119.html. Accessed 11 May 2018.

Gereffi, G., Humphrey, J., & Sturgeon, T. (2005). The Governance of Global Value Chains. *Review of International Political Economy, 12*(1), 78–104.

Gibson, C. S. (2007). Globalization and the Technology Standards Game: Balancing Concerns of Protectionism and Intellectual Property in International Standards. *Berkeley Technology Law Journal, 22*(4), 1403–1484.

Greenbaum, E. (2018). *5G, Standard-Setting, and National Security*. Available at: https://harvardnsj.org/2018/07/5g-standard-setting-and-national-security/

Huang, T., & Zhang, W. (2017, October 10). China's Own Standards Lead the Smart Audiovisual Era 中国自主标准引领智能视听时代. *China Electronics News 中国电子报*, p. 3.

Huawei. (2015). *Huawei CFO Meng Wanzhou Says Huawei Created Customer Value and Maintained Effective Growth in 2014*. Available at: http://www.huawei.com/en/press-events/news/2015/01/hw_411126. Accessed 25 October 2022.

Kanellos, M. (2004). *Intel, Others to Stop Shipping Wi-Fi to China*. CNET. Available at: https://www.cnet.com/news/intel-others-to-stop-shipping-wi-fi-to-china/. Accessed 25 October 2022.

Katz, M. L., & Shapiro, C. (1985). Network Externalities, Competition, and Compatibility. *The American Economic Review, 75*(3), 424–440.

Kennedy, S. (2006). The Political Economy of Standards Coalitions: Explaining China's Involvement in High-Tech Standards Wars. *Asia Policy, 2*(1), 41–62.

Kim, M., Lee, H., & Kwak, J. (2020). The Changing Patterns of China's International Standardization in ICT under Techno-Nationalism: A Reflection through 5G Standardization. *International Journal of Information Management, 54*, 102145.

King, I. (2015). *Qualcomm Fined $975 Million in China, Sets Licensing Rates*. Bloomberg. Available at: https://www.bloomberg.com/news/articles/2015-02-09/china-fines-qualcomm-975-million-sets-patent-licensing-rates. Accessed 14 August 2022.

Kohno, M. (1995). Ideas and Foreign Policy: The Emergence of Technonationalism in US Policy Toward Japan. In D. P. Rapkin & W. P. Avery (Eds.), *National Competitiveness in a Global Economy*. Lynne Rienner Publishers.

Kraemer, K., Linden, G., & Dedrick, J. (2011). *Capturing Value in Global Networks: Apple's iPad and iPhone*. Available at: https://webzoom.freewebs.com/phsworldhistory/AP%20WH%20Unit%20V/Value_iPad_iPhone.pdf

Kwak, J., Lee, H., & Chung, D. B. (2012). The Evolution of Alliance Structure in China's Mobile Telecommunication Industry and Implications for International Standardization. *Telecommunications Policy, 36*(10), 966–976.

Lee, H., & Oh, S. (2006). The Evolution of Alliance Structure in China's Mobile Telecommunication Industry and Implications for International Standardization. *The Journal of Strategic Information Systems, 15*(3), 177–195.

Lee, H., & Oh, S. (2008). The Political Economy of Standards Setting by Newcomers: China's WAPI and South Korea's WIPI. *Telecommunications Policy, 32*(9), 662–671.

Lemley, M. A., & Shapiro, C. (2006). Patent Holdup and Royalty Stacking. *Texas Law Review, 85*(7), 1991–2050.

Li, B., Xie, D., Cheng, S., Chen, J., Zhang, P., Zhu, W., & Li, B. (2005). Recent Advances on TD-SCDMA in China. *IEEE Communications Magazine, 43*(1), 30–37.

Liebowitz, S. J., & Margolis, S. E. (1994). Network Externality: An Uncommon Tragedy. *The Journal of Economic Perspectives, 8*(2), 133–150.

Lin, A. (2009). The WAPI Internationalization Process Has Made Important Progress, and There Are Hidden Secrets Behind the US. Compromise WAPI 国际化进程获重要进展 美方妥协背后暗藏重大玄机. *IT Times Weekly IT时代周刊* (13), 26–27.

Lu, J., & Gao, Z. (2010). A Research on TNCs Charging Patent Royalties from DVD Manufacturers in China 跨国公司在华DVD专利收费研究. *International Business 国际商务——对外经济贸易大学学报*, (3), 76–82.

McGregor, J. (2010). *China's Drive for 'Indigenous Innovation': A Web of Industrial Policies*. Global Regulatory Cooperation Project and US Chamber of Commerce. Available at: https://www.uschamber.com/sites/default/files/legacy/reports/100728_chinareport.pdf

Mudambi, R. (2008). Location, Control and Innovation in Knowledge-intensive Industries. *Journal of Economic Geography, 8*(5), 699–725.

Qin, L. (2010). *IPhones Supporting WAPI+WiFi Function Got Approved in China 苹果支持WAPI+WiFi功能iPhone在中国通过审批*. Available at: http://tech.sina.com.cn/t/2010-05-04/18204144259.shtml. Accessed 10 May 2018.

Shin, D. H., & Kim, W. Y. (2008). Forecasting Customer Switching Intention in Mobile Service: An Exploratory Study of Predictive Factors in Mobile Number Portability. *Technological Forecasting and Social Change, 75*(6), 854–874.

Shin, D. H., Kim, H., & Hwang, J. (2015). Standardization Revisited: A Critical Literature Review on Standards and Innovation. *Computer Standards & Interfaces, 38*, 152–157.

Shin, N., Kraemer, K. L., & Dedrick, J. (2012). Value Capture in the Global Electronics Industry: Empirical Evidence for the "Smiling Curve" Concept. *Industry and Innovation, 19*(2), 89–107.

Shintaku, J., Ogawa, K., & Yoshimoto, T. (2006). Architecture-based Approaches to International Standardization and Evolution of Business Models. *東京大学ものづくり経営研究センター, ディスカッションペーパ MMRC-96*.

Sunny Li, S., Hao, C., & Erin, G. P. M. (2010). Moving Upward in Global Value Chains: The Innovations of Mobile Phone Developers in China. *Chinese Management Studies, 4*(4), 305–321.

Suttmeier, R. P., & Yao, X. (2004). *China's Post-WTO Technology Policy: Standards, Software, and the Changing Nature of Techno-Nationalism*. The National Bureau of Asian Research.

Suttmeier, R. P., Yao, X., & Tan, A. Z. (2006) *Standards of Power? Technology, Institutions, and Politics in the Development of China's National Standards Strategy*. The National Bureau of Asian Research.

Taylor, J. (2013). *DVD Frequently Asked Questions (and Answers)*. Available at: https://www.dvddemystified.com/dvdfaq.html#1.5. Accessed 11 May 11.

Timmer, M. P., Erumban, A. A., Los, B., Stehrer, R., & de Vries, G. J. (2014). Slicing up Global Value Chains. *The Journal of Economic Perspectives, 28*(2), 99–118.

UNICTTF. (2005). *Measuring ICT: The Global Status of ICT Indicators*. United Nations ICT Task Force. Available at: https://www.itu.int/ITU-D/ict/partnership/material/05-42742%20GLOBAL%20ICT.pdf

USITC. (2011). *China: Effects of Intellectual Property Infringement and Indigenous Innovation Policies on the US Economy*. US International Trade Commission (USITC) Investigation No. 332–519. Available at: https://www.usitc.gov/publications/332/pub4226.pdf

USITO. (2014). *United States Information Technology Office (USITO) Recommendations for 2014 JCCT Information Communications Technology (ICT) Industry Priorities: Written Submission to the US Department of Commerce and the United States Trade Representative*. Available at: https://www.tiaonline.org/wp-content/uploads/2018/02/USITO-2014-JCCT-Joint-Submission-FINAL_0.pdf

USTR. (2004). *The U.S.-China JCCT: Outcomes on Major U.S. Trade Concerns*. Available at: https://ustr.gov/archive/Document_Library/Fact_Sheets/2004/The_US-China_JCCT_Outcomes_on_Major_US_Trade_Concerns.html

Wang, L. P., & Jia, F. (2010). Analysis on Supply Chain of Manufacturing Enterprise Product Service System. *2010 IEEE International Conference on Emergency Management and Management Sciences (ICEMMS)* (pp. 126–129). IEEE.

WIPO. (2017). *Record Year for International Patent Applications in 2016; Strong Demand Also for Trademark and Industrial Design Protection: Annex II*. PR/2017/804. Available at: http://www.wipo.int/pressroom/en/articles/2017/article_0002.html. Accessed: 10 May 2018.

Xin, Y., & Wang, J. (2006). *Four Major Telecom Operators Join the WAPI Alliance 四大运营商加盟WAPI联盟*. Available at: https://finance.qq.com/a/20060308/000428.htm. Accessed 11 May 2018.

Zhang, S. (2017). *China Telecom Announces the Official Opening of 5G Base Stations! Six Cities Were First Selected 中国电信宣布正式开通5G基站!首批选择这六大城市*. Available at: http://tc.people.com.cn/n1/2017/1207/c183008-29691245.html. Accessed 11 May 2018.

Zhao, Y. (2010). China's Pursuits of Indigenous Innovations in Information Technology Developments: Hopes, Follies and Uncertainties. *Chinese Journal of Communication, 3*(3), 266–289.

# 5

# China's Bilateral IP Engagement: A Look into the Chinese FTAs

## 5.1 Introduction

This chapter examines China's bilateral IP engagement. Specifically, it analyses how China has engaged with a range of countries in setting IP standards in its free trade agreements (FTAs) and implications for global distributive justice. As China has signed more than 20 FTAs, it is beyond the scope of this chapter to analyse in detail the IP provisions in each FTA. Instead, this chapter will focus on the relationship between Chinese FTAs and the TRIPS standards. Specifically, it classifies IP provisions in Chinese FTAs into four categories according to their relations with the TRIPS Agreement: passive defensive, active defensive, TRIPS-plus, and active promotion.

The relationship between Chinese FTAs and the TRIPS Agreement needs to be understood in the global context after the TRIPS Agreement. Developed countries—in particular, the US and members of the European Union—have long used bilateral FTAs as an instrument to promote more extensive IP protection (Drahos, 2002; Sell, 2010a). In the post-TRIPS era, FTAs have become a more effective instrument US to enhance TRIPS-plus standards because the most-favoured-nation (MFN) principle in TRIPS Agreement requires any advantage, favour, privilege or immunity in IP stipulated in one FTA to be available immediately and unconditionally to all other WTO members. The US has initiated vertical forum-shifting through FTAs and a couple of plurilateral IP agreements—in particular, the Anti-Counterfeiting Trade Agreement (ACTA) and Trans-Pacific Partnership (TPP)—to enhance global IP standards beyond the TRIPS Agreement (Sell,



W. Cheng, *China in Global Governance of Intellectual Property*, Palgrave Socio-Legal Studies, https://doi.org/10.1007/978-3-031-24370-7_5

2010b). While FTAs have become a critical node for the US and the EU to push up global IP standards, their strategies have encountered protests from both state and non-state actors. Developing countries opposed any TRIPS-plus standards because they had already made great concessions in the TRIPS negotiations. In addition to firmly adhering to TRIPS standards, developing countries actively promoted the Development Agenda at the WIPO. Developing countries also employed forum-shifting, promoting IP standards in the CBD and at the World Health Organization (WHO) on genetic resources, access to medicine and human rights. These practices unfolded a possible alternative standard-setting for valuable intangibles not originally included in the TRIPS Agreement.

The dynamics between FTAs and the TRIPS Agreement in the post-TRIPS era make China's bilateral IP engagement an important case, in particular, how Chinese FTAs have set IP standards as compared with the TRIPS Agreement. In terms of implications for global distributive justice, the dynamics between IP standards in bilateral FTAs and TRIPS Agreement can be simply stated in two dimensions: First, the TRIPS Agreement has already set higher standards than many developing countries could afford (Richards, 2004). So, the more TRIPS-plus standards are included in an FTA, the more protection will be offered to the IP rightsholders and the fewer policy spaces will be left in national law for balancing other social welfare. Second, this book has briefly introduced the Confucian golden principle of non-imposition in Chapter 1. The more coercion is used in a trade negotiation by the more powerful party, the further that party deviates from the Confucian golden principle of non-imposition.

### 5.1.1 IP Provisions in Chinese FTAs: An Overview

China first started its FTAs with developing countries such as the Maldives, Mauritius, and Costa Rica. In recent years, China also signed FTAs with developed countries like South Korea, Iceland, Switzerland, and Australia. So far, China has signed 21 FTAs since 2002, with 10 FTAs under negotiation and eight under consideration (Table 5.1).[1]

Intellectual property was not mentioned in the first few Chinese FTAs, which were concluded with the Association of Southeast Asian Nations (ASEAN), Pakistan, and Singapore. It was not mentioned in the internal

[1] *Source* China FTA Framework, Ministry of Commerce of China, Available from: http://fta.mofcom.gov.cn/english/index.shtml. In addition to the FTAs, China signed bilateral agreements that include IP provisions, including the European Union–China GI Cooperation and Protection Agreement (2020) and the United States–China Economic and Trade Agreement (2020).

**Table 5.1** IP provisions in Chinese FTAs (as of 16 April 2022)

| FTAs already signed (21) | |
|---|---|
| FTAs with IP provisions (12) | FTAs without IP provisions (9) |
| China–Chile FTA (2005) | China–ASEAN FTA (2002) |
| China–Chile FTA Upgrade (2017) | China–ASEAN FTA Upgrade (2015) |
| China–New Zealand FTA (2008) | China–Pakistan FTA (2005) |
| China–Peru FTA (2009) | China–Pakistan FTA (Phase II) (2019) |
| China–Costa Rica FTA (2010) | China–Singapore FTA (2008) |
| China–Iceland FTA (2014) | China–Singapore FTA upgrade (2018) |
| China–Switzerland FTA (2013) | China–Cambodia FTA (2020) |
| China–South Korea FTA (2014) | China Mainland and Hong Kong Closer Economic and Partnership Arrangement |
| China–Australia FTA (2015) | China Mainland and Macau Closer Economic and Partnership Arrangement |
| China–Georgia FTA (2017) | |
| China–Maldives FTA (2017) (text not available) | |
| China–Mauritius FTA (2019) | |
| *FTAs under negotiation (10)* | |
| China–Gulf Cooperation Council (GCC) FTA | |
| China–Japan–Korea FTA | |
| China–Sri Lanka FTA | |
| China–Israel FTA | |
| China–Norway FTA | |
| China–Moldova FTA | |
| China–Panama FTA | |
| China–Korea FTA Second Phase | |
| China–Palestine FTA | |
| China–Peru FTA Upgrade | |
| *FTAs under consideration (8)* | |
| China–Colombia FTA Joint Feasibility Study | |
| China–Fiji FTA Joint Feasibility Study | |
| China–Nepal FTA Joint Feasibility Study | |
| China–Papua New Guinea FTA Joint Feasibility Study | |
| China–Canada FTA Joint Feasibility Study | |
| China–Bangladesh FTA Joint Feasibility Study | |
| China–Mongolia FTA Joint Feasibility Study | |
| China–Switzerland FTA Upgrade Joint Feasibility Study | |

market coordination agreements with Hong Kong and Macau. Even as late as 2020, the Chinese–Cambodia FTA did not have an IP provision either. IP first appeared in China–Chile FTA as a single article in the chapter on cooperation. The China–Peru and China–Costa Rica FTAs take a similar approach as China–Chile FTA, introducing provisions that are of common interest to developing countries such as public health, protection for genetic resources, and traditional knowledge and cooperation. Except for border measures in China–Peru FTA, these FTAs did not introduce any TRIPS-plus obligations.

The China–New Zealand FTA was the first comprehensive Chinese FTA to cover trade in goods, services and investment, and the first FTA China signed with a developed country. An independent IP chapter in this agreement covered issues such as IP principles, contact points, notification and exchange of information, cooperation and capacity-building, genetic resources, traditional knowledge and folklore, and consultation. Much of the content is procedural. Like China–Chile FTA, the China—New Zealand FTA did not create any TRIPS-plus obligations.

In 2005, Iceland became the first European country to recognise the market economy status of China. Both countries started an FTA feasibility study in 2007; however, the negotiations lasted for eight years. In its IP chapter, this FTA confirms the principle of adhering to the TRIPS Agreement and the principle of balancing interests. It also lists other multilateral IP agreements both countries have joined. Unlike China's earlier FTAs with developing countries, which actively promoted protecting GIs, genetic resources and traditional knowledge, the agreement with Iceland does not involve any of these issues. Also differing from other FTAs with developed countries, this FTA does not include any substantive provisions either confirming TRIPS standards or promoting TRIPS-plus provisions.

The China–Switzerland FTA sets high standards for IP, especially on data exclusivity for biologics. With 22 articles over 12 pages, the IP Chapter in this agreement is among the longest in any Chinese FTA. Although Switzerland usually negotiates trade agreements together with Norway, Iceland, and Liechtenstein in the framework of the European Free Trade Association (EFTA) (SECO, 2018), China–Switzerland FTA was not negotiated under the EFTA.

In 2005 China and Australia started their marathon negotiations, which lasted for 10 years. As in China–Switzerland FTA, the FTA with Australia creates occasional TRIPS-plus standards in the IP chapter. South Korea is China's largest FTA partner, and their 2015 agreement includes the most detailed IP chapter with the largest number of TRIPS-plus standards among all Chinese FTAs (see Sect. 5.4). The FTAs with Georgia and Mauritius were concluded later than those with Switzerland, South Korea, and Australia, but they have shorter IP chapters with fewer TRIPS-plus provisions.

### 5.1.2 China's FTA Strategies in the Global Context

Among China's 21 FTAs, negotiations have accelerated since 2007 when China made FTA negotiation and implementation a national strategy at the Seventeenth National Congress of the CCP (Xinhua News Agency, 2007). The political will to promote Chinese FTAs was reinforced in a 2015 Opinion by the State Council.[2] The FTA strategy deploys objectives to facilitate trade liberalisation through FTAs. The short-term objective is to speed up FTA negotiations, further liberalise existing FTAs and promote negotiations with neighbouring countries and regions. By doing this, it is expected that China's trading values with FTA partners reach or exceed the level of most developed countries and emerging economies. The objectives in the mid-to-long terms are to create a global network of FTAs with neighbouring countries and regions, countries along the Belt and Road and priority countries on all five continents, and to liberalise and facilitate transnational trade for Chinese enterprises and bilateral investment.

As a response to backlashes against globalisation, Chinese President Xi Jinping's opening address at the 2017 World Economic Forum in Davos, Switzerland, declared that China would keep its door wide open and called for the international community to take steps to fix the current problems affecting free trade and economic globalisation, rather than backing away from them (Anderlini *et al.*, 2017). In this context, China has defended the WTO as the primary multilateral trade forum and accelerated its FTA negotiations to defend the international order of free trade.

### 5.1.3 Categories of Chinese IP Provisions in Its FTAs

This section categorises Chinese FTA provisions into four types according to their relations with the TRIPS Agreement: passive defensive, active defensive, TRIPS-plus, and active promotion. Specifically:

- Passive defensive (PD): FTAs that do not explicitly mention IP.
- Active defensive (AD): FTAs that explicitly refer to TRIPS Agreement or repeat specific TRIPS provisions in their text.
- TRIPS-plus: FTAs that provide more extensive protection than TRIPS or eliminate options available in TRIPS.

[2] State Council (2015) Several Opinions of the State Council on Accelerating the Implementation of the Strategies for Free Trade Areas国务院关于加快实施自由贸易区战略的若干意见 no. 69 [2015].

- Active promotion (AP): FTAs that promote a rival standard not originally covered in TRIPS.

Among the four categories, both passive defensive and active defensive FTAs maintain the TRIPS standards. TRIPS-plus provisions in FTAs refer to two circumstances: 1) FTAs requiring more extensive protection than TRIPs Agreement; and 2) FTAs eliminating an option for a member conferred by the TRIPS Agreement (Drahos, 2001). A typical example of the latter is that the TRIPS Agreement offers a member the option to decide whether 'visually perceptible' can be used as a requirement for trademark registration. China–South Korea FTA provides that 'visually perceptible' may not be used as a requirement for trademark registration. Without this requirement, the scope for trademark protection becomes broader: distinctive sounds and smells can be registered as trademarks.

Active promotion refers to rules that set alternative standards in areas the TRIPS Agreement has not touched, including overlaps between IP and other issues such as genetic resources. For instance, the disclosure obligation in Chinese FTAs belongs to the active promotion category. China and other developing-country trading partners consolidated alternative rulemaking in FTAs even though there is no treaty obligation to set such a standard. Table 5.2 illustrates the landscape of IP provisions in Chinese FTAs in these four categories.

## 5.2 Chinese FTAs Defending TRIPS Standards

### 5.2.1 Passive-Defensive Chinese FTAs

Of the 21 Chinese FTAs (excluding China–Maldives FTA for which the text is not available), nine FTAs do not mention IP at all and can be categorised as passive-defensive FTAs. These include the Chinese FTAs with ASEAN countries, Pakistan, and Singapore and their upgrades, China–Cambodia FTA, and China's closer economic arrangement with Hong Kong and Macau. Most ASEAN countries, Pakistan and Cambodia are developing countries, and the main purpose of these FTAs is to promote exports and imports by eliminating tariff barriers. Therefore, no IP provisions are consistent with their trade liberalisation objective. Singapore is a developed country, and it is not clear why there is no IP chapter in China–Singapore FTA. The China–Cambodia FTA, concluded in 2020, is the most recent to not have an IP provision.

Table 5.2 Intellectual property in Chinese FTAs: A comparison with the TRIPS agreement

| | | China–Chile | China–New Zealand | China–Peru | China–Costa Rica | China–Iceland |
|---|---|---|---|---|---|---|
| Issues included in the TRIPSAgreement | Adhere to TRIPS Agreement as a principle | AD | AD | AD | AD | AD |
| | The balance of interest and preventing abuse of IP | AD | AD | AD | AD | AD |
| | The exception to national treatment | | | | | |
| | Geographical indications | AP | | AP | AP | |
| | Border measures | AD | | AD | AD | |
| | Patentability | | | | | |
| | Protection of undisclosed information | | | | | |
| | Data exclusivity for biologics | | | | | |
| | Protection of industrial designs | | | | | |
| | 'Visually perceptible' as a trademark registration requirement | | | | | |
| | Protection of certification and collective marks | | | | | |
| | Well-known trademark | | | | | |
| | Protection of prior rights in trademark registration | | | | | |
| | Acquisition of the IP right | | | | | |
| | Opportunity for opposition | | | | | |
| | Provisional measures | | | | | |
| | Civil remedies | | | | | |
| | Criminal enforcement | | | | | |

(continued)

Table 5.2 (continued)

| | | China–Chile | China–New Zealand | China–Peru | China–Costa Rica | China–Iceland |
|---|---|---|---|---|---|---|
| Issues not covered by the TRIPSAgree-ment | Protect genetic resources and traditional knowledge | | AP | AP | AP | |
| | Public health | AP | | AP | AP | |
| | Incentives to enterprises for innovation | | | | AP | |
| | Contact point/IP committee | | AP | | AP | |
| | Information exchange, cooperation, capacity-building | AP | AP | | | AP |
| | Consultations before disputes | | AP | | | AP |
| | Limit the Internet Service Provider (ISP) liability | | | | | |
| | Exhaustion of rights | | | | | |
| | Obligations are minimum obligations | | | | | |
| | Transparency in IP granting procedure | | | | | |
| | Collective management of copyright | | | | | |
| | ISP liability | | | | | |
| | Publish judicial and administrative adjudications | | | | | |

| | | China–Switzerland | China–South Korea | China–Australia | China–Georgia | China–Mauritius |
|---|---|---|---|---|---|---|
| Issues included in the TRIP-SAgreement | Adhere to TRIPS Agreement as a principle | AD | AD | AD | AD | AD |
| | The balance of interest and preventing abuse of IP | AD | AD | AD | AD | AD |
| | The exception to national treatment | | AD | AD | | |
| | Geographical indications | AP | | AD | TP | |
| | Border measures | TP | TP | AD | | |
| | Patentability | AD | AD | | AD | |
| | Protection of undisclosed information | | AD | AD | | |
| | Data exclusivity for biologics | TP | | | | |
| | Protection of industrial designs | AD and TP | AD and TP | | | |
| | 'Visually perceptible' as a trademark registration requirement | | TP | TP | TP | |
| | Protection of certification and collective marks | | | TP | | |
| | Well-known trademark | | AD | AD | AD | |
| | Protection of prior rights in trademark registration | | AD | | | |
| | Acquisition of the IP right | AD | | | | |
| | Opportunity for opposition | | | AD | AD | |
| | Provisional measures | AD | AD | | | |
| | Civil remedies | TP | TP | | | |
| | Criminal enforcement | AD | AD | AD | AD | |

(continued)

**Table 5.2** (continued)

| | | China–Switzerland | China–South Korea | China–Australia | China–Georgia | China–Mauritius |
|---|---|---|---|---|---|---|
| Issues not covered by the TRIP-SAgreement | Protect genetic resources and traditional knowledge | AP | AP | AP | AP | |
| | Public health | AP | AP | AP | AP | AP |
| | Incentives to enterprises for innovation | | | | | |
| | Contact point/IP committee | | AP | | | |
| | Information exchange, cooperation, capacity-building | | AP | | AP | AP |
| | Consultations before disputes | | | | | |
| | Limit the Internet Service Provider (ISP) liability | | | AP | | |
| | Exhaustion of rights | | | AP | AP | |
| | Obligations are minimum obligations | | TP | TP | TP | |
| | Transparency in IP granting procedure | | | AP or TP | AP or TP | |
| | Collective management of copyright | | | TP | TP | |
| | ISP liability | | | AP | | |
| | Publish judicial and administrative adjudications | | TP | | | |

AD = active defensive; AP = active promotion; TP = TRIPS-plus

Most of the Chinese FTAs without IP provisions were negotiated at the beginning of the twenty-first century, just after China's WTO accession. Amendments to Chinese IP law on the eve of its WTO accession have been criticised because they set higher standards than required at that stage of development (Wei, 1997). Therefore, defending the TRIPS Agreement was a priority for China in negotiating its early FTAs. The China–Cambodia FTA is an exception to this early practice. In this negotiation, China could introduce more extensive TRIPS-plus standards as its domestic IP enforcement standards are already high. Nonetheless, the passive-defensive position in China–Cambodia FTA indicates that China has refrained from imposing TRIPS-plus standards on its developing trading partners.

In addition to the nine passive-defensive FTAs discussed above, the IP provisions in the remaining twelve FTAs can be further divided into three categories: active defensive, active promotion and TRIPS-plus. As one FTA may include provisions that can be classified into all three categories, these three categories are at the level of provisions. For instance, China–Switzerland FTA contains provisions reiterating the TRIPS provisions on border measures (active defensive), IP and public health, protection for genetic resources and traditional knowledge (active promotion), and six-year data exclusivity for biologics (TRIPS-plus). These categories will be discussed in the following sections.

### 5.2.2 Active Defensive Provisions in Chinese FTAs

The active defensive provisions have substantially increased in China's FTAs with Switzerland, South Korea and Australia. Specifically, these Chinese FTAs have made explicit reiterations of the TRIPS standards on the following issues:

- The principle of adhering to TRIPS standards. It appears as a basic principle in all eight Chinese FTAs explicitly mentioning IP.
- The possible exceptions to national treatment in TRIPS Agreement appear in China–Australia FTA.
- The requirement for patentability, which reiterates the TRIPS requirement in Article 27, in China–Switzerland FTA and China–South Korea FTA.
- The protection for well-known trademarks in China–South Korea, China–Australia and China–Georgia FTAs. These provisions refer further to relevant provisions of the Paris Convention. Given the Paris Convention has been incorporated into TRIPS Agreement, these provisions are still actively defensive of the TRIPS Agreement.

- Provisional measures and criminal enforcement in both China–Switzerland FTA and China–South Korea FTA. There are substantial similarities between Article 11.20.1of China–Switzerland FTA and TRIPS Article 50, Article 11.20.2 of China–Switzerland FTA and TRIPS Article 44, Article 11.21 of China–Switzerland FTA and TRIPS Article 61.
- TRIPS provisions on prior rights, IP acquisition and opportunity to submit opposition are reiterated in China–South Korea FTA, China–Switzerland FTA and China–Australia FTA, respectively.
- In regard to border measures, Chinese FTAs with Peru, Costa Rica and Australia contain provisions actively defending the TRIPS standards. In Chinese FTAs with Switzerland and South Korea, TRIPS-plus standards are provided on this issue.
- In the protection for undisclosed information, TRIPS provisions are reiterated in the FTAs with South Korea and Australia.

The specific rules mentioned above will not be elaborated on in this chapter, as the content for active defensive provisions is to reiterate what the TRIPS Agreement has already prescribed not to create new standards. Although active defensive provisions do not introduce additional international obligations for China, their effects vary with the types of rules they defend. Some active defensive provisions in Chinese FTAs were introduced to maintain the minimum standards of the TRIPS Agreement and to prevent derogation from such standards. Most of the active defensive rules appearing in China's FTAs with Switzerland, South Korea, and Australia fall into this group.

Another group of active defensive rules in Chinese FTAs repeats the flexibilities of the TRIPS Agreement, including the TRIPS principles and rules that are open to WTO members' interpretation or implementation. The principles of balance of interest (TRIPS Article 7) and preventing abuse of IP rights (TRIPS Article 8) appear in all Chinese FTAs that have IP provisions. For the balance of interest principle, Chinese FTAs reiterate the interests at stake—namely, that the IP system should 'achieve a balance between rights of right holders and the legitimate interests of users and the community with regard to the protected subject matter'.[3] These reiterations manifest China's expectation to balance IP protection and distribution of knowledge in these FTAs, instead of continuously promoting IP standards as what has happened in the US and EU FTAs. This principle helps to resist the entitlement-based

[3] See Article 110.1 of China–Chile FTA, Article 160.2 of China–New Zealand FTA, Article 144.2 of China–Peru FTA, Article 109.2 of China–Costa Rica FTA, Article 63.1 of China–Iceland FTA, Article 11.1.4 of China–Switzerland FTA, Article 15.1.2 of China–South Korea FTA, and Article 11.1.4 of China–Australia FTA.

IP framing developed by recent US and EU FTAs (Dreyfuss & Frankel, 2014). By emphasising the function of IP to both promote innovation and facilitate technological dissemination, this principle also enables Chinese FTAs to actively promote rules on the balance between IP and public health, as well as the disclosure obligation. With regard to the principle of preventing IP abuse,[4] such reiteration has practical significance for China. The recent judicial activism emerging from local courts and other anti-monopoly law agencies indicates the robust implementation of anti-monopoly regulations in China to prevent IP abuse (Xiang, 2021). Reiterating the principle of preventing IP abuse may also set a foundation for China to further export potential anti-monopoly norms through its FTAs in the future.

Provisions on certain IP issues were included as active defensive provisions in early Chinese FTAs but have evolved into TRIPS-plus provisions later on. A typical example is border measures. China's FTAs with Chile, Peru, and Costa Rica include active defensive provisions on this issue, but the FTA with South Korea introduced TRIPS-plus standards, both in the scope of the inspection and in the types of IP to be protected (see Sect. 5.4.4).

## 5.3 Active Promotion of New Standards in Chinese FTAs

As clarified in the previous definition, active promotion means both parties are committed to promoting a standard not mentioned in the TRIPS Agreement. These are standards that parties introduce to an FTA anyway when they are not obliged to do so. While active-promotion provisions are often voluntary soft rules with little legal consequences for non-compliance, they are particularly useful to understand the intentions and interests of the FTAs parties. This section explores active-promotion rules in Chinese FTAs on the following issues: protection for genetic resources and traditional knowledge, IP and public health, and limits to Internet service provider (ISP) liabilities. Active promotion rules for enhancing cooperation and information exchange will also be discussed.

[4] See Article 110.5 of China–Chile FTA, Article 144.4 of China–Peru FTA, Article 110.3 of China–Costa Rica FTA, Article 11.1.5 of China–Switzerland FTA, Article 15.2.3 of China–South Korea FTA, and Article 11.1.6 of China–Australia FTA.

### 5.3.1 Protection of Genetic Resources and Traditional Knowledge

As discussed in Chapter 3, China, as one of the mega-biodiverse countries in the world, has incorporated the disclosure obligation into its Patent Law. Provisions on genetic resources in Chinese FTAs are broader in scope than that for disclosure obligations in *Patent Law* (2008).

So far, China has actively promoted protecting genetic resources in its FTAs with seven countries: New Zealand, Peru, Costa Rica, Switzerland, South Korea, Australia, and Georgia. Among these FTA partners, Peru, and Costa Rica are developing countries, and both have domestic legislation in place on the disclosure obligation.[5] Australia and Costa Rica have signed the Nagoya Protocol while China, Peru, South Korea, and Switzerland have ratified it.[6] These mutual interests constitute the basis on which to include protecting genetic resources and traditional knowledge in these FTAs.

The focus of each of these seven FTA provisions on genetic resources is slightly different. The China–New Zealand FTA was the first Chinese FTA to mention the protection for genetic resources and traditional knowledge, with no binding requirement for the parties. The agreement with Peru was the first Chinese FTA to include provisions on the disclosure obligation, while China–Costa Rica FTA introduced the concept of access and benefit-sharing (ABS) for the first time. China–Switzerland FTA is the only Chinese FTA to address the legal consequences of the disclosure obligation. China–South Korea FTA, the first Chinese FTA signed after the Nagoya Protocol, reiterates certain requirements in that protocol.

Despite these differences, the Chinese FTA provisions on genetic resources and traditional knowledge share some commonalities. First, these provisions are more declarative than creating legally binding obligations and their inclusion demonstrates China's support for protecting genetic resources and traditional knowledge. However, since these rules are non-binding, there are flexibilities for the parties to choose the most suitable approach in terms of implementation within their capacity and available resources. For instance, while China–New Zealand FTA has a provision on this issue, the real commitment seems to be low—Article 165 of this FTA provides that 'subject to each Party's international obligations, the Parties may establish appropriate

5 In Peru, the disclosure obligation is provided in Article 4(c) No. 27811 *Biodiversity Law: A Law Introducing a Protection Regime for the Collective Knowledge of Indigenous Peoples derived from Biological Resources*, published 10 August 2002. In Costa Rica, the disclosure obligation is provided in Article 25, Rules on Access (2003).

6 From the website of the CBD: https://www.cbd.int/abs/nagoya-protocol/signatories/ [Accessed 19 September 2022].

measures to protect genetic resources, traditional knowledge and folklore' (emphasis added by author). Similar provisions can be found in Chinese FTAs with Switzerland and Australia.

The flexibilities in the genetic resource and traditional knowledge provisions are also indicated by the inconsistency of the provisions. If an FTA partner is not interested in such provisions, they can opt out and the FTA would not mention genetic resource protection at all. This explains why the issue does not consistently appear in all Chinese FTAs. In addition, later FTAs may derogate from stronger commitments previously. While China–Peru FTA first introduced disclosure obligation, this was not repeated in China's later FTAs with Australia, South Korea, and Switzerland. This is different from the IP provisions in US FTAs where a later FTA is negotiated based on the template of a previous one and a chain effect is expected over time (Morin, 2009). Such flexibility indicates that China may not attempt to dominate its FTA negotiations, but it also means that there is a lack of political will from China to promote alternative rulemaking in general.

In summary, protecting genetic resources and traditional knowledge demonstrates China's willingness to actively promote rules that were not originally included in the TRIPS Agreement. China has incorporated non-binding principles for protecting genetic resources into various FTAs, allowing for flexibility in implementation. However, the diversity of the Chinese FTAs also indicates a lack of structural design of their texts which may be due to the lack of coordination among different negotiating teams (Liu, 2016). Consequently, China's efforts for alternative rulemaking may not be sufficient to construct actionable and binding obligations for itself and its FTA partners.

### 5.3.2 Intellectual Property and Public Health

IP and public health were provided in six Chinese FTAs—those with Chile, Peru, Costa Rica, Switzerland, South Korea, and Australia—with similar clauses. IP and public health have been actively promoted in these FTAs by the reiteration of the principle in the *Doha Declaration on the TRIPS Agreement and Public Health* (2001), the *Decision on Implementation of Paragraph 6 of the Doha Declaration* (2003) and the *Geneva Protocol Amending TRIPS Agreement* (2005). The only exception is that the Geneva Protocol was not mentioned in China's FTAs with Chile or Peru.

FTA provisions on IP and public health are consistent with the progress of Chinese domestic IP laws, which is similar to the case of FTA provisions on genetic resource protection. The key issue addressed in the international negotiation of the Doha Declaration and its implementation is compulsory licensing. In China's *Patent Law* (2008), a whole chapter (Ch. VI, Arts 48–58) was devoted to the compulsory licensing mechanism. Article 49 of the *Patent Law* (2008) authorises the patent regulator to use compulsory licensing during a national emergency, when an extraordinary event occurs or when the public interests so require. Article 50 authorises the exportation of drugs manufactured under compulsory licences to other countries based on relevant international treaties. This provision is a domestic arrangement to implement Paragraph 6 of the Doha Declaration. Chinese FTAs with Peru, Costa Rica, Switzerland, South Korea, and Australia were signed after the promulgation of the *Patent Law* (2008), therefore, active promotion of public health in these Chinese FTAs will not introduce further implementation problems for China.

In addition to the reiteration of the TRIPS Agreement or subsequent revisions, China–Australia FTA adds a principle of retaining sovereign regulatory power over public health. Its Article 11.1(g) authorises the use of regulatory power by the parties to take appropriate measures to protect public health and nutrition as long as the measures are consistent with the TRIPS Agreement and the IP chapter of China–Australia FTA. This provision was probably proposed by Australia as a response to the regulatory chill led by its *Tobacco Plain Packaging Act* in 2011 (Tienhaara, 2011)and subsequent investor-state dispute settlement (ISDS) and WTO disputes (Hartmann, 2017).

### 5.3.3 Limit to ISP Liability

The Internet service provider (ISP) liability appears only in China–Australia FTA. ISP liability has never been an issue in multilateral negotiations. It is not mentioned in the TRIPS Agreement or the WIPO Internet treaties (the WIPO Copyright Treaty and the WIPO Performances and Phonogram Treaty). Rulemaking around ISP liability was first developed in US courts in the form of a judge-made law that tended to pose a direct, vicarious or contributory liability on ISPs before the US *Digital Millennium Copyright Act* (*DMCA*) in 1998 (Unni, 2001). The *DMCA* provides four types of limitations or 'safe harbours' on ISP liability: 1) transitory digital network communications, 2) system caching, 3) information residing on systems at the direction of users, and 4) information location tools. Although these safe harbours do not offer more relief from liability than has already been stipulated by the courts, they do offer courts grounds in later cases not to follow the decisions that have already been rendered (Yen, 1999).

However, the US legislative proposals, in particular, the Stop Online Piracy Act (SOPA) and Protect Intellectual Property Act (PIPA), have emphasised the reinforcement of ISP liability. ISP liability was also an important issue during both ACTA and TPP negotiations. The later development were intended to bypass the 'safe harbour' provision in the *DMCA* and impose more restrictive liabilities on ISPs (Carrier, 2012).

Australia issued its *Copyright Amendment (Digital Agenda) Act* in 2000, and one of its main purposes is to provide 'limited immunity' for telecommunications carriers and ISPs from liability for authorising infringement and contributory negligence (Rimmer, 2006). However, after the signature of the US–Australia FTA, Australia had to amend its copyright law. The Australian *Copyright Legislation Amendment Act* (2004) limits the scope of the exception for temporary copies made as part of a technical process of using an electronic copy of a work in § 3, Schedule 1 (Burrell & Weatherall, 2008).

The negotiation of China–Australia FTA started in 2005, just after the amendment of the Australian copyright legislation. During the 10-year negotiation of this FTA, China formulated its domestic legislation on ISP liability. The *Regulations on the Protection of Information Network Transmission Right* (2006), Tort Law (2010) and related judicial interpretations by the Supreme People's Court of China[7] address the issue of ISP liability. In this context, China–Australia FTA includes the following provision confirming the regulatory power of the state to limit ISP liability:

> Each Party may take appropriate measures to limit the liability of, or remedies available against, Internet service providers for copyright infringement by the users of their online services or facilities, where the internet service providers take action to prevent access to the materials infringing copyright in accordance with the laws and regulations of the Party.

This provision is an example of active promotion because it resists the diffusion of more restrictive provisions on ISP liabilities from the US and keeps open the door for further regulation on ISP liability—an issue that is not regulated by the TRIPS Agreement and other multilateral agreements.

[7] Supreme People's Court of China. (2012) Judicial Interpretation on Several Issues concerning the Application of Law in Hearing Civil Dispute Cases Involving Infringement of the Right of Dissemination on Information Networks, 17 December 2012 最高人民法院关于审理侵害信息网络传播权民事纠纷案件适用法律若干问题的规定.

### 5.3.4 Active Promotion of Cooperation and Dispute Settlement

In addition to active promotion of rules on specific issues, Chinese FTAs have actively promote IP rulemaking on:

- cooperation—including the exchange of information, capacity-building and established contact point or IP committee; and
- pre-WTO dispute settlement procedure.

Enhancing IP cooperation is mentioned in most Chinese FTAs that have an IP provision or IP chapter. IP cooperation provisions were the starting point for incorporating IP into Chinese FTAs. For instance, China–Chile FTA, the first Chinese FTA to explicitly mention IP in its text, places the IP provisions in the chapter on cooperation. The recent China–Mauritius FTA addresses IP cooperation as an important issue despite its relatively short IP chapter.

Different Chinese FTAs focus on different aspects of cooperation. China–Peru FTA requires the exchange of information on the conservation and sustainable use of biodiversity, actions to prevent illegal access to genetic resources and traditional knowledge, and domestic procedures concerning the practice of ABS (Article 148.3(a)). It is expected such information exchange would not only facilitate the learning of best practices from one another but also serve to provide evidence to support their respective positions in multilateral negotiations. A similar provision also appears in China–Costa Rica FTA (Article 117.1(c)). In Chinese FTAs with developed countries such as Switzerland and South Korea, the key issue for cooperation is to exchange information to reinforce IP enforcement. In China–Switzerland FTA, the use of genetic resources is not mentioned in the exchange of information.

Chinese FTAs also enhance cooperation on specific IP issues where there is a common interest. For instance, China–South Korea FTA specifically emphasises cooperation on the issue of utility models. Its Article 15.16.1 provides the following:

> Considering that both Parties have established utility model system, in order to facilitate the understanding and utilizing of utility model system by right holders and the public from both Parties and keep the balance of interests between right holders and the public, the Parties agree to enhance the cooperation on utility model legal framework of the Parties by exchanging information and experience on laws and regulations concerning utility models.

This provision reflects the common interests of China and South Korea in the utility model system. The utility model is a type of IP conducive to innovation and growth in developing economies (Kim *et al.*, 2012). As an integral part of the Chinese patent system, the *Patent Law* (2008) introduced some amendments to utility models (Ganea, 2010). South Korea has also relied on the utility model system to promote incremental innovation (Suthersanen, 2006). Thus, both countries have a mutual interest to agree to further cooperation in this area in their FTA. This provision manifests a 'win–win' outcome for both parties.

China's FTAs with New Zealand and Iceland introduce consultation as a pre-WTO dispute settlement procedure.[8] Both articles provide that consultation is a prerequisite for any IP dispute before a party pursues dispute resolution using the FTA or the WTO dispute settlement mechanism (DSM). With this consultation procedure, possible IP disputes between the parties could be solved in a more informal way. This provision would potentially benefit China, given it is more likely to be sued by than to sue developed countries.

In summary, on the protection of genetic resources and traditional knowledge and IP and public health, China has made efforts to promote alternative or additional rules in its FTAs. Instead of providing more extensive IP protection beyond the TRIPS Agreement, relevant Chinese FTA rules on the protection of genetic resources and traditional knowledge intended to include issues for which multilateral negotiations were not successful (Chapter 3), while provisions on IP and public health were to confirm flexibilities clarified by Doha Declaration and relevant implementation rules. On both issues, substantial progress was made in the FTAs after Chinese domestic laws were promulgated to articulate their positions. Chinese FTAs promoted these two issues by means of soft laws, so these provisions are more declarative than imposing obligations to the parties. In the case of GIs discussed in Chapter 2, rules on GI mutual recognition appeared in several Chinese FTAs. While overseas protection for Chinese GIs is consistent with China's interest, it did not require every FTA partner to have a mutual recognition mechanism. The limit to ISP liability was a case where China and Australia resisted the more restrictive standards of the US–Australia FTA. What was proposed was not a specific standard, but rather a confirmation of state power to regulate ISP liability.

[8] Article 166 of China–New Zealand FTA and Article 66.1 of China–Iceland FTA.

## 5.4 TRIPS-Plus Standards in Chinese FTAs

TRIPS-plus standards refer to protections more extensive than those conferred by the TRIPS Agreement or the closure of an option that is open in the TRIPS Agreement (Drahos, 2001). In the post-TRIPS era, these standards have been a battlefield of international IP rulemaking because these standards have encroached on flexibilities and policy spaces left open under the TRIPS Agreement (Kur & Grosse Ruse-Khan, 2011). TRIPS-plus IP provisions appear in recent Chinese FTAs with the developed countries of Switzerland, South Korea, and Australia, all of which include high IP protection standards. South Korea and Australia have signed FTAs with the US, respectively, that incorporated TRIPS-plus IP standards.

Whether TRIPS-plus standards in FTAs would introduce new obligations to a country depends on the comparison between such standards and IP protections offered by its existing domestic law. For countries that have already had high IP protection standards, newly signed FTAs do not necessarily result in new obligations for them to amend domestic law. This section compares TRIPS-plus standards in Chinese FTAs with relevant Chinese law and assesses the impact of these TRIPS-plus standards on China. This assessment will provide some insights into why China would agree to incorporate TRIPS-plus standards in its FTAs. Specifically, TRIPS-plus standards have been introduced to China on the following issues:

- data exclusivity for biologics,
- protection for designs,
- the abolition of 'visually perceptible' as a trademark registration requirement,
- border measures,
- strict transparency obligations, and
- accepting more extensive protection as a principle.

### 5.4.1 Data Exclusivity for Biologics

Test data are data generated in the development of drugs, including in relation to a drug's quality, safety and efficacy, as well as its physical and chemical characteristics (Correa, 2002). Test and other data are required by national authorities to register pharmaceutical products. The central issue concerning test data protection is a third party's use of those data for subsequent registration of similar products. There are two models for data protection and use by a third party. The first is trade secret protection. The TRIPS Agreement adopted this approach and protected test data and other data as undisclosed information in Article 39.3. The other approach is data exclusivity, which treats test data as a type of IP bearing an exclusive right. Before the TRIPS Agreement, the US and the EU introduced data exclusivity as part of their domestic/regional legislation. The US successfully incorporated data exclusivity into the North American Free Trade Agreement (NAFTA) but failed to have it incorporated into the TRIPS Agreement. Nonetheless, the US has incorporated data exclusivity into its post-TRIPS FTAs and TPP (Luo & Kesselheim, 2015).

Data exclusivity was a special condition for its WTO accession,[9] where China promise to grant six-year data exclusivity for test data. After its WTO accession, China complied with this WTO commitment by formulating *Regulations on Drug Administration* in which Article 35.2 stipulated a six-year data exclusivity for subsequent submissions for pharmaceutical products to get market approval (Cheng, 2019).

In China–Switzerland FTA, the parties agreed to provide six-year data exclusivity for biologics, which was not explicitly included in existing Chinese regulation. Switzerland is the home of three of the world's leading pharmaceutical companies, including Ciba-Geigy, Hoffmann-La Roche and Sandoz. Switzerland joined the US and EC in their proposal for data exclusivity in the TRIPS negotiation (Shaikh, 2016). As there is certain ambiguity about whether biologics could also enjoy data exclusivity as traditional pharmaceutical products, it seemed China had made a big concession to provide data exclusivity for biologics in this FTA, especially when considering the Swiss competitive advantage in pharmaceuticals and biologics.

As test data for biologics had not been explicitly protected by domestic Chinese laws when China–Switzerland FTA was concluded, the six-year data exclusivity period for biologics indeed introduced an additional obligation for China. Nonetheless, this gap was later filled by proposed domestic laws. In 2017, China Food and Drug Administration (now the National Medical Products Administration) proposed 10-year data exclusivity for biologics, original orphan drugs (drugs for rare diseases) and original drugs for children.[10] This was later updated by a new proposal for 12-year data exclusivity

[9] Para. 284, Accession of the People's Republic of China, 23 November 2001, WT/L432.

[10] China Food and Drug Administration. Notice on Calling for Comments on '*Policies Related to Encouraging Innovations in Pharmaceuticals and Medical Equipment and Protecting Interests and Rights of Innovators (Draft for Comments)*' 总局关于征求《关于鼓励药品医疗器械创新保护创新者权益的相关政策 (征求意见稿)》意见的公告.

for biologics and six-year data exclusivity for original orphan drugs or original drugs for children.[11]

## 5.4.2 Protection for Designs

Both China–Switzerland FTA and China–South Korea FTA include TRIPS-plus standards for industrial designs; however, the standards in the two FTAs are different. The FTA with Switzerland provides double protection, patent and copyright, to industrial designs. The FTA with South Korea includes a new right for design rightsholders in the form of the 'right of offer to sell'.

Article 11.12.1 of China–Switzerland FTA first confirms 10-year patent protection for industrial designs, equivalent to the TRIPS Agreement. In addition, it provides 25-year copyright protection for industrial designs that may also be 'considered works of applied art and fulfil the general condition required for copyright protection by the respective domestic legislation'.

China started to protect industrial designs in its *Patent Law* (1984), which granted five-year protection to designs with a possible renewal of another three years (Article 45.2). The Chinese *Copyright Law* (1990) did not include copyright protection for applied art. After China joined the Berne Convention in 1992, the State Council issued its *Provisions on the Implementation of the International Copyright Treaties*, which granted 25-year copyright protection for foreign works.[12] This was also considered supernational treatment of foreign works since Chinese rightsholders were not provided with the same protection. The term of patent protection for industrial designs was promoted to 10 years after China's WTO accession. Meanwhile, the supernational treatment of copyright protection for applied arts continues to be effective for foreigners. While domestic judicial decisions have confirmed the coexistence of copyright and patent protection for applied art, there have been

[11] China National Medical Products Administration. *Measures for the Implementation of Test Data Protection for drugs (Interim) (Draft for Comment)* 国家药品监督管理局《药品试验数据保护实施办法 (暂行) (征求意见稿)》.

[12] The definition of 'foreign works' conforms to the national treatment principle of the Berne Convention. Specifically, Article 4 of the Provisions defines the scope of foreign works as '1) works of which the author or one of the co-authors or the other owner of copyright or one of the co-owners of copyright is a national or a permanent resident of a country party to the international copyright treaties; 2) works of which the author is not a national or a permanent resident of a country party to international copyright treaties but which have been first published or published simultaneously in a country party of the international copyright treaties; or 3) works created by others by commission from a Chinese–foreign equity joint venture, a Chinese–foreign contractual joint venture or a foreign-capital enterprise which, by virtue of a contract, is the owner of copyright or one of the co-owners of copyright of the work'.

different opinions on their relations, in particular, whether double protection is available. While China–Switzerland FTA on copyright protection for designs did not introduce additional obligations to China as relevant provision has already existed in the 1992 regulation implementing international treaties and Chinese patent law, it is the only Chinese FTA indicating double protection may be available.

Article 15.20.2 of China–South Korea FTA provides that rightsholders of industrial designs can prevent unauthorised 'making, offering for sale, selling, or importing' of articles bearing or embodying the protected design. The offering for sale of such articles is a TRIPS-plus standard because it grants a right for designs not mentioned in Article 26.1 of the TRIPS Agreement. Again, this TRIPS-plus standard will not introduce a new obligation for China because the same level of protection has already been provided in Article 11 of its *Patent Law* (2008).

### 5.4.3 Abolition of 'Visually Perceptible' as a Trademark Registration Requirement

Article 15.1 of the TRIPS Agreement provides that '[m]embers may require, as a condition of registration, that signs be visually perceptible'. The China–Switzerland FTA reiterates this requirement in its Article 11.7.1; however, China–South Korea FTA closes this option from the TRIPS Agreement by stipulating that 'neither Party may require, as a condition of registration, that signs be visually perceptible, nor may either Party deny registration of a trademark solely because the sign of which it is composed is a sound' in Article 15.11.2. This is a TRIPS-plus standard because it expands the scope of trademark protection by decreasing the registration requirement.

It seems the abolition of the 'visually perceptible' requirement for trademark registration did not introduce an additional obligation for China. In the Chinese *Trademark Law* (2013), Article 8 stipulates that 'any signs, including words, graphs, letters, numbers, three-dimensional symbols, colour combinations, sound or any combination thereof, that are capable of distinguishing the goods of a natural person, legal person or other organization from those of others may be applied for registration as trademarks'. As China had abolished 'visually perceptible' as a condition for trademark registration before its FTA with South Korea, there was no new obligation introduced because of Article 15.11.2. Yet there could be an alternative interpretation that the law was amended just one year before China–South Korea FTA to implement what China had promised in the FTA.

### 5.4.4 Border Measures

Provisions on border measures are included in the Chinese FTAs with Chile, Peru, Costa Rica, Switzerland, South Korea, and Australia. Among these, the FTAs with Chile (Art. 11), Peru (Article 147), and Costa Rica (Article 114) mainly confirm the existing TRIPS standards on suspension of release, application, the requirement for security or equivalent assurance to protect defendants and prevent abuse, right of inspection and information and ex-officio action (Article 51–53, 57 and 58 in the TRIPS Agreement). In addition to these active defensive provisions, China–Switzerland, and China–South Korea FTAs also introduced TRIPS-plus standards for border measures (Table 5.3).

China accepted TRIPS-plus standards for border measures before the TRIPS Agreement. The TRIPS Agreement only requires WTO members to implement border measures for trademarks and copyright in the process of importation. Protection for other IP types and inspection in the process of exportation are optional according to TRIPS Article 51. Nonetheless, China accepted high standards on customs protection for IP during its bilateral negotiations with the US in the early 1990s. After the *US–China Intellectual Property Memorandum of Understanding* (1992), China formulated its *Regulation on the Customs Protection of Intellectual Property Rights* (1995), which protects copyright, trademarks and patents in both the importation and the exportation processes.[13] Although this standard turned out to be higher than that in the final text of the TRIPS Agreement, China may not derogate from this standard in its domestic legislation because of the treaty obligation contained in the 1992 MOU. Therefore, border measures for copyright and trademarks in the export process and border measures for patents, special signs for the Olympic Games, and World Expos in both exports and imports are TRIPS-plus standards. Such standards were incorporated in China's FTAs with Chile, Costa Rica, Australia, and Switzerland, but they has not introduced additional obligations for China.

The China–Peru and China–South Korea FTAs also include provisions on border measures for goods-in-transit. Border measures for goods-in-transit are controversial issues, especially after the case where the Netherlands seized generic drugs on their way from India to Brazil. The seizure was based merely on alleged patent infringement in the transit country (the Netherlands), although the drugs did not infringe any patents in either the country of origin (India) or the destination country (Brazil). India and

[13] Articles 3, 5, 14, 17, 19, 28, 29 and 31 of the *Regulation on the Customs Protection of Intellectual Property Rights* (1995) 海关知识产权保护条例().

**Table 5.3** Border measures in Chinese FTAs

| Content | Scope of protection | IP types under the protection |
|---|---|---|
| TRIPS Agreement | Importation | Suspected counterfeit trademark or pirated copyright goods |
| Regulation on the Customs Protection of Intellectual Property Rights of China (2010) | Importation and exportation (Article 3) | Patents, trademarks or copyright protected by the present Chinese legislation (Article 2)<br>Special signs for the Olympic Games and the World Expo |
| China–Chile FTA | Importation and exportation | Suspected counterfeit trademark or pirated copyright goods |
| China–Peru FTA | Importation, exportation, and goods in transit | Suspected counterfeit trademark or pirated copyright goods |
| China–Costa Rica FTA | Importation and exportation | Suspected counterfeit trademark or pirated copyright goods |
| China–Switzerland FTA | Importation and exportation | Goods infringing patents, industrial designs, trademarks or copyright |
| China–South Korea FTA | Importation, exportation, in transition, placement under a free zone and placement under a bonded warehouse | Trademarks and copyright, and goods which, according to the legislation of the party in which the application for customs action is made, infringe a patent, a plant variety right, a registered design or a geographical indication |
| China–Australia FTA | Importation and exportation | Suspected counterfeit trademark or pirated copyright goods |

Brazil requested a consultation with the European Union at the WTO (DS 408 and DS409). The WTO cases were settled later when the European Union and India reached an agreement to amend relevant EU Measures. The amendment of the EU regulation suggested the international standard is tilting towards no border measures for goods-in-transit. This issue has not yet been negotiated at multilateral forums, but ACTA indicated the efforts to push plurilateral rulemaking on border measures for goods-in-transit have been unsuccessful. Border measures for goods-in-transit have not been part of domestic Chinese law. However, relevant provisions in China–Peru and China–South Korea FTAs have locked China into the adoption of more restrictive border measures.

The China–South Korea FTA further extends the IP types under border measures to 'goods which, according to the legislation of the Party in which the application for customs action is made, infringe a patent, a plant variety right, a registered design, or a geographical indication' (Footnote 11 of the FTA). Existing Chinese regulations explicitly provide border measures only on copyright, trademarks, and patents. Border measures for plant variety rights and GIs have exceeded the level of protection to be found in China's domestic IP laws and introduced additional obligations for China. This coverage reflects a shadow of border measures to cover more types of IP than the TRIPS Agreement has provided—a shadow casted by the ACTA and other US and EU-led FTAs. For instance, border measures in the failed ACTA text cover patents, GIs and new plant variety rights (Articles 5(h) and 13). The EU–South Korea FTA provides border measures for all IP types.

Moreover, China–South Korea FTA extends border measures to goods 'in transition, placement under a free trade zone and placement under a bonded warehouse'. As with goods-in-transit, border measures for goods in a free trade zone or bonded warehouse are TRIPS-plus standards in the sense that these goods are not yet 'imported' into the territory of a state and are not intended to be protected under the TRIPS Agreement. The TRIPS-plus standards extending protection to more types of IP and processes beyond the importation of goods required China to amend its domestic law to incorporate these more stringent enforcement standards. In addition, through the TRIPS MFN principle, these protections will also be available for other WTO members.

### 5.4.5 Additional Transparency Obligation

Article 63 of the TRIPS Agreement provides a transparency obligation for WTO members, requiring a WTO member to publish its IP legislation, judicial decisions and administrative rulings in a national language. China–Australia requires parties to publish the database of invention patents, industrial designs, utility models, plant variety rights, geographical indications and trademarks via the Internet (Article 11.6.2). Requiring publication in other languages or through a certain medium (the Internet) and beyond the original scope required by the TRIPS Agreement introduces extra duties to China. While it is a TRIPS-plus standard because it limits China's choice in selecting the medium, China did accept it as the Internet is practically the most convenient way of information exchange.

### 5.4.6 Calculation of Damages

Although provisions on civil procedures in China's FTAs with Switzerland and South Korea are generally active defensive, relevant rules in both FTAs on the calculation of damages constitute TRIPS-plus standards. The specific ways for the calculation of damages were not stipulated in the TRIPS Agreement. Therefore, WTO members have the freedom to 'determine the appropriate method of implementing TRIPS provisions within their legal system and practice' (TRIPS Agreement, Article 1.1). The China–Switzerland FTA requires judicial authorities to consider the actual losses of the rightsholders or to presume a reasonable licence fee in determining the amount of damages (Article 11.19(b)). The China–South Korea FTA further specifies that the calculation of damages should consider 'the value of the infringed goods or services, measured by the market price, the suggested retail price, or other legitimate measures of value submitted by the right holder' (Article 15.24.2(b)). The above two FTA provisions have limited judges' discretion by specifying considerations for judges in relevant decision-making.

Nonetheless, the above two FTA provisions did not introduce further obligations to China. They are compatible with Chinese domestic IP legislation. Before China signed its FTAs with Switzerland and South Korea, the actual losses of rightsholders and reasonable royalties had already been laid out in domestic Chinese IP laws. For instance, actual lossse of the rightsholders, benefits gained by infringers and reasonable licence fees are stipulated in Article 63.1 in *Trademark Law* (2013) and Article 65.1 in *Patent Law* (2008). Chinese IP laws also provide statutory compensation as an additional method to calculate damages. Nonetheless, with the specific requirements in the FTAs, China is locked in by its treaty obligation to calculate damages in the above ways—in particular, this would constrain future legislative development to take a different approach.

### 5.4.7 Principle of Minimum Obligations

The China–South Korea FTA allows parties to provide more extensive protection for IP. Article 15.4 stipulates that 'each Party may, but shall not be obliged to, provide more extensive protection for, and enforcement of, intellectual property rights under its law than this Chapter requires, provided that the more extensive protection does not contravene this Chapter'. Article 11.3 of China–Australia FTA and Article 11.3 of China–Georgia FTA include similar provisions entitled 'Obligations are Minimum Obligations'.

This principle itself may not directly be TRIPS-plus, but it is an enabling provision. It enables the FTA to provide more extensive IP protection. It opens the door to a bilateral or plurilateral ratcheting up of TRIPS standards. This provision models Article 1.1 of the TRIPS Agreement and has a lock-in effect on the TRIPS-plus commitment made in any subsequent FTA. With this provision, states may not compromise any TRIPS-plus commitment they made in these FTAs. Together with the MFN principle in the TRIPS Agreement, these provisions of minimum standards in FTAs become a stepping-stone to more extensive protection.

## 5.5 Conclusion

This chapter examined Chinese FTAs through comparisons with the TRIPS Agreement and domestic Chinese IP legislation. It divided the Chinese FTA IP provisions into four categories based on their relations with the TRIPS Agreement: passive defensive, active defensive, TRIPS-plus, and active promotion. The primary finding is that most of the IP provisions in China's FTAs are TRIPS-defensive provisions, either passive defensive or active defensive. Chinese FTAs defend the TRIPS Agreement as the dominant multilateral IP agreement and defend the WTO as the major multilateral forum for IP rulemaking. China's position in these FTA provisions is manifested either through their explicit reiteration of specific TRIPS provisions or through the omission of IP entirely (so that the TRIPS Agreement automatically applies). This demonstrates that China mainly takes a pro-development, developing-country position in its bilateral IP engagement.

Active promotion and TRIPS-plus provisions are important to detect the 'novelty' that China has incorporated into the IP provisions in its FTAs. China's promotion of the genetic resource and traditional knowledge protection, IP and public health, and the limits to ISP liability, even if sometimes through non-binding declarative provisions, shows its support for alternative standard-setting on these issues. Some of these rival standards were proposed by its trading partners. For instance, Australia proposed provisions on ISP liability in China–Australia FTA. Others were issues that have been proposed by developing countries at multilateral negotiations, such as the issue of IP and public health. However, it is not clear to what extent China is interested to be a leader for alternative rulemaking on these issues, for instance, leading negotiations to consolidate ABS requirements to protect genetic resources and traditional knowledge.

This chapter identified TRIPS-plus provisions which include standards that exceed the TRIPS Agreement or eliminate TRIPS flexibilities. It further discussed implications of these TRIPS-plus for China, in particular, whether they created a new obligation for China. Among seven areas where TRIPS-plus standards are identified, additional obligations are introduced by China–Switzerland FTA on six-year data exclusivity for biologics and China–South Korea FTA on more restrictive border measures. The other TRIPS-plus standards essentially reiterate Chinese IP laws that are TRIPS-plus themselves and do not introduce any additional obligation.

The four categories of IP provisions in Chinese FTAs have different effects and implications. The TRIPS Agreement still applies to passive defensive and active defensive provisions. Active promotion FTAs may create binding obligations for both signatories and, in some cases, support alternative rule-making. A reiteration of domestic IP rules that exceed TRIPS standards in FTAs may lead to a lock-in effect for China. This is because once such provisions are included in FTAs, the standards are confirmed as international obligations and China will lose the flexibility of relinquishing such TRIPS-plus standards in its future domestic law amendment. TRIPS-plus provisions in Chinese FTAs have a further impact beyond the specific FTA partner. According to the MFN principle, any advantage, favour, or privilege that China provides to one FTA partner will be accorded immediately and unconditionally to other WTO members. This means once China agrees to a TRIPS-plus standard in one FTA, such a standard should also be open to all other WTO members. The dynamic of China's IP engagement at multilateral and bilateral levels reveals a clear inconsistency between China's general TRIPS-defensive position and its acceptance of TRIPS-plus standards. This inconsistency will be discussed in the strategy of dissembling in Chapter 9.

In addition to the FTAs analysed in this chapter, China's most recent IP engagement at the bilateral level includes the IP chapter in the USCETA, which includes TRIPS-plus IP standards on patent linkage, data exclusivity, broad definitions of confidential business information, and high-level criminal and civil enforcement rules such as the shifting of the burden of proof in civil proceedings of trade secret cases (Upreti & Vásquez Callo-Müller, 2020). It continues the history of US-China bilateral IP relations (Chapter 1) with yet another case that the US has exported its IP rules, particularly IP enforcement rules, to China. This agreement does not change the general conclusion of this chapter that most IP provisions in China's FTAs are pro-development TRIPS-defensive provisions that safeguard the multilateral IP system, but it indeed raises broader concerns when this agreement becomes part of the global IP ratchet.

In terms of implications for global distributive justice, the extensive TRIPS-defensive provisions in Chinese FTAs have maintained IP policy space for China. An FTA that includes a rival standard that promotes the balance between IP and public health can be considered one demonstrating the egalitarian principle for the distribution of primary resources beyond information. On the other hand, the increasing incorporation of TRIPS-plus standards into Chinese FTAs also raises concerns for global distributive justice. As will be discussed in Chapter 8, there is clear domestic momentum for the prevalence of the utilitarian and entitlement-based principles of distributive justice when it comes to IP protection. This has led to China's diminishing resistance to TRIPS-plus standards in its FTAs. Such diminishing resistance to high IP protection would further lead to shrinking domestic IP regulatory space for China and the prevalence of such TRIPS-plus standards internationally.

Previous analysis clearly shows that China has not imposed its own IP standards onto its FTA partners. There is no template for the IP chapter in its FTAs. When South Korea and Switzerland demanded higher IP protection, China expected that these countries would make a concession elsewhere. But in subsequent negotiations with Mauritius and Cambodia, China did not propose the same IP standards. Most provisions in China's FTA with Mauritius are defending the TRIPS Agreement. The 2020 China–Cambodia FTA was passive defensive to TRIPS Agreement without an IP Chapter. However, China-WIPO engagement in Chapter 6 demonstrates that China intended to enhance IP protection standards in the BRI countries. It actively engaged in dialogues with the BRI countries and sponsored WIPO technical assistance programmes to achieve this. In other words, the outcome that China has not imposed an IP standard on its FTA partners does not mean that China has deliberately pursued the Confucian golden principle of non-imposition to guild its global IP engagement. Chapter 8 will show that non-imposition is not an ethos in trade negotiation, but an outcome of managing contesting principles.

## References

Anderlini, J., Wang, F. and Mitchell, T. (2017) *XI Jinping Delivers Robust Defence of Globalisation at Davos*. Available at: https://www.ft.com/content/67ec2ec0-dca2-11e6-9d7c-be108f1c1dce (Accessed: 11 May 2018).

Burrell, R., & Weatherall, K. (2008). Exporting Controversy-Reactions to the Copyright Provisions of the US–Australia Free Trade Agreement: Lessons for US Trade Policy. *University of Illinois Journal of Law, Technology & Policy, 2*, 259–320.

Carrier, M. A. (2012). SOPA, PIPA, ACTA, TPP: An Alphabet Soup of Innovation-Stifling Copyright Legislation and Agreements. *Northwestern Journal of Technology and Intellectual Property, 11*(2), 21–32.

Cheng, W. (2019). Protection of Data in China: Seventeen Years after China's WTO Accession. *European Intellectual Property Review, 44*(5), 292–297.

Correa, C. M. (2002) *Protection of Data Submitted for the Registration of Pharmaceuticals: Implementing the Standards of the TRIPS Agreement.*

Drahos, P. (2001). BITs and BIPs. *The Journal of World Intellectual Property, 4*(6), 791–808.

Drahos, P. (2002). Developing Countries and International Intellectual Property Standard-Setting. *The Journal of World Intellectual Property, 5*(5), 765–789.

Drahos, P. (2021). *TRIPS Through a Military Looking Glass* (EUI Law Wroking Paper No. 2).

Dreyfuss, R., & Frankel, S. (2014). From Incentive to Commodity to Asset: How International Law Is Reconceptualizing Intellectual Property. *Michigan Journal of International Law, 36*(4), 557–562.

Ganea, P. (2010). China's Amended Legal Regime on Patents for Inventions and Utility Models. *Journal of Intellectual Property Law & Practice, 5*(9), 650–662.

Hartmann, S. (2017). When Two International Regimes Collide: An Analysis of the Tobacco Plain Packaging Disputes and Why Overlapping Jurisdiction of the WTO and Investment Tribunals Does Not Result in Convergence of Norms. *UCLA Journal of International Law and Foreign Affairs, 21*(2), 204–245.

Kim, Y. K., Lee, K., Park, W. G., & Choo, K. (2012). Appropriate Intellectual Property Protection and Economic Growth in Countries at Different Levels of Development. *Research Policy, 41*(2), 358–375.

Kur, A., & Grosse Ruse-Khan, H. (2011). Enough Is Enough-The Notion of Binding Ceilings in International Intellectual Property Protection. In A. Kur & M. Levin (Eds.), *Intellectual Property in a Fair World Trade System: Proposals for Reform of TRIPS* (pp. 359–407). Edward Elgar.

Liu, B. (2016). The Systematic Construction of the Intellectual Property Text in China's Free Trade Agreements中国自由贸易协定知识产权文本的体系化构建. *Global Law Review 环球法律评论, 4*, 179–192.

Luo, J., & Kesselheim, A. S. (2015). The Trans-Pacific Partnership Agreement and Implications for Access to Essential Medicines. *JAMA, 314*(15), 1563–1564.

Morin, J. F. (2009). Multilateralizing TRIPs-Plus Agreements: Is the US Strategy a Failure? *The Journal of World Intellectual Property, 12*(3), 175–197.

Richards, D. G. (2004) *Intellectual Property Rights and Global Capitalism.* ME Sharpe.

Rimmer, M. (2006) 'Robbery under Arms: Copyright Law and the Australia-United States Free Trade Agreement', *First Monday, 11*(3).

SECO. (2018). *Free Trade Agreements*. Available at: https://www.seco.admin.ch/seco/en/home/Aussenwirtschaftspolitik_Wirtschaftliche_Zusammenarbeit/Wirtschaftsbeziehungen/Freihandelsabkommen.html. Accessed 11 May 2018.

Sell, S. K. (2010a). *The Global IP Upward Ratchet, Anti-Counterfeiting and Piracy Enforcement Efforts: The State of Play*. American University Washington College of Law.

Sell, S. K. (2010b). TRIPS Was Never Enough: Vertical Forum Shifting, FTAS, ACTA, and TTP. *Journal of Intellectual Property Law, 18*(2), 447–478.

Shaikh, O. H. (2016) *Access to Medicine Versus Test Data Exclusivity: Safeguarding Flexibilities Under International Law.* Springer.

Suthersanen, U. (2006) *Utility Models and Innovation in Developing Countries.* International Centre for Trade and Sustainable Development (ICTSD).

Tienhaara, K. (2011). Regulatory Chill and the Threat of Arbitration: A View from Political Science. In C. Brown, & K. Miles (Eds.), *Evolution in Investment Treaty Law and Arbitration.* Cambridge University Press.

Unni, V. K. (2001). Internet Service Provider's Liability for Copyright Infringement-How to Clear the Misty Indian Perspective. *Richmond Journal of Law & Technology, 8*(2), 13.

Upreti, P. N., & Vásquez, M. (2020). Phase One US-China Trade Deal: What Does It Mean for Intellectual Property? *GRUR International, 69*(4), 389–393.

Wei, Z. (1997). The Amendment of the Chinese Copyright Law from a Perspective of Berne Convention从伯尔尼公约看中国著作权法之修订. *Peking Unversity Law Journal中外法学, 5*, 91–96.

Xiang, J. Y. (2021). *Intellectual Property, Antimonopoly Law and Sustainable Development in China* (WIPO-WTO Colloquium Papers, Special Issue).

Xinhua News Agency. (2007). *Interpretation of the 17th CPC National Congress Report Raised the Strategic Importance of Constructing Free Trade Agreements 党的十七大报告解读把自由贸易区建设提到战略的高度.* Available at: http://www.gov.cn/jrzg/2007-12/14/content_833950.htm. Accessed 11 May 2018.

Yen, A. C. (1999). Internet Service Provider Liability for Subscriber Copyright Infringement, Enterprise Liability, and the First Amendment. *Georgetown Law Journal, 88*(6), 1833–1894.

# 6

# China and Multilateral IP Governance

## 6.1 Introduction

This chapter focuses on China's engagement in global IP governance at the multilateral level, where WIPO and the WTO are the key forums to analyse. China has developed considerable trust in WIPO since the 1970s, and its engagement with WIPO has increased in recent years. The diplomatic conference for the *WIPO Treaty on Audiovisual Performances* was hosted in Beijing in 2012, and the treaty is also referred to as the *Beijing Treaty on Audiovisual Performances*. In addition, WIPO opened its Beijing office in 2014 and co-organised several IP and BRI events with SIPO. China's IP engagement with the WTO has been discussed in previous chapters. China amended its IP laws to comply with the TRIPS Agreement after its WTO accession, and another amendment was made to comply with the WTO dispute settlement resolution (Chapter 1). China co-sponsored the proposals with developing countries and the EU on GIs and the disclosure obligation (Chapters 2 and 3, respectively). China has by and large safeguarded TRIPS standards in most IP provisions in its FTAs (Chapter 5). These engagement generally shows China's classic pro-development position at the WTO. This chapter will focus on two cases of China's engagement in the WTO: its first proposal on IP in standardisation and its role in the IP waiver negotiations in the context of COVID-19.


W. Cheng, *China in Global Governance of Intellectual Property*, Palgrave Socio-Legal Studies, https://doi.org/10.1007/978-3-031-24370-7_6

## 6.2 China and WIPO: A Tale of Reciprocity

As one of the 15 specialised agencies of the United Nations (UN), WIPO has been an important forum in global IP governance since its establishment in 1967. Nonetheless, its significance declined when the US incorporated IP into the Uruguay Round of the GATT negotiations in the 1980s (Braithwaite & Drahos, 2000; Sell, 2003). The GATT negotiations led to the creation of the WTO, in which the TRIPS Agreement is the most comprehensive multilateral IP agreement with high enforcement standards. According to Abbott (2000), the inter-institutional relationship between the WTO and WIPO enabled the co-evolution of the two forums. Also, leaving enforcement to the WTO enabled the recent resurgence of WIPO with a greater focus on socialisation and norm-building (May, 2006, p. 35).

WIPO-administered 26 IP-related international treaties at the time of writing (WIPO, 2022a). Within these treaties, the Patent Cooperation Treaty (PCT) and the Madrid System (including the Madrid Agreement Concerning the International Registration of Marks and the Protocol Relating to the Madrid Agreement) are the most widely used. The administration of the PCT and the Madrid System makes WIPO a self-sufficient international organisation. According to its latest annual financial report released in 2020, 76.6% of WIPO's revenue comes from fees administering the PCT system and 16.3% from administering the Madrid System (WIPO, 2021, p. 8). Predominately relying on PCT administration fees could compromise its image as a technocratic, objective civil service organisation (Sell & Prakash, 2004). Indeed, WIPO has actively engaged developing countries as 'missionaries' in IP capacity-building—providing comments on drafting IP laws, personal training, technical assistance, and advice on TRIPS compliance (Drahos, 2010). It has also administered treaties with TRIPS-plus obligations. For instance, the WIPO Performances and Phonograms Treaty (WPPT) and WIPO Copyright Treaty (WCT) include higher standards than the TRIPS Agreement for online copyright protection.

Against this background, there has been a spirit of reciprocity in China–WIPO engagement. On the one hand, WIPO–China IP engagement began with WIPO's technical assistance to China in the early 1980s, when China had no IP law. On the other hand, China is currently home to the world's largest community using WIPO-administered treaties.

### 6.2.1 History of Trust-Building and Technical Assistance

The relationship between China and WIPO can be traced back to as early as 1973, one year after the UN recognised the People's Republic of China (PRC) as the representative of 'China' at that forum. From 1945 to 1972, that position was assumed by the Nationalist government based in Taiwan. Thereafter, WIPO, as a specialised organisation in the UN system, began to send invitations to China to attend its regular meetings. China first sent a civil organisation, the Chinese Council for the Promotion of International Trade (CCPIT), as its representative to observe the WIPO meeting in November 1973. While this delegation indicated China's intention to keep the first contact with WIPO informal, the contact was fruitful. After the meeting, the CCPIT assessed the feasibility of China joining WIPO and recommended China establish a patent system. Although this proposal was later shelved as China was still in the Cultural Revolution, the seed of a patent system had been planted (Zhao, 2008).

Árpád Bogsch, then Director General of WIPO, indirectly influenced the domestic debate on whether China should retain the inventor's certificate during the preparation of China's *Patent Law* (1984) and provided comments on one of its early drafts. After the establishment of the PRC, the patent right first provided in its early regulations was abolished as it was believed to be a capitalist right that was incompatible with China's socialist system. Following the model of the USSR, China established a system of inventor certificates under which only honorary titles were granted to inventors, without remuneration. To achieve a compromise, an early draft of the Chinese patent law designed a 'dual-track' system so that invention patents and inventor certificates could coexist. China sent a delegation to participate in the diplomatic conference for the amendment of the Paris Convention for the Protection of Industrial Property in 1980. During the breaks in this conference, Bogsch spent hours in private discussions with Chinese Patent Law drafters to advise on detailed technical questions. According to ZHAO Yuanguo, one of the drafters of the *Patent Law* (1984), the discussions with Bogsch were important for China to formulate a 'better, modern and more advanced patent law' and his comments helped China align its Patent Law with international standards (Zhao, 2008). In addition, WIPO provided technical assistance in 1986 on the early draft of China's *Copyright Law* (1990) (Liu, 2009). While China benefited from this early engagement, WIPO also made prominent achievements by advising the largest developing country in the world to establish IP laws.

In parallel with the legislative progress, China became a member of WIPO on 3 June 1980 and joined the Paris Convention on 19 March 1985. To date, China has ratified 16 and signed two WIPO-administered IP treaties (Appendix 1). China extensively participated in WIPO IP treaties not only because it is now the biggest user of the PCT and the Madrid System but also to demonstrate its endeavours to align its IP system with world standards. Meanwhile, China cooperates with WIPO in joint research projects, personnel training, and information exchange. Recent cooperation also extended to specific technical fields—for instance, trademark (SAIC, 2016) and patent classification.

While China was frequently criticised by the US for its ineffective and inadequate IP protection in the early 1990s, WIPO recognised China's progress. While the US put China on the Special 301 watch list and occasionally threatened it with unilateral trade retaliation, Bogsch, in a speech delivered in China in 1993, observed that 'China's intellectual property development in the last two decades was unprecedented in the history of intellectual property'. Bogsch's comment was quoted in the *China Intellectual Property White Paper* (1994) to demonstrate the progress that China has achieved in developing its IP system (SCIO, 1994). The endorsement by WIPO helped China to respond to the US criticism and further consolidated the China–WIPO relationship.

The number of IP filings from China has increased dramatically since the early 2000s through a pressure-driving mechanism (Cheng & Drahos, 2018). The China Trademark Office has received the largest number of annual trademark registrations among all trademark offices since 2001. Since the Global Financial Crisis, China has been the major contributor to the global increase in PCT applications. In 2016, SIPO received 1.3 million patent applications—more than the total of patent applications received by the US Patent and Trademark Office, the Japan Patent Office, and the Korean Intellectual Property Office combined (WIPO, 2017). WIPO has enhanced its liaison with China as a response to the pivotal role played by China in the WIPO-administered treaties. The recent development of the China–WIPO reciprocal relationship can be further examined through the following cases: 1) the opening of WIPO's Beijing office, 2) the decision to name the WIPO audiovisual treaty the Beijing Treaty on Audiovisual Performances, 3) WIPO's support for the BRI, and 4) China's support for WIPO to remain as the major forum for international IP rulemaking.

### 6.2.2 WIPO Beijing Office: A Response to Surging Chinese IP Applications

China became a contracting party to the PCT in 1994 and simultaneously one of the receiving offices for PCT applications. China was also the first developing country recognised as an International Search Authority and an International Preliminary Examining Authority for PCT applications. In 2016, the number of annual PCT applications from China increased by 44.7%. As reported by WIPO, China was the largest user of the PCT system from 2019 to 2021 (WIPO, 2022b).

The Madrid System provides streamlined services for the international registration of trademarks. China became a party to the Madrid Agreement in 1989 and the Madrid Protocol in 1995. The SAIC, representing China, signed an MOU with WIPO on 11 May 2016 to enhance cooperation on international trademark registration (SAIC, 2016). Following the US and Germany, China was the third largest user of the Madrid System for the international registration of trademarks in 2021 (WIPO, 2022b).

WIPO opened its Beijing office in October 2014 in response to China's rise as a significant user of both the PCT and the Madrid System—its fifth regional office beyond its headquarters in Geneva. Through the Beijing office, WIPO developed a deeper liaison with Chinese ministries in charge of IP (WIPO, 2016b). The Beijing office also enabled WIPO to collect and frequently update information about the Chinese economy and politics.

### 6.2.3 Beijing Treaty on Audiovisual Performances

The Beijing Treaty on Audiovisual Performances (the Beijing Treaty)[1] is a WIPO-administered treaty to enhance the protection of performers' rights. It is so far the only international IP treaty named after a Chinese city. Although China did not have significant influence in the treaty negotiations, hosting the diplomatic meeting and the treaty's naming after Beijing did have foreign policy significance for China. The well-documented interaction between the National Copyright Administration of China (NCAC) and WIPO also shows how WIPO and Chinese IP regulators engage with one another.

The issue of performers' protection originated from controversial provisions in the *International Convention for the Protection of Performers, Producers of Phonograms, and Broadcasting Organizations* (Rome Convention) in 1961.

---

[1] WIPO, *Beijing Treaty on Audiovisual Performances*, Adopted by the Diplomatic Conference on the Protection of Audiovisual Performances in Beijing, 24 June 2012.

The protection of performers' rights in the Rome Convention extends only to live performance and recording and reproduction through phonogram. The Rome Convention provides that 'once a performer has consented to the incorporation of his performance in a visual or audiovisual fixation, performers are not entitled to the rights granted by the Convention' (Article 19). When the Rome Convention was adopted, filmmaking was the only way to produce audiovisual works, but the convention was not enough to protect performers' rights with the development of digital technology and channels for dissemination. Although the issue of performers' protection was mentioned in the TRIPS Agreement and the WPPT, these treaties continued the logic of the Rome Convention.

The EU and US disagreed in the negotiations towards a new treaty. The EU has been active in developing regional rules to further protect performers,[2] but the US opposed international negotiations to extend performers' rights to audiovisual works for fear that such an extension would adversely affect the development of the US film industry. International negotiations on a new treaty on performers' rights in audiovisual works finally started in 2000 under the auspices of WIPO. This disagreement slowed the progress of a harmonised global governance of performers' rights. A consensus was ultimately reached in 2011. Although the treaty was later named after Beijing and China participated in the negotiations, China did not make a substantive contribution to the outcome. Like global governance of other issues, the protection of performers' rights was largely a deal between the EU and the US (Drezner, 2008, pp. 71–87).

YAN Xiaohong, then Vice-Minister of the NCAC, documented the history of the Beijing Treaty in his memoir. He mentioned it was WANG Bingyin, Deputy Director General of WIPO, who first contacted the NCAC: '[S]he will endeavour to facilitate Beijing to be the venue for the diplomatic conference if China would like to consider making the offer' (Yan, 2014, pp. 6–7). Hosting the IP diplomatic conference has symbolic significance for China, enabling it to display its recent IP achievements. As pointed out by Yan (2014, p. 7):

> Although China has made remarkable progress in recent years, there are still critics from the US, EU, and Japan. Hosting the conference in Beijing will introduce representatives from various countries to China to appreciate

---

[2] For instance, the European Economic Community (EEC) promulgated the *Council Directive 92/100/EEC of 19 November 1992 on Rental Right and Lending Right and on Certain Rights Related to Copyright in the Field of Intellectual Property.*

the development of China and acknowledge its development in intellectual property.

The proposal was later approved by the Chinese Government after whole-of-government deliberations, involving representatives from the Ministry of Foreign Affairs (MFA), MOFCOM, SAIC, SIPO, the Legislative Affairs Office of the State Council, and the Legislative Affairs Committee of the National People's Congress. This engagement was a typical case of reciprocity: WIPO found a perfect partner to host the diplomatic conference and China enhanced its image and showcased its recent IP achievements.

### 6.2.4 WIPO's Support for the Belt and Road Initiative

China started its Belt and Road Initiative (BRI) in 2013 (Swaine, 2015). Geopolitically, the BRI is important because it is extending China's outreach to Central Asia, Europe, South-East Asia, and Africa. The US sees it as a counterinitiative that will jeopardise its pivot to Asia (Overholt, 2015). The BRI connects Asia and Europe, with China positioned as the focal point. From the Chinese perspective, the grand initiative aims to enhance connectivity between China and more than 140 countries along the Belt and Road (BRI countries) via large infrastructure projects, such as express railways, ports, and pipelines. As China becomes a technology exporter, IP protection becomes an imperative issue in many BRI projects, and more comprehensive and higher IP protection standards across the BRI countries are aligned with China's interests. Yet, China is reluctant to impose IP standards on these countries. In this context, WIPO supported China to develop IP cooperation with BRI countries in various ways.

In 2016, WIPO initiated and co-organised with SIPO the High-Level Conference on Intellectual Property for BRI Countries. Francis Gurry, then Director General of WIPO, articulated the organisation's position of supporting the BRI. Gurry noted the significance of the close relationship between WIPO and the BRI and emphasised that 'this would ensure coherence in the architecture for the implementation of intellectual property worldwide' (WIPO, 2016a). He also encouraged the BRI countries to leverage WIPO tools, including its global IP services and databases, and participate in WPO-administered IP treaties (WIPO, 2016a). As China was reluctant to reach out to the BRI countries directly as IP 'missionaries', as Drahos (2010) described in *The Global Governance of Knowledge*; its collaboration with WIPO makes this much easier. According to WIPO's Intellectual Property Technical Assistance Database, China has hosted 448 IP-related technical assistance activities.[3] This number is only slightly smaller than that of the US (452) but higher than other countries, such as Japan (317), South Korea (302), and Germany (242). While not all activities are related to the BRI, the number and scale of these international technical assistance activities demonstrate how China has strategically used the leverage of WIPO as a platform for IP engagement with the BRI countries and how WIPO has responded to the geopolitical change in the international IP system.

### 6.2.5 China Supports WIPO to Remain a Major Multilateral IP Forum

Maintaining multilateralism in global IP governance has been important for China—in particular, as a response to the vertical forum-shifting strategies of the US and the EU (Sell, 2010). As discussed in Chapter 5, China has actively defended TRIPS standards in its FTAs. China's preference to maintain the multilateral trade system was also demonstrated by its implementation of the WTO Dispute Settlement Body's recommendations in its dispute with the US[4] (Scott & Wilkinson, 2013).

Multilateralism is also important for WIPO because its influence was compromised since the US shifted IP negotiations from WIPO to the Uruguay Round in the 1980s (Braithwaite & Drahos, 2000; Sell, 2003). After the creation of the TRIPS Agreement, WIPO was not as influential as a forum for international IP rulemaking as it had been in the pre-TRIPS period. Endorsement from China becomes important for WIPO. SIPO's Commissioner SHEN Changyu clearly articulated the Chinese position at WIPO's fifty-sixth General Assembly: 'WIPO should fully play the role as a major platform for international intellectual property rulemaking' (SIPO, 2016). On the other hand, China's extensive use of WIPO-administered treaties such as the PCT and the Madrid System means it has become the major source of revenue for WIPO. These factors further reinforced China's support for WIPO in multilateral IP rulemaking.

In summary, reciprocity has marked China's engagement with WIPO. Both parties have benefited from this relationship. To what extent this dynamic would impact (contribute to or compromise) global distributive justice in relation to IP needs to be analysed case by case. The opening of the WIPO Beijing office and China's hosting of the diplomatic conference

---

[3] WIPO, *Intellectual Property Technical Assistance Database (IP-TAD)*, available from: https://www.wipo.int/tad/en/index.jsp (Accessed 5 July 2022).

[4] WTO, *China: Measures Affecting the Protection and Enforcement of Intellectual Property Rights*, WT/DS362.

for the Beijing Treaty may not have broad implications for global distributive justice.

WIPO had supported the Chinese BRI through technical assistance on IP, focusing mainly on persuading developing countries to use WIPO tools and to respect IP by both foreign and domestic rightholders. This can be considered a recent example of China's effort of enhancing IP protection in these countries. Since many of these countries have been WTO members for years, therefore, China and WIPO's IP technical assistance may not result in a higher IP protection standard. While not imposing an IP standard on these countries, China influenced through dialogues, capacity-building, and information exchange with the support of WIPO. Still, for these countries, China has become another IP missionary to facilitate the understanding and adoption of IP rules in these countries. In terms of its appeal to distributive justice principles, China has encountered a potential conflict between the utilitarian and entitlement-based principles to protect its IP rights overseas and the Confucian principle as well as the egalitarian principle that guides non-imposition and provides knowledge as public goods. Cooperation with WIPO is a solution for China to find a middle ground.

Multilateral forums have a wider range of participants in negotiations and deliberations, so China's support for WIPO to remain the main forum for global IP rulemaking could help achieve more balanced rules than otherwise emerged in plurilateral forums, such as the TPP or ACTA. Even so, the impact of such engagement on global distributive justice ultimately depends on the nature of the rules. Most WIPO treaties have so far been specialised treaties to enhance IP protection or facilitate IP rightholders, except for the 2013 *Marrakesh Treaty to Facilitate Access to Published Works for Persons Who Are Blind, Visually Impaired or Otherwise Print Disabled* which has a clear humanitarian and social development dimension (Helfer *et al.*, 2017). The trust-building in the early days was also a process for China to understand IP and its utilitarian foundation. Later on, the fees from Chinese applicants are essential for the PCT and the Madrid System, both manifest the entitlement-based principle.

## 6.3 China and the TRIPS Agreement: Safeguarding Multilateralism Despite Limited Involvement in Agenda-Setting

The TRIPS Agreement defines IP as a trade-related issue. It harmonised global IP norms by setting 'minimum' protection standards and relies on the WTO's dispute settlement mechanism to safeguard compliance. China participated in TRIPS negotiations[5] and was one of the developing-country representatives in the '10 + 10' group.[6] Although China did not substantially contribute to the outcome of the TRIPS Agreement, which was mainly influenced by the 'Quad' of Canada, the EC, Japan, and the US) (Cottier, 2015, p. 86), participating in the negotiations allowed China to have direct access to the Draft Final Act (1991).[7] The information in this was particularly important for China in its parallel bilateral IP negotiations with the US from 1988 to 1996. The results of these negotiations were bilateral MOUs signed in 1992, 1995, and 1996.[8]

China participated in negotiations on multiple fronts, and the early involvement in the TRIPS negotiations allowed it to adjust its positions in US-China bilateral IP negotiations. They considered the IP protection standards provided in the *Draft Final Act* (1991) the basis for their bilateral negotiations with the US. China accepted IP standards equivalent to the Draft Final Act (1991) in preparation to re-enter GATT but refused to accept any US demands beyond it (Wang & Wu, 2001). Meanwhile, the US continued to persuade China to accept IP standards in its own TRIPS proposals from 1992 to 1995. It did succeed in some issues because the final draft of the TRIPS Agreement was not settled at that stage and there was a possibility that some of the US proposals would be adopted. After the TRIPS Agreement was concluded in 1995, it was almost impossible for the US to push China beyond the TRIPS Agreement.

This very early engagement at the pre-WTO stage set the tone for China's interaction with the WTO: China acknowledges the WTO as an important multilateral IP rulemaking forum, willing to comply with TRIPS standards. China systematically amended its IP laws in 2000 in preparation for its

[5] China was one of the co-sponsors for the GATT proposal MTN.GNG/NG11/W/71, 14 May 1990, which represented the developing countries' positions in the TRIPS negotiations.

[6] This '10 + 10' group was not a negotiating group, but a consultation group in the late phase of the TRIPS negotiations. It initially included 10 developed countries and 10 developing countries, but in practice, the group was open to any interested delegation. In the end, it included 14 developing countries (Argentina, Brazil, Chile, China, Colombia, Cuba, Egypt, India, Nigeria, Peru, Tanzania, Uruguay, Pakistan, and Zimbabwe).

[7] Trade Negotiations Committee of Uruguay Round, *Draft Final Act Embodying the Results of the Uruguay Round of Multilateral Trade Negotiations*, 20 December 1991, MTN.TNC/W/FA. The text of the TRIPS Agreement made two minor changes based on this *Draft Final Act* (1991): 1) the addition to Article 64 of paragraphs 2 and 3 on non-violation disputes and 2) the addition of the language in Article 31(c) in regard to semiconductor technology.

[8] These specifically included *US–China Memorandum of Understanding on the Protection of Intellectual Property* (1992), 17 January 1992; *China–United States Agreement Regarding Intellectual Property Rights Memorandum of Understanding* (1995), 26 February 1995; and *China Implementation of the 1995 Intellectual Property Rights Agreement* (1996), 17 June 1996.

WTO accession in 2001. China was sued by the US at the WTO in 2007 (WT/DS362). A well-documented area of China's engagement with the TRIPS Agreement is its record of compliance after the dispute (Gervais, 2009; Guan, 2014; Thomas, 2017; Yu, 2011). China also participated in post-TRIPS WTO negotiations on GIs and disclosure obligations (Chapters 2 and 3). In the case of disclosure obligations, the TRIPS Council was the most important platform for China to learn international practices and set its own standards when international law was not ready. China's proposals at the WTO manifested its classic pro-development, developing-country positions. Most of China's FTAs have either actively or implicitly defended TRIPS standards. This section analyses two under-investigated issues: China's first IP proposal at the WTO and its position in its recent IP waiver negotiations.

### 6.3.1 China's First WTO Proposal: IP in Standardisation

China submitted its first IP-related proposal to the WTO Committee on Technical Barriers to Trade (TBT), because interpretations of related parties for reasonable and non-discriminatory (RAND) principles were inconsistent and IP rightholders and users could not achieve consensus among its interpretations which further increased uncertainty of international standard adoption.[9] This has been a long-standing issue despite patent hold-up has been discussed in the literature (Farrell *et al.*, 2007), and RAND has been adopted by various international standard-setting organisations (SSOs) and recognised by case law in some jurisdictions.

China's WTO proposal on IP in standardisation is selected as a case to analyse China WTO interaction for two reasons. First, it was the first and by far the only independent WTO proposal initiated by China. This case offers insights into China's active engagement with the WTO. Second, it is a useful case to examine how China's appeal to certain distributive justice principles. The RAND principle benefits licensees—the weaker party in the negotiation of a licensing agreement. Since most US companies are technology exporters and licensors in the international market, the US prefers to letting the interpretation of RAND emerge *ex post* in dispute settlements. The litigation-oriented approach has caused considerable fragmentation and inconsistency in the conceptualisation of the RAND principle. Consequently, the lack of clear meaning benefits licensors. By contrast, the RAND principle is essential for Chinese companies as technology importers. Promoting

[9] WTO TBT Committee, *Intellectual Property Right (IPR) Issues in Standardization*, Communication from the People's Republic of China 25 May 2005, G/TBT/W/251.

RAND as an international standard at the WTO is part of the Chinese agenda to support its domestic companies. More broadly, such a proposal, if successful, would also benefit the technology licensees in general.

AN Baisheng, the key negotiator for the IP in standardisation proposal, pointed out that developing countries have been the victims of a unilateral standardisation process dominated by the US and the EU:

> Developed countries tend to be indifferent to the SSOs' behaviour that may undermine the productive efficiency of developing countries or require developing countries to accept the international standards they have formulated unilaterally or compel the international society to accept increasingly higher intellectual property standards without mentioning how to restrict the abuse of these intellectual property rights. (Liu, 2007, p. 10)

These remarks indicated China's intention to frame IP in standardisation as a development-related issue and gain support from other developing countries. Such framing constituted the basis for China's first WTO proposal.

As Article 15.4 mandates the TBT Committee review the operation and implementation of the TBT Agreement on a triennial basis, the fourth triennial review of the TBT Agreement took place in 2005. In May 2005, China proposed to the TBT Committee that IP in standardisation should be included in the triennial review among seven other issues.[10] China was the sole initiator of the proposal on IP and standardisation. The Chinese representative emphasised the significance of development in this proposal: '[T]o strike the right balance between the needs of international standards development and the implementation of adequate and fair protection of intellectual property rights'.[11] Further problems were identified, including insufficient disclosure of information by some SSOs and no sanctions for IP rightholders when they refused to trade (An, 2005). This proposal was questioned by other WTO members. For instance, Mexico asked for clarification of the proposal because IP was not within the remit of the TBT Agreement.[12]

[10] The other seven issues submitted for the fourth triennial review were: 1) implementation and administration of the agreement (proposed by the US), 2) good regulatory practice (proposed by the EC and US), 3) transparency (proposed by China and the EC), 4) conformity assessment procedures (proposed by the EC and the United States), 5) technical assistance (proposed by China and the EC), 6) special and differential treatment (proposed by China), and 7) labelling (proposed by the EC). See WTO TBT Committee, *Minutes of the Meeting of 22–23 March 2005*, G/TBT/M/35, 24 May 2005, Paras 74–76.

[11] Ibid., Para. 74.

[12] Ibid., Para. 78.

In response to this question, China clarified its position in its submission of G/TBT/W/251 to the TBT Committee after the meeting.[13] This submission focused on how prominent problems in IP and standardisation, including the lack of disclosure and the different interpretations of the RAND principle, have become obstacles to international trade. China recommended that the interpretation of RAND be included in the TBT triennial review. By framing IP in standardisation as an important development issue, China was trying to shift the forum for interpreting the RAND principle from international SSOs to the WTO TBT Committee.

This submission was supported by Brazil on the basis that patent rights should not constitute an obstacle to development objectives. Mexico again questioned the appropriateness of the TBT Committee as a forum to discuss the issue.[14] Canada and South Korea further questioned how IP in standardisation had become an obstacle for members to adopt international standards and facilitate international trade.[15] The US refused to discuss the Chinese proposal at the TBT triennial review. Without a consensus on this issue, the Chinese proposal was not included in the TBT triennial review. China's first and only IP proposal at the WTO failed.

After the TBT triennial review, China took the issue of IP in Standardisation to the forum of Asia–Pacific Economic Cooperation (APEC). This can be considered a strategy of forum-shifting as APEC could be a more convenient forum for China to promote this issue. Nonetheless, the proposal was not further pursued by China because of logistical considerations: China could not find a place and time for a meeting on which all parties would agree.

This may have been an excuse as there was no point for China to pursue this agenda further. The US position was already clear when the Chinese proposal was refused at the WTO, meaning it would be difficult for China to gain support from developing countries in the Asia–Pacific for the proposal, given the US is a key member of APEC. Notwithstanding China's framing of IP in standardisation as a development-related issue, it was more of a unique problem that China has faced as an emerging economy than a common development problem shared by all developing-country members of APEC. Moreover, APEC was not a key forum for international IP rulemaking, and it was unlikely APEC could establish rules mandating the adoption of

[13] WTO TBT Committee, *Intellectual Property Right (IPR) Issues in Standardization,* Communication from the People's Republic of China 25 May 2005, G/TBT/W/251.

[14] WTO TBT Committee, *Minutes of the Meeting of 2 November 2005*, G/TBT/M/37, Para. 120.

[15] WTO TBT Committee, *Minutes of the Meeting of 4 August 2005*, G/TBT/M/36, Paras 102–104.

RAND as a binding principle for technology licensing with an authoritative interpretation.

Although China's efforts at promoting a universal interpretation of the RAND principle were ultimately unsuccessful, the proposal indicated China's awareness of active engagement in the WTO. The trajectory of the proposal showed how China had learned to use the strategy of forum-shifting. The outcome of the proposal revealed the strong veto power of the US and its allies to block a proposal. In addition, there were dissenting opinions within the Chinese government. Some Chinese government officials were not confident about China's role in promoting the proposal even if the US did not disagree. They were concerned that RAND was a principle initially developed from judicial practices mainly in the US and the EU. Specifically, China, as an importer of IP rules, did not have the capacity and knowledge to further steer relevant negotiations. Should the US and the EC agree to review RAND at the TBT Committee, they would dominate the negotiations and China would not be able to guarantee the outcome would eventually benefit the technology licensees as the proposal intended.

### 6.3.2 China and the WTO Negotiations on 'IP Waiver'

The WTO has experienced a crisis since 2017. The US has blocked all appointments to the WTO Appellate Body, which has paralysed its dispute settlement mechanism—a central pillar of the multilateral trade system. The EU and China played a key role in addressing the consequences of the US block through their proposal for a Multiparty Interim Appeal Arbitration Arrangement (MPIA). The MPIA is an alternative system for resolving WTO disputes that are appealed by a member in the absence of a functioning and staffed Appellate Body. Among all proposals, this is the only rules-based solution that would deter future similar attempts to sabotage the WTO dispute settlement mechanism (Gao, 2021). This demonstrates the increasingly important role China has played in supporting the functioning of the WTO. On the other hand, among the nine ongoing disputes via the MPIA, China is the respondent in five cases.[16] While China has always implemented WTO rulings, its role as the respondent in such a high number

[16] These cases include DS589: *China—Measures Concerning the Importation of Canola Seed from Canada*; DS598: *China—Anti-Dumping and Countervailing Duty Measures on Barley from Australia*; DS602: *China—Anti-Dumping and Countervailing Duty Measures on Wine from Australia*; DS610: *China—Alleged Chinese Restrictions on the Import and Export of Goods, and the Supply of Services, to and from Lithuania*; and DS611: *China—Enforcement of Intellectual Property Rights*. These are only some of the continuing WTO disputes with China as respondent (updated on 11 July 2022.).

of cases reveals the discontent and challenges China is facing in the WTO system. As the focus of this book is China's (active) engagement in global IP governance, this section will not elaborate on these broader issues but focus on the recent WTO negotiations on the possible waiver of IP rights as a response to the COVID-19 pandemic. While negotiations on global IP rules are often prolonged, and the WTO IP waiver negotiations are continuing, they so far have offered an opportunity to observe China's WTO engagement more closely.

The global COVID-19 pandemic has raised the concern that the IP system (in particular the patent system) could become a barrier to equitable access to affordable COVID-19 vaccines and medicines. This has further escalated the call for restricting or relinquishing relevant IP rights to achieve equitable distribution of COVID-19-related vaccines and medicines. The global pandemic has crystallised the conflict of rights—COVID-19-related discoveries are primary goods that are essential for fundamental human rights, on which basis related IP rights should be waived so that COVID-19-related vaccines and medicines can be distributed following the egalitarian principle.

These concerns quickly developed into concrete agenda at the WTO. In October 2020, India and South Africa proposed to the WTO that members should

> work together to ensure that intellectual property rights such as patents, industrial designs, copyright and protection of undisclosed information do not create barriers to the timely access to affordable medical products including vaccines and medicines or to scaling-up of research, development, manufacturing and supply of medical products essential to combat COVID-19.[17]

One measure to reach this objective, according to India and South Africa, is a waiver on IP, which should continue until widespread vaccination is in place globally and most of the world's population has developed immunity.

An IP waiver would be a crucial step towards 'people's vaccines' (Gonsalves & Yamey, 2021). While the IP/C/W/669 proposal was supported by more than 350 civil society organisations and activists around the world, it did not obtain consensus support among all WTO members. Chad, Tanzania, and other African nations and South-East Asian and South American countries supported the proposal on behalf of the least-developed countries. China, Costa Rica, Chile, Colombia, Jamaica, El Salvador, and Senegal

[17] WTO TRIPS Council, *Waiver from Certain Provisions of the TRIPS Agreement for the Prevention, Containment, and Treatment of COVID-19*, Communication from India and South Africa, 2 October 2020, IP/C/W/669.

welcomed the proposal without seeking clarification. Yet, the rejection by Brazil, Canada, Norway, the UK, the US, Switzerland, and the EU meant the proposal could not go further at the WTO (Chattu *et al.*, 2021).

Opinions among the epistemic community have been divergent. IP scholars have argued the TRIPS Agreement incorporates sufficient flexibilities such as compulsory licensing of patents to prevent negative effects, so an IP waiver is unnecessary (Hilty *et al.*, 2021). However, other scholars have pointed out that the case-by-case and product-by-product approach of compulsory licensing is not enough (Labonte & Johri, 2020), and the mechanism is extremely complex to use (Drahos, 2021).

After the IP/C/W/669 proposal, the EU submitted to the TRIPS Council an alternative proposal, in June 2021 (IP/C/W/681).[18] While recognising that 'the WTO must step up its efforts to ensure that the rules-based global trading system plays its role in response to the COVID-19 crisis', this proposal avoided using the term 'IP waiver' and sought to reaffirm that the COVID-19 pandemic has met various conditions in TRIPS Articles 31 and 31*bis*. It is the IP waiver that signals pharmaceutical companies' IP rights should not be allowed to trump people's health rights and makes egalitarianism the basis for vaccine access. By avoiding using the term 'IP waiver', IP/C/W/681 did not attempt to seek further restrictions on IP other than confirming the applicability of the existing flexibilities available in the TRIPS Agreement.

In May 2021, the US also expressed willingness to engage in text-based negotiations for an IP waiver with narrower scope (vaccines only).[19] Thereafter, the EU, India, South Africa, and the US formed the Quad to engage in an informal process to produce a draft for text-based negotiations at the WTO. The outcome document from this process was disseminated among WTO members in early May 2022 (IP/C/W/688).[20] Some commentators have said this document is 'worse than no waiver' (Labonte, 2022). This is because it narrows the scope from the original IP/C/W/669 proposal's extensive coverage of technology including therapeutics, diagnostics, and other essential COVID-19-related health products to vaccines only. It includes an additional condition that companies producing generics must identify 'all related patents', which is a TRIPS-plus standard because TRIPS Agreement

---

[18] WTO TRIPS Council, *Draft General Council Declaration on the TRIPS Agreement and Public Health in the Circumstances of a Pandemic*, Communication from the European Union to the Council for TRIPS, 18 June 2021, IP/C/W/681.

[19] USTR, *Statement from Ambassador Katherine Tai on the COVID-19 TRIPS Waiver*, 5 May 2021, available from https://ustr.gov/about-us/policy-offices/press-office/press-releases/2021/may/statement-ambassador-katherine-tai-COVID-19-trips-waiver.

[20] WTO TRIPS Council, *Communication from the Chairperson*, 3 May 2022, IP/C/W/688.

did not have such a requirement. It also narrows the scope of the waiver to 'eligible members' instead of all WTO members. Footnote 1 provides two definitions of eligible members: Option 1 includes all developing countries but encourages those with the export capacity to opt out of the waiver; Option 2 defines eligible countries as developing countries which supplied no more than 10% of global vaccine exports in 2021. This eligibility requirement, no matter which option is adopted, confirms its TRIPS-plus nature as every WTO member can use Article 31 flexibilities. If the purpose of the IP waiver is to enhance production capacity through compulsory licensing, its provisions should not encourage countries with production and export capacity to opt out or establish an eligibility threshold. Arguably, generic drug companies in countries with export capacity are also those most capable of scaling up vaccine production. If a treaty or declaration on an IP waiver excludes these entities, it defeats its purpose of promoting equitable global access to affordable vaccines and medicines.

China would be effectively excluded from the deal should the second definition of an eligible member in IP/C/W/688 be adopted. At the WTO TRIPS Council meeting on 10 May 2022, Chinese representative LI Chenggang disagreed with the Quad text. He emphasised the fact that the outcomes of the negotiations should be fair and non-discriminatory; otherwise, it would be difficult to build consensus among those who were not involved in the process.

Specifically, China did not accept the second definition in Footnote 1, which used the criterion of export share to define eligible members. Ambassador Li said such an unreasonable and arbitrary criterion sent the wrong signal to the world and would have systemic implications for future negotiations:

> On one hand, this implies punishment to those who supplied a large amount of vaccines to others even when they themselves were suffering from shortages. On the other hand, this constitutes a tolerance or even an incentive for members to adopt inward-looking policies and apply export restrictions in difficult times when we should resist such temptations. So my question to everyone in this room is: is it a right signal that the WTO, a long-time advocate of free trade and multilateral cooperation, should be sending to the world? Should the contributions made by members during the pandemic be encouraged or discarded?[21]

[21] MOFCOM, *Statement by H.E. Ambassador Li Chenggang at Informal Meeting of TRIPS Council*, Ministry of Commerce of the People's Republic of China, 6 May 2022, available from http://wto.mofcom.gov.cn/article/newsupdates/202205/20220503310786.shtml.

China did not engage as actively as India and South Africa in the WTO negotiations on the IP waiver. At a TRIPS Council meeting in 2020, China welcomed the Indian and South African proposal for an IP waiver and explicitly mentioned its willingness to engage in discussions, but it did not co-sponsor the proposal.[22] This was similar to China's response to the negotiations on GIs and disclosure requirements when they were proposed at the TRIPS Council as new agendas. Three decades ago, the TRIPS negotiations expanded in ever-widening circles, and it was in the informal groups where much of the real negotiating was done and where the consensus and agreement that mattered were obtained (Drahos, 2007). This mechanism for WTO negotiations has not changed, while the Quad members were different—the US, EC, Japan, and Canada in the TRIPS negotiations and US, EU, India, and South Africa in the IP waiver negotiations. China's early reluctance to clarify its position and show genuine interest in the IP waiver negotiations excluded it from the core circle in the negotiations so far.

There are two explanations for China's engagement on this issue. First, it seems China has own its agenda to help make vaccines available globally, in particular, for developing countries. Participating in the IP waiver is only part of this agenda and may not be the most important part. At the 2020 World Health Assembly, President Xi pledged that once China had invented a vaccine, it would become a global public good and China would share it with other countries (Gretler, 2020). This set the foundation for China's position at the WTO TRIPS Council meeting:

> China has taken good note of the capacity constraints that developing countries encounter in using TRIPS flexibilities such as compulsory licensing, as pointed out by the proposal. China has made serious commitment that COVID-19 vaccine development and deployment in China, when available, will be made a global public good and developing countries will be our priorities.[23]

In addition to this declaration, China participated in the COVID-19 Vaccines Global Access (COVAX), the global pooled procurement mechanism for COVID-19 vaccines to facilitate fair and equitable access to vaccines for all 190 participating economies. China also emphasised the importance of information-sharing and the need to seek a solution to scale up the timely supply of vaccines. China briefed the WTO members on the 'Information

[22] WTO TRIPS Council. *Minutes of Meeting: Held in the Centre William Rappard on 15–16 October and 10 December 2020*, 16 February 2021, IP/C/M/96/Add.1, para. 977.

[23] Ibid., para. 976.

Sharing Platform for Patents on Epidemic Prevention against COVID-19' as the basis for information exchange.[24]

These more unilaterally and bilaterally oriented efforts were partly the result of pragmaticism to get things done in time. As pointed out by Drahos (2021, p. 7), international IP negotiations 'can be seen as linear functions competing against exponential functions of growth (the virus) and decline (the death of people)'. Indeed, by the time the WTO produced a document for text-based negotiation on the deal that was considered worse than no waiver in May 2022, the vaccine supply issue was no longer so urgent. China contributed to relieving the shortage of supply before the document. By August 2021, China's vaccine donations through foreign aid and exports had reached 700 million doses, exceeding the total number of vaccines donated and exported from all other countries combined (Qu, 2021). This number reached 2.2 billion in May 2022, including technology transfers and joint production in Africa.[25] In certain periods in 2020 and 2021, the EU, India, and the US, three members of the Quad, enacted export restrictions on vaccines to meet their domestic demand.[26] In this context, even though China's vaccine donations and technology transfers did not obtain publicity in Western media and have been framed as 'vaccine diplomacy' (Lee, 2021), they did enhance the provision of vaccines as global public goods.

There could be deeper reasons for China's greater focus on vaccine exports and donations at the bilateral level rather than on becoming a core member of the WTO IP waiver negotiations. First, China is confident in its innovation capacity to develop its own vaccines. Chinese biological and pharmaceutical industries have experienced significant development in the past decade (Chapter 3). Chinese scientists were the first to publish the genome sequence of COVID-19 to the WHO and the first to start research on a vaccine. Some Chinese institutions accumulated research capacity after the 2003 Severe Acute Respiratory Syndrome (SARS) pandemic. More than two-thirds (363) of the 500-plus patents for biologics to treat and prevent SARS and MERS were for vaccine development (Liu *et al.*, 2020). This means China could benefit from its existing research foundations on SARS, which fast-tracked the overall process of vaccine development (Deb *et al.*, 2020). In addition, as the world's leading producer and exporter of active pharmaceutical ingredients (APIs), China provides almost 70% of APIs for Indian pharmaceutical

---

24 Ibid., para. 89.

25 'Statement by H.E. Ambassador Li Chenggang at Informal Meeting of TRIPS Council'.

26 WTO, *COVID-19: Measures Affecting Trade in Goods as of May 30, 2022*, available from: https://www.wto.org/english/tratop_e/covid19_e/trade_related_goods_measure_e.htm.

companies (Chatterjee, 2020). This added to China's confidence in scaling up domestic production capacity once a vaccine was developed.

Second, even though China's Patent Law incorporates compulsory licensing, this mechanism has never been used domestically by generic drug companies. In the Patent Law amendment in 2000, China precisely reiterated the provisions in Article 31 of the TRIPS Agreement on compulsory licences as domestic law. On 29 November 2005, SIPO issued its *Measures for Compulsory License of Patents Concerning Public Health*,[27] as part of the implementation of the *Doha Declaration on the TRIPS Agreement and Public Health*. Since then, civil society and domestic pharmaceutical companies have tried to apply for compulsory licences. There has been only one reported such case, where the community of Chinese hepatitis and HIV/AIDS sufferers submitted a petition to grant a compulsory licence for the drug Lamivudine to the MOFCOM, the Ministry of Health, SIPO, the Chinese Centre for Disease Control and Prevention and the China Food and Drug Administration (Fang & Zou, 2012). However, no compulsory licences were issued as there was simply no application by Chinese genetic drug companies. So far there has been no announcement of a single case of compulsory licensing in the 18 years since SIPO's measures were announced in 2005. This suggests China may not think negotiations on compulsory licensing are a practical solution to vaccine shortages—in particular when the mechanism is so complex and has never been used. In the context of the WTO crisis and the potentially prolonged negotiations, China has decided to rely more on its innovation and unilateral and bilateral engagement to enhance equitable access to medicines, rather than being actively involved in the IP waiver negotiations. Nonetheless, not actively engaging in the IP waiver negotiations came with the cost that China was excluded from the list of eligible members for the waiver according to IP/C/W/688. After Ambassador Li's speech, the WTO's Director General appreciated China's bold move to show leadership (WTO, 2022). As this is a fast-evolving issue, that are still opportunities for China to participate in the negotiation to extend the IP waiver from COVID vaccines to COVID treatment and tests.

In terms of implications for global distributive justice, the China–WTO engagement presents a more complex picture. China's first WTO proposal was a simple case to show the difficulty it had in promoting alternative and more favourable rules for patent users (licensees). Even though the RAND proposal had a clear development orientation, it did not obtain much support when tabled at the WTO, not even from the developing-country

---

[27] These measures were replaced with *Measures for Compulsory Licence of Patent Implementation*, Promulgated by Order No. 64 of SIPO, 15 March 2012.

members. The WTO's decision-making mechanism requires consensus, and the proposal failed when the US refused to discuss it. Despite the China having a good record in its compliance with WTO dispute settlement decisions and support for the establishment of the MPIA, the IP waiver negotiations demonstrate that China has still tangentially participated in WTO rulemaking.

Assuming the limited impact of compulsory licensing on its domestic practices, China took a pragmatic approach by focusing on measures that can directly enhance vaccine availability, rather than participating as a core member in the WTO IP waiver negotiations. Yet, without its participation, the text of IP/C/W/688 set unreasonable and arbitrary criteria for eligible members, which went against the WTO's general principle of non-discrimination. The key lesson for China here is it needs to understand WTO negotiations as ever-widening circles and the importance of active participation. For the international IP order to be fairer, states need to actively engage in negotiations, even though there can be more effective measures to be taken in parallel.

Nonetheless, the case also reveals China's agenda for promoting access to COVID-19 vaccines as global public goods. It has engaged in multiple ways to achieve this goal, including self-innovation, scaling up domestic production capacity, and bilateral engagement through vaccine exports and donations. With the donation and export of 2.2 billion vaccine doses up to May 2022, China's measures have contributed to enhancing global equitable access to vaccines in the early stages of COVID-19. This was a significant contribution considering in the same period other major jurisdictions with production capacity were stockpiling vaccines through export controls. Such measures demonstrate China's appeal to cosmopolitanism as a principle for global distributive justice to enhance the availability of vaccines beyond its national border (Collste, 2022).

## 6.4 Conclusion

This chapter examined China's IP engagement with WIPO and the WTO, the two major multilateral forums for global IP rulemaking. The continuing WTO negotiations on IP waiver add uncertainty and difficulty to assessments of the future direction of China's international IP engagement. There are, however, some general observations that can be made of China's multilateral engagement—in particular, when these engagements are considered together with its engagement bilaterally (Chapter 5) and plurilaterally (Cheng, 2019).

China's positions on the same issues can be inconsistent at different forums. China's engagement with WIPO aims to facilitate its rising IP applications and to better serve the interests of Chinese IP rightholders. At the WTO, China seeks to take a pro-development position that is aligned with other developing countries. Bilaterally, however, it included TRIPS-plus standards in its FTAs (Chapter 5). At the plurilateral level, China collaborated with WIPO in IP capacity-building in BRI countries through its provision of technical assistance. This observations constitute the basis for China's strategy of 'dissembling' in its engagement in global IP governance, which will be discussed in Chapter 9.

This chapter also shows the Chinese strategy of multi-forum engagement in navigating the international IP regime complexity (Chapter 9). Unlike the US strategy of forum-shifting and new forum creation, China tends to play a multi-forum game. While China advocates its own regional or plurilateral IP arrangements, it simultaneously supports WIPO and the WTO as pillars of IP multilateralism. This is consistent with findings that in its engagement in international financial regulation where China did not seek to demolish or exit from current international organisations and multilateral regimes but construct additional channels, partly complementary and partly competitive, to shape the international order beyond what the Western leadership has promised (Heilmann *et al*., 2014).

## References


Abbott, F. M. (2000). Distributed Governance at the WTO-WIPO: An Evolving Model for Open-architecture Integrated Governance. *Journal of International Economic Law, 3*(1), 63–81.

An, B. (2005) *Intellectual Property Issues in Standardization 标准化中的知识产权问题*. http://it.sohu.com/20050425/n225329829.shtml. Accessed 11 May 2018.

Braithwaite, J., & Drahos, P. (2000). *Global Business Regulation*. Cambridge University Press.

Chatterjee, P. (2020). Indian Pharma Threatened by COVID-19 Shutdowns in China. *The Lancet, 395*(10225), 675.

Chattu, V. K., Singh, B., Kaur, J., & Jakovljevic, M. (2021). COVID-19 Vaccine, TRIPS, and Global Health Diplomacy: India's Role at the WTO Platform. *BioMed Research International, 2021*, 6658070.

Cheng, W. (2019). China Engages with the Global Intellectual Property Governance: The Recent Trend. *The Journal of World Intellectual Property, 22*(3–4), 1–16.

Cheng, W., & Drahos, P. (2018). How China Built the World's Biggest Patent Office—The Pressure Driving Mechanism. *IIC-International Review of Intellectual Property and Competition Law, 49*(1), 5–40.

Collste, G. (2022). 'Where You Live Should Not Determine Whether You Live'. Global Justice and the Distribution of COVID-19 Vaccines. *Ethics & Global Politics, 15*(2), 43–54.

Cottier, T. (2015). Working Together towards TRIPS. In J. Watal & A. Taubman (Eds.), *The Making of the TRIPS Agreement: Personal Insights from the Uruguay Round negotiations* (pp. 79–94). WTO Online Bookshop.

Deb, B., Shah, H., & Goel, S. (2020). Current Global Vaccine and Drug Efforts against COVID-19: Pros and Cons of Bypassing Animal Trials. *Journal of Biosciences, 45*(1), 1–10.

Drahos, P. (2007). Four Lessons for Developing Countries from the Trade Negotiations Over Access to Medicines. *Liverpool Law Review, 28*(1), 11–39.

Drahos, P. (2010). *The Global Governance of Knowledge: Patent Offices and Their Clients*. Cambridge University Press.

Drahos, P. (2021). *Public Lies and Public Goods: Ten Lessons from When Patents and Pandemics Meet* (EUI Working Paper LAW 2021/5).

Drezner, D. W. (2008). *All Politics Is Global: Explaining International Regulatory Regimes*. Princeton University Press.

Fang, S., & Zou, S. (2012). China Began a New Era of Patent Compulsory License?—Comment on the New *Measures for the Compulsory License of Patents* 中国开始专利强制许可新时代?—评新的《专利实施强制许可办法》. *Lexis Chinese Legal Perspective 律商中国法律透视*(59).

Farrell, J., Hayes, J., Shapiro, C., & Sullivan, T. (2007). Standard Setting, Patents, and Hold-up. *Antitrust Law Journal, 74*(3), 603–670.

Gao, H. (2021). Finding a Rule-Based Solution to the Appellate Body Crisis: Looking Beyond the Multiparty Interim Appeal Arbitration Arrangement. *Journal of International Economic Law, 24*(3), 534–550.

Gervais, D. (2009). China-Measures Affecting the Protection and Enforcement of Intellectual Property Rights. *American Journal of International Law, 103*(3), 549–555.

Gonsalves, G., & Yamey, G. (2021). The COVID-19 Vaccine Patent Waiver: A Crucial Step towards a "People's Vaccine". *British Medical Journal*, 373. https://doi.org/10.1136/bmj.n1249

Gretler, C. (2020). *Xi Wows China Will Share Vaccine and Gives WHO Full Backing*. Bloomberg. https://www.bloomberg.com/news/articles/2020-05-18/china-s-virus-vaccine-will-be-global-public-good-xi-says. Accessed 11 July 2022.

Guan, W. (2014). *Intellectual Property Theory and Practice: A Critical Examination of China's TRIPS Compliance and Beyond*. Springer.

Heilmann, S., Rudolf, M., Huotari, M., & Buckow, J. (2014). *China's Shadow Foreign Policy: Parallel Structures Challenge the Established International Order*.

https://merics.org/sites/default/files/2020-05/China_Monitor_18_Shadow_Foreign_Policy_EN.pdf. Mercator Institute for China Studies.

Helfer, L. R., Land, M. K., Okediji, R. L., & Reichman, J. H. (2017). *The World Blind Union Guide to the Marrakesh Treaty: Facilitating Access to Books for Print-disabled Individuals.* Oxford University Press.

Hilty, R., Batista, P. H. D., Carls, S., Kim, D., Lamping, M., & Slowinski, P. R. (2021). COVID-19 and the Role of Intellectual Property: Position Statement of the Max Planck Institute for Innovation and Competition of 7 May 2021. *Max Planck Institute for Innovation & Competition Research Paper* (21-13).

Labonte, R. (2022). We Still Need a Vaccine Patent Waiver, but Not the One on Offer at the World Trade Organization Meeting. *The Conversation.* https://theconversation.com/we-still-need-a-vaccine-patent-waiver-but-not-the-one-on-offer-at-the-world-trade-organization-meeting-181235. Accessed 11 July 2022.

Labonte, R., & Johri, M. (2020). COVID-19 Drug and Vaccine Patents Are Putting Profit before People. *The Conversation.* https://theconversation.com/covid-19-drug-and-vaccine-patents-are-putting-profit-before-people-149270. Accessed 25 October 2022.

Lee, S. T. (2021). Vaccine Diplomacy: Nation Branding and China's COVID-19 Soft Power Play. *Place Branding and Public Diplomacy.* https://doi.org/10.1057/s41254-021-00224-4

Liu, C., Zhou, Q., Li, Y., Garner, L. V., Watkins, S. P., Carter, L. J., Smoot, J., Gregg, A. C., Daniels, A. D., & Jervey, S. (2020). *Research and Development on Therapeutic Agents and Vaccines for COVID-19 and Related Human Coronavirus Diseases.* ACS Publications.

Liu, G. (2009). *The History of China Joined International Copyright Conventions 我国加入国际版权公约的前前后后.* http://www.ncac.gov.cn/chinacopyright/contents/537/20672.html. Accessed 11 May 2018.

Liu, R. (2007, January 17). Intellectual Property Issues in Standardization 标准化中的知识产权问题. *China Intellectual Property News 中国知识产权报.*

May, C. (2006). *World Intellectual Property Organization (WIPO): Resurgence and the Development Agenda.* Routledge.

Overholt, W. H. (2015). One Belt, One Road, One Pivot. *Global Asia, 10*(3), 1–8.

Qu, S. (2021, August 1). The Number of China's Foreign Aid and Exports of COVID-19 Vaccines Has Exceeded Those from Other Countries Combined 中国对外援助和出口新冠疫苗数量超过其他国家总和. *People's Daily 人民日报.*

SAIC. (2016). *China Reinforced Its Cooperation with WIPO in Trademarks 中国加强与世界知识产权组织在商标领域的合作.* http://www.saic.gov.cn/jggk/zjld/zm/zyhd/201605/t20160517_172148.html. Accessed 22 May 2017.

SCIO. (1994). *The Situation for Intellectual Property Protection in China 中国知识产权保护状况.* http://www.fmprc.gov.cn/ce/cept/chn/zt/zgzfbps/t95340.htm

Scott, J., & Wilkinson, R. (2013). China Threat? Evidence from the WTO. *Journal of World Trade, 47*(4), 761–782.

Sell, S. K. (2003). *Private Power, Public Law: The Globalization of Intellectual Property Rights*. Cambridge University Press.

Sell, S. K. (2010). TRIPS Was Never Enough: Vertical Forum Shifting, FTAS, ACTA, and TTP. *Journal of Intellectual Property Law, 18*(2), 447–478.

Sell, S. K., & Prakash, A. (2004). Using Ideas Strategically: The Contest Between Business and NGO Networks in Intellectual Property Rights. *International Studies Quarterly, 48*(1), 143–175.

SIPO. (2016). *Speech of SHEN Changyu at the 56th Assembly of WIPO (Full Text) 申长雨在第56届WIPO成员国大会上的发言 (全文)*. http://www.sipo.gov.cn/zscqgz/1100762.htm. Accessed 27 May 2017.

Swaine, M. D. (2015). *Chinese Views and Commentary on the 'One Belt, One Road' Initiative*. Hoover Institution.

Thomas, K. (2017). *Assessing Intellectual Property Compliance in Contemporary China: The World Trade Organisation TRIPS Agreement*. Springer.

Wang, L., & Wu, H. (2001). *China-US Intellectual Property Negotiation Review 披尽黄沙始见金—中美知识产权谈判再回顾*. http://www.cpo.cn.net/zscqb/zhuanban/t20011116_2735.htm. Accessed 4 May 2017.

WIPO. (2016a). *High Level "Belt and Road" Conference Urges Closer IP Collaboration for Economic Growth*. http://www.wipo.int/about-wipo/en/offices/china/news/2016a/news_0008.html. Accessed 15 May 2018.

WIPO. (2016b). *WIPO Director General Wraps up Official Visit to China*. http://www.wipo.int/about-wipo/en/dgo/news/2016b/news_0037.html. Accessed 22 May 2017.

WIPO. (2017). *China Tops Patent, Trademark, Design Filings in 2016*. http://www.wipo.int/pressroom/en/articles/2017/article_0013.html. Accessed 16 May 2018.

WIPO. (2021). *Annual Financial Report and Financial Statements*. https://www.wipo.int/edocs/pubdocs/en/wipo_pub_rn2021_18e.pdf

WIPO. (2022a). *WIPO-Administered Treaties*. https://www.wipo.int/treaties/en/. Accessed 5 July 2022.

WIPO. (2022b). *WIPO IP Facts and Figures 2021*. https://tind.wipo.int/record/44650

WTO. (2022). *Members Welcome Quad Document as Basis for Text-based Negotiations on Pandemic IP Response*. https://www.wto.org/english/news_e/news22_e/gc_10may22_e.htm. Accessed 11 July 2022.

Yan, X. (2014). The Milestone for Chinese Copyright Cause: The History for the Promulgation of the Beijing Audiovisual Performance 中国版权事业的里程碑—《视听表演北京条约》出台始末. *China Copyright 中国版权年鉴, 3*, 5–9.

Yu, P. K. (2011). TRIPS Enforcement Dispute. *Nebraska Law Review, 89*(4), 1046–1131.

Zhao, Y. (2008). The Establishment of the Chinese Patent System Manifested Efforts of Comrade DENG Xiaoping 专利制度的建立凝聚了小平同志的心血. *Intellectual Property and Reform and Opening-up in the Past 30 Years 知识产权与改革开放三十年*. Intellectual Property Publishing House 知识产权出版社.

# Part III

## Discussion

Chapters 7–9 adapt the analytical framework from Braithwaite and Drahos' *Global Business Regulation* (Braithwaite & Drahos, 2000) and analyse data from the case studies in terms of actors, principles and strategies. The discussion draws on data from the previous chapters as well as China's plurilateral engagement, which the author has discussed elsewhere (Cheng, 2019a). Chapter 7 will address the actors involved in China's international IP engagement, with the Chinese state as the focus. This analysis will be complemented by that of the various substate actors involved in determining policy (ministries affiliated with the State Council) and non-state actors (epistemic communities and private actors). Drawing on case studies, Chapter 8 will identify principles for China's international IP engagement. Chapter 9 will discuss the strategies China uses, including those related to forums and principles.

# 7

# Who Governs? Actors in China's International IP Engagement

## 7.1 Introduction

One basic assumption of realism, a school of international relations theory, is that states are the major actors in international society. However, focusing on China as a unitary actor is not sufficient to understand its international engagement in IP issues. Viewing China as a unitary actor may not enable detailed observation internally—for instance, who represents China in negotiations at various forums, and who builds transnational networks with substate actors of other states. Further, an analysis of domestic deliberations, which could influence China's international IP engagement, is not possible if China is considered a unitary actor. Based on previous case studies, this chapter will produce a more detailed analysis of the actors involved in China's international IP engagement. This level of analysis is helpful to understand the different outcomes of China's engagement in different cases and the different strategies China has used.

## 7.2 Substate Actors

For present purposes, 'substate actors' refers to Chinese ministries affiliated with the State Council that have the mandate to regulate specific IP issues and can represent China in its international engagements. Table 7.1 provides a summary of substate actors involved in multilateral, plurilateral, and bilateral IP engagement in the cases examined in Chapters 2–6.


W. Cheng, *China in Global Governance of Intellectual Property*, Palgrave Socio-Legal Studies, https://doi.org/10.1007/978-3-031-24370-7_7

**Table 7.1** Substate actors as Chinese representatives in international IP forums

| Issue area | Forums | Substate actors |
|---|---|---|
| Geographical indications | WTO TRIPS Council | MOFCOM |
| | WIPO IGC | SAIC |
| | Bilateral FTAs | MOFCOM |
| | EU–China Agreement on GI Mutual Recognition | MOFCOM, AQSIQ |
| | National level | SAIC, AQSIQ, MOA |
| Disclosure obligation | CBD and Nagoya Protocol | Ministry of Ecology and Environment (MEE), SIPO (now the China National IP Administration, CNIPA) |
| | WTO TRIPS Council | MOFCOM |
| | WIPO IGC | SIPO |
| | National level | SIPO |
| IP and standardisation (the WAPI case) | National standard-setting | MIIT, SAC, AQSIQ |
| | ISO/IEC JCT1 SC6 | SAC |
| | Bilateral: JCCT | Vice-Premier of China, MOFCOM |
| | Domestic implementation | Local Chinese courts and NDRC |
| IP provisions or chapters in FTAs | Bilateral | MOFCOM |
| RAND proposal | WTO TBT, APEC | MOFCOM, SIPO |
| Beijing Treaty on Audiovisual Performances | WIPO | NCAC, MFA, MOFCOM, SAIC, SIPO, LAO and LAC |
| Patent prosecution highway | Bilateral | SIPO |
| International patent classification (IPC) proposal | WIPO | SIPO |
| Hague Agreement | WIPO | SIPO |
| Patent-related cooperation among major patent offices | IP5 (the world's five largest patent offices) | SIPO |
| IP and public health, data exclusivity and patent linkage | US-China IP Cooperation Dialogue | CFDA (now the National Medical Products Administration, NMPA) |

MOFCOM, as the trade negotiator for China, has been the ministry most extensively involved in international IP negotiations and other forms of engagement among the 31 IP-related regulators in China at the central government level (see Appendix 2). These regulators are members of the State Council Inter-Ministerial Joint Meeting for the Implementation of the

National IP Strategy with its general office located at the SIPO. Several ministries that regulate a specific IP issue (ministries in charge) are also mandated to represent China in international engagement or cooperation on that issue, which is set out in each ministry's *Provisions on the Main Mandates, Setup of Internal Bodies and Staffing*. Over time, these ministries have developed transnational networks with their counterparts in other jurisdictions. Such networks of technocrats have played an important role in the global diffusion of IP norms (Drahos, 2008). Among Chinese substate actors, SIPO has already developed into a new node in international patent regulation. This section will analyse MOFCOM, SIPO and rule-implementing actors, as well as some ministries missing from China's global IP engagement.

### 7.2.1 MOFCOM: The Checkpoint for China's IP Engagement

MOFCOM was established in 2003, two years after China's WTO accession. It has comprehensively regulated domestic and international trade and economic issues, including designing strategies and policies for domestic and foreign trade and international economic cooperation and participating in multilateral, regional, and bilateral trade negotiations. MOFCOM essentially functions as the 'checkpoint' for China's international IP engagement—a metaphor that has two meanings: First, MOFCOM coordinates China's international IP engagement, implemented by ministries in charge; and second, if an issue is agreed to by MOFCOM in negotiation, it will usually be implemented in China without further checks.

MOFCOM is the key negotiator on IP issues on almost every front indicated in Table 7.1. As China's trade negotiator, it has the resources and capacity to bargain across issues and coordinate negotiations with transnational and international actors. IP is one of the many issues it can juggle with. China needs to have MOFCOM in coordinating positions at various forums to best represent the country's interests—as illustrated by the GI case.

With CNIPA and MOA establishing three GI protection mechanisms (Chapter 2), GI regulation in China is a typical example of regulatory competition. Both ministries regulating GIs have developed networks with international IP organisations or their counterparts from other states. When more than one ministry could represent China in international engagement, a trading partner can approach the most convenient ministry with which to undertake negotiations. This selective negotiation could undermine China's overall bargaining capacity.

In its bilateral cooperation with China, the European Union (EU) insightfully selected AQSIQ (instead of SAIC) with which to negotiate the mutual recognition of GIs. As early as October 2006, the European Commission Directorate-General for Agriculture and Rural Development and Directorate-General for Trade agreed with AQSIQ on the mutual recognition of GIs, and the two sides each nominated 10 GIs in a pilot '10 + 10' project (AQSIQ, 2009). In 2007, the EU–China intellectual property rights (IPR2) project was launched, in which MOFCOM began to represent China in the bilateral GI negotiations with the EU. The negotiations with MOFCOM became slower for the EU than its previous negotiations with AQSIQ. The '10 + 10' programme took another five years to finalise. Its upgraded version, '275 + 275', was concluded after the US-China bilateral IP agreement in 2020 (Chapter 2).

The GI case shows that it is easier for a trade partner to make a deal with a specialised IP ministry than with MOFCOM. By negotiating with AQSIQ, the EU could focus only on GIs and the parties could quickly get to the technicalities without being influenced by broader bilateral relations. However, MOFCOM negotiates everything related to trade, and IP is only one of the issues. Simultaneously, negotiating many issues with one trading partner enabled MOFCOM to arrange reciprocal coordination (Braithwaite & Drahos, 2000). Thus, the EU would have had to concede on other issues to make a deal on GIs with China.

A domestic IP regulator tends to make decisions based on the technocratic trust built with its counterparts. The EU and the US have focused on IP-related capacity-building in China for years. Through exchange and training programmes, study tours and seminars since the 1990s, Chinese IP regulators and epistemic communities have been convinced that the EU and US IP systems are the 'most advanced' in the world and China needed to 'learn from the best'. Chinese officials attending technical training also absorbed the norms and values of the training programme.

When the EU and China undertook negotiations on the mutual recognition of GIs, AQSIQ, the Chinese negotiator in the early stage, genuinely believed that the GI system would help rural prosperity and that mutual recognition would benefit Chinese agriculture and exports. This trust led negotiators into detailed discussions regarding the technical issues and implementation mechanisms, rather than calculating where China would relatively gain from the deal as compared with the EU.

The second dimension of the checkpoint metaphor essentially means that the MOFCOM ensures compliance there are no further checks once

MOFCOM agrees. For example, after the 2004 JCCT, the implementation of WAPI as a national compulsory standard was indefinitely suspended (Chapter 4). MOFCOM's assent was fundamental in this case. MOFCOM's checkpoint role makes it possible for China to implement systematic strategies in its international IP engagement—in particular, dissembling (Chapter 9).

### 7.2.2 SIPO: A New Node for International Patent Regulation

SIPO[1] has been one of the ministries most extensively involved in China's international IP engagement. As a result of the surge in patent applications from Chinese residents, since 2011, SIPO has become the biggest patent office in the world (WIPO, 2012). It has come to play an increasingly important role in global patent regulation. In addition to representing the Chinese government, SIPO has developed its own transnational networks with its counterparts (the patent offices of other states) and international organisations (WIPO and the WTO). For instance, SIPO has been one of the 'IP5', the world's five largest patent offices, and 'ID5', the five largest offices for industrial designs. SIPO has also established a patent prosecution highway (PPH) with 31 patent offices globally. The pilot PPH programme for IP5 launched in September 2013 (EPO, 2016), and thereafter, the Chinese PPH expanded to smaller patent offices such as Austria, Mexico, Iceland, and Israel.[2]

In addition to cooperation on patent examinations with other major patent offices, SIPO began to contribute to discussions about harmonisation of international patent classification, under the WIPO-administered treaty *Strasbourg Agreement Concerning the International Patent Classification* (IPC). China has distinctive traditional knowledge, particularly in plant pesticides. At the thirty-fifth Committee of Experts of the IPC Union meeting in October 2004, SIPO proposed a detailed classification of botanical pesticides. To persuade others to accept this classification, SIPO skilfully framed its demand as a specific issue related to one of the meeting's agenda items—consideration of the need for further development of IPC concerning biodiversity. Chinese representatives proposed that botanical pesticide technologies

[1] Although the official English name of this regulator was changed to the China National Intellectual Property Administration (CNIPA) in September 2018, this chapter uses the old name, SIPO, as it is more commonly known and most of the issues discussed happened before the name change.

[2] These include. For a full list of patent offices that have established PPH with China, see https://www.cnipa.gov.cn/col/col46/index.html, Accessed 16 July 2022.

cover the relevant subject matter relating to 'developing new pesticides with biocompatibility'.[3] They requested a more detailed patent classification in IPC A01N65/00 concerning botanical pesticides, to facilitate patent document searches in this area. One month later, at the twelfth meeting of the IPC Revision Working Group, SIPO submitted its proposal for the detailed classification of IPC A01N65/00 for plant pesticides, as a solution to the search problem. It took SIPO more than two years to undertake intensive negotiations with patent offices in Germany, the UK, the US, Japan, the EU, Sweden, and WIPO. The proposal, finally adopted by WIPO in 2007, was the first Chinese proposal on IPC (The New Century of Agrochem, 2007).

SIPO then participated in six IPC revision projects. For instance, China volunteered to be a rapporteur for the WIPO Five-Year Plan for the Revision of IPC in 2013.[4] Among the six revision projects, SIPO played the role of rapporteur in two: C462 (IPC revision in the field of transmission in electronic communication techniques) and C464 (IPC revision in the field of food or foodstuffs and their preparation or treatment).[5] Both projects have been completed and SIPO's proposals have been adopted by WIPO (Wu, 2016).

India has created Traditional Knowledge Digital Library (TKDL)—a database designed to protect India's centuries-old traditional knowledge. The TKDL plays a defensive role within the existing IP protection system by preventing the misappropriation of traditional knowledge. From 2009 to 2011, the EPO used the TKDL to identify 36 patents making use of Indian traditional knowledge (WIPO, 2011). SIPO also developed its own Traditional Chinese Medicine Patent Database (TCMPD) (Liu & Sun, 2004), which is different from the TKDL because it is a database of the patented traditional Chinese medicines granted by SIPO, not a database of traditional knowledge itself. While the Chinese proposals are complementary to the existing IPC and do not involve rival standards, these cases show that SIPO is moving closer to the centre stage in international patent regulation and is interested in facilitating relevant patent examinations among WIPO members.

[3] WIPO Special Union for the International Patent Classification Committee of Experts, Thirty-Fifth Session, *Classification Tools Relating to Traditional Knowledge and Biodiversity*, IPC/CE/35/7, 21 September 2004.

[4] WIPO International Bureau, Project CE 453, *Five-Year Plan for the Revision of the IPC*, 7 February 2013, see Para. 5 for the issue areas to be revised and Para. 11 for the responsibilities of the rapporteurs.

[5] WIPO Special Union for the International Patent Classification Committee of Experts, Thirty-Fifth Session, *Report*, IPC/CE/45/2, 22 March 2013, see Para. 20 for the list of projects.

From a nodal governance perspective (Burris *et al.*, 2005), SIPO has become an important node of global patent governance. With its integration into the international IP (particularly patent) system, SIPO began to identify itself as a somewhat independent actor to promote international IP regulation. The recent development of SIPO's IP engagement in forums and various programmes on IP capacity-building also signals its intention to become an IP regulatory exporter. It has quietly experimented with exporting its IP regulation by providing technical assistance, training, and exchange programmes to the BRICS and BRI countries. IP capacity-building has been deemed necessary when Chinese companies invest extensively overseas and export their own patented technologies.

As an 'independent' node, SIPO has made efforts to expedite the number of patent applications or to benefit potential rightholders as clients of the patent system. This level of normative integration has indeed diverged from China's general position in its international IP engagement as a developing country that insists the TRIPS Agreement should balance IP protection and effective technology dissemination. Moreover, as SIPO has been deeply integrated into the private insiders' governance network with other big patent offices, it increasingly thinks within rather than outside the international patent paradigm. Abbott *et al.* (2013) suggested that emerging economies such as China, India, and Brazil would be the potential force for change in the global patent order, but the above analysis on SIPO would add more nuances to the role played by substate actors.

### 7.2.3 Rule-Implementing Actors: Judicial Activism

Chinese rule-implementing actors include both the courts in judicial enforcement and IP administrations in administrative enforcement. Administrative enforcement has been a legacy before the TRIPS Agreement and is increasingly institutionalised in its procedure. The role of rule-implementing actors will become important for the GIs, in particular European GIs that would be challenged by the New World countries as generic names (Chapter 2). Nonetheless, rule-implementing actors have played an important role so far in the case of IP and standardisation in Chapter 4—the only arena in which China has attempted to promote a rival standard. Rule-implementing actors in this case could substantially influence an outcome through their interpretation of the law. For example, although China did not successfully make WAPI a compulsory national standard in the rulemaking game, relevant standards are patent protected and the owner of WAPI can sue licensees (Sony and Apple) for royalties in court.

Courts are involved in China's international IP engagement when they have jurisdiction over a case. This requirement is usually satisfied when civil IP litigation involves 'foreign-related civil relations'[6]—in particular when one of the parties is a foreign citizen or a foreign legal person. However, getting involved does not necessarily mean active engagement. This section will focus on cases of 'judicial activism', where courts and local IP regulators creatively articulate laws. These include applying rules in the deliberative process before they are codified or deciding a case following a specific interpretation when more than one interpretation is available.

Chinese courts and other rule-implementers began to engage in the international IP system in the 1980s. Chinese courts and local IP regulators began to enforce IP based on international treaties before domestic IP laws were in place. For instance, GIs for Danisa and Champagne were first protected in China by local branches of SAIC based on the Paris Convention, before any GI legislation was promulgated (Chapter 2). Another example is *Disney vs Beijing Publishing House* in 1994.[7] In this case, Disney had licensed its copyright in Chinese publications to Maxwell, and Maxwell agreed not to license the right to a third party. When Maxwell breached the agreement by licensing the copyright to Beijing Publishing House, Disney sued only Beijing Publishing House for copyright infringement. The US-China bilateral MOU (1992)[8] included a clause on reciprocal protection of copyright, manifesting the beginning of China's protection of US copyright. However, the licensing agreement between Maxwell and Beijing Publishing House was signed before the 1992 US-China MOU. That meant at least between the signature of the licensing agreement and the effectiveness of the 1992 US-China MOU, China was not committed to protecting the copyright owned by US rightholders. After the MOU was effective, there were also issues about automatically applying international treaties as law by a Chinese court and whether the MOU could be considered a treaty at all in this case. There was no agreed practice at that time on the first issue (Chen *et al.*, 2000). The court nonetheless applied the bilateral MOU directly as a treaty, on which basis it

[6] 'Foreign-related civil relations' are regulated by the Law on the *Application of Laws to Foreign-Related Civil Relations of China* 涉外民事关系法律适用法 (2010). The specific circumstances that may constitute 'foreign-related civil relations' are further defined in Article 1 of the Supreme People's Court Interpretations on Several Issues Concerning Application of the Law to Foreign-Related Civil Relationships (I) 最高人民法院关于适用《涉外民事关系法律适用法》若干问题的解释 (一).

[7] *The Walt Disney Company, US v. Beijing Publishing House* etc. *(Copyright Infringement Dispute)* 美国沃尔特·迪斯尼公司诉北京出版社等侵犯著作权纠纷案, Beijing Intermediate People's Court Decision No. 141, 中经知初字第141号 (1994), available in SPC Gazette 最高人民法院公报 1996 (4).

[8] *US-China Memorandum of Understanding on the Protection of Intellectual Property* (1992), 17 January 1992.

further confirmed the copyright infringement and ordered Beijing Publishing House to pay damages to Disney. These early cases of judicial activism aimed to prove that China had an effective system for IP protection, in particular those owned by foreign rightholders (Jiang, 2009).

In the case of standardisation, Chinese rule-implementing actors no longer provide favourable treatment to foreign parties. Instead, they tend to look to stimulate indigenous innovation and assist Chinese companies to gain technological independence. In the case of *IWNComm vs Sony*,[9] the Beijing Intellectual Property Court ordered Sony to pay treble damages to IWNComm for the licensing of the SEPs before the concept of treble damages had been enacted in the patent law (Chapter 4). In the case of *Huawei vs Inter Digital Technology Corporation*[10] (Zhang & Lee, 2016; Zhang, 2015), the Shenzhen Intermediate People's Court creatively based its decision on the principle of fair, reasonable, and non-discriminatory (FRAND). At the time the decision was made, this principle had not yet been incorporated explicitly into Chinese law.

The function of rule-implementing actors and instances of judicial activism is not confined to specific cases or isolated from the bigger picture of competitiveness among companies and states. Instead, they should be considered as part of China's national strategy of technological catch-up, specifically cultivating indigenous innovation and improving the core competitiveness of Chinese companies. This orientation has been clearly articulated by a Supreme People's Court opinion in 2009, which mandated the various levels of Chinese domestic courts to:

> raise the sense of crisis, hardship, big thinking and overall thinking, and pay more attention to expanding the space for innovation, promoting the cultivation of indigenous intellectual property, local brands and new economic growth areas, and enhancing the market competitiveness of enterprises and raising the core competitiveness of China.[11]

[9] Xian Xidian Jietong Wireless Communication Co., Ltd. (IWNComm) v SONY mobile communication products (China) Co. Ltd., 西电捷通诉索尼发明专利侵权纠纷案 (2017) 京民终454号.

[10] Huawei Tech. Co. v. InterDigital Communications, Inc. 华为技术有限公司诉交互数字通信有限公司, Shenzhen Intermediate People's Court, No. 858 深中法知民初字第858 号 (2011). For the decision of the second instance, see Guangdong High People's Court, No. 305 粤高法民三终字305号 (2013).

[11] *Supreme People's Court Opinions on Several Issues Concerning (Using) Intellectual Property Trials to Serve the Overall Objective under the Current Economic Situation* 最高人民法院关于当前经济形势下知识产权审判服务大局若干问题的意见, No. 23 (2009) 法发 (2009) 23 号.

As a rule of thumb, courts could decide according to the law, so the opinions should not be interpreted as the SPC encouraging courts to bend the law to achieve these objectives. These guidelines are particularly relevant for cases where judicial activism is possible to fill a gap or promote a specific interpretation of a rule.

### 7.2.4 The Missing Actors in Developing Potential Engagement

Substate actors represent China in its international IP engagement when they are mandated to do so. When domestic regulatory competition exists, the ministries in charge are often motivated in their international engagement by a desire to consolidate their regulatory legitimacy (e.g. AQSIQ in regulating GIs). However, in other cases, one can observe regulatory neglect, where substate actors, which would otherwise be expected to be involved, are missing from the engagement. The reasons for regulatory neglect could be other ministries share the regulatory power, or the international engagement on that issue is not clearly mandated. Since regulatory neglect presents as inaction, it is difficult to identify in the first place.

China's international engagement on the disclosure obligation could be considered a case of regulatory neglect—in particular, its role in the Nagoya Protocol negotiations. XUE Dayuan, one of the experts advising China in these negotiations, pointed out that the lack of coordination, communication, and mutual support among various ministries in China was a crucial problem (Xue, 2015; Xue & Cai, 2009). This can be a case of regulatory neglect because of shared regulatory power: The Chinese delegation on the Nagoya Protocol was led by the Ministry of Environmental Protection; SIPO, as a member of the delegation, was not active in promoting the disclosure obligation.

Regulatory neglect could provide a plausible explanation for China's comparatively inactive engagement in the issue of IP and public health, where IP is only one pillar of the challenges. As shown in Chapter 6, no compulsory licence has been issued in China since the relevant law was promulgated in 2003 to implement the *Doha Declaration on the TRIPS Agreement and Public Health*. Nonetheless, China has directly provided vaccines to other countries during the COVID-19 pandemic without actively participating in the WTO IP waiver negotiations. This indicates that regulatory neglect could be caused by the consideration that relevant engagement on IP is not the most effective way to get things done.

### 7.2.5 Discussion

Among the substate actors involved in China's international IP engagement, this section has highlighted MOFCOM, SIPO, rule-implementing actors, and some missing actors. The coordination (and lack of coordination) among these substate actors, as well as regulatory competition and regulatory neglect, directly impact China's international IP engagement. Externally, the technocratic trust built through participation in transnational networks has also influenced the positions of Chinese ministries to assimilate with those of the EU or the US.

In summary, the checkpoint role of MOFCOM emphasises its mandate to arrange reciprocal coordination. When SIPO identified itself as an independent node in the global governance of an issue for which it has an official carriage, it deployed its nodal power and status which may diverge from the general Chinese IP positions in international engagement. Rule-implementing actors in China have, through judicial activism, influenced outcomes in the implementation game. Some substate actors do not engage as much as they are expected internationally in cases of regulatory neglect, due to either a lack of coordination or a lack of confidence in international IP rulemaking.

## 7.3 Non-state Actors

Two types of non-state actors have been involved in China's international IP engagement: IP epistemic communities and private actors. Unlike the substate actors, their engagement does not represent the position of the Chinese government.

### 7.3.1 Chinese IP Epistemic Communities

The epistemic community concept refers to networks of professionals with recognised expertise and competence in a particular domain and an authoritative claim to policy-relevant knowledge within that domain or issue area (Haas, 1992). Although the IP system has been officially established in China for just four decades since its *Trademark Law* (1982), there has been a dramatic growth in epistemic communities in this area. Chinese IP epistemic communities (mainly trained by IP lawyers) have been building networks and endeavouring to disseminate a view of IP that is based either on utilitarian or entitlement-based theories. While public interests are part of their consideration, they are often marginalised.

IP epistemic communities play a critical role in the strategy of modelling (Chapter 9), which is the key strategy for diffusing IP knowledge in China. The absorption of new regulatory models relies on epistemic communities comprising technical experts who study, adapt, and finally adopt models presented by foreign experts. For instance, WIPO and the EU have regularly seconded expert advisors to help with the amendment of IP legislation in China (Chapter 6). Chinese patent examiners, IP judges and other technocrats, as well as academics in universities, have also been dispatched to study the 'more advanced' IP systems of other states—mostly in the US and the EU.

Because the composition of these epistemic communities is heterogeneous and the function of different communities varies, I divide them into two groups: IP elites who can influence lawmaking and IP practitioners who are active in the law implementation game. Their relationship can be thought of as a 'ripple', where IP elites are at the centre as opinion leaders and IP practitioners are on the periphery to augment the message. This section focuses on their role in transnational networks and how such networks influence their positions and ultimately Chinese IP law and regulation.

#### 7.3.1.1 IP Elites

The term 'IP elites' in China refers to opinion leaders in IP issues, including celebrated IP academics and retired high-level government officials. Among all IP epistemic communities, they are among the few who can influence IP law and regulation directly. For instance, Professor LIU Chuntian, the Dean of the Intellectual Property Academy at Renmin University, was named one of the World's 50 Most Influential People in IP in 2014 in the category of 'policymakers'. According to the official website of Renmin University: 'Professor Liu is the only academic who is listed in the category of policymakers. This … reflected the recognition of international society of the special role played by Chinese academics in the development of China' (RUC News, 2014). Professor Liu was also the Chinese coordinator of the US-China IP Cooperation Dialogue. Co-organised by Liu's academy and the US Chamber of Commerce in 2013, the Dialogue comprised five from each country, including governmental officials, business experts, judges, lawyers, and academics (Sun, 2016). The Dialogue has developed into an important informal bilateral forum for the US to influence Chinese thinking on

IP issues in particular after the US-China WTO dispute. Feasibilities for higher IP protection in China, such as patent linkage and copyright for live streaming of sports broadcasting, can be found in its periodic reports (US-China IP Cooperation Dialogue, 2013; US-China IP Cooperation Dialogue, 2014–2015; US-China IP Cooperation Dialogue, 2016).

Patent linkage and data exclusivity are two examples of US influence. The US-China IP Cooperation Dialogue (2014–2015, p. 2) first claimed that China's potential for innovation in the pharmaceutical industry was hampered by its IP protection regimes and recommended that China should 'improve the patent linkage system and provide effective protection for clinical data of new chemical entities by using the ongoing effort to amend the Patent Law and the Drug Administration Law' (p. 2). At the conference to launch the Dialogue's 2016 report viewed by 60,000 audiences online, the US and Chinese experts who drafted the report again advocated for a patent linkage scheme in China (Zhang, 2017).

As these Dialogue reports were submitted to high-level officials in the Chinese government, they may have a direct policy impact. In addition, Chinese IP elites as opinion leaders have produced academic publications or organised workshops that could further influence decision-making. After the launching conference of the Dialogue's 2016 report, CHENG Yongshun, a former judge of the Beijing People's High Court and one of the Chinese experts in the Dialogue, organised a symposium to promote patent linkage in China (Beijing Intellectual Property Institute, 2016). The symposium was attended by former government officials from SIPO and former IP judges as well as representatives from the generic companies in China. Although most former government officials agreed that patent linkage would be a fair and transparent mechanism, Chinese generic companies were concerned that domestic companies could not adapt well to the system. However, opinions of generic companies seemed not being heard as they were only mentioned in passing in the symposium brief.

While the US-China IP Cooperation Dialogue seemed to be suspended as there were no sessions after 2016, the US took a more coercive approach during the negotiation of the USCETA 2020. In 2017, China Food and Drug Administration (CFDA) proposed a patent linkage mechanism[12] that modelled the US *Drug Price Competition and Patent Term Restoration Act of 1984*. It also proposed up to 10 years of data exclusivity for biologics,

[12] China Food and Drug Administration (CFDA) 中国食品药品监管总局, *Notice of Calling for Comments on 'Policies Related to Encouraging Innovations in Pharmaceuticals and Medical Equipment and Protecting Interests and rights of innovators (Draft for Comments)* 关于鼓励药品医疗器械创新保护创新者权益的相关政策 (征求意见稿), No. 55, 12 May 2017.

orphan drugs, and original drugs for children (Cheng, 2019b), another issue that was closely advocated by the dialogue. Eventually, the patent linkage mechanism was included in the *Patent Law* (2020), partly influenced by the informal US-China IP Cooperation Dialogue and partly to implement China's commitment to the Article 1.12 of USCTEA 2020.

The utilitarian or entitlement-based philosophy for intellectual property underpins the position of the Chinese IP elites, which could be a contributor to China's insufficient engagement in the current IP waiver negotiations at the WTO (Chapter 6). For instance, Xiong and Zhang (2022) treated the IP waiver and access to medicines or vaccines as separate issues, arguing that public health objectives could not be achieved by only waiving IP rights, more needs to be done by promoting the efficiency of access to COVID-19 vaccines or scaling up production. This is very similar to the position of leading Western IP scholars who question the necessity for or effectiveness of the IP waiver (Hilty *et al.*, 2021).

#### 7.3.1.2 IP Practitioners

IP practitioners are a rising group in the Chinese IP epistemic community, which includes technocrats and IP intermediaries such as IP lawyers and patent agents. The recent patenting surge in China, as well as a series of policies to develop the IP service industry, has stimulated the expansion of intermediaries. According to the Deputy Director of SIPO's Planning and Development Department, China had more than 31,000 IP agencies with more than 600,000 employees by 2014 (Liu, 2015). Statistics from the All-China Patent Attorneys Association indicate there were over 48,000 qualified patent attorneys in China as of 2020 (Shen, 2020).

IP practitioners are located on the periphery of the 'ripple' of the Chinese IP epistemic communities. Messages from IP elites are disseminated to them via different channels. The fact that over 60,000 people watched the launch of the US-China IP Cooperation Dialogue, 2016 via live streaming was a typical example of how IP practitioners got to know where the wind blows.

Various transnational networks have also been established between Chinese IP technocrats and their counterparts in the US and the EU. For instance, starting in 1994, SIPO began to send selected employees as visiting scholars to the John Marshall Law School in the US. More than 400 individuals from SIPO participated in this programme for 20 years. As pointed out by TIAN Lipu, then Commissioner of SIPO, at the twentieth anniversary of the SIPO-John Marshall cooperation:

> [T]hose who once attended the John Marshall program now become departmental leaders and backbones of SIPO. Such programs help develop technical ties across time and culture. When problems arise those trained in the US will likely look to how the US has addressed the problem. (Zhang, 2013)

In addition, Chinese lawyers are also keen to pursue an LL.M. degree from US law schools. IP lawyers are part of this trend and, when they return to China, they apply what they have learned into practice and spread US-specific IP norms into the Chinese IP system. Although the number of IP practitioners is large, this community is narrowly constituted, comprising mainly those legally trained in IP law and dedicated to maximising the interests of IP rightholders.

### 7.3.2 Private Actors

Private actors—in particular, MNCs—are important nodes in international IP regulation (Tusikov, 2016). In the case of IP and standardisation (Chapter 4), Intel developed sophisticated strategies to launch Wi-Fi-enabled personal computers into the Chinese market, formed strategies of coalition building, threatened embargoes, lobbied the US government and influenced the standard setting of the IEEE. Other less powerful MNCs have also attempted to pressure the Chinese government through their national or regional industrial associations. For instance, the American Chamber of Commerce in China represented high-tech MNCs doing business in China. It questioned China's indigenous innovation policies, helped to place those policies on JCCT negotiations and played a role in suspending their implementation.

Most Chinese companies are still in the middle of global value chains and are dependent on MNCs (Chapter 4). However, Chinese companies such as ZTE and Huawei have become two of the top PCT patent applicants worldwide. They have also inclined to an entitlement-based theory for IP so that their interests can be better protected both within China and in other jurisdictions.

In the case of IP and standardisation, there are two paths for Chinese companies to obtain supportive regulation. The first is through the ministries in charge. For instance, the MIIT supported the tie-in strategy of the WAPI alliance by requiring every mobile phone entering the Chinese market to have WAPI installed (Chapter 4). However, such reliance on the Chinese government has been criticised as a black box operation. The lack of transparency and its close connection to the state turned WAPI into an example of China's technological nationalism (Suttmeier & Yao, 2004; Suttmeier *et al.*, 2006). The Chinese Government and Chinese companies learned from the WAPI case. Later, China did not exclude foreign companies from involvement in developing the 4G standard. MNCs like Qualcomm came on board and the standard development process became more transparent. In this way, China further integrated into the global ecosystem of developing telecommunications standards (Higgins, 2015).

The second path for supportive regulation is initiating litigation or anti-monopoly investigations against MNCs. This means Chinese companies can resort to the courts as rule-implementing actors—in particular, when MNCs breach the FRAND principle in the Chinese market. Large Chinese companies have also become more active in initiating legal action in other jurisdictions. As the various markets in China mature and Chinese players become more experienced, the significance of rule-implementing actors also grows. The telecommunications sector in China is an obvious case of this maturing process.

## 7.4 Conclusion

This chapter analysed various substate actors and non-state actors that have involved in China's international IP engagement in previous case studies. Substate actors mainly include MOFCOM, SIPO and rule-implementing actors, and non-state actors include the IP epistemic communities and private actors. This chapter also analysed the roles that should be played by Chinese regulators in its global IP engagement but are not yet fulfilled, sometimes caused by the lack of coordination among ministries and sometimes out of pragmatism.

Instead of making consolidated efforts, the substate actors show a spectrum of positions behind China's international IP engagement. For instance, while China's trading partners have selected the most accommodating ministry with which to negotiate a deal on IP, MOFCOM functioned as the checkpoint through reciprocal coordination over a much broader range of issues. However, SIPO has increasingly developed into an independent node in global patent regulation, taking more responsibilities in establishing PPH with other patent offices and rulemaking around the ICP. These activities ultimately serve the interests of the rightholders.

Rule-implementing actors get involved in China's global IP engagement through their judicial activism. They have developed innovative interpretation of law or filled gaps when the law has not yet been established, which makes the implementation game increasingly complex.

Chinese IP epistemic communities have developed transnational networks with their counterparts in the US and EU, absorbing various legal approaches and ideas about IP, especially those underpinned by the entitlement-based theory. Prominently, the US-China IP Cooperation Dialogue has contributed to the enhanced the Chinese IP protection standards on pharmaceutical patents through their advocacy for the establishment of the patent linkage mechanism.

## References


Abbott, F. M., Correa, C. M. and Drahos, P. (2013). Emerging Markets and the World Patent Order: The Forces of Change. In F. M. Abbott, C. M. Correa, & P. Drahos (Eds.), *Emerging Markets and the World Patent Order* (pp. 3–33). Edward Elgar.

AQSIQ. (2009). *China-Eu GI Mutual Recognition Project Is Progressing Smoothly 中国欧盟地理标志互认项目进展顺利*. http://www.gov.cn/gzdt/2009-11/26/content_1474017.htm. Accessed 6 October 2022.

Beijing Intellectual Property Institute. (2016). *Brief on Pharmaceutical Patent Link System Salon '药品专利链接制度沙龙'简报*. http://www.bipi.org/index.php/6/406.html. Accessed 6 October 2022.

Braithwaite, J., & Drahos, P. (2000). *Global Business Regulation*. Cambridge University Press.

Burris, S., Drahos, P., & Shearing, C. (2005). Nodal Governance. *Australian Journal of Legal Philosophy, 30*, 30–58.

Chen, H., Zhou, W., & Jiang, H. (2000). Relationship between International Treaties and National Law: Its Practice in China国际条约与国内法的关系及中国的实践. *Tribune of Political Science and Law政法论坛, 02*, 117–123.

Cheng, W. (2019a). China Engages with the Global Intellectual Property Governance: The Recent Trend. *The Journal of World Intellectual Property, 22*(3–4), 1–16.

Cheng, W. (2019b). Protection of Data in China: Seventeen Years after China's WTO Accession. *European Intellectual Property Review, 44*(5), 292–297.

Drahos, P. (2008). "Trust Me": Patent Offices in Developing Countries. *American Journal of Law & Medicine, 34*(2–3), 151–174.

EPO. (2016). Patent Prosecution Highway Pilot Programme between the IP5 Offices Based on PCT and National Work Products. *European Patent Office Official Journal, 12*, A106.

Haas, P. M. (1992). Introduction: Epistemic Communities and International Policy Coordination. *International Organization, 46*(1), 1–35.

Higgins, V. (2015). *Alliance Capitalism, Innovation and the Chinese State: The Global Wireless Sector.* Springer.

Hilty, R., Batista, P. H. D., Carls, S., Kim, D., Lamping, M., & Slowinski, P. R. (2021). *COVID-19 and the Role of Intellectual Property: Position Statement of the Max Planck Institute for Innovation and Competition of 7 May 2021.* Max Planck Institute for Innovation & Competition Research Paper (21–13).

Jiang, Y. (2009). The Application of US-China Intellectual Property MOU in a Copyright Dispute by Chinese Court for the First Time《中美知识产权谅解备忘录》在著作权案件中的首次适用. *China Copyright 中国版权, 6*, 32–34.

Lee, J.-A. (2016). Implementing the FRAND Standard in China. *Vanderbilt Journal of Entertainment & Technology Law, 19*(1), 37–86.

Liu, J. (2015). The Present Situation and Development of China's Intellectual Property Service Industry 我国知识产权服务业现状与发展目标思考. *Journal of Science, Technology and Law 科技与法律, 4*, 674–694.

Liu, Y., & Sun, Y. (2004). China Traditional Chinese Medicine (TCM) Patent Database. *World Patent Information, 26*(1), 91–96.

RUC News. (2014). *Professor Liu Chuntian Was Selected Again as "50 Most Influential Intellectual Property Figures in the World" 刘春田教授再度入选"全球50位最具影响力知识产权人物"*. http://news.ruc.edu.cn/archives/85923. Accessed 6 October 2022.

Shen, C. (2020). *Speech by SHEN Changyu, Director of the State Intellectual Property Office, at the 10th National Congress of the All-China Patent Attorneys Association国家知识产权局局长申长雨在中华全国专利代理人协会第十次全国会员代表大会上的讲话.* http://www.acpaa.cn/article/content/202003/4861/1.html. Accessed: 6 October 2022.

Sun, D. (2016). *Chinese and US Expert Enthusiastically Discussed Intellectual Property in Shenzhen 深圳: 中美专家热议知识产权* Intellectual Property Daily. http://www.chinaiprlaw.com/index.php?id=3527. Accessed: 6 October 2022.

Suttmeier, R. P., & Yao, X. (2004). *China's Post-WTO Technology Policy: Standards, Software, and the Changing Nature of Techno-Nationalism*: The National Bureau of Asian Research.

Suttmeier, R. P., Yao, X., & Tan, A. Z. (2006). *Standards of Power? Technology, Institutions, and Politics in the Development of China's National Standards Strategy.* The National Bureau of Asian Research.

The New Century of Agrochem. (2007). China's Plant Pesticide Patent Proposal Was Adopted by International Convention for the First Time 我国一植物农药专利提案首次被国际公约采用. *The New Century of Agrochem 农化新世纪, 7*, 16.

Tusikov, N. (2016). *Chokepoints: Global Private Regulation on the Internet.* University of California Press.

US-China IP Cooperation Dialogue. (2013). *US-China IP Cooperation Dialogue Report 中美知识产权学者对话纪要 (2013)* http://www.theglobalipcenter.com/wp-content/uploads/2013/01/US_China_IP_Cooperation_FINAL-FULL.pdf

US-China IP Cooperation Dialogue. (2014–2015). *US-China IP Cooperation Dialogue中美知识产权学者对话纪要 (2014–2015).* http://www.theglobalipcenter.com/wp-content/uploads/2015/08/US-China-IP-Dialogue_2014-2015.pdf

US-China IP Cooperation Dialogue. (2016). *US-China IP Cooperation Dialogue中美知识产权学者对话纪要 (2016).* http://www.theglobalipcenter.com/wp-content/uploads/2017/06/ChinaReportEnglishFinalPDF.pdf

WIPO. (2011). *WIPO and India Partner to Protect Traditional Knowledge from Misappropriation.* http://www.wipo.int/pressroom/en/articles/2011/article_0008.html. Accessed 16 May 2018.

WIPO. (2012). *World Intellectual Property Indicators.* http://www.wipo.int/edocs/pubdocs/en/intproperty/941/wipo_pub_941_2012.pdf

Wu, Y. (2016, August 12). China's Patent Classification Capacity Has Steadily Improved 我国专利分类业务能力稳步提升. *China Intellectual Property News 中国知识产权报* (p. 4).

Xiong, Q., & Zhang, W. (2022).疫情应对中的知识产权保护取舍 Intellectual Property Protection and Its Response to A Pandemic. *法治研究 Research on Rule of Law* 01: 63–73.

Xue, D. (2015). On Establishing the National Synergy Strategy for the Implementation of International Agreements Related to Biodiversity Conservation 建立生物多样性保护相关国际公约的国家履约协同战略. *Biodiversity Science 生物多样性, 5*, 673–680.

Xue, D., & Cai, L. (2009). China's Legal and Policy Frameworks for Access to Genetic Resources and Benefit-Sharing from Their Use. *Review of European, Comparative & International Environmental Law, 18*(1), 91–99.

Zhang, G., & Zhang, G. (2015). *A review of Huawei v IDC.* http://www.managingip.com/Article/3440420/A-review-of-Huawei-v-IDC.html

Zhang, W. (2017, May 30). Chinese and US Experts Jointly Call for Introducing the Patent Linkage Mechanism to China 中美专家联合呼吁引入专利链接制度. *法制日报 Legal Daily.*

Zhang, Z. (2013). *Successful Cooperation between SIPO and John Marshall Law School for 20 Years 国家知识产权局与马歇尔法学院成功合作20年.* http://www.iprchn.com/Index_NewsContent.aspx?newsId=58878. Accessed 6 October 2022.

# 8

# Principles for China's International IP Engagement

## 8.1 Introduction

This chapter focuses on the principles that have guide or sometimes constrained China's international IP engagement. Two sets of general principles are identified in this chapter: One concerning the theories about domestic IP protection in China and the other on foreign policy principles that guide China's international engagement on various issues. Both sets of principles are drawn from the case studies (Chapters 2–6). The domestic justification of IP protection is particularly relevant to understand which distributive justice principles China has appealed to in its international IP engagement. While some foreign policy principles to be discussed in this chapter have also been officially advanced by the Chinese government, this chapter also discusses those more implicit behavioural guidelines directly related to IP.

This chapter discusses lower-level principles guiding China's international IP engagement. These contrast with common higher-level principles in China's foreign policy agenda, like 'pragmatism', 'rationalism', or 'reciprocity', which will not be discussed here. This is because, with principles that are not sufficiently specific, it can be difficult to identify directly related implementation measures, tensions between them, and strategies to manage such tensions.



W. Cheng, *China in Global Governance of Intellectual Property*, Palgrave Socio-Legal Studies, https://doi.org/10.1007/978-3-031-24370-7_8

## 8.2 Underpinnings for Domestic IP Protection: IP Instrumentalism

China's understanding of the value of an IP system has been instrumental, which is similar to the utilitarian principle in Western countries (Chapter 1) following a 'means-to-ends' philosophy. Nonetheless, the narrative in China is not that IP would maximise the utility of rightholders to innovate, but it is useful to facilitate China to achieve its various objectives, including enhanced innovative capacity and technological competitiveness and economic growth.

There are two reasons why China has focused on IP's instrumental value. First, instrumentalism was an embedded justification when China imported the IP system. Modern China first encountered IP in the context of colonialism. China reintroduced IP in the late 1970s as part of its quest for foreign technologies. China had to establish its IP system to begin science and technology cooperation with the US as required by the US-China Agreement on High Energy Physics (1979) and the US-China Agreement on Trade Relations (1979). Considering China's socialist system was dominated by egalitarian distribution of resources, officials from then Ministry of Machine Industry condemned the proprietorial nature of patents when the drafts of the first Patent Law were deliberated in the early 1980s, arguing the patent system was incompatible with China's socialism (Zhao, 2003). Nonetheless, the patent system survived initially because of its instrumental value. Establishing a patent system was a prerequisite for reciprocal coordination with the US and other developed countries so that these countries would release restrictions on their exports of high technology to China or increase their foreign direct investment (FDI) in China. In the post-TRIPS era, the instrumental value of IP was still dominant, while it gradually reoriented to serve domestic interests when Chinese entities started to own patents and trademarks.

Second, IP theories were imported to China from the West with the institution, meaning that there was no equivalent concept to IP in the long history of China. In the bilateral IP negotiations in the 1990s, US negotiators framed China as a 'born pirate' and threatened it with unilateral trade retaliation if Chinese IP protection standards did not meet the US expectation. After the early antagonistic approach of imposition, the US took a softer approach using dialogues, framing IP as the means to promote innovation. China bought into this reframing as the emphasis on the instrumental value of IP to promote innovation matched its enthusiasm for enhancing the development of science and technology and achieving technological catch-up.

The Chinese public, by and large, took a defiant position when the alien IP system was introduced in the early 1980s as the overarching egalitarian distributive principle at that stage. Repetitive, large-scale and sometimes organised IP infringement took place everywhere. The lack of consideration of local conditions by the Chinese government partly contributed to the defiant attitude (Braithwaite, 2009). Such defiance conversely led to the high costs and low effectiveness of IP enforcement.

Nonetheless, IP regulators have taken a hard approach to repress the defiance under the mentality that the Chinese IP system should serve the 'big picture 大局' following instrumentalism. In Chinese, its literal meaning is 'grand chessboard', which also indicates having a sense of panoramic vision in decision-making. DENG Xiaoping identified two 'big pictures' for China in the 1980s, one domestic and the other international. The objective of the international big picture is to maintain a peaceful world, and the objective of the domestic big picture is to achieve China's development. Deng argued that the two big pictures are mutually conducive, and they have been considered the essence of his diplomatic thinking (Zhang, 2016). President XI Jinping has also emphasised this idea (Xi, 2013). There are two dimensions in which IP instrumentalism can serve the big picture—by stimulating innovation and by contributing to China's economic transformation.

### 8.2.1 The Innovation Stimulation Theory

In the early stages of its adoption of IP law, China faced the problem that its IP system was protecting key technologies belonging to foreign rightholders. The DVD case discussed in Chapter 4 clearly showed how patents and standards together prevented the diffusion of knowledge from MNCs to Chinese companies. Over time, the innovation stimulation theory in China has developed along two dimensions: To provide incentives for innovation and to serve China's grand strategy of technological catch-up.

The first dimension is consistent with the original explanation of the utilitarian theory in Western countries, while the second is a further derivative of the theory to fit the Chinese context. The innovation stimulation theory is based on utilitarianism, meaning IP will promote innovation by rewarding the innovators and providing incentives to invest in knowledge creation. As pointed out by Schroth (2008), when it comes to distributive justice, the utilitarian principle leaves the best outcome as an open question: The greatest amount of well-being (maximising incentives to innovate in the IP case) or the fairest distribution of burden and benefits (IP as one component serving the fair distribution of overall social warfare). In the Chinese context, there is also a question about whether such an outcome is expected now or in the foreseeable future. For a regulatory importer, these questions mean policy space since the theory still allows China to make its own decisions as far as international law permits.

In China, the balancing theory (Xu, 2003) was also influential which emphasised fair distribution of well-being and the need to balance different interests before 2008. But the 2008 National IP Strategy has leaned towards maximising incentives to innovate. The strategy, initiated by SIPO and issued by State Council, clarified the priorities on IP creation, utilisation, protection, and development, generating further pressure on various levels of local government to implement such goals (Cheng & Drahos, 2018).

Thereafter, the innovation stimulation theory has been the foundation for Chinese national IP agendas. IP has been incorporated as an instrument to promote innovation into even higher-level national agendas: *National Strategy on Innovation-driven Development*[1] and *Made in China 2025*.[2] In the *National Strategy on Innovation-driven Development*, IP is incorporated, together with the strategies of standardisation, quality, and brand, as forces to further enhance innovation. *Made in China 2025* is the first step towards building China into an innovation power by 2045, and the IP indicator (number of valid invention patents per 100 million yuan of main business income in sizeable enterprises in manufacturing industries) was adopted to measure innovative capacity. Both agendas demonstrate the instrumentalism of employing IP to stimulate innovation as well as an increasing recognition of the significance of IP among Chinese regulators that are not directly in charge of IP.

IP has gained wider recognition from various Chinese regulators on development agenda and industrial policies mainly because its function to stimulate innovation serves achieving technological catch-up. China first attempted to achieve this goal through technology transfers from foreign countries. While the US and the EU recently complained that this amounted to forced technology transfer, the need for cross-border technology transfers is not unique to China. It has been a common feature of national laws in many developing and emerging countries to require foreign investors to partner with local enterprises as a condition of FDI. While forced technology transfer is an issue beyond the jurisdiction of the TRIPS Agreement (Abbott, 2020,

[1] Central Committee of the Communist Party of China, State Council of China, *National Strategy on Innovation-Driven Development* 国家创新驱动发展战略纲要, 19 May 2016.

[2] State Council, *Notice of the State Council on Issuing Made in China 2025* 国务院关于印发《中国制造2025》的通知, No. 28 (2015), 8 May 2015.

p. 261), having one's IP law aligned with international standards has been integral to achieving technological catch-up.

China established IP protection standards well beyond the demands of local companies and the stage of domestic technological development in order to attract MNCs to transfer their technology. It was the temporal dimension of innovation stimulation that suggested the concession of IP would be worthwhile for China. It was hoped that with local companies absorbing transferred technologies and starting self-innovation, the level of Chinese IP protection would one day fit its domestic needs. This justified promoting IP as a priority on the national agenda before opportunities matured.

### 8.2.2 The Economic Contribution Theory

The function of IP has also been associated with China's broader economic development goals, in particular, transforming its manufactueconomic contribution theoryring industry from mass quantity to high quality, changing the production model from labour-intensive to technology-intensive, and balancing economic development with environmental sustainability. This led to the second dimension of IP instrumentalism in China, the, the proposition that IP should contribute to China's economic transformation. Within this economic transformation agenda, economic growth and job creation have been central goals, but the role of IP in promoting innovation that meets environmental and sustainable development goals has also come into focus recently.

Numerous econometric studies have addressed the economic contribution of IP (Chu *et al.*, 2014; Gould & Gruben, 1996; Park & Ginarte, 1997; Thompson & Rushing, 1996; Yang & Maskus, 2001). However, the links between IP and economic growth in the literature remain uncertain or at least have many caveats. For example, the economic effect of patents differs across industries, and different types of IP have different economic impacts. While not empirically proven, the economic contribution theory makes a normative argument about the contribution of IP to economic development, with innovation stimulation as an intermediate variable.

In the context of regulatory import, ministries in charge of IP are inclined to frame IP in a way that serves the grand agenda of China directly so that its value could also be recognised by other domestic regulators who would further support IP-related work. The specific interpretation of the economic contribution theory evolved accordingly. In the 1990s, the theory focused more on how an IP system could contribute to attracting foreign investment in China. The belief was that only a relatively comprehensive IP system could convince MNCs to transfer technology to Chinese companies. In the absence of technology transfers, China would still be trapped in the vicious circle of 'equipment importation, equipment ageing, and equipment reimportation'. This broad narrative has supported China's acceptance of high IP standards till the TRIPS Agreement. Since the National IP Strategy stated that the goal of IP is to serve economic and social development, SIPO incorporated IP as one of the issues that have an impact on economic transition. For instance, Chinese economic growth entered into the 'New Normal' phase in the past decade with a slower annual economic growth rate of 6–7% (Zhang & Chen, 2017). SIPO Commissioner SHENG Chagyu stated at the 2015 Conference of Directors of Local IP Offices that 'intellectual property is a very important factor to support [the] economic new normal. In order to better support the new normal, intellectual property should be deeply mixed with [other aspects of] social and economic development' (Shen, 2015). In the *Several Opinions on Accelerating Building China as an IP Power under New Conditions*,[3] the function of IP to directly contribute to an increase in the gross domestic product (GDP) was emphasised. Since 2016, the National Bureau of Statistics (NBS) has incorporated IP products into the calculation of the System of National Accounts (National Bureau of Statistics, 2017). When the central government was committed to reviving the manufacturing industry through *Made in China 2025*, Commissioner SHEN further stated that IP should serve the development of China's real economy (Zhang, G. 2017). The National Copyright Administration of China (NCAC) has also striven to consolidate the direct contribution of the copyright industry to economic growth. Since 2007, the NCAC has been investigating the contribution of the copyright industry to economic growth. It is reported that the Chinese copyright industry contributed 7.3% to China's overall GDP in 2015 (Hou, 2017). In addition, SAIC has emphasised the contribution of the trademarks to economic development, specifically through its function to adapt to supply-side reform, enhance product quality and promote increases in consumption (Cui, 2017a, 2017b). In addition, SAIC and AQSIQ have addressed the pivotal role of GIs in solving problems in agriculture and rural development (Chapter 2).

IP-related measures have also been incorporated into various industrial policies in recent years. For instance, after the State Council decided on

[3] State Council of China, *Several Opinions on Accelerating Building China as an IP Power under New Conditions* 国务院关于新形势下加快知识产权强国建设的若干意见, No. 71 (2015), 18 December 2015.

cultivating strategic emerging industries,[4] SIPO, with nine other ministries, jointly issued *Opinions for strengthening IP in strategic emerging industries*,[5] which further specified that an IP assessment mechanism should be established to facilitate the development of these industries. When such a national agenda is implemented by local governments, such incorporation means IP indicators become part of the performance evaluation of the overall agenda.

Ultimately, IP instrumentalism has directed China to set higher IP protection standards domestically. Even though Chinese IP instrumentalism has its own focus which differs from Western utilitarianism, the above discussion indicates that various Chinese IP policies are also based on enhanced IP creation and effective IP enforcement to achieve the broader national objectives of technological catch-up and economic transformation. Therefore, to serve the big picture, such measures also serve the interests of IP rightholders, home and abroad. In this sense, there is little difference between traditional utilitarianism and IP instrumentalism as principles of distributive justice.

## 8.3 China's Foreign Policy Principles

As shown in Chapters 5–6, IP has been one of the central issues in China's bilateral and multilateral negotiations. China has long developed its basic principles for foreign policy, which guided its international engagement including in the IP area. The foreign policy principles relating to China's international IP engagement include non-alignment under the independent foreign policy of peace, adhering to the position that China is a developing country, and safeguarding the multilateral trade system.

### 8.3.1 Non-alignment in the Independent Foreign Policy of Peace

China's foreign policy agenda changed greatly in its first three decades: From leaning towards the Union of Soviet Socialist Republics (USSR) (1949–58) to opposing the two hegemons of the US and USSR in the 1960s, to the 'big-triangle strategy' in the 1970s (Deng, 2005; Ding, 2003; Liu, 1999;

---

[4] State Council, *the Decree on Accelerating the Cultivation and Development of Strategic Emerging Industries*国务院关于加快培育和发展战略性新兴产业的决定, No. 32 (2010), 10 October 2010.

[5] The General Office of the State Council, *Notice on Forwarding Several Opinions of the State Intellectual Property Office and Other Departments on Strengthening the Work of Intellectual Property Rights in Strategic Emerging Industries* 国务院办公厅转发知识产权局等部门关于加强战略性新兴产业知识产权工作若干意见的通知, No. 28 (2012), 28 April 2012.

Zhang, 2000; Zheng, 1991). By and large, these early policies were to identify 'who are our enemies and who are our friends' in the Maoist era when China endeavoured to survive between the two superpowers. As China abolished its IP system entirely in the 1960s, it was not part of the early foreign policies.

China has developed a relatively stable foreign policy agenda since the 1980s, namely 'the independent foreign policy of peace', the theme of which is:

> China may not ally with any superpowers, and China will not join one superpower to oppose the other. In dealing with foreign affairs, China will decide its own position on the basis of the merits of the issue, and the fundamental interests of the Chinese people and the people of the world (Zhang, 1997, pp. 48–49).

The independent foreign policy of peace was developed along with the changing situation globally and has guided China's bilateral relations with other states. As pointed out by Zhang (1997), the core of this policy is non-alignment, specifically not making coalitions with other countries. This guideline, however, has hindered China from clearly co-sponsoring proposals at the WTO on both issues of GIs and disclosure obligation (Chapters 2–3). Its first WTO proposal on IP in standardisation also failed partly because it did not actively seek alliances from other WTO members to support the proposal (Chapter 6).

When the general guideline for Chinese foreign policy changed from keeping a low profile to striving for achievement (Yan, 2014), the position of non-alignment also evolved into partnerships with other countries. China's Foreign Minister WANG Yi has explained that the core idea of partnership that China has established is 'partnership without alliance' (Wang, 2015), which differs from a conventional alliance in two ways. First, it does not emphasise security as the alliance system does; second, it does not target any third party as a potential enemy or exclude or coerce a third party (Sun, 2012). This can also be manifested by China's bilateral engagement via FTAs with various countries where China did not seek to impose its IP standards on its FTA partner (Chapter 5).

### 8.3.2 China's Support for Developing-Country Agendas

China's status in the world has been a controversial issue due to its dual identities. It has become the world's second-largest economy while still a lower-middle-income country (Nolan, 2012). From this dual identity, one can infer that China is either a leading world economy or a developing country. China has given full play to its dual identity to best serve its national interests. In terms of international IP engagement, China's self-identification as a developing country has been consistently maintained. For instance, in the case of the disclosure obligation investigated in this book, the Chinese representative at the WTO TRIPS Council stated the following to support the disclosure obligation (Chapter 3):

> *Many developing countries* possessed plenty of genetic resources and related traditional knowledge but, due to some constraints on their technological capacities, most of them were unable to make full use of these resources and knowledge for patented innovation ... The TRIPS Agreement did not extend protection to genetic resources and traditional knowledge, thus encouraging biopiracy and damaging the interests of *many developing countries*. The proposal for the amendment of the TRIPS Agreement made by *some developing Members* was meant to enhance the mutual supportiveness of the TRIPS Agreement and the CBD ... China, together with *many developing Members*, believed that the work under the TRIPS Council should be intensified ... ensuring that the source of genetic resources and traditional knowledge obtained from *developing countries* was disclosed in patent applications. He agreed with Brazil that this item be included in the final single undertaking.[6]

These comments vividly show how China has situated itself as a developing member of the WTO in post-TRIPS IP negotiations to promote the protection of genetic resources and traditional knowledge.

The case studies in the book indicate that in terms of IP, China has consistently supported the following positions that align its developing-country identity. First, China backed multilateralism in general, opposed TRIPS-plus standards and the new trend of plurilateralism (such as ACTA and the TPP) (Cheng, 2019). Second, China supported developing countries' IP proposals at multilateral and bilateral forums. This can be seen in China's stance at the WTO TRIPS Council in cases of GIs and disclosure obligation (Chapters 2 and 3). In addition, the active-promotion provisions in Chinese FTAs (Chapter 5), while often being voluntary soft rules, represent China's preference and prospect for various issues at the bilateral level. Third, China supported the development agenda at WIPO and promoted the dissemination of knowledge when there is a potential conflict between IP and other paramount public interests. This is evident in China's stance on the issue of

[6] WTO TRIPS Council, *Minutes of Meeting Held in the Centre William Rappard on 13 February 2007*, IP/C/M/53, 22 March 2007. [Emphasis added.]

access to medicines.[7] Interestingly, China took a more pragmatic approach to enhance the supply of vaccines for COVID-19 and other medical equipment instead of being actively involved as a core member in the recent WTO negotiations on IP waiver.

### 8.3.3 China's Support for the Multilateral IP Regimes

China has safeguarded the TRIPS Agreement mainly through its compliance with WTO rules. China comprehensively amended its IP laws to comply with WTO rules in 2000 and again to comply with the DSB decision on the US-China WTO IP dispute (DS362). China has been slowly building itself as a pillar to support the multilateral trade system. When the US signalled its intention to back to bilateralism under the Trump administration (Gertz, 2017), GAO Hucheng, Chinese Minister for Commerce made the following statement in December 2016:

> China has participated in, protected and contributed to the multilateral trade system by observing WTO rules and fulfilling its promises and responsibilities. After the outbreak of the global financial crisis, China continued its efforts on multilateral trade rules. When the Doha Round met with impasse, China, at both ministerial meetings in Bali and Nairobi, played a leading role as a responsible major trading country, in a bid to help the WTO move forward, bolster global prosperity and boost [the] multilateral trade system. (Gao, 2016)

Gao also emphasised that the WTO is a rules-based multilateral trading system and compliance with its rules plays a key role in the prosperity that international trade and investment can bring. Interestingly, 15 years after its WTO accession, China began to adopt the same discourse the US used when it tried to establish the WTO—the 'rules-based international order'—and urged the EU and the US to comply with the rules of the system (Zhang, X. C. 2017). As discussed in Chapter 6, China later played a critical role in establishing the Multiparty Interim Appeal Arbitration Arrangement for the WTO when the US paralysed the WTO's Appellate Body.

In summary, the non-alignment principle deals with the basic position of whether China can make alliances in IP negotiations. The developing-country identity and the imperative to support multilateralism influence what positions China should take substantively in its international IP engagement. It seems that the principle of non-alignment has, to a certain extent,

---

[7] WTO TRIPS Council, 'Intellectual Property and the Public Interest', Communication from Brazil, China, Fiji, India and South Africa, IP/C/W/630, 6 June 2017.

constrained China from actively forming coalitions with other developing countries to promote its own agenda, this is what can be expected when an approach of non-imposition is taken.

Also, one can see the nuances that China applied different foreign policy principles in practice. There have long been discussions about when to keep a low profile and when to strive for achievement. For another instance, in recent years, China started to resort to the narrative of the rules-based international order to urge other countries to comply with the multilateral trade rules. Yet China was not dogmatic to relying on international rulemaking as the only solution to a problem. In its effort to provide COVID-19 vaccines as global public goods, China took a more pragmatic approach by engaging with countries in need directly and exporting or donating vaccines to them instead of becoming a core member in the WTO IP waiver negotiation.

## 8.4 The Development of Principles and Their Contestation

The primary principles guiding China's engagement have evolved in the past four decades with the increase of IP filings from domestic rightholders. Gradually, substate actors have come to recognise the value of IP and started cultivating an IP culture. In the area of foreign policy, one can see an emphasis on striving for achievements instead of hiding capabilities and biding time.

### 8.4.1 From IP Instrumentalism to the Entitlement-Based Theory

China's IP filings from residents have been the highest in the world for more than a decade, IP is not only the means but also the end—the entitlement-based principle gains popularity quietly. While 'entitlement' is not exactly the term used in the Chinese context (there is no equivalence in the Chinese language at all), IP has been recognised as an exclusive right in the Chinese Civil Code 2020 (Wei & Cheng, 2022). This is the confirmation that IP rights should be protected as legitimate rights conferred by the law, not to achieve a national objective as the innovation stimulation theory has entailed.

There have been several factors for the popularity of the entitlement-based justification for IP. Most prominently, it was first accepted by epistemic communities and technocrats under the influence of the transnational networks they formed. These networks often take the form of technical assistance, training and exchange programmes (Chapter 7). Wyzycka and

Hasmath (2017, pp. 556–557) argued in their research on EU-China IP cooperation projects that 'probably the greatest achievement of the EU's norms transfer to China is that there seems to be an increasingly positive attitude at the central level of Chinese administration, in particular, MOFCOM, towards IP'. WIPO has been another important influencer promoting IP protection to Chinese regulators, not only during the early days when the first Chinese IP laws were drafted (Chapter 6) but also in their recent cooperation. For instance, in November 2016, the Shanghai Municipal People's Government and WIPO co-organised an international conference with the theme 'Building Respect for Intellectual Property: Stimulating Innovation and Creativity' (Gurry, 2016). This title precisely captures the essence of the theory in the Chinese context—IP rights should be respected (and it does not really matter why) as long as they are legitimately acquired.

Domestic rightholders who have benefited from the IP system began to advocate for more effective IP enforcement. For instance, ZHENG Yuanjie, a celebrated author of children's books in China, spoke at various events about the importance of IP for authors (Wang, 2017). Administrative IP enforcement has been emphasised in various domestic forums, and special campaigns against counterfeiting have been launched by different ministries and implemented by local IP authorities, in response to calls from rightholders. Meanwhile, judicial IP enforcement has also been enhanced in the most recent round of law revision, through a clarification of the basis to decide punitive damages for IP infringement (Wei & Cheng, 2022).

Over the years, Chinese regulators have made efforts to educate the public and cultivate an IP culture. In 2013, *Several Opinions on Reinforcing the Construction of Intellectual Property Culture* were jointly issued by six IP regulators,[8] setting medium and long-term goals for the cultivation of an IP culture:

> By 2015, the social identity of the core values of intellectual property and the sense of honour and shame related to intellectual property will have been significantly improved, and public awareness of intellectual property will have been further enhanced. By 2020, the core values of intellectual property will have been an important part of universal recognition by the public.

Among various strategies to implement these opinions, IP education has been emphasised and extended to primary and secondary schools. SIPO and the

[8] SIPO, Ministry of Education, Ministry of Culture, SAIC, State Administration of Press, Publication, Radio, Film and Television and NCAC jointly issued *Several Opinions on Reinforcing the Construction of Intellectual Property Culture* 关于加强知识产权文化建设的若干意见, No. 22 (2013).

Ministry of Education initiated a campaign to cultivate children's awareness of IP and respect for its intrinsic value.[9] These measures were introduced to gradually transform public attitudes towards IP from defiance to acceptance and respect among the next generation. In addition, in its latest grand strategy to build China into a global IP power,[10] China also aims to raise cultural awareness of IP. As will be discussed in Chapter 9, subscription to the entitlement-based theory has already influenced China's strategies for global IP engagement.

On the other hand, some domestic regulators have begun to address the adverse impacts of IP. Anti-monopoly regulators, for instance, have recognised the impact of IP monopolies on restricting knowledge dissemination. They formulated anti-monopoly guidelines on the abuse of IP to manage these negative effects.[11]

### 8.4.2 From 'Keeping a Low Profile' to 'Striving for Achievements'

DENG Xiaoping first proposed the principle of 'keeping a low profile and getting things done 韬光养晦, 有所作为' in the early 1990s as China's foreign policy principle to respond to the end of the Cold War. This guideline set the tone for China's multilateral engagement in many issues, emphasising keeping a low profile. For years, China has kept a low profile by hiding capabilities and biding time, avoided confrontations with other countries, and focused on its domestic development,taking advantage of the peaceful and stable international environment. China also expanded its trade relations, entered the WTO, and enhanced its technological competitiveness during this period.

Gradually, 'getting things done' became the priority, which further transitioned into a more proactive principle of 'striving for achievements' (Yan, 2014). China's international IP engagement was influenced by this transition. Building 'fairer and more reasonable international IP rules' has been

[9] SIPO and the Ministry of Education, *Work Plan for Implementing the National Pilot and Demonstration Program of Intellectual Property Education at Primary Schools and Secondary Schools (Trial)* 全国中小学知识产权教育试点示范工作方案, in 2015.

[10] The Central Committee of the CCP and the State Council, Outline for Building a Powerful Intellectual Property Country (2021–2035) 知识产权强国建设纲要 (2021–2035年).

[11] Anti-monopoly Commissioner of the State Council, *Anti-monopoly Guidelines in the Field of Intellectual Property*, 4 January 2019.

State Administration for Market Regulation, *Provisions on Prohibition of Abuse of IP Rights to Exclude and Restrict Competition (Draft for Comment)*, 27 June 2022.

part of China's objective in its IP engagement,[12] and most activities discussed in the case studies in this book happened as part of this transition. Yet, the case studies also show that in the area of global IP engagement, China has not imposed its own IP standards onto other countries in its effort for achievements. China has kept its FTAs diversified to meet the demands of its trading partners (Chapter 5). When it did want to influence the BRI countries to enhance their IP capacity, it cooperated with WIPO to undertake training and organise events together. When IP waiver negotiations were not the most effective way to enhance global COVID-19 vaccines, striving for achievements further guided China to think out of the box to provide vaccines directly to countries in need (Chapter 6).

## 8.5 Summary

This chapter discussed principles that have guided China's international IP engagement, including both IP principles (theories for having an IP system in China) and foreign policy principles. While IP instrumentalism is the primary principle justifying establishing, maintaining, and strengthening the IP system in China, it differs from the Western version of utilitarianism. Instead of maximising the welfare of the rightsholders, the Chinese version of IP instrumentalism focuses on how the IP system can serve the imperatives of the country. In other words, it emphasises IP's instrumental role for China's technological catch-up and economic development. In the past decade, the entitlement-based theory has also gained popularity, with the call for respect for the intrinsic value of IP and the cultivation of an IP culture.

China's contemporary foreign policy developed in a history of seeking survival and independence between the two superpowers from the 1950s to the 1970s. It later clarified its foreign policy principle as keeping a low profile and getting things done which directly guided China's international IP engagement since the 1980s. The case studies show that China followed that principle, avoiding making alliance with other countries and supporting developing country proposals as well as the multilateral trade system. This principle of keeping a low profile, however, has also constrained China from more active engagement. In the past decades, China started striving for achievement in its participation in global governance. This indeed led to its more active engagement in incorporating IP into its FTAs and enhancing IP capacity-building in BRI countries.

[12] Para. 25 of the *Several Opinions in Accelerating Building China as an IP Power under New Conditions* (2015).

The interaction of different principles has become more complicated and potentially contested. While IP instrumentalism and the emphasis on the intrinsic value of IP would require more extensive IP protection, a developing-country position can only be manifested through defending the TRIPS Agreement without going beyond its standards. Next chapter will discuss the strategies that China has developed to manage the contesting principles.

## References

Abbott, F. M. (2020). Under the Radar: Reflections on 'Forced' Technology Transfer and the Erosion of Developmental Sovereignty. *GRUR International, 69*(3), 260–263.

Braithwaite, V. A. (2009) *Defiance in Taxation and Governance: Resisting and Dismissing Authority in a Democracy.* Edward Elgar Publishing.

Cheng, W. (2019). China Engages with the Global Intellectual Property Governance: The Recent Trend. *The Journal of World Intellectual Property, 22*(3–4), 1–16.

Cheng, W., & Drahos, P. (2018). How China Built the World's Biggest Patent Office – The Pressure Driving Mechanism. *IIC - International Review of Intellectual Property and Competition Law, 49*(1), 5–40.

Chu, A. C., Cozzi, G. and Galli, S. (2014) 'Stage-Dependent Intellectual Property Rights', *Journal of Development Economics,* 106(Supplement C), pp. 239–249.

Cui, S. (2017a) 'Interpretation of the "Thirteenth Five-Year Plan": Implementing Trademark Brand Strategy to Improve the Quality of Economic Development "十三五" 规划解读——实施商标品牌战略 提升经济发展质量', *China Industry and Commerce Daily 中国工商报,* 8 April 2017.

Deng, X. (2005). From "Leaning to One-side" to "New-type Partnership": The International Strategic Thought of Three Generations of Chinese Leadership 从"一边倒"到"新型伙伴关系"—三代领导核心的国际战略思想. *Academic Forum 学术论坛, 9,* 9–12.

Ding, M. (2003). Post-war International Relations and the Formation of China's "Leaning to One-side" Policy 战后国际关系与我国建国初"一边倒"方针的形成. *Contemporary China History Studies 当代中国史研究, 10*(2), 92–99.

Gao, H. (2016) *China Will Firmly Protect Its Legitimate Interests and Multilateral Trade System.* Available at: Official website of MOFCOM http://english.mofcom.gov.cn/article/newsrelease/significantnews/201612/20161202196164.shtml (Accessed: 9 October 2022).

Gertz, G. (2017) *What Will Trump's Embrace of Bilateralism Mean for America's Trade Partners?* Available at: https://www.brookings.edu/blog/future-development/2017/02/08/what-will-trumps-embrace-of-bilateralism-mean-for-americas-trade-partners/ (Accessed: 9 October 2022).

Gould, D. M., & Gruben, W. C. (1996). The Role of Intellectual Property Rights in Economic Growth. *Journal of Development Economics, 48*(2), 323–350.

Gurry, F. (2016). *Building Respect for Intellectual Property – Stimulating Innovation and Creativity*. WIPO Magazine. Available at: WIPO Magazine http://www.wipo.int/wipo_magazine/en/2016/si/article_0001.html. Accessed 9 October 2022.

Hou, W. (2017). *Copyright Industry Continues to Contribute to the Economic Development of China 版权产业对我国经济贡献持续提升*. Available at: http://ip.people.com.cn/n1/2017/0502/c136655-29247297.html. Accessed 9 October 2022.

Liu, J. (1999). MAO Zedong's Perception of the US and the Formation of PRC's International Strategy of "Leaning to One Side" 毛泽东的美国观与新中国"一边倒"国际战略的形成. *Social Science in China 中国社会科学, 5*, 155–171.

National Bureau of Statistics. (2017). *Official from the National Bureau of Statistics (NBS) Responded to the Reporters' Questions Concerning the State Council's Approval of the "System of National Account of China (2016)" Proposed by the NBS. 国家统计局有关负责人就国务院批复国家统计局《中国国民经济核算体系 (2016) 》有关问题答记者问*. Available at: Official website of the National Bureau of Statistics (NBS) http://www.stats.gov.cn/tjsj/sjjd/201707/t20170714_1513205.html. Accessed 9 October 2022.

Nolan, P. (2012). Is China Buying the World? *Challenge, 55*(2), 108–118.

Park, W. G., & Ginarte, J. C. (1997). Intellectual Property Rights and Economic Growth. *Contemporary Economic Policy, 15*(3), 51–61.

Schroth, J. (2008). Distributive Justice and Welfarism in Utilitarianism. *Inquiry, 51*(2), 123–146.

Shen, C. (2015). *Intellectual Property Rights Should Further Deepen Its Integration with Economic and Social Development 知识产权要进一步实现与经济社会发展深度融合*. Available at http://culture.people.com.cn/n/2015/0116/c172318-26399702.html. Accessed 9 October 2022.

Sun, D. (2012). Chinese Quasi-alliance Diplomacy in the New Era 论新时期中国的准联盟外交. *World Economics and Politics 世界经济与政治, 3*, 57–81.

Thompson, M. A., & Rushing, F. W. (1996). An Empirical Analysis of the Impact of Patent Protection on Economic Growth. *Journal of Economic Development, 21*(2), 61–79.

Wang, Q. (2017, April 21). ZHENG Yuanjie Denounces "Seven Sins" for Infringement: Awareness for the Protection of Intellectual Property Rights Should be Raised among Kids 郑渊洁痛斥侵权"七宗罪": 呼吁保护知识产权从娃娃抓起. *Beijing Morning News 北京晨报*.

Wang, Y. (2015). *China on a New Road of Partnership without Alignment and Has Made More Friends 中国走出结伴不结盟的新路 "朋友圈"越来越大*. Available at: http://np.china-embassy.gov.cn/zgwj/201503/t20150308_1544371.htm.

Wei, Z., & Cheng, W. (2022). The Concept of Intellectual Property Rights in the Chinese Civil Code. *European Intellectual Property Review, 44*(1), 43–47.

Wyzycka, N., & Hasmath, R. (2017). The Impact of the European Union's Policy Towards China's Intellectual Property Regime. *International Political Science Review, 38*(5), 549–562.

Xi, J. (2013). *Explanation on the "Decision of the Central Committee of the Communist Party on Several Major Issues Concerning the Comprehensive Deepening of Reform" 关于《中共中央关于全面深化改革若干重大问题的决定》的说明*. Available at http://cpc.people.com.cn/xuexi/n/2015/0720/c397563-27331312.html. Accessed 9 October 2022.

Xu, X. (2003). Justification of Intellectual Property: Also on Consideration and Equity in the Law of Intellectual Property 知识产权的正当性——论知识产权法中的对价与衡平. *Social Sciences in China 中国社会科学, 4*, 144–154.

Yan, X. (2014). From Keeping a Low Profile to Striving for Achievement. *The Chinese Journal of International Politics, 7*(2), 153–184.

Yang, G., & Maskus, K. E. (2001). Intellectual Property Rights, Licensing, and Innovation in an Endogenous Product-cycle Model. *Journal of International Economics, 53*(1), 169–187.

Zhang, B. (2000). From " Leaning to One-Side" to "All-around": Reflection on the Structural Evolution of China's Diplomatic Policy in the Past 50 Years 从"一边倒"到"全方位"——对50年来中国外交格局演进的思考. *Journal of Chinese Communist Party History Studies 中共党史研究, 1*, 21–37.

Zhang, G. (2017). *SHEN Changyu Calls for Strengthening the Creation and Utilization of Intellectual Property and Boosting the Development of the Real Economy 申长雨: 加强知识产权的创造和运用 助推实体经济发展*. Available at: http://ip.people.com.cn/n1/2017a/0905/c136655-29516407.html. Accessed 9 October 2022.

Zhang, J., & Chen, J. (2017). Introduction to China's New Normal Economy. *Journal of Chinese Economic and Business Studies, 15*(1), 1–4.

Zhang, X. C. (2017) *Opening Statement by Ambassador ZHANG Xiangchen as a Part of the Oral Statement of China at the First Substantive Meeting of the Panel in the Dispute: European Union—Measures Related to Price Comparison Methodologies (DS516)*. Available at: http://images.mofcom.gov.cn/wto/2017b12/20171213174056990.pdf. Accessed 9 October 2022.

Zhang, X. M. (1997). The Four Strategic Foreign Policy Choices of the PRC in the Cold War Period 冷战时期新中国的四次对外战略抉择. *Research of Contemporary Chinese History 当代中国史研究, 5*, 41–51.

Zhang, Y. (2016). Coordinate the Domestic and International Two Big Pictures and Actively Participate in Global Governance 统筹国内国际两个大局 积极参与全球治理. *China Review of Political Economy 政治经济学评论, 7*(4), 41–43.

Zhao, Y. (2003). *The Preparation and the Birth of the Chinese Patent System 中国专利制度的孕育与诞生*. Intellectual Property Publishing House 知识产权出版社.

Zheng, X. (1991). The Origin and Transformation of the "Leaning to One-Side" Diplomatic Policy "一边倒"外交方针的产生和转变. *Journal of Chinese Communist Party History Studies 中共党史研究, 1*, 49–56.

# 9

# China's Strategies to Engage in Global IP Governance

## 9.1 Introduction

International regime complexity has created legal fragmentation and rule ambiguity (Gomez-Mera, 2015). Consequently, even the most powerful actors need to pay attention to their strategies for engagement in global governance because problem-solving ceases to be straightforward for anyone (Alter & Raustiala, 2018). Based on the findings from the previous chapters, two broad groups of strategies are identified and discussed in terms of China's strategies in its global IP engagement: Forum and agenda-related strategies and principle-related strategies. Forum and agenda strategies relate to the questions of where and how to advance an agenda in the context of international regime complexity, including multi-forum engagement, dissembling, and more cohesive responsive engagement. As China's international IP engagement is guided and conditioned by the principles discussed in Chapter 8, principle-related strategies are those to achieve a certain principle or manage contesting principles. Two major principle-related strategies, modelling and balancing, will be discussed.

## 9.2 Forum and Agenda-Related Strategies

Forums-related strategies often include forum-shifting and competitive forum creation (Braithwaite & Drahos, 2000; Helfer, 2009; Morse & Keohane, 2014). When more than one forum exists in international regime




W. Cheng, *China in Global Governance of Intellectual Property*, Palgrave Socio-Legal Studies, https://doi.org/10.1007/978-3-031-24370-7_9

complexity, states have the opportunity to strategically choose to pursue its agenda in the most convenient forum. When the US could not advance its IP agenda at WIPO in the 1980s, it shifted negotiations to the Uruguay Round of GATT where it was the most influential actor. This strategy eventually led to the WTO and the TRIPS Agreement. In the post-TRIPS era, the US and the EU used the vertical forum-shifting strategy to shift negotiations from the WTO to bilateral and plurilateral forums (Sell, 2010). Forum-shifting is an important strategy, yet only the powerful players are likely to be successful, because they are well resourced with legal and negotiation expertise, personnel, and other organisational supports (Drezner, 2009). China has used forum-shifting once in the cases examined in the book. In IP in standardisation, China shifted its proposal for adopting the RAND principle from the WTO to the Asia–Pacific Economic Cooperation (APEC). However, this was not because APEC was a more convenient forum to reach its objective; rather, China shifted to APEC as a retreat strategy to continue discussion on relevant issues when China's proposal at the WTO was not successful. This also indicates that the Chinese forum-related strategies may be different from those being used by the US or the EU in the literature. Based on data from this book, there are two forum-related strategies that China has taken in its global IP engagement: Multi-forum engagement and dissembling.

### 9.2.1 Multi-forum Engagement

Several cases in this book show China's strategy of multi-forum engagement, by which China participated in negotiations and discussions in all relevant forums rather than prioritising one forum over another. Unlike forum-shifting as an agenda advancing strategy, multi-forum engagement is a strategy of participation. China's engagement in a 'new' forum was not to promote its failed agenda to a more promising forum either. For instance, IP was incorporated into the new forums of the BRICS and BRI (Chapter 5), but the main activities in both forums were enhancement of IP cooperation, and China did not promote any failed agenda in other forums. In the cases of GIs and the disclosure obligation, China participated in negotiations at the WTO and WIPO at the same time. Both issues were also incorporated into China's bilateral trade agreements, with GI provisions in its FTAs are more prescriptive and specific than those on the protection of genetic resources. In both cases, China's participation in multilateral negotiation was not purported to advancing its own proposition.

China has benefited from multi-forum engagement in three ways. First, this strategy helps China to aggregate information about the nuances of positions taken by different parties at various forums and the progress of negotiations. Such information is crucial for China not to make unnecessary compromises. When China and the US were undertaking the second round of bilateral IP negotiations in the late 1980s, China also participated in the TRIPS Agreement negotiation as an observer. Before China had access to the draft TRIPS text, it had agreed to some TRIPS-plus standards bilaterally, such as providing customs protection for IP on export goods. This was based on the assumption that the US requirement would become part of the TRIPS Agreement, but this assumption could not be verified without access to the TRIPS text. After having access to the TRIPS text, China was able to use TRIPS standards as the baseline for its bilateral negotiations with the US and resisted TRIPS-plus requirement. Second, the diverse positions presented at international forums are a source of information to support Chinese domestic decision-making. As will be discussed in the modelling strategy, China's domestic IP rulemaking has followed the models of the TRIPS Agreement and IP laws of other jurisdictions that China may deem as 'advanced' IP laws. Indeed, there are a lot for China to learn in terms of the specifics of institutional design. Multi-forum engagement provides China with information about the pros and cons of institutional design so that it can design implementing mechanisms that are most suitable to its local conditions. A case in point was that China learned about disclosure requirements from proposals by the EU and Norway and joint proposals by developing countries at both the WTO and WIPO, and it further created its own institution of genetic resource protection by absorbing different proposals. Third, participating in discussions and negotiations in various forums provides opportunities for taking the dissembling strategy.

The multi-forum engagement strategy was also manifested in China's engagement in global governance of finance (Hameiri & Jones, 2018; Heilmann et al., 2014). One explanation for China to take this strategy instead of forum-shifting or new forum creation is the diverse effect of international regime complexity on different actors. International regime complexity is more beneficial to the powerful actors that have the resources and knowledge (Alter & Raustiala, 2018), and China is not one of them yet. For instance, when the US refuse to discuss RAND at the WTO TBT council, the Chinese proposal went nowhere. Its shifting to APEC was more a retreat than a strategic manoeuvre to further advance the agenda. Another explanation is the potential constraint from China's foreign policy principles, in particular non-alignment and keeping a low profile. This will be further discussed in the balancing strategy.

### 9.2.2 Dissembling

Dissembling is another forum-related strategy. China takes this strategy to support different, sometimes inconsistent, principles at different forums. China often takes a relatively unambiguous position in one international forum at one time, but its positions on the same issue at different forums are inconsistent with one another. Dissembling is deployed systematically and is evidenced in the data comparing China's engagement at different levels. At the national level, China reinforces IP protection to achieve technological catch-up and facilitate economic development. The innovation stimulation principle has prevailed at the domestic level: Some Chinese domestic IP laws and regulations are much stricter than TRIPS standards. At the multilateral level, China still supports IP multilateralism at the TRIPS Council, aligns its positions with those of other developing countries and resists forum-shifting attempts led by the US via TPP or ACTA. At the bilateral level, China's positions vary. Most IP provisions in Chinese FTAs uphold TRIPS standards, either implicitly or explicitly, indicating its support for multilateralism. Most of the active-promotion provisions are vague and open-ended, without creating a rival standard or introducing a treaty obligation. Chinese FTAs with developing countries usually do not mention TRIPS-plus standards, following an non-imposition approach. Nonetheless, China has adopted considerable TRIPS-plus IP standards in its recent FTAs with Switzerland, Australia, and South Korea on a range of issues (Chapter 5).

These seemingly inconsistent stances can be a result of using the dissembling strategy. China's domestic IP protection level is high, so it is no longer a concession for China to accept TRIPS-plus standards. Still, its FTA partners aiming for higher IP standards (for instance, Switzerland, Australia, and South Korea) had to go to the bilateral forums to negotiate TRIPS-plus provisions with China. By opening a bilateral FTA door to TRIPS-plus provisions with a developed country, China has turned IP into a bargaining chip. As FTAs are individually negotiated, TRIPs-plus provisions in one Chinese FTA will not affect a forthcoming FTA that adopts a lower IP protection standard. China does not insist negotiation be based on a template. With dissembling, TRIPS-plus provisions at the bilateral level do not interfere with China's support for developing countries' positions at the multilateral level either.

However, variated positions on one issue are not always a result of dissembling. They can be an outcome of a lack of coordination among different substate actors (Chapter 8) or non-intended consequences, both of which are non-strategic in nature.

### 9.2.3 More Cohesive Responsive Engagement Than Active Promotion

Agenda-related strategies can be active and responsive. Responsive strategies are important for China even though they are less visible. Case studies show that China has a clearer agenda and more cohesive approach for its responsive engagement than actively promoting its own agenda. Among the distributive justice principles discussed earlier (Chapter 1), technologically advanced countries tend to rely on utilitarianism or entitlement-based theory to justify higher IP protection standards while technologically retarded countries call for more egalitarian distribution of information and knowledge at the global level emphasising other paramount values including human rights and the right to development. As the US, the EU, and private actors constantly take initiatives to advance the global IP ratchet , other impacted countries, mainly developing countries, must respond to these initiatives. Otherwise, they will be disadvantaged by high IP protection standards that do not serve their own interests. For decades, China has been affirmative in making defensive coalitions in response to TRIPS-plus standards proposed by developed countries, including China's response to ACTA and TPP (Cheng, 2019a). BRICS is the major forum for China's responsive engagement. In these defensive coalitions, China adopts classic pro-development positions.

China's active IP engagement is diversified. At the multilateral level, China has always been a co-sponsor of developing-country proposals, including those for the GI Extension, enhancing the disclosure obligation, the protection of traditional knowledge, and the IP waiver for COVID-19-related vaccines and medicines. Nonetheless, China usually backs these proposals as a follower rather than an initiator. When it was indeed an initiator in its only WTO proposal on IP in standardisation (Chapter 6), the proposal was not widely co-sponsored by other countries. Recently, China has engaged more actively in plurilateral initiatives at forums of RCEP and the BRI. Its positions differ between these forums. In the RCEP, China neither led the IP negotiations nor resisted TRIPS-plus standards when other states proposed them. This can also be considered another example of dissembling. In the BRI, China took small steps to incorporate IP into the initiative, built networks for information exchange, and collaborated with WIPO in capacity-building among the BRI countries (Chapter 6). While these activities help gradually assimilate the BRI countries to the theory of IP instrumentalism.

## 9.3 Principle-Related Strategies

### 9.3.1 Modelling

Modelling refers to a process of undertaking active learning, working with models from international organisations, studying the experiences of other industrialised countries, and sometimes refining these to fit local conditions. As pointed out by Braithwaite and Drahos (2000), modelling is more than mere imitation because the actor that models others can have considerable discretion to adapt processes.

China modelled Western IP systems to establish its own IP system, especially through a process of regulatory importation. As part of the legislative process, text of IP laws of many countries was translated into Chinese, and their differences were studied carefully. IP experts from the EU and the US were invited to China to provide technical assistance, and Chinese officials and IP scholars took study tours, training, and personnel exchanges overseas to learn more about different institutional designs of the IP system. Chinese IP scholars actively followed and analysed the latest developments in the international system and foreign legislation. After China's WTO accession in 2001, China systematically amended its IP laws to model TRIPS. When TRIPS was not specific enough, the EU or US model (the EU and US models in the case of GIs) was further followed to enhance the implementation of TRIPS standards. China has long modelled other international IP regulation beyond TRIPS, including WIPO-administered treaties and the UPOV Convention where China made autonomous decisions at a pace consistent with its domestic conditions. For instance, China has joined the UPOV 1978 text instead of the 1991 text as the former recognised farmers' privilege. In the case of the disclosure obligation, China modelled weak disclosure from the EU and Norwegian proposals at the WTO with its own institutional innovation.

#### 9.3.1.1 Modelling for Foreign Policy Objectives

China was a latecomer to modernisation and has aspired to catch up with advanced technologies in many fields. In the early days of the PRC, China followed the egalitarian principle which allowed the unconstrained dissemination of knowledge within China, but the lack of IP protection also excluded China from the global market as well as access to the world's most advanced technologies. The USSR model that China followed was influenced by its grand foreign policy agenda in that time (Chapter 8). After the normalisation of foreign relations with the US, China accepted in the 1978 bilateral agreement to establish patent law and trademark law as a condition to start cooperation on high-energy physics technology with the US. The early IP law in China set the foundation for other technologies to be transferred to Chinese companies in a way that a foreign party could get royalties from patents and know-how. Therefore, having a domestic IP system in place was a cost China had to pay to integrate itself into market globalisation and achieve its objective of technological catch-up.

However, in the domestic context where the egalitarian distribution of production resources was the predominant principle, the IP rights of foreign parties were not well protected. China was criticised as a born pirate and three rounds of US-China bilateral IP negotiations were held in the late 1980s and early 1990s, which were accompanied by threats of trade retaliations and counter-retaliations. Reciprocal coordination between the parties was achieved: The US agreed on MFN treatment for China and the release of restrictions on technology transfers, while China agreed to increase IP protection standards and enforcement. In 2000, China modelled the TRIPS Agreement on the eve of its WTO accession, and thereafter, the two parties relied mainly on the WTO to solve their disputes. Nonetheless, the recent USCETA 2020 is another example of China modelled the US IP law.

While the case studies of this book did not explore how China has modelled US IP law, it was part of the historical context (Chapter 1) and has been well documented (Yu, 2000, 2005). For the present purpose, what is important is the underpinning for these early modelling—China's intention to calm and restore its bilateral relations with the US, which put IP on the broader foreign policy chessboard. Still, serving the foreign policy priority did not mean China lost its autonomy in selecting the model law. In the 1980s, China invested considerable time and personnel in studying and comparing IP systems from different jurisdictions, and China did not always model US law—for instance, when SIPO began accepting patent applications in 1985, it signed an agreement with the European Patent Office (EPO) for technical assistance. Such modelling to operationalise the patent institution is equally important to modelling at the level of rules. For more than 30 years, the Chinese Patent Office modelled the EPO extensively in areas of policy and rulemaking, personnel training, patent examination, machine translation, Cooperative Patent Classification, and patent archives (Tuo & Tang, 2015).

#### 9.3.1.2 Modelling Rival Standards

Although the starting point for Chinese IP law was to fulfil treaty obligations with the US in the late 1970s, case studies in this book show a more diverse picture than China modelling IP law from the US as a single source. In areas where there is no international consensus, China has actively modelled rival standards that were supported by the EU and other developing countries. In the case of GIs, China modelled the US trademark protection and the EU *sui generis* protection for GIs respectively (Chapter 2). In the case of the disclosure obligation, Chinese representatives undertook active learning at the WTO TRIPS Council and the WIPO IGC. Consequently, China supported a rival weak disclosure model similar to the EU and Norwegian proposals. Further, China's *Patent Law* (2008) created a complementary 'linkage' arrangement to protect genetic resources. This case indicates China's unique learning curve in the post-TRIPS era, and its active modelling on disclosure obligations has also brought it closer to the positions of megadiverse countries and further to those of the US. China's active modelling of rival standards in both cases facilitated the practices based on rival standards to become customary international law before an international agreement is reached.

#### 9.3.1.3 Active Modelling and Model Export

Since China's *National IP Strategy* in 2008, China's IP law rulemaking has started to follow the innovation stimulation theory to serve domestic technology and economic development priorities. Chinese decision-makers, as well as epistemic communities, have been convinced by the innovation stimulation theory which guided China to actively model 'more advanced foreign IP systems'. TRIPS-plus standards adopted in domestic IP laws and accepted in bilateral FTAs (Chapter 5) demonstrate this emerging trend. Typical examples of the more advanced IP rules include data exclusivity and patent linkage where the advocacy of IP epistemic communities played a crucial role (Chapter 7).

The past decade also witnessed China's transition into an IP model exporter, particularly through the forums of BRICS and the BRI. China enhanced its IP engagement by collaborating with WIPO in capacity-building in developing countries (Chapter 6). Through dialogues instead of coercion, China provided technical assistance and disseminated its 'successful experiences and best practice' to these countries. Such engagement was motivated to better protect Chinese IP overseas when Chinese entities engage in foreign direct investment and exported their technologies to these countries. Nonetheless, analysis of IP provisions in Chinese FTAs (Chapter 5) indicates China did not impose TRIPS-plus standards on these countries in its role as a model exporter. Meanwhile, being a model exporter does not mean China has stopped model importing—China still modelled the US IP laws in the USCETA 2020. This shows China has engaged in modelling bidirectionally.

The economic history has revealed that modelling IP rules was not required when Switzerland, the Netherlands, Germany, and other industrialised countries sought to introduce more advanced technologies from other countries in their early stage of industrialisation (Chapter 1). Instead, they kept domestic IP standards low so that foreign technology and knowledge, when flown into their countries, could be further disseminated. The nineteenth-century international law did not prevent them from doing so. China integrated into the globalised market at the neoliberal phase of world capitalism which emphasises property rights and market-based management, accompanied by significant growth of new forms of regulation including intellectual property. China had to integrate the globalised IP regulations. Ignoring the TRIPS Agreement and the WTO would be a cost that China, a developing country relying on export growth, could not afford. While China's modelling strategy can be said to have come from autonomous decisions, the above mentioned context for such decisions should not be forgotten. Indeed, the TRIPS Agreement and some subsequent bilateral FTAs have restricted the space for its sovereign discretion. On the other hand, benefiting from the characteristics of the Chinese economy, unprecedented demographic dividend, and many opportunities brought by globalisation in the 1990s and 2000s, China went through the process of industrialisation and technology acquisition much faster as compared with the industrialisation of other countries previously. When imported technologies were assimilated and indigenous innovation was accelerated within these couple of decades, the apparent contestation between foreign policy principles and domestic innovation stimulation principle has also been concealed. This is the basis for China's recent active modelling even without external pressure and its activities in exporting its own IP practices to other developing countries. It is noted that China's regulatory export so far has manifested the approach of non-imposition, which the Western countries failed to do when they exported their IP regulatory standards globally.

### 9.3.2 Balancing

As Braithwaite and Drahos pointed out in *Global Business Regulation*, principles are not mutually exclusive. Different principles can coexist and contest (Braithwaite & Drahos, 2000), principles need to be managed. China used the strategy of 'balancing' to reconcile the contestation of principles, in particular the potential contestation between the innovation stimulation theory and some of its foreign policy principles. One of the foreign policy principle is China's self-recognition as a developing country and the other is China's foreign policy agenda. First, supporting innovation stimulation internationally may conflict with China's position on maintaining its developing country status. The innovation stimulation principle encourages China to promote more extensive IP protection. However, maintaining a developing country status requires China to act as a developing country—for example, supporting developing country positions at various international forums. The contestation of principles becomes prominent when different principles guided China to both promote TRIPS-plus standards as well as to oppose TRIPS-plus standards and developed countries' forum-shifting. Second, as discussed in the modelling strategy, innovation stimulation may not always be consistent with the foreign policy priority. The management strategies were discussed by Yang Jiechi, State Counsellor and Director of the CCP Central Foreign Affairs Office:

> We have to emphasise that foreign affairs must take care of both domestic and international respects, plan comprehensively, deploy uniformly, and implement under coordination; this requires central and local governments, civil society and other foreign-related departments firmly to establish a sense of '外交一盘棋foreign policy chessboard', perform their duties, and make a concerted effort (Yang, 2013, p. 10)

Following this guideline, IP negotiations, bilaterally or multilaterally, should serve China's overall interests and foreign policy priorities. This means that when there is potential contestation between the innovation stimulation principle and China's grand foreign policy agenda, the foreign policy agenda prevails; when there is an internal conflict between different positions on IP negotiations, the one that serves China's foreign policy objective prevails.

Case studies of this book show that the balancing strategy has been implemented in three ways: reticence, serving the foreign policy priority and rule complexity.

#### 9.3.2.1 Reticence

Reticence is a strategy that China takes in its active engagement. When participating in international IP negotiations, China often refuses to make alliances, abstains from expressing a clear substantive position, or keeps implementation to a minimum. This strategy partly contributed to the diminishing resistance to strong IP protection in China's responsive engagement.

Through the practice of reticence, China aimed to reconcile the tension between the innovation stimulation theory and its foreign policy principles. Domestically, China continued to support IP creation and use, strengthened its administrative enforcement, and created specialised IP courts to streamline judicial enforcement. This makes the Chinese IP system increasingly similar to more advanced IP systems in the world, in particular those of the EU or the US. Internationally, this caused diminishing resistance to TRIPS-plus standards as discussed previously. Yet, China's foreign policy principle maintains that it is a developing country and should support pro-development agendas. Moreover, China must participate in negotiations because this is key to the strategy of multi-forum engagement. Under all these constraints, reticence was useful to mitigate tensions when China participated in multilateral and plurilateral trade negotiations with countries that prefer more flexibility in IP protection.

China's reticence mainly takes the form of inaction or being a quiet follower instead of an initiator when it comes to pro-dissemination and pro-development proposals. At the WTO TRIPS Council, China has only supported the IP waiver for COVID-19 vaccines in principle. Unlike India and South Africa, it was more of an observer of the progress of international debates without trying to influence or steer the debates . On this issue, China has taken different positions at different forums, which can be considered a case of combining the strategies of dissembling and reticence. China has focused on supporting domestic innovation in vaccines and medicines as a response to COVID-19, guided by the principle of IP instrumentalism, and it has been the leading origin of patent filings related to vaccines and therapeutics (WIPO, 2022). At the 2020 World Health Assembly, President XI Jinping pledged that once China invented vaccines, they would become global public goods and China would be willing to share its vaccines with other countries. China indeed exported or donated its vaccines when other countries with production capacity were stockpiling. However, this was coordinated at bilateral forums, and China has not been active in negotiations for an IP waiver at the TRIPS Council (Chapter 6). The cost for China's pragmatism and reticence in multilateral negotiation was that it was disadvantaged in the proposed negotiation text IP/C/W/688. Meanwhile, dissembling allows China's abundant domestic vaccine patent filings, bilateral vaccine exports and donations as well as the multilateral reticence to coexist.

#### 9.3.2.2 Serving the Foreign Policy Priority

When there is a contestation between IP and the foreign policy agenda in China's IP engagement, the rule of thumb is that foreign policy prevails. IP becomes a pawn on the 'big chessboard of foreign policy'. As mentioned in the modelling strategy, the initial momentum for China to draft IP laws in the early 1980s was to fulfil its obligations under bilateral treaties with the US on high-energy physics and trade relations.

The foreign policy priority also means that when a regulatory issue or a judicial dispute is 'foreign related', it would be resolved efficiently, and in most cases favouring the foreign party. Foreign companies have long been aware of such guidelines when they first started business in China. The European GI owners of Danisa and Champagne managed to pressure the Chinese government to protect their GIs through case-specific administrative decrees (Chapter 2). In the Disney case the court applied US-China MOU as a legal basis in its decision, which was a rare decision in terms of applicable law. Some early IP related decrees offered 'supernational treatment' to foreign IP rightholders as the protection for domestic rightholders was not equally high—for instance, when foreign GI names were protected based on the Paris Convention in the 1980s, Chinese domestic geographical names were not protected.

When a decision is related to a foreign policy priority, coordination and deliberation processes take place with all relevant ministries involved. But after a decision is made, all relevant ministries will have a concerted position even though they may have disagreed in the earlier deliberation process. An example of this is the deliberation process for hosting the diplomatic conference of the WIPO Treaty on Audiovisual Performances. While China did not make a substantive contribution to the treaty negotiation, the decision of whether to host the conference had foreign policy significance as it was at odds with the foreign policy guideline of hiding capabilities and biding time. The deliberation process involved not only the National Copyright Administration of China as the copyright regulator, but also the Ministry of Foreign

Affairs, MOFCOM, SAIC, SIPO and the Legislative Affairs Office of the State Council and Legislative Affairs Committee of the National People's Congress. After careful consideration, it was decided that Beijing would host the diplomatic conference and the treaty would also be referred to as Beijing Treaty following common practices. The involvement of many stakeholders in deliberation achieved two objectives—first, a consensus was needed as hosting such a conference would be an exception to the hiding and biding principle; second, the deliberation would guarantee that everyone would recognise the salience of the issue and support its implementation.

#### 9.3.2.3 Rule Coexistence and Complexity

Modelling rules from different sources and rationales led to a status of rule coexistence. In the case of GIs, three independent GI protection mechanisms coexisted till 2018. China also provided dual protection for test data, namely trade secret protection as required by the TRIPS Agreement and data exclusivity as required by the WTO's *Report of the Working Party on the Accession of China* (Cheng, 2019b). The coexistence of rules modelled from different sources further led to a certain level of legal fragmentation and regulatory competition domestically. In particular, GI provisions in the recent Chinese agreements concluded with the EU and the US have competing demands that could render compliance with both agreements impossible. First, protecting 275 EU GIs through an agreement of mutual recognition gives exclusivity to the EU rightholders to use certain names in China, and enforcing such exclusivity will potentially conflict with China's promise in the USCETA 2020 that US market access will not be undermined by other international agreements. Second, following the US definition of generic terms may lead to large-scale cancellation of EU GIs in China. While the implementation of both agreements is still in progress, it seems China has started to create more complex rules to reconcile competing demands. Despite the potential inconsistency, rule complexity would help avoiding direct conflict of rules with each other— as different rules could be issued by different regulators, they could cover different scopes, they could use ambiguous language to avoid conflict, they could include a gap-filling provision to cover any other circumstances the rule can be applied, or they could delegate discretion to competent regulators at the implementation stage. Whether there will be a real conflict is uncertain in the context of rule complexity, as the resolution to the potential conflict is often deferred to processes of rule implementation and rule interpretation, on a case-by-case basis.

## 9.4 Potential Effects of the Strategies

In summary, China adopted a strategy of multi-forum engagement, participating in relevant IP negotiations at all multilateral forums, incorporating IP into its bilateral trade agreements and dissembling its positions across different forums. In terms of responsive engagement, it has constantly resisted TRIPS-plus standards so far, but its resistance is diminishing, as demonstrated in the USCETA 2020. Its active engagement has been diverse, but the common feature is that China does not impose IP standards on other countries in its global IP engagement, in particular at the bilateral level. This may manifests the Confucian golden principle concerning global distributive justice. To manage different principles, China has also taken the modelling and balancing strategies. As an ending note, it is worth discussing the potential effects of the strategies, especially those perhaps beyond the original intention of taking a strategy.

### 9.4.1 Institutional Isomorphism and Constructed Inconsistency

Modelling has two potential effects: Compliance and institutional isomorphism. Modelling guarantees that Chinese domestic IP laws are consistent with various multilateral and bilateral standards and that China meets its treaty obligations. Modelling makes Chinese IP rules, rationales, procedures or even its entire IP institution resemble those of the model countries. Through modelling, Chinese IP regulators (and epistemic communities) established and consolidated transnational networks with their international counterparts. Innovation stimulation theory and the entitlement-based theory disseminated through these networks and took root in China. Consequently, China tends to take positions similar to those countries from which it modelled IP laws. This may further prevent China from identifying opportunities for alternative rulemaking.

China's balancing strategy has led to its constructed inconsistency and obscurity in positions on many IP issues at the international level. Constructed inconsistency is a result of maintaining versatile positions across levels and forums on the same issue. On many TRIPS-plus standards, China is a rule-taker at the national level; it has resisted more extensive IP protection at the multilateral level but keeps open opportunities to negotiate such rules at the bilateral level. Constructed inconsistency in the form of rule complexity can also be a result of implementing competing treaty demands through domestic law and regulations. It has already caused legal fragmentation and wasted public resources with the creation of dual protection mechanism for text data and triple protection mechanisms for GIs. Nonetheless, the compliance dilemma in the GI case is a relatively recent phenomenon. Rule complexity will potentially impact the stability and predictability of the rules when decision-making are postponed until implementation. The foreign policy priority and reticence lead to China's invisibility in many international IP debates. China's uniform foreign policy consideration hinders bottom-up initiatives. On the foreign policy chessboard, IP is only one piece and, on most occasions, not the most important one. Interests in IP may sometimes be sacrificed for other paramount interests, even when such sacrifices can be devastating to certain domestic stakeholders. Reticence, on the other hand, prevented China from making coalitions with other developing countries on important issues such as access to medicines. By taking this approach, China has departed from other developing countries that support pro-dissemination and pro-development agendas on global IP governance—a result that is seemingly inevitable in the long term.

### 9.4.2 Diminishing Resistance to TRIPS-Plus Standards

While traditionally China has resisted TRIPS-plus standards with other developing countries concertedly, observation of China's IP engagement in the USCETA 2020 and RCEP indicates its resistance to high IP protection standards is diminishing. Okediji (2004) pointed out that developing-country coalitions on IP are fracturing as some emerging powers (India and Brazil) have developed their technology, which subtly changes their positions in IP negotiations. Similar to these countries, China's diminishing resistance to TRIPS-plus standards is also a result of its enhanced domestic innovation capacity (Chapter 8).

Diminishing resistance to TRIPS-plus standards is a trend in China's decades-long global IP engagement. Despite not being a dedicated case study, the USCETA 2020 was discussed in various places in this book. Prominently, China agreed to the US to provide IP protection over confidential business information (Upreti & Vásquez Callo-Müller, 2020) and establish a patent linkage mechanism (Chapter 7). The level of IP protection was unprecedented among US bilateral trade agreements. China has accepted the IP standards in the USCTEA 2020 as it is an area where China can make a concession as compared with other more controversial issues. With domestic companies also enhancing theirced technological competitiveness, accepting such high IP standards will neither cost China as much as its concession on

IP in its 1980s bilateral agreements or as much as its concession on other issues in this agreement.

The diminishing resistance also indicates that constructed inconsistency through dissembling may not work for China in the future. The only way to implement the USCETA 2020 is by amending domestic Chinese IP law. After the USCETA, China has already amended its Patent Law and Copyright Law, issued the Criminal Law (11th amendment) and issued nine judicial interpretations for adjudicating IP cases (CNIPA, 2020, pp. 18–20; CNIPA, 2021, pp. 15–17). With high domestic IP protection standards as such, there would be little practical interest for China to join other developing countries in resisting global TRIPS-plus standards at multilateral forums.

China's diminishing resistance to TRIPS-plus standards may have broader implications for global distributive justice. Powerful actors can always use coercion to force others to enhance IP protection standards, but such strategies may not always be successful when facing concerted resistance. In international IP regime complexity, with an increasing number of IP rules in bilateral agreements, it is already difficult for developing countries to make defensive coalitions; they are divided and conquered. As the largest developing country in the world, China's resistance to high standards is something on which other smaller and powerless countries can rely. If China had resisted the unprecedentedly high IP protection standards in the USCETA 2020, made the negotiation process open, and provided reasons for its resistance (by resorting to egalitarianism for instance), it would have been difficult for the US to make the deal in its current form. Such a precedent would help other developing countries to resist the same standards when negotiating the same issue in their own FTA with the US. However, when China gave up its defence in USCETA negotiation, a new row of dominoes with TRIPS-plus standards equivalent to that agreement started to fall—similar provisions have reappeared in the United States-Mexico-Canada Agreement (USMCA) which was signed in July 2020.

## References

Alter, K. J., & Raustiala, K. (2018). The Rise of International Regime Complexity. *Annual Review of Law and Social Science, 14*(1), 329–349.

Braithwaite, J., & Drahos, P. (2000). *Global Business Regulation.* Cambridge University Press.

Cheng, W. (2019a). China Engages with the Global Intellectual Property Governance: The Recent Trend. *The Journal of World Intellectual Property, 22*(3–4), 1–16.

Cheng, W. (2019b). Protection of Data in China: Seventeen Years after China's WTO Accession. *European Intellectual Property Review, 44*(5), 292–297.

CNIPA. (2020). *IP Protection in China (2020) 二〇二〇年中国知识产权保护状况*. https://www.cnipa.gov.cn/module/download/downfile.jsp?classid=0&showname=%E4%BA%8C%E2%97%8B%E4%BA%8C%E2%97%8B%E5%B9%B4%E4%B8%AD%E5%9B%BD%E7%9F%A5%E8%AF%86%E4%BA%A7%E6%9D%83%E4%BF%9D%E6%8A%A4%E7%8A%B6%E5%86%B5%EF%BC%88%E7%BB%88%E7%89%88%EF%BC%89.pdf&filename=1bbc55548e3d4f298f666465c3359aaa.pdf

CNIPA. (2021). *IP Protection in China (2021) 二〇二一年中国知识产权保护状况*. https://www.cnipa.gov.cn/module/download/downfile.jsp?classid=0&showname=%E3%80%8A%E4%BA%8C%E3%80%87%E4%BA%8C%E4%B8%80%E5%B9%B4%E4%B8%AD%E5%9B%BD%E7%9F%A5%E8%AF%86%E4%BA%A7%E6%9D%83%E4%BF%9D%E6%8A%A4%E7%8A%B6%E5%86%B5%E3%80%8B.pdf&filename=fa28f809b1af42a6bfa35c3e465305f4.pdf

Drezner, D. W. (2009). The Power and Peril of International Regime Complexity. *Perspectives on Politics, 7*(1), 65–70.

Gomez-Mera, L. (2015). International Regime Complexity and Regional Governance: Evidence from the Americas. *Global Governance, 21*(1), 19–42.

Hameiri, S., & Jones, L. (2018). China Challenges Global Governance? Chinese International Development Finance and the AIIB. *International Affairs, 94*(3), 573–593.

Heilmann, S., Rudolf, M., Huotari, M., & Buckow, J. (2014). *China's Shadow Foreign Policy: Parallel Structures Challenge the Established International Order*. Mercator Institute for China Studies. https://merics.org/sites/default/files/2020-05/China_Monitor_18_Shadow_Foreign_Policy_EN.pdf

Helfer, L. R. (2009). Regime Shifting in the International Intellectual Property System. *Perspectives on Politics, 7*(1), 39–44.

Morse, J. C., & Keohane, R. O. (2014). Contested Multilateralism. *The Review of International Organizations, 9*(4), 385–412.

Okediji, R. L. (2004). The Institutions of Intellectual Property: New Trends in an Old Debate. *Proceedings of the Annual Meeting (american Society of International Law), 98*, 219–222.

Sell, S. K. (2010). TRIPS Was Never Enough: Vertical Forum Shifting, FTAS, ACTA, and TTP. *Journal of Intellectual Property Law, 18*(2), 447–478.

Tuo, Y., & Tang, S. (2015). *30 Years of Sino-European Intellectual Property Cooperation: From Technical Support to Strategic Partnerships 中欧知识产权合作30年：从技术辅助发展到战略伙伴关系*. http://world.chinadaily.com.cn/2015-10/12/content_22161247.htm. Accessed 12 May 2018.

Upreti, P. N., & Vásquez Callo-Müller, M. (2020). Phase One US-China Trade Deal: What Does It Mean for Intellectual Property? *GRUR International, 69*(4), 389–393.

WIPO. (2022). *COVID-19-related Vaccines and Therapeutics: Preliminary Insights on Related Patenting Activity During the Pandemic*. https://www.wipo.int/publications/en/details.jsp?id=4589

Yang, J. (2013). Chinese Diplomatic Theory and Practice Innovation in the New Situation 新形势下中国外交理论和实践创新. *Qiushi 求是, 16*, 7–10.

Yu, P. K. (2000). From Pirates to Partners: Protecting Intellectual Property in China in the Twenty-First Century. *American University Law Review, 50*(1), 131–243.

Yu, P. K. (2005). From Pirates to Partners (Episode II): Protecting Intellectual Property in Post-WTO China. *American University Law Review, 55*(4), 901–1000.

# 10

# Conclusion

This book analysed how China has engaged in global IP governance, with a focus on the period after it acceded to the WTO in 2001. Three thematic cases, geographical indications, the disclosure obligation, and IP and standardisation, were examined in Chapters 2–4. In these areas, international rules were unsettled, and China had opportunities to contribute to international rulemaking at various levels and in various forums. Cases of China's bilateral and multilateral IP engagement (Chapters 5–6) were also analysed to capture its activities in global IP governance on broader issues. The discussion chapters analysed the actors involved in China's international IP engagement, identified the principles that guided or constrained this, and discussed strategies actors have used in their international IP engagement. This chapter discusses broader implications of findings from this book for China's domestic IP regulation, its role in the international IP system, and global distributive justice.

## 10.1 Effects of the Strategies: China's IP System Increasingly Resembles Those of the US and/or the EU

Identifying the strategies China has used in its engagement in global IP governance could be the most important contribution of this book to the


W. Cheng, *China in Global Governance of Intellectual Property*, Palgrave Socio-Legal Studies, https://doi.org/10.1007/978-3-031-24370-7_10

extant literature. China's strategy of multi-forum engagement and dissembling, while both were initially taken as a response to regime complexity in global IP governance, has helped it manage the contesting principles. When IP instrumentalism guided China to accept higher IP enforcement standards, it also opened the opportunity to negotiate such standards at the bilateral level. At the multilateral level, China still generally supports developing country positions as guided by its foreign policy agenda. China has deployed the strategy of dissembling to take inconsistent positions at the different international forums, as far as international IP regime complexity allows such behaviour. China further used the modelling strategy to implement the innovation stimulation principle, which can be considered utilitarianism with Chinese characteristics. It also takes the strategy of balancing, including reticence, serving foreign policy priorities, and rule coexistence and rule complexity, to manage potentially contesting principles. The consequences and ramifications of these strategies have gone beyond their original intention of managing contesting principles.

One prominent effect is that the Chinese IP system has moved closer to the US or EU systems than might have been expected, most prominently in the area of IP enforcement. This is mainly because the strategy of modelling has led to institutional isomorphism and a close technocrat network among IP regulators. Four decades of modelling make China similar rather than different to developed countries, also in deeper issues such as recognising the value of IP and designing IP institutions. There is a clear trend that the underpinning rationale for the Chinese IP system is transitioning from a system based on utilitarianism to one recognising the intrinsic value of IP as a proprietary right. The consolidation of transnational networks of technocrats and epistemic communities has reinforced the trend. China has also quietly emerged as an IP model exporter in its engagement with the BRICS and BRI countries. When the US and the EU disagree with each other in the GI case, China's strategy of rule complexity was only an expedient solution to the compliance dilemma. It may further lead to fragmented domestic IP regulation where the resolution to such uncertain legal issues is deferred to the implementation stage.

## 10.2 Tipping Point for China to Become an International IP Rule-Maker?

The variations of China's role in specific cases confirm that it is not possible to capture its role with a simple binary categorisation of China as either an international IP rule-taker or rule-maker. However, as this question is central in various debates, it is useful to discuss how findings from this book would inform answers to it. There can be different angles to approach this rule-taker versus rule-maker question. This book takes a positivist approach, asking whether China's large-scale IP deployment in various markets also means that it has become a global IP regulatory power—in the sense of being an agenda setter and source of global influence over IP rules. The UK in the nineteenth century and the US in the twentieth century were regulatory IP powers in this sense. This approach differs from one based on the *status quo* versus revisionist dichotomy, assuming existing international IP law based on the TRIPS Agreement is part of the rules-based international order and alternative (revisionist) rulemaking would be detrimental to this order. The diverse principles of distributive justice discussed in Chapter 1, however, indicates that IP rules based on one distributive justice principle may not necessarily be supported by another principle. Therefore, there is no inherent justification that the existing IP rules are more ethical than rival ones, and IP waiver for COVID-19 vaccines and medicines is a case in point.

Following this approach, previous case studies indicate that China has some way to go before it can claim a regulatory agenda-setting influence to match its status as the world's second-largest economy. In the case of GIs, disclosure obligation, IP waiver, and IP and public health, there was a lack of political will to influence international negotiations. Even where China looked to promote a rival standard, as in the WAPI case, its attempts were opposed by the US and ultimately defeated. Nonetheless, China's recent IP engagement with the BRICS and BRI reveals intentions for more active engagement.

Given that China's IP system increasingly resembles those of the US and the EU, it is unlikely that China would advance alternative IP rules that correct the global IP ratchet trend by following an egalitarian or cosmopolitan principle of distributive justice. Concerning IP rules that aim to further enhance IP protection, like those included in the USCETA, China has barely absorbed such high standards itself. This means China would not actively promote such standards internationally either. For other TRIPS-plus standards that have already been consolidated in its domestic law, the answer to this question would depend on what happens in China's foreign policy space. Chapter 5 shows that China has so far safeguarded the TRIPS standards in its IP chapters in FTAs even though considerable TRIPS-plus standards have already been consolidated into domestic IP laws. As long as China's self-identification as a developing country is unchanged, the foreign policy priority of supporting developing country agendas will still prevail over the principle of IP instrumentalism to guide China's global IP engagement. In this context, it is unlikely for China to openly support TRIPS-plus standards multilaterally, but TRIPS-plus standards will still appear in a Chinese FTA if such a standard conforms with the mutual interests of China and its FTA partner.

In addition, while the strategy of multi-forum engagement may indicate China's more active engagement in various ways, the primary purposes of this strategy were to aggregate information, support domestic policymaking, and leverage positions across forums through dissembling. In one way or another, it is a responsive or following strategy, not an active rulemaking strategy. Therefore, multi-forum engagement together with dissembling may not lead China to a position of global IP agenda setter.

From a structural perspective, even if China becomes more active in international IP regulation, there is still a question whether China is able to exercise the kind of dominance that the US demonstrated during the making of the TRIPS Agreement. International regime complexity provides powerful states with more opportunities to play cross-institutional games or create an entirely new regime, but it also means no single state can be the rule-maker in all regimes. Nowadays, no state can dominate the IP rulemaking game in the way that the US and EU once did in TRIPS negotiation due to legal fragmentation, rule ambiguity and rule complexity created by international regime complexity. China has entered a game of great networked complexity in which IP is one key global issue, but only one. Where China will end up on IP is hard to say, not just because of China's speed of development, but also because there are many other players in the game responding to and affecting this networked complexity.

## 10.3 China's Global IP Engagement and Global Distributive Justice

There is a clear trend in China's appeal to distributive justice principles in its domestic IP regulation, starting from egalitarianism after the establishment of the PRC. Since the late 1970s, China had to response to the US demands on IP to continue their cooperation in science and technology and to gain membership in the WTO. Also in this period, Chinese IP regulators began to consolidate their regulatory power, and a strong domestic IP epistemic community began to grow. China used IP as a fulcrum to leverage its trade and export capabilities and attract FDI. Once advanced technologies were introduced to China, they took root—first absorbed by local partners, then integrated with existing technologies, and further adapted to fit local conditions. From the 2008 National IP Strategy, China genuinely subscribed to the utilitarian principle, which justified IP as an instrument for its innovation-driven development. More recently, China has started transitioning towards an entitlement-based principle, which concerns respect for the intrinsic (property) value of IP and cultivating a cultural awareness of IP. China's evolving appeal to different distributive justice principles domestically has reflected its imperatives of economic reform and transition and technological import and development over time.

Case studies in this book show varied implications of China's IP engagement for distributive justice. In the case of GIs, China suffered from a compliance dilemma by accepting potentially conflicting GI standards in its 2020 agreements with the EU and the US respectively. Without China's resistance to the rules causing this compliance dilemma and urge the EU and the US to solve the issue directly, these rules may become templates for forthcoming EU and US FTAs with other third countries. In the case of disclosure obligation, China's support for the amendment of TRIPS Article 29*bis* was part of the effort to enhance global distributive justice from a cosmopolitan point of view. In the USCETA, China has accepted the highest IP standards among all US FTAs. As compared with early US-China MOUs in the 1990s and China's struggle in revising its domestic law to comply with TRIPS in the early 2000s, China's resistance to high IP enforcement standards is diminishing. The weakened resistance from China could be detrimental to global distributive justice from the cosmopolitan point perspective.

Two caveats remain for this implication. First, China's assimilation to the entitlement-based principle for distributive justice is distinct from its role in providing global public goods. While China was reluctant to participate in the WTO's IP waiver negotiations, it has provided COVID-19 vaccines directly to other countries through exports and donations (Chapter 6). Second, the dynamics of substate actors in Chinese IP regulation could introduce more uncertainty in terms of whether China can indeed develop a holistic preference for the entitlement-based principle. The recent rise of anti-monopoly regulations over IP is an example of restricting the scope of entitlement-based rationale. In the end, China's vast internal IP networks of epistemic communities and private actors will add yet another layer of network complexity.

Chinese FTAs with developing countries and China's plurilateral engagement in forums like the BRICS and BRI also show that China has refrained from imposing its high IP protection standards on other countries. Prominently, there is still no IP chapter in China–Cambodia FTA when the FTA was concluded in 2020. China–Mauritius FTA (2019) has also introduced considerable limitations to IP. Both countries have retained their regulatory flexibilities over IP when concluding trade agreements with China. Although these practices are consistent with the Confucian golden principle of non-imposition, China does not declare that it is the moral guidance it follows. In fact, the *Outline of Building a Powerful Intellectual Property Country* (2021–2035) has mainly envisaged enhanced international cooperation in only in the area of IP protection in 2035. The analysis of this book shows that the consequence of non-imposition is more an outcome of managing contesting principles than deliberately following non-imposition as moral guidance.

# Appendix 1: Multilateral Treaties Effective in China

| Administer/Forum of negotiation | Name of the Treaty | Date effective to China |
|---|---|---|
| WIPO-administered Treaty (16 ratified, 2 signed but not ratified) | The Convention Establishing the World Intellectual Property Organization | June 3, 1980 |
| | The Paris Convention for the Protection of Industrial Property (1967) (the Paris Convention) | March 19, 1985 |
| | The Madrid Agreement Concerning the International Registration of Marks (1989) (the Madrid Agreement) | October 4, 1989 |
| | The Berne Convention for the Protection of Literary and Artistic Works (1971) (the Berne Convention) | October 15, 1992 |
| | The Convention for the Protection of Producers of Phonograms against Unauthorised Duplication of their Phonograms (1971) | April 30, 1993 |

(continued)




W. Cheng, *China in Global Governance of Intellectual Property*, Palgrave Socio-Legal Studies, https://doi.org/10.1007/978-3-031-24370-7

(continued)

| Administer/Forum of negotiation | Name of the Treaty | Date effective to China |
|---|---|---|
| | The Patent Cooperation Treaty (1970), as amended in 1979, and modified in 1984 and 2001 | January 1, 1994 |
| | The Nice Agreement Concerning the International Classification of Goods and Services for the Registration of Marks (1957), as amended in 1979 (the Nice Agreement) | August 9, 1995 |
| | The Budapest Treaty on the International Recognition of the Deposit of Microorganisms for the Purposes of Patent Procedure (1977), as amended in 1980 (the Budapest Treaty) | July 1, 1995 |
| | The Madrid Protocol | September 1, 1995 |
| | The Locarno Agreement Establishing an International Classification for Industrial Design (1968), as amended in 1957 (the Locarno Agreement) | September 19, 1996 |
| | The Strasbourg Agreement Concerning the International Patent Classification (1971), as amended in 1979 | June 19, 1997 |
| | WIPO Copyright Treaty (WCT) (1996) | June 9, 2007 |
| | WIPO Performances and Phonograms Treaty (WPPT) (1996) | June 9, 2007 |
| | Beijing Treaty on Audio-visual Performances (2012), (Beijing Treaty) | April 28, 2020 |

(continued)

(continued)

| Administer/Forum of negotiation | Name of the Treaty | Date effective to China |
|---|---|---|
| | Hague Agreement Concerning the International Registration of Industrial Designs | May 5, 2022 |
| | Marrakesh Treaty to Facilitate Access to Published Works for Persons Who Are Blind, Visually Impaired or Otherwise Print Disabled (2013), (Marrakesh Treaty) | May 5, 2022 |
| | Washington Treaty on Intellectual Property in Respect of Integrated Circuits (1989) (the Washington Treaty, not yet in force) | Signed in 1989, not effective yet |
| | Singapore Treaty on the Law of Trademarks | Signed on Jan 29, 2007, not effective yet |
| WTO | Agreement on Trade-Related Aspects of Intellectual Property Rights (1994) (TRIPS) | December 11, 2001 |
| UNESCO | The Universal Copyright Convention (1971) | October 30, 1992 |
| | The Convention for the Safeguarding of the Intangible Cultural Heritage (2003) | April 21, 2006 |
| | The Convention on the Protection and Promotion of the Diversity of Cultural Expressions (2005) | December 29, 2006 |
| UPOV | The International Convention for the Protection of New Varieties of Plants (1978) | April 23, 1999 |
| COP of the Convention of Biological Diversity | The Convention on Biological Diversity (1992) | January, 1993 |

(continued)

(continued)

| Administer/Forum of negotiation | Name of the Treaty | Date effective to China |
|---|---|---|
| | The Cartagena Protocol on Biosafety to the Convention on Biological Diversity (2000) | April 27, 2005 |
| | Nagoya Protocol on Access to Genetic Resources and the Fair and Equitable Sharing of Benefits Arising from their Utilisation to the Convention on Biological Diversity (2014) | September 6, 2016 |

Data collected on February 10, 2017, referring to the WIPO and CBD websites: http://www.wipo.int/treaties/en/summary.jsp, and https://www.cbd.int/

# Appendix 2: Intellectual Property Regulators in China

The following table contains the names of all 31 members to the State Council Inter-Ministerial Joint Meeting for the Implementation of the National Intellectual Property Strategy both in Chinese and in English.

| | |
|---|---|
| 中共中央宣传部 (国务院新闻办) | Central Propaganda Department of the Chinese Communist Party |
| 最高人民法院 | Supreme People's Court |
| 最高人民检察院 | Supreme People's Procuratorate |
| 外交部 | Ministry of Foreign Affairs |
| 国家发展改革委员会 | National Development and Reform Commission |
| 教育部 | Ministry of Education |
| 科技部 | Ministry of S&T |
| 工业和信息化部 | Ministry of Industry and Information Technology |
| 公安部 | Ministry of Public Security |
| 司法部 | Ministry of Justice |
| 财政部 | Ministry of Finance |
| 人力资源和社会保障部 | Ministry of Human Resources and Social Security |
| 环境保护部 | Ministry of Environmental Protection |
| 农业部 | Ministry of Agriculture |
| 商务部 | Ministry of Commerce |
| 文化部 | Ministry of Culture |
| 卫生和计划生育委员会 | National Health and Family Planning Commission |

(continued)


W. Cheng, *China in Global Governance of Intellectual Property*, Palgrave Socio-Legal Studies, https://doi.org/10.1007/978-3-031-24370-7

(continued)

| | |
|---|---|
| 人民银行 | People's Bank |
| 国务院国有资产监督和管理委员会 | State-owned Asset Supervision and Administration Commission of the State Council |
| 海关总署 | General Administration of Customs |
| 工商行政管理总局 | State Administration of Industry and Commerce |
| 质量监督检验检疫总局 | General Administration of Quality Supervision, Inspection and Quarantine |
| 新闻出版广电总局 (版权局) | State Administration of Press, Publication, Radio, Film and Television (National Copyright Administration) |
| 国家林业局 | State Forestry Administration |
| 国家知识产权局 | State IP Office |
| 国务院法制办公室 | Legislative Affairs Office of State Council |
| 中国科学院 | Chinese Academy of Sciences |
| 国防科技工业局 | State Administration of Science, Technology and Industry for National Defence |
| 中央军委装备发展部 | Central Military Commission Equipment Development Department |
| 中国国际贸易促进委员会 | China Council for the Promotion of International Trade |

Source of the list: website of the General Office of the State Council Inter-Ministerial Joint Meeting for the Implementation of the National Intellectual Property Strategy http://www.sipo.gov.cn/zlssbgs/#, last retrieved on January 24, 2018

# Appendix 3: IP Targets in the Action Plan for Further Implementing the National IP Strategy (2014–2020)

| Target | 2013 | 2015 | 2020 |
|---|---|---|---|
| Invention patents by residents (unit: patent numbers/10,000 people) | 4 | 6 | 14 |
| Patent applications filed via the "Patent Cooperation Treaty" (unit: 10,000) | 2.2 | 3.0 | 7.5 |
| Average years of maintenance of an invention patent applied for by a resident | 5.8 | 6.4 | 9.0 |
| Number of copyright registrations (unit: 10,000) | 84.5 | 90 | 100 |
| Copyright registrations for computer software (unit: 10,000) | 16.4 | 17.2 | 20 |
| Total amount of trading in technology contracts registered at technology exchange market nationally (unit: 100 billion) | 0.8 | 1.0 | 2.0 |
| Annual amount of IPR pledge financing (unit: 100 million) | 687.5 | 750 | 1800 |
| Royalties and license fees from export of exclusive rights (unit: USD 100 million) | 13.6 | 20 | 80 |
| Annual increase in the revenue of intellectual property services (%) | 18 | 20 | 20 |
| Social satisfaction with intellectual property protection (score) | 65 | 70 | 80 |
| Average period for substantive examination of an invention patent (months) | 22.3 | 21.7 | 20.2 |
| Average period for registered trademarks (months) | 10 | 9 | 9 |


W. Cheng, *China in Global Governance of Intellectual Property*, Palgrave Socio-Legal Studies, https://doi.org/10.1007/978-3-031-24370-7

# Appendix 4: Different Positions on the Disclosure Obligation Based on Relationship Between CBD and TRIPS


W. Cheng, *China in Global Governance of Intellectual Property*, Palgrave Socio-Legal Studies, https://doi.org/10.1007/978-3-031-24370-7

| Relationship between CBD and TRIPS | Representative supporters | Proposals | Positions related to the disclosure obligation |
|---|---|---|---|
| Inherent conflict | African Group, Brazil, China, Colombia, Ecuador, EC, India, Indonesia, Peru, Thailand, Turkey, Venezuela | IP/C/W/195<br>IP/C/W/284<br>IP/C/W/356<br>IP/C/W/403<br>IP/C/W/420<br>IP/C/W/429<br>IP/C/W/438<br>IP/C/W/441<br>IP/C/W/442<br>IP/C/W/443<br>IP/C/W/459<br>IP/C/W/470<br>IP/C/W/474<br>IP/C/W/475<br>TN/C/W/52<br>TN/C/W/59 | – Two proposals<br>(1) amend Article 27.3(b), incorporating disclosure of origin as well as PIC and ABS as part of the requirement for patentability<br>(2) amend of Article 29 bis of TRIPS to incorporate the disclosure of origin as part of the disclosure obligation<br>– the nature of disclosure should be substantive: without disclosure, the patent application will not be processed before grant or be invalidated after grant<br>– the scope of information to be disclosed is extensive, including associated traditional knowledge |

(continued)

(continued)

| Relationship between CBD and TRIPS | Representative supporters | Proposals | Positions related to the disclosure obligation |
|---|---|---|---|
| – No inherent conflict; but<br>– International action should be enhanced in relation to the patent system to ensure implementing the mutual supportiveness of both Agreements | EC, Norway, Switzerland | Switzerland: IP/C/W/284 IP/C/W/400 IP/C/W/423 IP/C/W/433 IP/C/W/446 Norway: IP/C/W/473 IP/C/W/491 European Communities: IP/C/W/383 WIPO/GRTKF/IC/8/11 (proposal to the WIPO IGC) TN/C/W/52 | Disclosure obligation with three proposals: Amend Patent Cooperation Treaty (PCT) to explicitly incorporate the disclosure obligation (Switzerland); Amend existing international legal framework for patents, such as the proposed Patent Law Treaty (PLT), or the Patent Cooperation Treaty (PCT) to incorporate the disclosure obligation. Disclosure should be the formal requirement in patent application (EC); Amend Articled 29 TRIPS to incorporate the disclosure obligation. Disclosure is the formal requirement and penalties for non-compliance outside the patent system (Norway) |

(continued)

(continued)

| Relationship between CBD and TRIPS | Representative supporters | Proposals | Positions related to the disclosure obligation |
|---|---|---|---|
| No conflict | Australia, Canada, Japan, Korea, United States, New Zealand | IP/C/W/257<br>IP/C/W/434<br>IP/C/W/449<br>IP/C/W/469 | – No amendment of TRIPS;<br>– No disclosure obligation<br>– Alternatively, tailored national solution based on contracts are recommended |

*Note* Red text indicates proposals co-sponsored by China

# Index




W. Cheng, *China in Global Governance of Intellectual Property*, Palgrave Socio-Legal Studies, https://doi.org/10.1007/978-3-031-24370-7

D

Kolibri 360 GmbH
Ferdinand-Jühlke-Straße 7
99095 Erfurt, Deutschland
produktsicherheit@kolibri360.de